SERVING GOD
BEHIND ENEMY LINES

The Incredible True Adventures of

RON REASONER

The Autobiography of a 25-Year
Veteran Missionary to Russia

Disclaimer: This book is a work of nonfiction. Nothing in this book should be construed as medical or legal advice.

Copyright © 2022 Ronald William Reasoner

First Edition, 2022

All Rights Reserved. No part of this book may be reproduced, or any derivative work produced, in any form, including, but not limited to, photocopying, recording, taping, word processing, scanning, or by any information storage retrieval system, without permission from the author, except as permitted by U.S. copyright law.

Permission is granted to Christian churches, organizations, and schools to make up to 10 copies of 10 or fewer pages for Bible study purposes. Permission is also granted to make brief quotations in book reviews. To request additional permission, please contact Ron Reasoner: copyright@RonReasoner.com

Cover by Janae Reasoner
Maps by Janae Reasoner
Design & Layout by Jonathan Burley
Chief Editors: Kathy Reasoner, Jim Elstad, Jonathan Burley

ISBN: 979-8-9874315-0-4 (paperback)
ISBN: 979-8-9874315-1-1 (hardback)
ISBN: 979-8-9874315-2-8 (eBook)

Library of Congress Control Number (LCCN): 2022923876

This book is published by Reasoner Publishing in the United States, and is available for wholesale and individual purchase. Contact the author here: www.RonReasoner.com

All scripture quotations are taken from the King James Version, public domain.

Jeremiah 33:3

Call unto me, and I will answer thee, and show thee great and mighty things, which thou knowest not.

— King James Version

Table of Contents

Table of Contents iv
Author's Note ix
Prologue xiii

Childhood Adventures 1
My Journey to God 12
Bible College Bound 22
First Year of Bible College 28
Second Year of Bible College 32
Marriage & Early Ministry 40
Ministry Lessons 46
Corridor Baptist Church 53
Church Growth 62
Tires & Splits 67
When Thou Vowest a Vow 74
Called to Russia 76
Calling a New Pastor 80
God Calls Kathy 84
Trials of Deputation 87
The Survey Trip 101
My First Day in Moscow 106
The Train Ride 112
The Smolensk Campaigns 119
The Decision 139
Meeting the General 142
Blessings of Deputation 146
The End of Deputation 151
Saying Goodbye 156
Russia, At Last! 162
First Day in Russia 171
Finding Roman 177
Surveillance 181
Tears for Babushka's Bible 186
Raising Children in Russia 193
2,000 Churches by 2000 202
Buying a Home in Russia 211
The Uphill Battle 222
Andre & Gala 230
Moving Forward 240

Eur-Asia Baptist Bible College	245
Heading North	251
Norilsk	256
Dudinka	263
The Town of Hello	268
Rehearsing All That God Did	271
Preparing for the 2nd Trip	275
Leaving on the 2nd Trip	282
Labytnangi & Salekhard	287
The Value of One	294
Polyarnyy Ural, Asia	301
The Tank Ride	305
A Reindeer Village	309
The Journey Back	318
Back to Salekhard	321
Train Ride of Terror	324
Trust in the Lord	328
The White Reindeer	333
The Safe Haven	349
The Camel People	353
The College Boys & The Nenets Translation of Luke	357
Mother Russia	363
Buddhists & Spiritual Warfare	371
A Reindeer Pastor	382
Idols & The Fishermen	390
Winter Bible Conference	398
Our Last Reindeer Trip	410
The Red Brick Church	422
An Old Friend	428
Ever the Spy Suspect	445
Many Other Things	451
Health Problems	458
The Valley of Decision	461
I Left My Heart in Russia	467
Back in the U.S.A.	476
The Next Journey	480
Epilogue	xv
Special Thanks	xxi
Scripture Index	xxii
Maps	xxiv

This book is dedicated to:

My precious wife, Kathy, of 39 years who followed me around the world.

My five lovely children who were excited to partake in this adventure with us: Joel, Micah, Keturah, Hannah and Jeremiah

Most of all, my Wonderful Saviour Who answered when I called unto Him and shewed me the great and mighty things recorded in this book.

Author's Note

In 2022, the world population topped 8 billion souls. A vast harvest is being born. Who will preach the Gospel to these souls?

Before Jesus Christ ascended into Heaven, His Last Command was,

But ye shall receive power, after that the Holy Ghost is come upon you: and ye shall be witnesses unto me both in Jerusalem, and in all Judea, and in Samaria, and unto the uttermost part of the earth. (Acts 1:8)

His Last Command should be our first concern! That is what missions is all about—preaching the Gospel around the world. Unless people go, others cannot know.

As we look back on our missionary journey, we see how undeserving we were to answer God's call to missions. What an honor to serve the Lord God of Heaven! People often ask, "How did you have the faith to do it?"

I love Psalm 119:105:

Thy word is a lamp unto my feet, and a light unto my path.

A lamp shines several feet in front of us, allowing us only to see the next few steps. Real faith is found one step beyond absolute surrender. The Lord gave this faith to us, and He will give it to you as well. I see young people today struggling to make the leap into ministry because they can't see where a life of faith will take them. They need to just jump and trust the Lord.

This book contains many stories. They are the Lord's stories of how He worked in our lives. This is also a narrative biography. As such, please do not expect pinpoint accuracy. The words in quotes are rough approximations of what was said. The details of what happened have been recounted to the best of my memory, my wife's journals, and those of my family and friends. Every effort has been taken to be as accurate as possible. Some names have been changed to protect both the innocent and the guilty. Some conversations happened through interpreters and may not be noted.

Some details may seem unbelievable. Please know that they seemed just as unbelievable to me at the time they occurred. We serve a powerful God, and I was blessed to see Him work miracles repeatedly.

Over the years, individuals and churches supported our ministry through prayers and giving. Without their obedience to the Lord's prompting and faithfulness, we could not have done as much to reach the lost.

As you read this book, I hope you see practical ways in which your support for a missionary helps them on the mission field. The joy we felt in reaching the lost should be shared by everyone who prayed and financially supported us. Thank you for trusting us with your missions giving.

The Apostle Paul wrote to one of his supporting churches:

> *Not because I desire a gift: but I desire fruit that may abound to your account. (Philippians 4:17)*

When you support missions, the souls saved around the world abound to your account in Heaven. What a great opportunity to be a blessing and receive eternal blessings in return.

As I travel the country preaching at Missions Conferences, I often reflect upon and question the effectiveness of our current missions programs. The churches in Macedonia begged Paul for the opportunity to support his missionary journeys.

> *For to their power, I bear record, yea, and beyond their power they were willing of themselves, praying us with much intreaty that we would receive the gift, and take upon us the fellowship of the ministering to the saints. (2 Corinthians 8:3-4)*

In truth, the Church is privileged to partner with missionaries. Instead of missionaries asking for support from churches, churches should be begging the missionaries for the incredible opportunity to reach souls together.

It is my prayer that this testimony blesses you and causes you to ponder what role the Lord would have you do in fulfilling the Great Commission. Nothing is too small for God. He takes the little we give and multiplies it into eternal rewards

> *Then saith he unto his disciples, The harvest truly is plenteous, but the laborers are few; Pray ye therefore the Lord of the harvest, that he will send forth laborers into his harvest. (Matthew 9:37-38)*

Ron Reasoner

If God has called you to be His servant,

Why stoop to be a King?

— Charles Spurgeon

Prologue

Somewhere near the Arctic Circle in July of 2000

I stared at the clerk in disbelief. "I need to get up North to the town of Hello. My documents say I'm free to travel in this district!" I waited for Andre to translate.

The clerk shook his head. "You don't have authorization to enter a restricted military zone."

Lord, there must be a way. I've been arrested at the airport and interrogated for hours. I've exposed my lungs to perilous green gas, and I've been nuclear radiated. Surely these trials were not in vain! I must go North to the Reindeer People. Please show me what to do.

I sighed and maintained eye contact with the clerk, "Isn't there anyone in authority I can appeal to?"

The man laughed and pointed across the way, "There's a General in that tower who could give you permission." The smirk on the clerk's face told me there was little to no chance, but I had to try.

As I walked across the gravel lane towards the military base, I shivered, and not just from the cold. There was an eerie silence across the tundra. The only sound was our footsteps as the wind blew wisps of charcoal-colored dust in our faces.

Why am I doing this? I'm walking into a trap! Russians this far North are still bitter about losing the Cold War. As an American, I am still their enemy.

Townsfolk watched from a safe distance as this crazy American and his interpreter approached the military gate. The entrance to the base was heavily guarded with razor-sharp fences, machine guns, and German Shepherd/wolf guard dogs. The dogs went livid as I drew near. Even from behind the fence, they were violently trying to attack. It seemed obvious that they had been trained on American meat and I was the only American within a thousand miles! I felt intimidated.

Lord, give me strength. I can do all things through Christ which strengtheneth me.

The highest-ranking soldier pursed his lips and pointed his weapon at me. "What do you want?"

I was tired and suffering from sleep deprivation. It seemed as if every step of our journey was met with one more roadblock. Perhaps the machine gun pointed at my head clouded my judgement. My mouth was not working in Russian like I wanted. I did not wait for my interpreter and demanded in Russian: "Take me to your leader!"

What? Was I crazy?

I swallowed hard and softened my voice. "I mean, can I please talk to someone about getting permission to go up North?" The guard yanked the passport out of my hand and zeroed in on the USA emblem. The look on their faces told me what they were thinking, "What was an American doing this far North in the Russian tundra?"

The guard disappeared up the steep metal stairs to the tower. He soon returned, restrained the dogs, and opened the gate. Despite the near freezing temperature, sweat dripped from my brow. I walked up the steps to a large set of doors. A tall soldier scowled as I walked past. I was between two burly soldiers. The clomping of their boots and my soft footfall told me I was no match.

But like David when he went against Goliath, they are no match for my God.

The guards guided me into an office. "Wait for our commander." They then left with Andre.

I waited in the small office. My mind began to panic.

I am in the middle of the Russian Arctic North, inside a secret military base. No one, not even my wife knows where I am. This could be where my journey ends. They could keep me, and the American Embassy would have no idea where to find me. Where did they take Andre?

With each passing minute my fear of joining the unnamed political prisoners of the Cold War grew exponentially. Finally, I heard someone coming up the steps.

Clunk! Clunk! Clunk!

The door opened. A huge man, roughly 300 pounds and six feet five inches tall, lowered his head to walk through the door. My eyes were drawn to my passport in his hand. He paused just inside the doorway and waited for me to acknowledge his presence. He towered over me as our eyes locked, and said, "Now that I've got an American, I think I'll keep you."

Lord, how did I get here? What will become of me?

That is when my whole life flashed before my eyes—

CHAPTER ONE

Childhood Adventures

And David said unto Saul, Thy servant kept his father's sheep, and there came a lion, and a bear, and took a lamb out of the flock: And I went out after him, and smote him, and delivered it out of his mouth: 1 Samuel 17:34-35a

"Honey, I'm home," Dad shouted as he closed the door. He walked into the kitchen and saw Mom resting in a chair, breathing hard. "Is it time?" he asked as he hurried to rub her back.

She whispered through clenched teeth, "The contractions are about 7 to 10 minutes apart. We better hurry. Robert and Michelle were born soon after the contractions reached 5 minutes apart."

Dad grabbed the two children, Mom's valet bag and headed for the car. He was so excited he almost forgot Mom. Running back into the house he hurried to help her from the chair, "I'm so sorry! I almost left without you!" He put his arm around Mom's waist and escorted her to the car.

Through her labored breath, Mom whispered, "Drop the kids off at Debbie's."

Fifteen minutes later, Dad squealed to a stop in front of the Emergency Room. A nurse quickly appeared and wheeled Mom away.

"How far apart are your contractions?" the nurse asked as she pushed the elevator button to the maternity ward.

"About five minutes. I have two little ones at home, so I know we are getting close."

"We'll get you settled. The doctor will check on you shortly."

Mom screamed as the pain increased, "Please tell him to hurry, the baby is coming!"

Serving God Behind Enemy Lines

I arrived just before midnight on May 20, 1963. I was told I did not cry, which concerned everyone. The doctor gave me that swat on the behind newborns got before spankings became frowned upon in the delivery room. I still did not cry. But when the nurse put me on that cold hospital scale, I let out a scream heard all over the hospital. I obviously had an aversion to cold.

Little did I know it was a foreshadow of my future. Many years later in Russia, I would be reminded of my dislike for the cold. Some of my missionary journeys took me to places where minus 40-degree temperatures stayed for weeks. Once we almost froze to death in Kalmykia.

Me (far left) with my siblings Rob, Michelle & Jeff, 1965

I was born into a Catholic family. My father is the kindest and most amiable person anyone could ever hope to meet. My mother is a retired public-school teacher. Her worldview centered on learning and growing through every situation.

Robert Francis, two-and-a-half years older, is my eldest sibling. Second in line is my sister, Michelle, 16 months older. Lastly, my younger brother, Jeff, is 21 months younger. My siblings were a big part of my childhood. There was never a dull moment in our household, and most of the time, I was in the middle of the excitement.

Our Omniscient Creator

God uses our past to take down the giants in our future. Looking back, I can see there were situations and events in my childhood that prepared me to be a missionary. I was even born in the mission field of Portland, Oregon! The unofficial motto of the city is *Keep Portland Weird*. It is a town of great diversity, free thinkers, and socialistic liberals. I learned early that I did not have to agree with someone's worldview to be their friend nor did I have to compromise my biblical beliefs because someone was offended.

Childhood Adventures

The weather in the Pacific Northwest is perfect for three months every summer but the rest of the year can be prolonged periods of overcast, wet days. I learned not to let the weather dictate my mood. I would later need that mindset in Russia with the seven to nine months of winter.

Gravity is real

My first childhood memory was learning the laws of gravity. Like most toddlers, I could not separate television from reality.

It was a rainy afternoon. Mom was tired of playing referee. She looked at her watch and smiled, "Okay, kids, cartoons are on! Mommy needs to get dinner ready. Sit down while I cook dinner. Please be quiet. Baby Jeff is sleeping."

She turned on the TV to afternoon cartoons. A man dressed in blue tights with a red cape appeared on the screen. I squealed, "It's my favorite." She spaced us evenly on the couch and headed for the kitchen.

We became mindless robots, glued to the TV. I hated commercials but they gave me time to run to the bathroom or get a drink of water. At almost three years old, I saw the commercial break as an opportunity to practice my flying skills. I grabbed one of Jeff's receiving blankets, tied it around my neck and climbed onto the dining room table. "Watch me!" I cried as I took a running jump and flew horizontal like a superhero—for one second. I landed a perfect belly flop, knocking the wind out of me.

My siblings laughed hysterically. I don't remember much, but I do remember feeling like I was dying. Their laughs brought Mom into the living room. When she saw me on the floor gasping to breathe, she exclaimed, "Ronnie! Are you O.K?"

When I finally caught my breath, I let out a blood curdling scream that awakened Baby Jeff. Mom felt my arms and legs, decided there were no broken bones and scolded me, "What were you thinking?"

"I got a cape, but I no fly!" I gasped between short breaths.

"No, people don't fly and now you've awakened Jeffy! How will I get dinner ready, keep you off the table, and care for Jeff?" Mom scowled. She stood up to get the screaming baby. Dinner was late that night.

Such events were almost daily occurrences in our household. My imagination never slept. A few years later, I decided to try the umbrella jump off the roof of the house. It was a perfect storm. Someone had left a ladder standing against the house. Mom had left an umbrella open to dry out on the front porch. I had seen this in a movie, and it looked amazing. Again, there were no broken bones, but it took two weeks to recover from that one.

What I learned from these situations was that you cannot believe everything you see on TV. Learning to discern fact from fiction (propaganda) was vital to our ministry in Russia. I found both Russia and America's media to be full of half-truths and fact distortions.

Doggie Doors are not for People

When I was six years old, new neighbors moved in next door. They installed a dog entrance in the back door. One day the neighbor came over. Mom answered the door, "Hello, John. How are you doing?"

"I'm fine, Helen. Umm, my family is going on vacation for two weeks, and I was wondering if you could keep an eye on our house."

Mom smiled, "No problem."

"Thank you," John said as he turned to leave, "We appreciate it."

At that time, I was the leader of the five- and six-year-olds in our neighborhood. We were our own Little Rascals gang. I gathered the gang and devised a plan, "Hey guys, John next door told my mom they are going on vacation for two weeks. I want to play a prank on them. Let's climb through their doggie door and re-arrange their furniture!"

One of the girls piped up, "Isn't that breaking the law?"

"No!" I replied, "We aren't going to take anything. We are going to re-arrange their living room furniture. They won't know what happened when they return. It will be fun."

We headed to John's back yard. The little kids climbed through it with no problem, but I was a bit bulkier. You might see where this is going. I could not fit through the dog door, yet I was determined. There was no going halfway in my personality and character.

"Pull me in!" I yelled to the children already in the house, "I need help!" The two strongest boys pulled at my arms, but I did not budge. "Pull harder!" I screamed.

"We are!" They yelled back.

I was wedged halfway in, and I could not get out. I tried to back out, but I was stuck.

Now what?

One of the boys sighed, "Ron, this was your idea. What should we do?"

Being jammed so tightly in the door was starting to hurt. I saw no other choice but to get my mom involved. "Get my mom," I mumbled in a panic.

Boy am I in trouble!

"What?" they asked in unison.

I spoke a little louder, "Go get my mom!" With that, they walked out the front door and I was alone.

This was not my brightest idea.

Soon my mom appeared. She took one look at me and yelled, "Ronnie! What were you thinking?" She took both of my arms and pulled hard.

"OUCH!" I screamed, "STOP! It hurts. My sides are coming off!"

Mom was mad. "Well, I don't see any choice but to call the fire department." She walked over to the phone on the wall. She looked back at me, "Last year the phone company created a new number to call for emergencies. I didn't think I would ever have to use it! I should have known better. What is it—9—1—1? I'll give it a try."

Me around age 6

The fire department soon arrived. They laughed. "This is something my kid would do." One of them said. Another one looked at me and asked, "What were you thinking, kid?"

"Everyone else got through. I thought I could too." I answered.

"Whose idea was this?" asked another fireman.

The other children had gathered around the front door, watching the show. Several of them announced in unison, "It was his idea!"

The firemen and the growing crowd laughed, "Figures." He held a chainsaw over me so I could see it. "This is going to hurt!" I held up bravely until he fired it up. I started to cry. He laughed and stopped the chainsaw.

After everyone had their fun jeering at me, two firemen went around back, grabbed my legs, and yanked me out, tearing off some of my hide along the way. This was how I learned my number one life's principle: STUPID HURTS.

My mom thanked the firemen, locked up the neighbor's house and sent everyone home. The look on her face as she grabbed my arm and hurriedly walked me home, told me that not only was I going without dinner, but Hot Wheels tracks were in my immediate future.

Mom was the disciplinarian in our family. She gave out most of the discipline by way of spankings. I had it all; spoons, belts, handpicked switches from the willow tree, and 2x4s. But her all-time favorite was the Hot Wheels tracks. We three boys shared a room and loved cars. Not just any cars—we had Hot Wheels. There were always stray tracks lying on the floor. They became the spanking stick of convenience.

I learned something can be wonderful and enjoyable, but when used the wrong way, it can become extremely painful. This is another principle: THINGS ARE JUST THINGS. THEY BECOME GOOD OR EVIL BY THE WAY IN WHICH THEY ARE USED. I'm not calling my mom "evil", but boy could she give a painful spanking.

"Ronnie, you embarrassed me today. I was tasked with keeping John's house safe and now the whole neighborhood knows they are on vacation."

"Sorry, Mom I—" my words turned to screams as the Hot Wheels track hit my raw hide.

From the Doggie Door Dilemma, I learned not to be in places I did not belong. Often in Russia there were 'do not enter' signs. I did not enter. Others did not heed the signs. Some had guns drawn on them, others were arrested, and several were shot. They had not learned the lesson to not go where you do not belong.

Baseball

From the time I was 10 years old, I was sent off each summer to make money picking strawberries. I was small, but I made enough money to buy school clothes.

When I got home from work, it was time to play. Baseball was my passion. We lived next to a baseball park, and I played every day. I would watch games and catch foul balls for free snow cones. Our yard was the biggest one on the street, so it was a makeshift baseball lot when the fields were occupied. We scrounged an old catcher's mitt and a mask; we had real baseball in our front yard.

One day I heard a knock on the front door. I opened it to find a group of seven boys with baseball gloves in their hands. "Hey, Ron, can you guys come out and play?"

I called to Rob and Jeff. Even though Jeff was younger, we would let him run after the foul balls. "There is a group of guys waiting to play ball. Anyone up for a game?"

We grabbed our mitts and headed outside. I worked my way from shortstop to pitcher and finally to batter. Picking up two bats, I weighed them in my hands, put them together, swung a few times, and decided on the heavier bat.

Childhood Adventures

"Okay, pitcher! Give me a homerun ball!" The first ball was too high—ball one. The next was too low—ball two. But that third pitch was right over the plate and coming at good speed. I waited for just the right moment and swung as hard as my 11-year-old arms could swing. I hit the sweet spot and heard the beautiful sound of a perfect connection—*Crack!* I took off running while watching the ball fly over the road. It was pure ecstasy and celebration until I heard a second and dreaded—*Crack!*

As I rounded second base, Rob fell on his stomach and laughed uncontrollably. "Great, Ron! You broke Mr. Nick's picture window again."

I enjoyed the sweet victory of a homer and then went in the house. "Mom!" I yelled out of obligation, "Mom? Where are you?"

She walked out of the laundry room. The mitt in my hand and the look on my face told her all she needed to know. "Really, Ronnie? You broke Nick's window again?"

"It was a perfect pitch, Mom. I didn't know it would go so far."

Mom walked me over to Nick's house to apologize, retrieve the ball, and arrange for me to work off the price for the large picture window.

"I'm too frustrated to spank you. Go to your room and your dad will deal with you."

The thrill of victory turned into the agony of defeat as I sat on my bed until Dad came home.

God would someday use my passion for baseball to draw people to Christ in Russia. I coached a Little League Team in Moscow and taught baseball workshops in our little town of Domodedovo, Russia. It was a great evangelistic tool of our ministry.

The Tree House

"Pull me up, Ron!" my little brother Jeff shouted from the ground. I was sitting in our tree house with a few friends. We had built it from scrap wood and there were no railings.

I looked over the edge and yelled down, "No, Jeff, it's too dangerous. You're too young."

"Please, Ron. I promise I'll be careful. I want to come up! Please drop the rope."

I looked at my friends. They shrugged and nodded. I grabbed the rope and threw one end down. "Hold on tight and I'll pull you up!"

Jeff grabbed the rope with both hands and wrapped his legs around the end. I began to pull. Five feet, six—I put my full weight into pulling my little brother up. Suddenly, he let go and fell to the ground.

Serving God Behind Enemy Lines

"Help!" I yelled to my friends as I stumbled back. I was off balance, struggling to stay on the platform. It happened too quickly. No one had time to catch me. I fell 15 feet to the ground, landing awkwardly on my arm. It broke in three places.

I learned that day how important it is for both people to hold the rope. If one lets go, the other will fall. This was an important lesson. Years later, I learned the importance of the teamwork of missions.

William Carey, Missionary to India, once said, "I will go down, if you will hold the rope." The missionary goes, but it is the responsibility of supporting churches to hold the ropes of prayer and finances. More than once, I got letters in Russia from churches letting go of the rope. Some of them folded, others got a new pastor who wanted to support his own missionaries. Sadly, several changed their philosophies of ministry and missions. We suffered brokenness because they let go.

The Water Tower

One day while walking home from school with Jeff and his friends, I noticed graffiti on the Aloha Water Tower. I stopped and commented, "It looks like someone was able to climb the water tower and spray paint graffiti. That's cool. I'll bet the view of the city is beautiful up there."

They looked up at the tower. "I could do that. It's no big deal." Tom said as he shrugged.

"I bet it's harder than it looks," I replied with my eyes on the ladder, "Look, the first part is easy, it's just like any ol' ladder, but as it reaches the tank, it curves out. That's gonna be hard to hang on."

Tom smirked, "I could do it."

At 11 years old, I was the oldest in the group. I should have had the brains to stop such nonsense. I was still working to pay off Nick's broken window. I should have gone home, but I was never one to back away when the gauntlet was thrown down.

Our first hurdle was to get over the fence protecting the tower. We finally found an area where someone had taken wire cutters and made a hole big enough to crawl through. I squeezed through, stood up, and called as I ran for the ladder, "I'm first! Tom, wait until I get back down before you try. We'll see who gets farther."

As I suspected, the first part was easy. But it was tiring to climb straight up 60 feet in the air.

I stopped to rest and yelled down at the other kids, "I'm tired. I'll rest a minute, then climb higher."

Thirty seconds later, I continued. As the ladder began to curve outward, my good sense got the better of me and I climbed back down.

"Is that all you got?" Tom teased as I hopped off the bottom rung.

"It's harder than you think and a lot higher than it looks! Let's see how far you get."

With that, Tom started up. I cannot say how far he got because just as he reached the curve, we heard sirens in the distance.

Jeff spoke first, "You don't think someone called the police on us, do you?"

As the sirens got closer, I realized they were indeed headed for us. I yelled, "The police are coming. Everyone, run!"

Those on the ground made an easy escape. We crawled through the fence and made a beeline for the forest. "This way!" I directed, "It leads to our house."

"What about Tom?" asked Jeff as we ran through the forest maze.

"It seems like this was his idea to start with. Serves him right," I replied.

Immediately, my curiosity got the better of me. I stopped and turned to look at the water tower. "Let's sneak back and see what happens."

We hid in the bushes as we watched the police scold Tom. When I was sure the police were not going to arrest him, I motioned for the boys to follow me. As soon as we were out of earshot, we took off at a steady run. I slowed to a walk as we approached our house. Opening the

front door, I led the gang to the living room, turned on the TV, sat down, and pretended to have been there all afternoon. We waited for a knock on the door from the police, but it never came.

Years later God would use my skill to climb a lookout tower in a small village in Kalmykia, Russia. My sons and I, along with one of their college buddies, climbed a tower (see previous page). That evening, many Kalmykians came to the cultural house to meet the Americans who climbed the tower. Once there, they heard the Gospel of Jesus Christ.

Am I in Heaven?

One day in my sophomore year of high school, I got home first from school. "Stink!" I said to my best friend, Lance, "I left my housekey in my room." We quickly checked all the doors and windows. Only the side garage door was unlocked.

"I guess we'll have to wait." Lance grumbled as he sat on the front porch.

I did not want to wait until someone got home with a key. "I think I can climb through the garage attic into the house. There is another entrance to the attic in the house hallway. It will be easy!"

"I don't know man; it could be dangerous."

I laughed, "Danger is my middle name."

I pulled the stairs down and ascended into the attic over the garage. I knew to walk only on the wooden planks but when I stepped on a long one over the living room, I heard a terrible crack. The plank gave way, and I fell through the ceiling, landing on my back.

I must have momentarily passed out because when I came to, all I saw were small white clouds floating through the air.

Did I die? Am I in Heaven? Am I floating in the clouds?

Suddenly I felt great pain in my back. I rolled over to discover blood on the carpet. The pain was unbearable, and I almost fainted again at the sight of my own blood.

Am I in Hell?

I heard singing.

Definitely Heaven.

But it was off key.

Maybe Hell?

I caught something out of the corner of my eye. It was Lance standing at the sliding glass door, yelling.

Not singing; but yelling.

I crawled to the door and let him in.

Childhood Adventures

"Ron! Are you okay? The back of your shirt is covered in blood!"

I turned to look at the ceiling and the insulation still floating to the ground. "I thought the insulation was clouds and I had died and gone to Heaven. But the pain in my back made me think I went to the other place."

Lance looked at the mess, "Boy are you going to be in trouble! There's a hole in the ceiling and blood on the carpet." He lifted the back of my shirt. "Let's get you cleaned up—you're bleeding bad! You'll have rows of scars from this." I still do.

Lance patched me up as best he could. He vacuumed the insulation while I tried to get the blood out of the carpet. After the floor was somewhat clean, I commented, "Do you think my parents will notice the hole in the ceiling?"

He looked up, "They'll notice." They did.

From falling through the attic, I learned not to take shortcuts, but to patiently wait for help. Many years later, I would still struggle with patience on our first Reindeer Trip.

I admit, I was not the best-behaved kid. Most of the trouble was harmless fun and I regret any frustration I caused my parents, neighbors, and emergency services. God used those situations to teach me valuable lessons that would shape and help our Russian adventures. I am living proof that God does not look at our past to determine if He will use us. He looks at our heart to determine if we are willing to be used.

THOUGHTS

- God uses the most unlikely people.
- Think for a moment about the most challenging child in your life. It might be your own child, the neighborhood troublemaker or perhaps a bus kid at church.
- Now, imagine the plans that God has for that young child.
- If someone invests the time to help that child fall in love with God and instill in them a desire to serve Him faithfully, they might turn the world upside down.
- Write down a prayer to God for this challenging child in your life.

CHAPTER TWO

My Journey to God

And brought them out, and said, Sirs, what must I do to be saved? Acts 16:30

A Search for the Truth

The smell of Mom's homemade oatmeal wafted to my room. It drew me out of bed and into the kitchen. "Good morning, Ron, how did you sleep?"

"I keep dreaming that I'm in a hot air balloon and trying to save as many people as I can from dying. I reach over the side to pull people into the basket. I can't reach everyone. The basket gets full and yet there are so many that need to be saved. A string of people is hanging on to me as the balloon rises. I'm afraid I'll drop them."

My mom gave me a questioning look. I knew an interrogation was coming, "Did you go into that church booth at the county fair yesterday? We are Catholics, Ron! You are 10 now and don't need to be looking for God anywhere else."

"I know, but I like to collect the brochures and see what people are selling. A church has a booth where I can sit in front of a fan and watch free Bible Stories. I enjoy it when they read from the Bible. Besides, they give away balloons and candy if I stay through the whole presentation. It's cool."

"Well, I wish you wouldn't do that. We are Catholic. Maybe your dream is God calling you to be a priest."

I furrowed my brow, "Maybe."

As I got older, I appreciated the exposure to different religions. My parents were lenient and said that if I went to Catholic mass first, then I could visit other churches. They were confident that I would always be a Catholic. They taught me to question everything and make wise decisions.

My Journey to God

Confessions & Hail Marys

"Hurry! We'll be late!" Mom yelled from the front door. All four kids scurried to the car.

"I call front seat!" I said grabbing the passenger door and jumping in. I almost got it closed but was not quick enough. Rob pulled me by the collar and dragged me out.

"No way, Jose! You had it last time. It's my turn!" he demanded.

I struggled to get into the front seat, but Mom's hand on my neck stopped me. I turned to her and asked, "Why do we have to go to confession anyway? It's just weird telling someone else about my sins. I don't really have anything to confess."

Mom guided me to the back seat with her hand still on my neck. "Perhaps you can confess how you always fight with your siblings and drive your mother crazy!"

Soon we were at church, and it was my turn to go into the confessional booth. I needed to tell the priest something. Fighting with my siblings and driving my mom crazy were not bad sins to me. I decided to make something up. I blurted out, "I had a bad week, Father. I smoked a pack of cigarettes, drank a six pack of booze, and littered the forest with the butts and bottles."

Father Mark grunted. I'm not sure he believed me, but he said, "Do five Hail Marys for your penance."

I did the penance and felt clean from my imaginary sins. This was important because the next day at church was my day to serve as an altar boy. Our church practiced transubstantiation, the belief that the bread and wine became the actual body and blood of Christ once the priest prayed over it. My job was to catch the bread that fell off the tongue of people taking communion. The whole process was strange to me. The priest would do five services every Sunday. He would drink wine—a whole goblet each service. I was supposed to mix the water and the wine together, but the priest never allowed me to put in water. By the third service the priest was tottering back and forth. He would occasionally pass out at the fifth service. If the altar boys stood too long, they would pass out too. Church became about seeing who would pass out first—an altar boy or the priest.

When I turned 12, it was time to prepare for Confirmation Day. This was a profoundly serious time. I already had my baptism as a baby—Sacrament number one. My first communion at seven—Sacrament number two. Now it was time for Confirmation—Sacrament number three. The sealing of the Holy Spirit. On the way to church, Rob asked,

"Did you pick a patron saint who will protect you in life and help you stay out of *Purgatory*?"

"Yeah, I studied the book of saints and I've picked Saint Trixie." We both smiled at the name.

During the Confirmation, Father Mark asked, "Who have you picked for your saint?"

I proudly proclaimed, "Saint Trixie."

The Father stifled his response, "I confirm you under Saint Mark."

After my Confirmation, my parents sat us down for a talk. "Children, you all need to take your Catholic religion seriously. We have decided to put you in St. Cecilia's School this year."

We groaned in unison and the bickering began, "What about my baseball team at school?" Rob asked.

"Will I have to wear a uniform?" Michelle asked in horror.

"You can't be serious!" I proclaimed, "I'm starting seventh grade. My life is just about to begin!"

Jeff had no comment.

While my parents were concerned that we remain true Catholics, going to that school is where God changed my life. However, not in the way my parents anticipated.

My first day of school was interesting. A group of boys had been in this school since first grade. They wanted to prove who was boss. They picked the toughest kid to fight me.

"Come on, Reasoner. Show us what you got!" He said as he punched my arm.

Are you kidding me? I would not even get this in public school. Oh well, if you want an education.

I stepped closer and gave the kid a warning, "I live in a rough neighborhood where fighting is a way of life. You Catholic boys have no idea what is about to unleash on your head!" He sneered and threw the first punch. I punched back again and again. Soon the boy was on the ground crying, and I was on my way to the principal's office. The nun hit my hands with a ruler. Ouch! It was not a good first day.

I could not believe the religion class. They had extra books in the Bible that seemed more like fairy tales than Bible stories, especially the Book of Maccabees. It is here that the Catholics get their doctrine of *Purgatory* (a middle-earth between Heaven and Hell where sinners go to suffer for their sins and earn their way to Heaven). If *Purgatory* was real, why was it not in any other books of the Bible? I was confused.

Then a tragic event happened that changed my life.

My Journey to God

"Students, we have a very sad announcement to make," came a voice over the loudspeaker, "Father John has died. He was a great priest and hero in the Northwest Diocese. We will remember him properly and with respect. Tomorrow we will lay his body out in the chapel. One by one we will file in and kiss his body to transfer his holiness to us."

Everyone thought he was holy, but I knew he was a drunkard. I was the altar boy that poured his wine. How could I kiss the dead body of a drunk and get holiness?

Father John's death caused me to contemplate my own mortality. Suddenly my 12-year-old life was not just about the here and now; I began to think of eternity and the fact that I would someday die. How could I be sure of a spot in Heaven?

I am a sinner and I need to find God!

The nuns and priests who had been studying religion all their lives should be able give me a heads up on how to get to Heaven. I approached a nun. "Sister Susie, how do I get to Heaven when I die?"

She towered over me, "Oh I miss Father John too. I know this is hard on you, but we will see him again in Heaven someday."

"But how?" I repeated, "How do I get to Heaven?"

She looked me in the eye, "Well, you start with saying your *rosary* (a religious exercise in which prayers are recited and counted on a string of beads) every day and being a good person all the time. When you die, you will spend a thousand years in *Purgatory* until you are good enough to get into Heaven."

"But I don't want to go to *Purgatory*. How do I get straight to Heaven?"

Sister Susie took a moment to examine my attitude. Satisfied that I was serious and not just trying to get out of class, she answered, "Go see Father Matthew."

I knocked on the head priest's door. "Come in."

I entered and quickly said, "Sister Susie sent me because I want to know how to go straight to Heaven without going to *Purgatory*. She said I should talk to you."

"There is a way. Come in, take a seat, and I'll tell you." I was all ears. I sat down on the couch, folded my hands, and waited. The Priest began, "You must do two miracles in your lifetime."

My eager eyes fell to the ground. I was already defeated.

I've never performed any miracles and don't see any on the horizon.

He continued, "You must live a near perfect life."

Serving God Behind Enemy Lines

There was no hope. I was the neighborhood troublemaker. Everyone knew I was not perfect.

Was the priest still talking?

"After you are buried 20 years, the church digs up your body and according to the decomposition of your body, votes on whether you are a saint. If they determine you are a saint, you get to go straight to Heaven!"

Dejected and confused, I stood to leave. "Thank you for your time."

What he said sounded like he was making it up.

From that moment on, I could no longer be a Catholic. I had to find the Truth.

The Search for How to Get to Heaven

Our neighborhood was diverse. It gave me a great opportunity to ask several religions about how to get to Heaven. Sally was a Mormon. I asked, "Sally, tell me about the Mormon church."

She was excited, "We are a Christian Church."

"What makes you different from the Catholics?"

"We have an extra Bible. We had a leader named Joseph Smith who found angel Moroni in the woods. The angel gave him special glasses to read an illegible manuscript. He wrote the Book of Mormon." I ruled this one out right away as fiction. Why go from one fairy tale to another?

Ralph was a Lutheran. He might know something. "Hey Ralph," I yelled across the parking lot after baseball practice, "I have a question for you. Can we walk home together?"

"Sure," he said, "What's your question?"

"You're a Lutheran, right?"

Ralph paused for a moment.

He doesn't even know what I'm talking about!

Suddenly his eyes lit up with understanding, "Oh, my religion? Yes, I'm Lutheran."

"So, I'm wondering, how does your church say you get to Heaven?"

"Um, to be honest, I don't listen to sermons. We only go on Christmas and Easter. I don't remember hearing anything about going to Heaven—just the birth and resurrection of Jesus. I suppose we just believe in God, and we are good to go."

I was done supposing and hoping, I was looking for knowing how to get to Heaven. I continued my search. Some churches talked more about their song service and activities than Bible teaching. Others asked if I was predestinated.

Predestinated? I have no clue.

My Journey to God

I continued searching. I was frustrated. Every time I thought I was getting closer to the truth, it led to a dead end. Finally, I met a backslidden Christian. He was the stepfather of my best friend, Lance. Lance convinced me that his stepfather knew how to get to Heaven. So, I met with his father. He had a cigarette in one hand and a beer in the other.

Not too promising but I'll hear him out.

I started the conversation, "Lance says you know how to get to Heaven."

He answered, "Yes. I am 100% sure I'm going to Heaven." Mr. Mog put out his cigarette, finished his beer, and stood to retrieve his Bible. He opened it to John 3:16 and started to read:

"For God so loved the world..."

I joined him in the last half of the verse,

"...that he gave his only begotten Son, that whosoever believeth in him should not perish, but have everlasting life."

"Oh, you know that verse?" Mr. Mog was surprised, "Then you know that God loves you so much, He sent His only Son to die for you."

Nothing new so far...most religions teach this.

Mr. Mog turned his Bible to Romans 3:23 and read:

"For all have sinned, and come short of the glory of God;"

He paused to look at me, "Are you a sinner, Ron?"

"Well, yeah, but isn't everyone?" I proudly countered.

Mr. Mog flipped one page and continued, "Romans 6:23 says,

"For the wages of sin is death; but the gift of God is eternal life through Jesus Christ our Lord."

He stopped, looked me in the eye and said, "You're right. We are all sinners and deserve death, but God sent Jesus to save us from our sins."

I tried to remember my catechism responses from Catholic Sunday School, "Yeah, Jesus died on the cross for Adam's sin nature in us. We have to work our way to Heaven."

Mr. Mog flipped through his Bible again. He found 1 John 1:7 and read,

"But if we walk in the light, as he is in the light, we have fellowship one with another, and the blood of Jesus Christ his Son cleanseth us from all sin.

"It says right here that Jesus cleanses all our sin, not just the original sin from Adam."

Serving God Behind Enemy Lines

I was interested, but I was also proud. Honestly, it was impressive this man opened his Bible and showed me what he believed with Scripture. But 13 years of Catholicism reigned in me. I said, "The Catholic church is the oldest church in the world. What church do you go to?"

Mr. Mog answered, "We attend a Baptist Church."

"How old is the Baptist Church?" I smugly asked knowing the Catholic Church was over a thousand years old.

Rubbing his chin, Mr. Mog paused before answering, "I don't rightly know, but I know that it is not the Baptist Church that will get me to Heaven, it is my faith in Jesus that saves me. I don't know all the answers, but this one thing I know, I was a sinner on my way to Hell and now I am a saved sinner on my way to Heaven."

I stood to leave, but he stopped me, "Ron, just let me read one more verse and then I'll let you go. Ephesians 2:8-9 says,

"For by grace are ye saved through faith; and that not of yourselves: it is the gift of God: Not of works, lest any man should boast.

"See here, you can't work your way to Heaven."

"Thanks for talking with me, Mr. Mog, but I still believe my church is the oldest and good works are necessary for Heaven."

As I walked away, I felt I was victoriously defending my religion. But I felt unsettled. That night, the Scriptures he read kept going over and over in my mind. Mr. Mog told me he did not have all the answers, but still, he had opened his Bible to talk to me. This was new. No one had ever opened their Bible and shared the Gospel like he had. I had to find out more. Perhaps his pastor could answer all my questions.

Still Searching for the Truth

The next day I called out, "Hey, Lance, what is the name of your church?"

"Aloha Berean Baptist Church. Do you want to come to church on Sunday? We leave our house at 9:45 a.m."

"I could go to early mass, then make it to your house by 9:45 a.m."

When I entered the Baptist Church, I immediately noticed differences. The basin of holy water was missing. There were no confessional booths or icons. The people were smiling as they entered with Bibles tucked under their arms. The pastor dressed in a suit.

This should be interesting.

I started for the auditorium, but Lance grabbed my arm, "No, we have Sunday School first. The youth group meets in their own room. Follow me."

My Journey to God

I followed Lance to the youth room. I saw familiar faces from my school and neighborhood. By this time, I was back in public school. Catholic school lasted one year. There was also a group of pretty girls smiling and giggling in the corner.

This could get interesting.

The youth director made a beeline for me, "Hi, I'm Brother Greenjeans. What is your name?"

Trying to contain my laughter at his name, I coughed, "Ron Reasoner."

"It's great to have you visiting with us today. I assume you are a friend of Lance's?"

"Yeah, I asked him if I could come to church."

During Sunday School we played a game, sang Gospel songs, and had a short Bible lesson. Afterwards, we filed into the auditorium for the main service. Pastor Wood preached a message on the God of the Bible and how to know Him personally. This was exactly what I was looking for. I went forward at the invitation, "Sir, I need God."

Pastor smiled and motioned for a man to take me to the altar. We knelt and this man opened his Bible to the same Scriptures that Mr. Mog had shown me; John 3:16, Romans 3:23, Romans 6:23 but also Romans 10:9-13,

> *That if thou shalt confess with thy mouth the Lord Jesus, and shalt believe in thine heart that God hath raised him from the dead, thou shalt be saved. For with the heart man believeth unto righteousness; and with the mouth confession is made unto salvation. For the Scripture saith, Whosoever believeth on him shall not be ashamed. For there is no difference between the Jew and the Greek: for the same Lord over all is rich unto all that call upon him. For whosoever shall call upon the name of the Lord shall be saved.*

This man was nervous; like it was his first time to lead someone to Christ. He barely looked at me and mumbled, "Would you like to call upon the name of the Lord to save you?"

"Yes!" I exclaimed.

"Then you need to pray a prayer."

I did not understand what kind of prayer to pray. The first one that came to my mind was the Hail Mary. So, I prayed, "Hail Mary, full of grace, The Lord is with thee; blessed are thou among women, and blessed is the fruit of thy womb, Jesus. Holy Mary, Mother of God, pray for us sinners now and at the hour of our death. Amen."

Serving God Behind Enemy Lines

The man squirmed, scratched his head, and coughed, "Well—I guess you are saved!"

Really? I've been saying that prayer since I could talk. I guess I've always been saved. This does not make sense.

We rose from our knees. The Pastor stood me before the church and asked, "Ron, did you ask Jesus to save you just now?"

"Yes." I replied. 'Amens' were heard all over the auditorium. The Pastor asked me to stay up front. After the closing prayer, people in the church came by and shook my hand.

I continued to attend Mass early with my family and then rushed over to the Baptist Church sporadically for several years and even got baptized.

When I was 15, my next-door neighbor, Brother Cookston, became our interim youth director. He had Saturday night youth meetings in his basement. One Saturday evening, I felt the Holy Spirit working in my heart during the devotion. At the end, Cookston asked, "Is there anyone who is not sure of their salvation? Please raise your hand so I can pray for you."

I had been going to the church for about three years and while my head was processing the Gospel story, my heart was still confused. I still could not understand salvation by grace. I raised my hand and made another profession of faith. In my mind, I was still earning my salvation. I got baptized again.

Our next youth director was a motivational speaker. He announced, "We are going to have a contest. Whoever brings the most visitors during the month of September will receive a $50 bill."

I brought the high school football team. They came once and heard the Gospel.

We often went soul winning, and I believed I was earning salvation through good works. We would lead children, teens, and adults to Christ every time we went out. Even though I was not saved, God was using me.

My life was a dichotomy, yet somehow, I was able to compartmentalize the areas where I did not meet the standard of a true Christian. In my heart of hearts, I knew I was still missing something. On one hand, I was miserable. On the other hand, I was praised by the church for being an example of the believer.

Sadly, the time I devoted to the Baptist church came with a heavy price tag. When I was 17, my parents told me to stop going to the Baptist church. In tears, my mom said, "If you are going to continue witnessing to people on the streets, you will need to find another place to live."

Looking back, I think my mom was just upset. Our lives were in transition. My family had moved from Hillsboro to Molalla. The stress from the move was overwhelming to all of us. I was unhappy and missed my football buddies on the Hillsboro team. I do not think Mom really wanted me to leave home, but I took her seriously.

I told the church the situation with my parents and a gracious couple allowed me to live with them. I transferred back to Hillsboro High. After a few months, the family kicked me out. I am sure I deserved it. It would be hard to take a young man into your home.

On the High School Football Team

I soon got an apartment, worked, played sports, and kept up on my homework. School had never been a struggle, but sleep deprivation wreaked havoc on my mind. I battled to get good grades my senior year. I had enough money to pay the rent and put gas in my car to go to church, school, and work. I grew up far too quickly my senior year of high school.

Looking back, I see how the Lord used my Catholic background in Russia for His glory. The national religion, Russian Orthodoxy, has the same basic tenets as the Catholic Church. God used me to lead many religious people to Him. I understood their mindset and knew how important it was for them to set aside their ideology that good works would get them to Heaven. I knew to emphasize that only by grace, through faith in Jesus Christ, can one be saved.

THOUGHTS
- When you witness to others, do you consider their religious background and worldview when explaining the Gospel?
- People must understand they are lost before they can be saved.

CHAPTER THREE

Bible College Bound

This man was instructed in the way of the Lord; and being fervent in the spirit, he spake and taught diligently the things of the Lord, knowing only the baptism of John. Acts 18:25

Off to California

"California, here we come!" Yelled my friend out the window as we crossed the Oregon/California state line. It was 1981 and Fall classes were about to start at college. I had packed all my belongings and motorcycle into a trailer. The farewell with my parents had been full of tears, but this was a good step in my life.

The choices we make after high school determine our life's trajectory. I had several scholarship offers to play college football but was determined to serve the Lord.

What better way to secure my place in Heaven than to go to Bible College?

My pastor had suggested I move to California before school started and jump into the job market before other students arrived. He had given me the address of a pastor friend in Puente who found a family to house me until the campus dorms opened.

High School Graduation

Bible College Bound

We were exhausted when we found the Fawn home. It was the days before cell phones and the Internet. One had to use maps and pay phones to get where they were going. Mrs. Fawn opened the door, "Oh, Ron, you made it! It is a long drive from Portland to Los Angeles. Please come in. I'm Lucy and this is my husband, Jack."

Jack noticed my motorcycle in the driveway, "Brave man to drive that in L.A. traffic!"

I nodded, "Yeah, I had no idea. I'll get a car when I find a job."

"Have you eaten?" Lucy asked as we walked into the house. "I can heat up leftovers."

"Thank you. That would be wonderful!" I waved goodbye to my friend before walking into the house. Jack sat across from me. He watched as I practically inhaled the food. "This is delicious!" I managed to say between bites.

"Have you gotten any leads on a job?" Jack asked. I shook my head, so he continued, "I have a friend who is hiring. It isn't a glamorous job by any means and it's not in a very safe neighborhood." He stopped to size me up, "But it looks like you can take care of yourself. Did you play football in high school?"

I nodded, "Halfback—" Was all I got out before he continued.

"Well, the job is at a fabric company."

Really? Does it look like I would work at a fabric store?

Jack saw the look, "Not a fabric store, but a factory that dyes material and then sells it to fabric stores."

Okay. that's better.

"Interesting. Where do I apply?"

"I've got the phone number. You can call on Monday."

I finished my plate, rinsed it, and put it in the sink. Jack stood, "I'll show you where you will be staying. Tomorrow is Sunday. Would you like to go to church with us?"

"Sounds good." I turned to Lucy and smiled, "Thank you so much for the dinner. It hit the spot."

God had led me to a good family. The Fawns were strong Christians who helped me out spiritually and physically. I got the job working in the garment district putting dyes on silk screens to print on fabric. It was awful, messy, and smelly, but it was a job. It gave me enough money to enroll in college and buy a car.

Orientation

Once the dorms opened, I gathered my belongings, thanked the Fawn family for their hospitality, and drove to Pacific Coast Baptist Bible College. I had only been in L.A. three weeks, but I already felt like I needed a vacation. The hustle and bustle of big city life was taxing on this young man from Oregon.

As I drove down South Valley Center Road in San Dimas, it appeared to end.

I'm lost again.

As I was about to turn around, I noticed a narrow road.

Could this be the campus?

I saw a small *PCBBC* sign and an arrow pointing down a hill. The road wound down past an equestrian park, over a bridge, around a hairpin turn and up a steep hill. Once I crested the hill, a majestic green oasis appeared amid the craziness of California.

As I approached the beautiful *Pacific Coast Baptist Bible College* sign, a uniformed guard immediately stepped out of a small shack and signaled for me to stop.

"Can I help you?" he asked.

"I'm Ron Reasoner, a new student. Could you please direct me to Oak Knoll Dorm?"

"Welcome to Pacific Coast Baptist Bible College, Ron. Turn right just past the shack. Oak Knoll Dorm is the second building on the right."

"Thank you." I nodded and drove onto the campus. I had no idea how much my life was about to change.

I turned my motorcycle off, grabbed my bags, and headed across the grass to the front door of the dorm. "Hey!" someone called, "Get off the grass or you'll get hours! Didn't you read the student handbook before coming on campus?"

I jumped onto the sidewalk. "Sorry, I looked it over, but haven't memorized it. I did read the part about getting hours. Isn't that where you must work for the school for free because you broke a rule? Let me guess, walking on the grass is an infraction?"

"Yes, on both accounts. It's okay," the man said, "We give new students some grace the first few weeks while they get accustomed to campus life. My name is Mark."

"I'm Ron Reasoner."

"Oh, you're Ron, I'll be your dorm monitor. Welcome to campus. Come, I'll show you your room."

As I followed Mark, he asked over his shoulder, "Do you have a job yet?"

"I've been here a few weeks already. I'm working in downtown L.A."

"Let me know if you get tired of the commute, I have numerous contacts for jobs." Mark stood in the center of the room, "I'll leave you to the unpacking. The bed assignments are first come, first served. You are the last to arrive." He scanned the beds. "It looks like you got stuck with a top bunk."

At registration, I had to pick a major: Pastoral, Missions, Youth, or Music. Music was definitely out. The registrar saw my hesitation, "Don't worry, Pastoral, Youth, and Missions majors have all the same classes the first year. You don't have to decide today."

Relieved, I marked Missions, bought my textbooks, and paid the first installment of tuition. Everyone was friendly and I felt good about my decision to attend Bible College to secure my salvation.

Red-Light District

Truly, L.A. traffic was dangerous, so I bought a 1963 Ford Falcon. I thought it was a steal of a deal but soon discovered it had bad brakes. In fact, everything about the car was bad. I worked the swing shift at the fabric company and got off at 11:30 p.m., just as the L.A. gangs began their night life. One evening on my way home, my car broke down right in the middle of the Red-Light District.

The gangs were out in full force, harassing people, and causing chaos. There was nothing I could do but pray.

Lord, please help. My car is broken, and I need You.

Serving God Behind Enemy Lines

Five gangsters headed my direction. I felt the Lord telling me to get out of the car.

Really Lord? There are five of them and one of me.

I looked around and saw a phone booth just a few feet away. Could I make it?

Okay, Lord, here I go. Please protect me!

I stepped out of the car. Before I even made a break for the phone booth, the gang members took a side glance at me, halted their approach, and turned away.

That was cool, Lord.

They were more afraid of me than I was of them. The multicolored dyes from work had stained my clothes and face giving me the look of a psychedelic crazy man. I got to the pay phone and called the guard shack on campus. Someone was sent to pick me up. God's protection grew my faith.

Still Searching for the Truth

Pacific Coast Baptist Bible College did not have a campus church. The administration encouraged students to try several "approved" churches in the area to see where God would lead them to minister. I was already attending Puente with the Fawn Family, but I wanted to try other churches.

One of the nearby churches was Calvary Baptist Church of San Dimas. The pastor was one of my professors. I really liked his classes, so I thought I would give his church a try.

The next Sunday, I sat through the morning service. God was working on my heart. I had been on campus long enough to know that I was different from the others. They had something I did not have. I talked differently. Not profane, just unpolished. Many of the students came from Christian homes, even pastors' homes, and knew how to talk the talk and walk the walk.

Christianity comes so easily for them.

As a first-generation Baptist, I was struggling but I knew God was calling me. At the close of the pastor's message, I went forward at the invitation. This was my third time seeking to have a personal relationship with Christ.

"I don't believe I'm really saved," I told the altar worker. I recognized him as my Theology professor, Mr. Smith. I poured out my heart, "I went forward when I was 12, but I prayed the Hail Mary to receive Jesus. I later prayed in the basement of my youth pastor and repeated a prayer but I don't believe I have ever truly repented."

Mr. Smith patted me on the back and smiled, "Son, don't worry. I doubt my salvation all the time. Here, read this and you will be fine." He handed me a pamphlet from his Bible, placed his hand on my shoulder and prayed, "Lord, thank You that this young man wants to know You. Bless him! Amen."

I returned to my seat more confused than ever.

What just happened?

Mr. Smith said it would be fine, but it did not seem fine. The Holy Spirit was convicting me, but Satan did all he could to deceive me. I did not get saved that day, but I did realize the need to be genuinely saved. No pamphlet could justify why I should feel good about being unsaved and headed for Hell.

I decided to return to Puente Baptist Temple with the Fawns. I joined the church and continued to work my way to Heaven.

THOUGHTS
- Have you doubted your salvation?
- What would you say to someone who doubts?

CHAPTER FOUR

First Year of Bible College

A man that hath friends must show himself friendly: and there is a friend that sticketh closer than a brother. Proverbs 18:24

Rapture Practice

"Mike, stop taking all the hot water!" I yelled in frustration one day. I was settling into college life. The first semester entailed learning how to get along with my dorm mates and prioritizing my time so I could work full time, study, and still have a social life.

This guy, Mike, was an only child. He would wake up early to shower and use all the hot water. We only had one large hot water tank for about 30 guys.

"Let's teach Mike a lesson," Mark said, "I am tired of cold showers, and I have devised a plan. Tomorrow while he is taking his long shower, we will fake the rapture."

"How?" I asked, "What's the plan?"

We huddled as Mark lowered his voice, "While he is in the shower, we put our clothes in piles throughout the dorm. We'll run the faucets, leave blow dryers and razors running. Then everyone will hide."

"I'll put my pile of clothes in the hallway and leave my glasses on top," one student said.

Another offered, "I'll dangle my blow dryer from its cord between the sinks and leave it on. Then I'll place my towel below it like I was drying my hair and suddenly was raptured."

A third conspirator chimed in, "I'll leave my electric razor turned on and put my suit under the sink. It needs to be dry cleaned anyway."

Another mused, "I'll leave my alarm clock beeping."

First Year of Bible College

I joined in, "I'll drop my toothbrush and tooth paste with the cap off in the sink and leave the water running."

The next day, we got up while Mike was showering. By the time we finished prepping, even I would have believed the rapture had happened. Mike turned off the shower and we ran to hide. Piles of clothes, electric razors, and blow dryers on, water running, but no people.

It only took a few moments before Mike screamed, "The rapture! I missed it!" We heard him running down the hall, opening all the doors and yelling our names. Before anyone could stop him, he flew out the front door and sprinted across campus in only his towel.

He ran to the Dean's office. Brother Moody was knelt in prayer when Mike swung open the door and screamed, "Brother Moody. We missed the rapture! We must not be saved!"

Brother Moody arose. "Mike, slow down! What seems to be the problem?"

"Everyone is gone. There are piles of clothes on the floor. Blow dryers and electric razors are still running. Several alarm clocks are beeping throughout the dorm. Everyone is gone!"

"Not again!" Brother Moody sighed, "Come, let's get you back to the dorm. Here, put my jacket on, you're practically naked."

Mike threw on Brother Moody's jacket and held his towel as he ran back to the dorm. When Brother Moody entered, he put both hands around his mouth and yelled, "Okay, Boys, fun's over. Come on out."

We stayed put, but to no avail. Brother Moody knew the scam. Students did the same stunt every few years to the most annoying and gullible student. We came out of our hiding spots and were promptly issued some serious campus service hours.

Mike was furious, "I can't believe you guys scared me like that! I wet myself! Why?"

"Mike, we've told you countless times to quit taking all the hot water. We needed to get your attention. QUIT TAKING ALL THE HOT WATER!"

From then on, most of us got hot showers.

Boy Meets Girl

Living in the dorms on a Bible College campus is not all Kumbaya. We had thieves and cheaters just like secular college campuses. I kept a jar of change on my dresser. The money randomly disappeared. Someone else must have needed it more than me. God is their Judge. I worked swing shift and tried to get my school assignments finished before leaving for work. Often, I came home at midnight and found that my homework was ruffled through and even missing on occasion.

Some students were 'Mama called, and Papa sent.' That means they were not called into the ministry by God, but their family sent them to college to find a good wife/husband or to get straightened out spiritually. Many lives have been ruined when pure, young girls married hypocrites pretending to be men of God. The opposite is also true— ungodly young women married godly young men, only to ruin their ministries later in life.

In the days prior to computers, our professors seemed to think we had time to sit in front of an electric typewriter and type our class notes, papers, and assignments. I did not have a typewriter and did not type fast. Therefore, I paid girls to do it for me.

Near the end of the second semester, a large group of us were signed in after curfew to the annex building. Curfew was at 10:30 p.m. and if you needed to do homework after that, you had to sign in at the guard shack to whatever building you planned to be in. This evening, most of us were typing papers. I hired Lori to type mine. It was late. I had just returned from work to dictate my paper to her. It was due the next day.

I was not in the annex long when I saw a commotion at the other end of the table. John yelled at a short blonde girl, "Come on, Kathy, quit making so many mistakes on my notebook! I'm going to get a bad grade! You aren't getting the lines even after you use the white out."

I looked questioningly at Lori, and she said, "I know! John's been yelling at that girl all night. Get this: she's already finished all her notebooks, papers, and assignments yet she's here past midnight typing this guy's notebook and all he does is yell at her. That girl works a fulltime job and gets straight A's. John doesn't have a job, yet he has that girl staying up all night to do his assignment. I think they are boyfriend and girlfriend so she's probably not even getting paid."

I shrugged my shoulders and dictated as Lori continued to transcribe my Theology paper. It was hard to concentrate with John continually belittling that girl. Finally, I could take it no more. I stood up, walked over, and rebuked him, "John, you need to treat this woman with respect. She's done with all her homework and she's only here to help you. How dare you treat her like this!"

John stood up, "She's MY girlfriend. I'll treat her as I please."

I looked at the girl cowering in embarrassment and asked, "What's your name?"

She shyly answered, "Kathy."

First Year of Bible College

"Kathy, you don't have to take this garbage from anyone. It's way past midnight, why don't you go to bed?"

She looked from me to John and then around the room. All eyes were on her. Kathy rose and timidly said, "I'm tired—I'm going to bed. Good night, everyone. Good luck with your papers." She looked at me and smiled, "Thank you. Good night."

After my intervention, Kathy and John broke off their relationship. John did not return to school the next year. This was my first encounter with Kathy Longest, but certainly not my last. Years later, she told me after that night, she secretly called me her 'knight in shining armor.'

THOUGHTS
- Part of life is about learning to get along with others.
- People you meet in college will become lifelong friends if you treat everyone with respect.
- Give much—you never know when you will need others to give unto you.
- Many of my college friends supported us on the mission field.
- Name an area of your life where you can improve on inter-personal relationships.

Chapter Five

Second Year of Bible College

Study to show thyself approved unto God, a workman that needeth not to be ashamed, rightly dividing the word of truth.
2 Timothy 2:15

A New Job

"Hey, Ron," Don said, "What do you think you'll do in Heaven?" It had been a long shift. I was tired and not thinking straight.

"I suppose all those mansions have doorknobs. Maybe God is preparing one of us to polish them." I responded.

During the second semester of my first year, I got a job working with most of the married students at Kwikset Lock and Key Factory in Anaheim. Kwikset loved hiring PCBBC students because we had a strong work ethic. It was drilled into us by Dr. Jack Baskin, our college Vice-President,

And whatsoever ye do, do it heartily, as to the Lord, and not unto men; (Colossians 3:23)

Landing a job at this factory was a huge blessing, so when my first year of college was over, I did not dare quit and go home for the summer. Instead, I moved off campus into an apartment with an older single student. I survived the first year of living with people I knew deep down had a relationship with God which I did not have.

The shift was 3-11:30 p.m. It was a 48-minute drive each way, so many students car-pooled. My carpool buddies became lifetime friends. We had great theological debates to and from work. My favorite was 'Did Adam have a belly button? If he did, was it an innie or an outie?'

Second Year of Bible College

Courage

During my second year, I began hanging out with Kathy Longest—the girl who had been mistreated by her boyfriend. She was looking for someone to help her with the Junior High Class at Calvary Baptist Church in San Dimas—I volunteered. While I had initially decided to not go to this church, I was excited about this ministry opportunity, not to mention spending time with her.

Through it we became good friends, but that was all, because I was engaged to my high school sweetheart back in Oregon.

Not long after meeting Kathy, she went forward at church to make assurance of her salvation.

I asked her, "Do you feel any different?"

"I went forward when I was six years old. I remember it, but I'm not sure I repented. I remember thinking I was a good kid and I'm not sure I really saw myself as a sinner at six years old. So, I went forward to make assurance of my salvation because I don't want to miss Heaven by twelve inches."

"Twelve inches?" I asked.

"Yeah, the distance between my head and my heart. In my head I knew that Jesus is God and died for me, but I wasn't sure I believed that in my heart. I needed assurance. I have peace now, knowing beyond a shadow of a doubt that I'm going to Heaven."

What courage it took Kathy to admit she had doubts! Her testimony spoke to my own heart about my salvation uncertainties.

The next Sunday she gave her testimony to the Jr. High Youth Group. She held up a jar with a cockroach inside, "See this cockroach? We hate them. They are disgusting. That is how God sees our sin. We think we are good, but God sees us as cockroaches—if we have never asked Jesus to forgive us of our sins. Isaiah 64:6 says,

"But we are all as an unclean thing, and all our righteousnesses are as filthy rags; and we all do fade as a leaf; and our iniquities, like the wind, have taken us away."

Several of the teens repented and asked Jesus to save them.

Finding the Truth

One day we drove to Azusa Canyon. Kathy was athletic and thought she could beat me in a one-mile race to the Azusa Canyon waterfall.

"Are you ready?" I asked as we stood at the trailhead.

"Are YOU ready to be beaten by a girl?" Kathy smiled back. She took off running and yelled over her shoulder, "Go!"

I quickly passed her and ran ahead on the winding trail. I looked behind, but she was nowhere in sight. I soon reached the waterfall and waited. No Kathy. I had given it my all. I was hot and sweaty. I jumped in the pool at the bottom of the fall to cool off. Still no Kathy. I got out and sunned myself to dry my clothes. I waited. No Kathy. Where was she?

Perhaps she sprained an ankle?

I headed back down the trail to find her. I met her just past the first bend. She was huffing and puffing, but still coming.

"I've already been to the waterfall, swam, and dried off!" I laughed, "What's taking so long?"

Kathy gave me a weak smile, "I guess I'm a little out of shape. How much farther?"

"Just around the bend. You're almost there." With that I took off for the waterfall yelling over my shoulder, "I'll beat you twice!"

We had a great time together. Kathy had packed a lunch. We watched the squirrels frolic in the trees and talked about how to grow the Junior High Class. At every turn, Kathy acknowledged our need to trust God and seek His face. I could see her relationship with God was genuine, and I wanted that same kind of relationship with God.

Conviction overcame me as I compared my life to that of a real Christian. I had so much trouble overcoming sin. I never felt at peace. I was tired of working my way to Heaven. I wanted God's free gift and the Holy Spirit's help and guidance.

Sitting behind the wheel of my truck in Azusa Canyon, I called upon the Lord, "God, I'm tired of playing religion. I'm tired of working my way to Heaven. I just keep failing. I have asked You to save me several times, but I have never accepted Your gift of salvation. Today, I ask You to be my Personal Savior. At this moment, I repent and realize I no longer need to work my way to get to Heaven. Jesus Christ, You did all the work and I accept Your free gift of salvation."

I looked at Kathy. She was crying, "Did you just get saved?"

Through my tears, I whispered, "Yes. I did."

The burden was finally gone! I trusted God, not myself for my salvation. The peace is real. In fact, it is surreal. I met the Savior that night and He became my First Love, Hope and Desire.

The next day, I humbled myself to my Pastor, "I got saved last night. I need to be baptized."

My Pastor was surprised, "What is it with the Junior High staff? You are the third one this year to get saved. There must be a revival going on in that department! We will have a baptism next Sunday."

Second Year of Bible College

Now that I was genuinely saved, I struggled with the idea of Christian service. If I only now was truly saved, how was I called into the ministry in high school? What was I doing in Bible College?

I needed wise counsel. I made an appointment with Dr. Jack Baskin. "Dr. Baskin, I got saved last week and now I'm wondering what I'm doing at Bible College."

"Ron, do you want to serve the Lord?"

"Yes, I owe everything to my Savior. I thought God called me in High School, but I wasn't even saved."

Dr. Baskin smiled, "Do you need a call to serve the Lord? Give me your phone number, and I'll call you!"

I was confused. He smiled, "Ron, you are in my missions classes. You know that we don't need a call when we have a command to go. God will use anyone who is willing to be used. I want to pray with you right now." He laid his hands on me and began to pray, "Lord, Ron is willing and ready to serve You. I pray that You will call him to be a missionary and that he will serve You with gladness all the days of his life."

I smiled as I left Dr. Baskin's office. I thought back to my dream as a child in that hot air balloon saving people. It had been a nightmare because I could not help them all.

Maybe being a missionary was a way to save people.

My motivation for going to Bible College had not been right. I was looking to earn my salvation, but God had different plans. So often in life we think we are in control. As a Christian, we cannot be. If we are in control, then we are going the opposite of what God intended for us in our lives. The most important part of the Christian life is to live by faith and keep doing whatever God wants you to do.

If you are going the wrong way, God has a way of doing a course correction. The Bible is filled with people going the wrong way and God intervening with what He likes to call the 'Right Way.' Moses, Jonah, Matthew, Zacchaeus, and Paul are just a few examples. This was a defining moment in my life. God made a huge course correction.

Harm's Way

Not long after my salvation, God gave me an opportunity to feel the peace that passes all understanding—something He gives when one is truly His child. At work I was tasked with being a material handler. I ran around the warehouse with a hand truck carrying parts from one machine to the next. I would run into some of the most dangerous people in Orange County. There was a gang leader who did not like white people. I had to pick up his parts every day. He constantly bullied me.

One day Big Boy waited until I was alone in the warehouse aisle. With no witnesses around, he approached me pulling out a big switch blade, "White boy, what is your problem? I told you; you can't run your parts through my area."

I looked him in the eye and said, "It's my job. I must or I'll get fired."

Big Boy did not care about my job security. "I'm going to kill you. I kill people like you all the time." Horrific hatred was written on his face, in his eyes, and evident in his threatening words.

While he was holding his knife on me, I calmly replied, "You can't kill me."

He put the knife closer to my neck and asked, "Why not?"

I answered, "You will only change my address from earth to Heaven. I am a Christian, and I will live forever."

Suddenly, Big Boy doubled over in pain. He grabbed his stomach and ran out of the warehouse. I watched paralyzed as he rushed out. Sweat was pouring down my face. I shook uncontrollably.

Lord, thank You for protecting me. Please help me calm down so I can go back to work.

As I strolled past Big Boy's machine the next day, I overheard a co-worker say, "Hey, did you hear the guy who worked on this machine is now in jail for multiple murders? The police arrested him last night."

I had no idea that Big Boy really had murdered people. I was supposed to be his next victim, yet God had different plans for me.

On yet another occasion, I was on campus doing homework until it was time to leave for Kwikset. I left my truck there and rode in the campus carpool. We got to work, completed our shift, and got ready to drive back to campus.

Before I could leave, my boss called me into his office, "Ron, I have a job that will only take ten minutes if you work fast."

I asked the campus carpool to wait, but they left.

How am I going to get back to campus?

I was upset and anxiously looked around to see if anyone was still there to carpool with. I saw a man from another carpool still finishing his shift and asked, "Hey, Jack, can you wait for me? My boss has a ten-minute job for me. I'll hurry."

"Sure," Jack replied, "I've got about ten minutes of work as well."

"Thanks!" I called back as I hurried to complete the project.

Ten minutes later, we piled into Jack's old Oldsmobile. "Thanks again for waiting. I guess the other campus students wanted to get going."

Second Year of Bible College

On the drive home, we noticed a huge wreck alongside the road. "Hey," someone said, "It looks like a tornado dropped a car in a tree."

"There aren't tornados in Southern California!" I replied. We thought nothing more of it.

It was not until we got back to the campus parking lot, that we heard the bad news. That car in the tree was the campus carpool. They had driven through a green light unaware of a firetruck about to sail through the intersection.

A high school friend was in that car and died on impact. A fireman was also killed. Several of the students suffered life-long health issues. I was upset they took off without me, but God again intervened and kept me out of harm's way. I would continue to experience this lesson of God re-arranging my schedule to save my life.

It is humbling when one comes that close to death. I had no idea of the plans God had for me, but I knew there was a reason He spared me that night. Jeremiah 29:11 came to my mind:

> **But I know the thoughts that I think toward you, saith the Lord, thoughts of peace and not of evil to give you an expected end.**

Choosing a Help Meet

Kathy was smart, funny, and helpful. Her testimony was a big part of my salvation story. I knew she was falling for me. I needed to talk to her about my future. I caught her as we were leaving Missions class, "Hey, Kathy, we need to talk. Can you meet me at the pond after classes are over?"

"Sure! See you then!"

I did not hear much of the lesson in my Church Administration class. I was too busy formulating my plan of how to tell Kathy I was engaged. My fiancé and I had an on-again, off-again, relationship throughout high school. She was three years younger, but she was working hard to finish her A.C.E. paces and graduate in the Spring so we could get married in the summer. She was underage but her parents were eager for us to get married.

Kathy was sitting on one of the benches near the pond as I approached. She smiled, "Isn't it beautiful here on this campus? You'd never know that just across the valley is the chaos and confusion known as Los Angeles. God is good to give us such a wonderful place to learn more about Him! I love the birds, the flowers, and I think Herman just popped his head up in the pond!"

She paused as we both scanned the pond to see if the large catfish named Herman Munster was still visible. The water was calm. Herman had once again descended to the bottom of the old cement swimming pool.

Finally, our eyes met, and she asked, "But hey, what's up?"

I gathered the courage to speak, "I called my fiancé, Sandy, this past weekend. We've been unofficially engaged since she was 14. I've mentioned her to you before, haven't I?"

She nodded and I hurried on, "Her grandmother gave me the family wedding rings. It looks like she will be able to graduate in the Spring, so we have decided to get married this summer."

Kathy's face flashed a look of shock. She quickly composed herself and smiled, "Oh! Well, if that's God's will for your life, that's great—uhm, I need to go. I forgot I need to leave early for work."

She stood, gave me a weird look, opened her mouth to speak, pointed at me, then waved her hand in dismissal as she walked away.

Her sudden exit bothered me all night at work. When I got home, I could not sleep. I had no peace. I knew I was making the wrong decision. God kept saying to me—

Favour is deceitful, and beauty is vain: but a woman that feareth the LORD, she shall be praised. (Proverbs 31:30)

Sandy was beautiful, but Kathy feared the Lord. After a night of wrestling with the Lord, I realized Kathy was God's will for me.

The next day I asked Kathy to have another talk. She politely sat down, "What's up?" she began, "Did you want a woman's prospective on how to officially propose to Sandy? I'm probably not the person to talk to—"

I interrupted her, "No! I couldn't sleep at all last night. I felt like I was making the wrong decision for my wife. God kept saying, 'Beauty is vain but a woman that feareth the Lord, she shall be praised.' And I don't know of anyone who loves and fears the Lord more than you. God is telling me that you should be my wife."

A whole array of emotions crossed Kathy's face: shock, disbelief, confusion, and finally an understanding smile. She threw her head back and laughed.

"Why are you laughing?"

"It wasn't until you told me that you were going to marry someone else, that I realized I had feelings for you. When I left yesterday, I went back to the dorm, grabbed my best friend, Teresa, and we decided to pray after we got off work. We prayed all night in Voorhis Chapel that God would change your heart if it was truly His will."

Second Year of Bible College

I too laughed, "God really loves you. I'm glad I will be the one to lead you on great adventures for Christ. He obviously answers your prayers. You do know I'm called to be a missionary, don't you?"

Voorhis Chapel where Kathy prayed all night for Ron to know God's will

"Yes, I know. I prayed about that last night too. God reminded me that I surrendered to whatever He wants me to do when I came to Bible College. I am willing to go anywhere. Just lead, and I will follow."

It does not get any better than that!

THOUGHTS
- Have you ever fervently prayed all night for God to answer a need?

CHAPTER SIX

Marriage & Early Ministry

Whoso findeth a wife findeth a good thing, and obtaineth favor of the LORD. Proverbs 18:22

Love & Marriage
The next morning, I waited for Kathy outside her dormitory. She soon appeared and came toward me laughing. "What's so funny?" I asked.

"The girls in the dorm are mad at you."

"Why? What did I do?"

"They were watching us when we discussed God's will for our lives. They could tell something had changed and as soon as I walked in the dorm, they grilled me. I told them how God impressed upon you that you were to marry me instead of Sandy because, 'beauty is vain but a woman that feareth the Lord, she shall be praised.'"

"So? What's wrong with that?"

"They all looked at me in horror and said, 'He called you ugly?' I didn't—"

"Wait!" I interrupted, "I didn't mean it that way! I meant you are a godly woman and I choose that over anything else!"

Kathy laughed, "Don't worry. I didn't take it that way. But if any of the girls from my dorm give you the stink eye today, you'll know why." And they did.

Now that I knew God's will in whom I was to marry, we began our plans. First off was for me to tell Sandy, her family, and my home church how God had worked in my life. They did not respond kindly. Sandy hung up on me, her father called to chew me out and my home pastor told me I was no longer welcome at that church. I felt bad for hurting them, but I knew God had called me to Bible College to get saved and to marry Kathy.

I surprised Kathy with a trip to Idaho, her home state, for Christmas. Teresa, Kathy's best friend, agreed to come along as our chaperone. We drove through Oregon, stopping to spend Christmas Eve with my family. They liked Kathy a lot.

We left early Christmas morning to celebrate with Kathy's family. We wanted to surprise her parents and arrived just in time for lunch. They always hosted Christmas Dinner for about 25 people. Someone got to her mom before us, "Judy, I thought you said Kathy wasn't coming."

"She isn't." she replied.

"Why is she in your living room?"

Our Engagement Picture

Judy turned to see Kathy standing behind her. I stood back while they embraced and cried. Finally, Kathy turned, "Mom, I'd like you to meet a friend of mine, Ron Reasoner. He brought me home."

Of course, my whole reason for going to Idaho was to get alone with Kathy's father, Ben, and ask permission to marry Kathy. When everyone left that evening, I asked Ben for a moment alone, "I have come to ask for Kathy's hand in marriage. I love her and I want us to spend the rest of our lives together serving the Lord."

Ben looked me in the eye, "Well, that's up to Kathy. If she wants to marry you, I'm all for it, but if she doesn't, then I'm against it as well."

We spent several days with Kathy's family before returning to college. Kathy began planning a summer wedding during the two-week shutdown Kwikset had in July.

Meanwhile, I got a promotion. The Lord allowed me to move up from the bottom to the top of my pay grade, and I now was paid for piece work in addition to getting a base pay. This meant I received a bonus for each doorknob I polished over the nightly quota. I doubled my pay by working smarter and harder.

We decided to have the wedding in Idaho. My family could easily carpool from Portland. Kathy spent hours writing to her mother and planning. She was determined to plan it all by mail, saving every penny possible for our lives together.

The time quickly approached. Kathy flew home two weeks before the wedding to iron out the final details. I stayed in California working and planning our honeymoon. Kathy wanted to drive up to Canada and stay in Banff Castle. She had seen a photograph of that old castle when she was a child and had always wanted to go there. I do not remember much about those final weeks before the wedding except I fell asleep each night with the ceiling lights glaring in my face.

Three days before the wedding, my best man, the photographer, an usher, and I drove up in Kathy's Datsun B210. When I got to Kathy's home, she and her mom had everything ready: the flowers, the cake, the napkins, the punch, the mints, and nuts.

That accounted for everything except for the call we received the night before the dress rehearsal. Our pastor in California was supposed to officiate our wedding, but his father-in-law passed away and he could not come. Thankfully we had already asked Kathy's pastor to sing and pray, so he easily slipped into officiating.

The much-anticipated day finally arrived on July 16, 1983. We only had a few surprises, but the wedding turned out beautifully. First, Kathy was nervous and when she repeated her vows, she said, "All my love to me I pledge—" instead of saying "all my love to thee I pledge." The other surprise was I swooped and leaned her back when the Pastor said, 'you may now kiss the bride.' We had waited to kiss on the lips until our wedding day. I wanted to make the kiss memorable. Kathy held on for dear life fearing I might drop her, but my sudden plan went smoothly. The look on Pastor's face sent everyone into laughter.

After the reception, we drove to McCall, Idaho where Kathy's parents had paid for a night in the hotel on the lake. We never made it to Banff, Canada. Instead, we went camping.

This was my first encounter with misunderstandings between husbands and wives. Camping to me meant buying a tent and grilling the fish we caught over an open fire. Camping to Kathy meant an RV. I'm not sure where she thought I was hiding an RV, but she was deeply disappointed in the two-man tent I brought along. Not surprisingly, we cut our camping trip short and went back to her parents' home. I helped

Marriage & Early Ministry

Ben lay the concrete foundation of a cabin they were building. We also went waterskiing. Kathy learned to ski when she was 10 and I was just happy I got up on my first try.

After our honeymoon, we returned to California so I could get back to work. I had rented an apartment two months earlier, and now it was time to settle into our lives as a married couple.

Our First Child

Nine-and-a-half months after our wedding, on April 29, 1984, we welcomed Joel Christopher into our family. He was born during finals week. Kathy and I were both graduating with a Missions degree. She was the valedictorian. I, on the other hand, could not even spell it. I thought it was called "valevictorian". So, no, I was not in the running.

In the 1980's everyone preached the imminent return of Jesus Christ. The signs of the times were everywhere, and we needed to get busy! To hurry into ministry, I decided to graduate with a three-year degree instead of four. However, that summer God impressed upon my heart to get my bachelor's degree in Theology, so I started up classes again in the Fall. Years later in Russia, that bachelor's degree kept me out of jail and allowed me to preach repeatedly in schools and universities. I had no idea how important education and degrees were to the rest of the world.

Graduation & Our Second Child

In May 1985, I graduated. It was time to get on staff somewhere. I talked to a pastor I knew from Portland during Graduation/Fellowship Week. "Hello, Brother Jones, do you remember me? I'm Ron Reasoner. I grew up in Oregon. I'm from Aloha Berean Baptist Church. I graduate this week with a bachelor's degree in Theology with a Missions emphasis, and I'm looking for a place to serve my internship. Do you have any staff positions available?"

Brother Jones looked me up and down, "Yes, Ron, I remember you from youth camps and rallies. As a matter of fact, I am looking for a young marrieds' director. Are you married?"

"Yes, Sir, and I have one child and another on the way."

"Do you have a resumé?"

I retrieved a copy from my briefcase. "Good!" he said as he took it, "I'll call you next week."

Brother Jones called a few days later, "Ron, I'd like to offer you a staff position at my church. When can you start?"

College Graduation Picture

"Well, Sir, my wife is eight months pregnant. We need to have the baby here in California where my work insurance will cover it. We can come after the baby's six-week checkup."

"Oh, I kind of need someone immediately, but I guess we can wait three months. I'll keep in touch."

Six weeks later, on July 26, 1985, we had our second son, Micah Duane. True to his father's form, Micah did not cry when he was born. When describing his birth, Kathy says, "I thought, 'How nice, a quiet child' and Micah's been deceiving us ever since."

Micah's birth was the end of an era. We were now ready to leave the student path and step into ministry. This meant leaving the safety of my job at Kwikset. When I gave my notice to leave, they asked me to stay in an executive position. This was a six-figure income. My flesh wanted the security of a good job, but I knew God had bigger plans. It was time to walk by faith.

Marriage & Early Ministry

It was also time to say good-bye to our Junior High Class at Calvary Baptist Church. We had invested our money, time, prayers, and lives into these teenagers. Several went on to become pastors and missionaries.

After our last service, Kathy, the boys, and I went back to our packed apartment. I called Brother Jones, "Hello, Pastor Jones, this is Ron Reasoner. I'm just calling to find out more information about where we will live once we move to Oregon."

Brother Jones cleared his throat and stumbled over his words, "Oh! Ron, did I forget to call you? I gave the staff position to someone in our church. So, we won't be needing you after all. Sorry for any inconvenience. Have a good day. God bless!" He hung up.

Great! I had already given notice at Kwikset. This was a hard blow. I knew from experience that the men who stuck around the college after graduation, often do not make it into ministry. They start careers and get comfortable. I did not want to be one of them. I knew God wanted me in ministry.

"Kathy, we have a problem!"

She came into the room with Joel on her hip and Micah nestled in her other arm, "What's wrong?"

"He hired someone else."

"What will we do?"

"We pray." I grabbed her hand, "Lord, we are Your servants, ready to do Your will. Lead us where You need us until we are home with You." That started our routine family times of prayer when a situation seemed bleak and only the Lord could help.

When I finished, Kathy said, "Maybe you should call my pastor in Idaho. Perhaps he needs help."

I called and he invited us to come to their church as the young marrieds' director. I would have to work a full-time job, but he promised if I got 10 givers in my class, he would give me a salary.

After Micah's six-week checkup, at the end of August 1985, we loaded up my Ford truck and Kathy's Datsun B210 and drove to Idaho. We were so excited to be done with Bible college and starting full-time ministry. This is what we had waited for and what we had gone to Bible college to learn. The 850 miles to Boise, Idaho seemed like an eternity.

THOUGHTS

- Has a spiritual figure in your life ever let you down?
- How did you deal with that disappointment?

CHAPTER SEVEN

Ministry Lessons

And the apostles said unto the Lord, Increase our faith.
Luke 17:5

When we arrived in Idaho in the mid-1980s; it was going through an economic slump. I remember there were 300 applicants waiting in line at McDonald's for a job. The Lord provided and blessed us when I got a job as a school bus driver and Kathy worked in a daycare where she could keep the children with her. We would not have made it financially if Kathy's parents had not given us a place to live.

My in-laws moved into the beautiful cabin they spent three years building in the mountains. They offered to let us live in Kathy's childhood home which was old and needed to be remodeled before they could sell it. They let us live there rent free if we agreed to move out when they started to remodel.

Between us, we made just enough for a car payment and utilities, but there was little left over for food. We ate lots of macaroni and cheese and potatoes. Meat was a luxury.

After six months, we moved into a two-bedroom apartment. The $300 a month for rent only added to our financial burdens.

The young marrieds' class met Sunday nights, so it was difficult to get people to attend. On our first Sunday, there were two people. In our second month we had 15, and in the third month we had 33. The class slowly grew, but sadly it never worked out to get a salaried position. Instead, I learned to deal with broken promises. The Lord would teach me this lesson many times in the coming decades.

Moving Into Ministry

Personal disappointments aside, we had the opportunity to lead and disciple many young couples. I was excited when two men surrendered to full time ministry. Besides sharing the Gospel and seeing people make decisions to follow Jesus, there is nothing more exciting than seeing people catch the vision to spread the Gospel and reach the lost.

Micah's Illness

Eventually I switched jobs and started working swing-shift on the "green chain" at a sawmill. It was hard work. Within a few months, I got promoted to the day shift. It was a blessing to now have evenings free for ministry, plus dayshift got health insurance!

One day I heard my name called over the loudspeaker, "Ron Reasoner, you have a phone call on line one."

No one calls me at work. What could be the problem?

"Hello?" I asked as I reached the office and grabbed the phone from the secretary.

Kathy blurted out, "Ron, I'm so glad I got ahold of you. Micah is sick. When he woke up this morning, his eye was swollen, and he has a fever. The swelling keeps getting bigger. Do we have insurance? Can I take him to the doctor?"

I put my hand over the phone and asked the secretary, "Do I have health insurance? My child needs a doctor."

The secretary asked, "How long have you been on days?"

"Just over two months."

"Then, yes, you have insurance."

"Kathy? Yes! Take Micah to the doctor and let me know how it goes. Love you. Gotta go." I said a quick prayer and went back to work.

When Kathy arrived at the clinic, the doctor took one look at Micah, and said, "Take your son and go directly to St. Luke's hospital. He is horribly sick and if it is what I think it is, his life is in danger. Before you go, I want to show his eye to the optometrist downstairs. He is new and probably has never seen this."

Kathy followed the doctor to the optometrist's office. When he saw Micah's eye, he exclaimed, "Who hit you, Son?"

The pediatrician immediately spoke up, "No! This is periorbital cellulitis. It is so rare, I thought you might want to see it. In the future, if someone comes to you with this disease, you must be able to diagnosis it."

Turning to Kathy, the pediatrician said, "Now, go straight to the hospital. I will let them know you are coming. I will be there this evening after office hours."

Kathy called from the hospital, "It's serious, Ron. They admitted Micah. I guess this is a bacterial infection. The doctor said it is the same bacteria that causes Spinal Meningitis, and we are lucky it settled in his eye instead of his spine where it could go undiagnosed until it is too late. They have hooked Micah up to an I.V. on top of his head so he cannot touch it. It looks awful. Please hurry."

I was devastated.

What are You doing, Lord?

We got Micah on the church prayer chain. I called everyone I knew. When you go through hard times, you call your spiritual friends and ask them to pray in case your prayers are not making it through to God. We needed faithful prayer warriors praying!

On the third day of Micah's stay, my boss called me into his office. He shuffled his feet and had trouble looking me in the eye, "I checked, and you don't have insurance."

"But I have been on the day shift for more than two months and the company policy says I get it after one month on day shift."

The boss looked down at his feet and mumbled, "I didn't file the paperwork. I was trying to save money."

I was shocked, "But it is company policy."

The boss said, "What's done is done. I can't change it."

Lord, how will I pay for Micah's hospital stay? We hardly have money for food, let alone hospital bills. How much money will this cost us? Why are You allowing this to happen?

Ministry Lessons

Micah was in the hospital for a week. Many people from our church visited to encourage us and pray for Micah. There was a little girl in the next room. She was 18 months old with cancer. Her family watched as we had a steady flow of visitors. Her mother finally asked, "Who are these people? Are they family?"

I explained, "They are our church family who love us and come to pray." I gave her a tract and invited her to church.

As soon as their little girl got out of the hospital, they came to church. We rejoiced to see the mother and father both come forward and receive Jesus as their Savior.

This is what You were doing Lord! You placed us in their lives to lead them to the One who gives eternal life and hope!

They became faithful members of my young marrieds' class. I learned so much about ministry through their lives and the trial of their little girl having cancer. I was allowed the privilege of being the pastor who comforted and counseled them when God called their little girl to Heaven. They taught me about grief, suffering, and dealing with the death of a child.

I will never forget the night I went over to comfort them after their daughter's death. I was expecting chaos, but I found peace. The mother told me this story:

> "My little girl woke up crying in pain two nights ago. I called the doctor and he said, 'Get some rest. We'll admit her into the hospital in the morning. Prepare yourself. There is nothing else we can do. She has had her lifetime doses of everything.
>
> "I fell back to sleep and dreamt that my girl was in the room at the end of the hall on the pediatric floor. My baby was in so much pain, I could hardly stand to be in the room with her. I couldn't stop crying. The agony! Then, suddenly she stopped crying and began to smile. She stood up in her crib and put her hands out. I started toward her but realized that she was not reaching out to me, but Someone behind me. I looked and saw Jesus.
>
> "He gave me a gentle smile, walked past me, and picked up my little girl. Immediately she was whole. He took a final look at me, hugged my girl, and showed me she was no longer crying. Then Jesus walked out of the room with my child in His arms. My baby was happy and pain free. She waved good-bye as Jesus carried her away from the pain and suffering of life.

> *"The next day, I asked for the same room that had been in my dream. That night, while I slept, Jesus came and got my little girl. I did not see Jesus, but my dream comforted me. I know what happened to my baby."*

Until a month before the little girl died, she was so active and normal. You would never know by looking at her that she was full of cancer eating away her life. It was a day of celebration when she got promoted to Heaven.

Cancer is a perfect picture of the natural man. On the outside, we look fine, but on the inside, sin is eating away at us. Only by dying to self and becoming alive in Christ Jesus can we be made whole again.

Though I was upset with my boss for not putting my family on the health insurance plan, I desperately needed the job and dared not file a complaint. There were hundreds of men out of work.

The next week, the company owner made a surprise visit. When he saw how my boss ran the company, he got fired. This was the first time God showed me the principle of dealing honestly with those in spiritual leadership. My boss (a backslidden Christian) cheated us, but God judged him. I still did not have insurance, but the hospital directed us to a charity who covered the bill.

I also learned an important lesson about how people are watching you when God allows trials into your life. They want to see if your God on the mountain is still real when you are suffering in the valley. This lesson became a life changer in Russia. People wanted to see Christ in us before giving up their family and culture to follow Christ.

Living by Faith

Math does not work when you are dealing with God's economy. He fed 5,000 people with five loaves and two fish. It is hard to understand how faith changes your whole life. When you live and think logically, one plus one always equals two. However, when you live by faith, everything is turned upside down. God increased our faith by allowing us to live a whole year on $800 a month. All the bills were paid including our tithes and offerings and we never missed a meal.

Miracles happened along the way. One such miracle was when we finally hit rock bottom. We had no food and the money we had was for our faith-promise missions giving. Kathy came to me, "What are we going to do? We have enough money to either give our tithe and faith-promise, or we can buy food."

Ministry Lessons

"We will do God's will and trust Him," I answered. We went to church, and I deposited every penny we had into the offering plate.

When we got home, Kathy looked at me, "What are YOU going to do now? You gave God everything. Now what?"

There is only one proper response for the child of God. Pray. But first, I took one final inventory of our cupboards. Often when your wife says, "There's no food in the house," she means there is no food we like. But I found that our cupboards were indeed empty. The refrigerator had a dried-up carrot. We would have to divide it up four ways. We needed a miracle from God at that moment. We did not tell anyone about our predicament, we trusted God.

"Come," I said to Kathy and the boys, "Let's kneel here in the living room and pray for God to send manna from Heaven." We were teaching the boys to bring the family together in times of need, asking God to answer our prayers. It is important for parents to not only teach their children to live by faith, but to involve them in the process of applying their faith.

Kathy settled two-and-a-half-year-old Joel and 18-month-old Micah on their knees between us and I cried out to God, "Lord, we have given all. We come before You with empty stomachs asking You to fill them. You fed the 5,000 with just a little bit of food. Perhaps You will multiply that carrot and make us a stew. I don't know what else to do but ask You to intervene."

I have rarely prayed so fervently as I did that night. My prayers were motivated by great need and great hunger. While we were praying, there was a knock on the door. We were too busy doing business with God to answer it.

Eventually, curiosity got the best of me. When Kathy finished praying, I walked over to open the door. There was no one there. But, on our porch were two sacks of groceries. My wife saw them and jumped up and down. "Hurry up! Bring them in! I want to see where God shops!"

Are you kidding me? We are experiencing a miracle and you want to know where God shops?

Even in one of our darkest hours, Kathy had not lost her sense of humor. I looked at the bags and replied, "He shops at Albertsons."

We lined the food on the counter with oohs and ahhs. Just when we thought we would miss our first meal in the ministry, God gave us groceries in time for a late dinner.

We rejoiced in God's faithfulness and told the story repeatedly. I do not believe we would have gone to Russia without this experience. It increased our faith to know that God will answer if we pray. He takes care of all our needs according to the riches of His grace.

A faith-promise commitment really allows one to walk by faith. If one takes that important leap of faith into depending upon God, He will supply. Faith is found one step beyond absolute surrender. It is no longer the hearing or even the committing, it is the doing.

God continued to supply our needs. Once I shook hands with a deacon and he slipped a $100 bill into my hand. He will find out in Heaven how desperately we needed that money.

Another time we received a money order for $50. The address of the sender said, "Bank of Heaven."

Groceries do not last forever. Soon we were down to slim pickings. It is amazing how many ways one can prepare macaroni and cheese. Being a vegan was not yet popular, but we were often forced to go without milk and meat for days at a time.

One Sunday, the church was gearing up for a potluck dinner. The pastor asked for volunteers from the pulpit. "Who will bring a potato salad?" My wife quickly ran through the ingredients needed: potatoes, mayonnaise, mustard, pickles, onions, and eggs. We had them all. She raised her hand. "Okay. Kathy, you bring a potato salad and make sure you put eggs in it."

As we walked out of the church, one of our young married couples ran over. "We volunteered to make a potato salad too. Pastor said to put eggs in it, and we don't have any. Can we borrow some?"

I immediately answered, "Sure. Come on over and get them right now."

When we got in the car, Kathy sighed, "I only have two eggs and we don't have money to buy more. I'll have to make my potato salad without eggs and hope Pastor doesn't notice."

That evening at church, someone grabbed my hand as they walked past. I looked down, and there was a $50 bill. We had given all, and God replaced it 100-fold. Just like He promised!

These are the kinds of situations that God used to prepare us for the mission field. We stepped off the cliff of faith repeatedly. God caught us every single time.

THOUGHTS

- Can you think of a situation in your life where someone meant you harm but God meant it for good?

Chapter Eight

Corridor Baptist Church

And he said unto them, Let us go into the next towns, that I may preach there also: for therefore came I forth. Mark 1:38

Decision Time

One evening after Kathy put the boys to bed, we sat on the couch in our small apartment. I needed to share my heart, "Kathy, I feel like God is moving us again."

She frowned, "We've only been at this church for 18-months. I know it's been hard. We are so poor, but God has always provided. Do you think we have learned all God has for us here?"

"Well, the Associate Pastor has taken me under his wing and taught me a lot about the practicalities of church ministry. We've grown in Idaho mentally, spiritually, and practically."

"But definitely not financially!" Kathy interjected.

True.

I ignored her negative comment and continued, "I've been praying for about a month, and I feel it is time to move on."

"Well," Kathy said as she pulled her head off my shoulder, "We were Missions majors. When we met, you felt the call to the Philippines, then Nigeria. Are you still considering Nigeria?"

"You know I have this deep desire to go where no one has ever preached the Gospel. Like Paul said in Romans 15:20-21,

"Yea, so have I strived to preach the gospel, not where Christ was named, lest I should build upon another man's foundation: But as it is written, To whom he was not spoken of, they shall see: and they that have not heard shall understand.

"Every time a missionary comes through our church, I pray about that foreign field, but God keeps telling me, 'Wait.' I've been asking God where He could use me the most and my hometown of Hillsboro keeps popping into my head. There is no Independent Baptist Church there."

"Hillsboro? Have you never read that verse in the Bible?" She teased, "'A prophet hath no honor in his own country.'"

"I know, but I can't get Hillsboro out of my mind. For some reason, God wants us there for five years before we go to the foreign fields. If we can't make it in America, we certainly won't make it on the foreign field."

Kathy half smiled, "Thank you for sharing your heart with me, Ron. The good thing is, we can't get any poorer. If you believe it's God's will, I'll start packing."

Grabbing her hand, we began our family prayer, "Lord, we are Your servants, ready to do Your will. Lead us where You need us until we are home with You."

Oregon, Here We Come

In March of 1987, we left Boise, Idaho and moved to Oregon. All our belongings fit into the back of a truck. We did not know that young church planters often spend a year or two traveling to churches asking for financial support. We just went by faith. The church in Boise sent us $200 a month for two years. How hard could it be? My, how naïve we were!

The Oregon State Baptist Fellowship did not support new pastors. They felt you should make it on your own for the first year. If you were still around after a year, they would consider supporting you. They did not want to waste mission's dollars on someone who would not 'stick and stay and make it pay' but the first year is when a young preacher boy needs the most encouragement and support. When a support check comes, the knowledge that people are praying for you is as important as the money itself.

The First Service of Corridor Baptist Church — June 7, 1987

"Is everything ready?" I asked Kathy for the 10th time.

"I think so. We should get to the Oak Hills Recreation Center about 30 minutes early so we can set everything up. They have chairs there, right?"

"Yes, but we need to bring our electric piano and a pulpit. Can you think of anything else?"

"Did you pack the box of hymnals that Oak Harbor Bible Baptist Church sent us?"

Ministry Lessons

"Check." I frowned, "I can't believe we sent over 200 letters to Baptist Churches and Oak Harbor was the only church to respond and offer to help."

"We are young, Ron. People want to see what we are made of before they put money into us. It's okay. God will provide. He's already provided an apartment."

I smiled, "Yes. Last week we had no money to pay the rent. We haven't even started the church yet, and we are already struggling."

Kathy laughed and sat on the arm of my chair. "We thought God had failed us because we couldn't pay our bills. We kept praying and praying, thinking God had not answered."

I looked into her eyes. Now we both were enjoying the moment. I finished our story, "We asked God to send in the funds, but we forgot to check the mail! When I finally remembered, a $1,000 check had been waiting there two days. It covered our rent, our utilities and bought us a portable electric piano."

"He's never failed, Ron. Why do we doubt?"

I drew her hand to my mouth and gently kissed it. "Indeed! But now we must concentrate on tomorrow. I've knocked on every door in Oak Hills and Bethany. We've had Tuesday night meetings for a month. They have averaged 10 people. My sermon is ready. Let's pray for visitors." We bowed down on our knees and prayed, "God, we have sown, we have watered, but only You can give the increase. Help us, Lord, to glorify You tomorrow."

The next day, God blessed Corridor Baptist Church with 38 people in attendance. Obviously, some people just came out of courtesy because the next Sunday we had 15.

We called it Corridor Baptist Church because Hillsboro is situated near Highway 26 which runs between Portland and the Pacific Coast. The locals called it the Sunset Corridor. Our vision was to someday buy property near the highway. The word 'corridor' also has the double meaning of a hallway between two places. The church is like a hallway connecting people with Christ.

Our First Picnic

Soon we averaged 20 people in church. Since we had been meeting for several months. we decided to have our first church picnic at Shute Park in Hillsboro. We invited everyone we knew. I had met Lisa knocking on doors and she had repented at her door. She visited several times and was excited about coming to the picnic.

The day arrived. We came early to set up for our church. "Kathy, let's take those tables under the large tree," I said, my arms laden with a cooler and charcoal, "It is off the beaten path and I'm praying that God will give us a good group."

Kathy directed Joel to sit at a table and gave him the impossible task of keeping Micah seated while she helped get more supplies from the car. Soon everything was setup and people began to arrive.

"Let's play catch. I brought some mitts and a softball," someone said. Another family brought a volleyball net and set it up. An elderly couple volunteered to man the grill. Things were beginning to look like a real BBQ.

The group was having a good time when suddenly we heard shouting and cussing. The sound was getting closer. We turned and saw Lisa yelling obscenities to people in the park along the path towards our area, "Where is Corridor Baptist Church's picnic?" Kathy ran to meet her, directing her to our tables.

"I parked really far away," Lisa said, "I need to go get my BLANK car."

Kathy replied, "Okay. I'll go with you and help find a closer spot. Ron, please keep an eye the boys while I help Lisa." A lady in the church offered to watch Lisa's young boy.

Now, understand that Kathy is from a Christian home. She never went to parties and was never around drunk people. She had no idea this young lady was drunk. Kathy spoke softly all the way to the car, trying to calm her down.

When they got to the car, Lisa got behind the wheel and had trouble starting the car. Kathy thought that was odd. As soon as she pulled onto the street, a police car turned on its lights. Lisa began cussing and fuming. "I don't have a driver's license. I lost it last year for drunk driving."

"Park the car here near our group and stay calm," Kathy nervously said.

Two officers approached us, one on each side of the car. "Ladies, would you please step out of the car."

Kathy opened the door. "Please put your hands on the top of the car," the policeman ordered. She readily complied. "Ma'am, have you been drinking?"

Kathy looked shocked, "Officer, I have never had a drink of alcohol my entire life."

The policeman smirked and asked, "Then why did you get into the car with a drunk woman? You do realize that she is drunk, don't you?"

Ministry Lessons

"No, I didn't realize that. I have never been around drunk people."

The policeman rolled his eyes and continued, "We were called because she was going through the park cussing and creating trouble with her child in tow. Is she your friend?"

"Well," Kathy replied sheepishly, "We are having a church picnic and she was invited."

A slight grin came across the policeman's face as he asked, "A church picnic? Let me guess, are you the pastor's wife?"

"Yes, I am." Kathy smiled back.

The other policeman looked across the roof of the car at Kathy, "You are free to go, but we will have to arrest this lady for disorderly conduct, public drunkenness, and driving without a license. Can you take the child with you?"

At this point, I and half the park showed up. Lisa went nuts. She resisted arrest, kicking and screaming words I had never heard. They put her in the police car, and she began screaming and kicking at the windows. The policeman approached me and asked, "Are you the Pastor of this church?"

"Yes, Sir. I am."

"What kind of church is this? What is the name of it?"

I wanted to say the name of any church but ours. However, half the congregation was standing behind me and I could not lie, "Corridor Baptist Church, sir. We believe in reaching out to the lost."

The policeman smiled, shook my hand, and walked away.

We went back to grilling burgers and playing games while Kathy took the little boy home to his grandmother.

It was a church picnic we would never forget!

Greg gets Saved

One rainy day I knocked on a door near where we were meeting. A middle-aged lady answered the door, "Hi, I'm Ron Reasoner from Corridor Baptist Church. We meet in the Oak Hills Recreation Center. What is your name?"

"I'm Glenda. I used to go to church. Please come in, you'll get soaked out there."

Glenda directed me to the couch. I sat down and began my invitation, "We are a new church. You said you used to go to church. Do you mind me asking where?"

"It was a Baptist Church in Cottage Grove. I miss God in my life. I want Him back! I'm ready to come to church."

Wow. That was easy. Thank you, Lord!

Glenda became a faithful member of our church. She opened her home to have Vacation Bible School on her back deck.

Vacation Bible School at Glenda's House
Kathy Pregnant with Keturah

I visited Glenda weekly, hoping to connect with her husband. Finally, it happened. "Greg, I see you have a boat outside in the driveway. It's a good sized one. Do you ocean-fish?"

Greg's eyes brightened as he began to talk about his passion for fishing. We conversed for a while and eventually I was able to steer the conversation to spiritual things. "So, what is your religious background?"

"I'm a Catholic. I'm a good person. God and I have our own thing going," he proudly replied.

"If you were to die today, stand at the gates of Heaven and God asked you why He should let you into Heaven, what would you say?"

"I've lived a good life. My good deeds far outweigh my bad deeds. I think I'm safe."

"Do you mind if I show you a few verses from God's Word about salvation?" I opened my Bible to Ephesians 2:8-9:

"For by grace are ye saved through faith; and that not of yourselves: it is the gift of God: Not of works, lest any man should boast."

I looked Greg in the eye, "Do you understand what this verse is saying?"

He thought for a moment and answered honestly, "I'm not sure."

"It says that salvation is a free gift from God. We can't earn it. God says it's all about Him, so man has no reason to boast."

"But I'm a good person!" Greg adamantly stated.

For the next two hours, I showed him scripture after scripture about how man cannot work his way to Heaven, that it is all God's grace. Finally, Greg saw his need for Christ. He bowed his head and asked Jesus to save him, "God, I'll never be good enough to make it to Heaven on my own. I ask You to forgive my sins and save me. I believe Jesus died on the cross for my sins, was buried and rose again. I accept You as my Savior."

Greg became a great encouragement. One Sunday he came to me and said, "I'm alive! I see people differently now. I meet someone and I wonder, do they know the secret of life—Jesus came to save them? I pray for the courage and knowledge to tell others of Jesus."

Don't Jump Ahead of God

Though we had a small group of people regularly attending services, God had much to teach us about depending upon Him. The offerings were only enough to pay the church rent and sometimes the rent on our apartment. There was no money left to buy food. We did not take any kind of government assistance, not even W.I.C. (Women, Infants, and Children). We lived by faith and felt as missionaries in training we should depend upon God for our needs. I knocked doors 50 to 70 hours a week and begged God to bring them in.

One Tuesday morning I found Kathy crying. I sat down beside her, took her hand, and asked, "Kathy, what's the problem?"

"I did something terrible. I knew you wouldn't approve so I did it without your permission."

All kinds of scenarios were floating in my head, "What happened?" I asked as calmly as I could muster.

"It's been two weeks since our children have had any milk. I couldn't stand it anymore. I remembered those children in my high school health book who had rickets. It's hard to watch our children go without nutrients that are essential for a healthy childhood. One can only eat so many bowls of macaroni and cheese made with water instead of milk. We ran out of margarine this week too. I couldn't stand it anymore!"

"What did you do?" I asked less calmly.

"Friday night I went to the store and wrote a check for $2.39 for a gallon of milk. I figured we would get at least $5 in the offering on Sunday. I would deposit the church's offering and then write us a check to cover my hot check before it bounced. It usually takes at least a week for a check to clear."

"But?" I snapped.

"The grocery store banks at the same bank we do. They must have taken their deposit in right after I wrote the check, and it bounced. The store is charging us a $15 return fee and the bank is charging us a $15 return fee. My gallon of milk is going to cost us $32.39! I got ahead of God and I'm so sorry."

"Wow!" I wanted to say so much more, but I held my tongue, "Did we get enough money in the offering to cover everything?"

"Yes, plenty. I should have waited on God, but I ran ahead and now I've wasted $30 of God's money! I'm so stressed and miserable! I hate being poor!" Kathy burst into a new round of tears. She was usually so strong, but not today. It was too much for her.

It took everything within me to calmly say, "I'll watch the boys while you go and pay the return fees. Get cash. I doubt they'll take a check."

Kathy left on her errand, and I fell on my knees, "God, we need You to help us. We won't take government help. We must depend on You. Give me wisdom, Lord."

My eyes fell on the Sunday paper someone had given us for the food coupons. I opened the 'help wanted' section and saw they were hiring bus drivers. I called and by the time Kathy got home, I had good news. I got a job driving a school bus for a private school. It was only four hours a day; two in the morning and two in the afternoon. It was not a lot of money, but at least the children would have milk and I would still be able to door knock between shifts.

God supplies Nourishment

My sister-in-law, Audrey, is from a fishing family. When her father learned that we were starting a church, he stopped by our apartment. I opened the door and saw him holding a large plastic bag. I took it and looked inside. I heard Kathy gasp over my shoulder, "Salmon! My favorite. Thank you so much, Mr. McNear!"

I stepped aside to invite him in, "You have made my wife a happy woman! Thank you for bringing this. Please come in."

Mr. McNear pointed to his car, "I can't, I'm late for a meeting. Audrey told me you are starting a church and struggling a bit financially. I caught that this morning. I have plenty where that came from so let me know when you need more. Enjoy!"

I closed the door and walked into the kitchen. Kathy's smile covered her face, "I'll cut it up, freeze some for later and bake some for dinner." We had baked salmon with green beans that night, salmon patties for breakfast the next day, and fried salmon for lunch.

By dinner, I was done with salmon, "Honey, don't you have anything else to cook?"

Kathy frowned, "I'm sorry, Ron. This is the only meat in our freezer. I can change up the sides from green beans to potatoes, but we can't afford meat."

Now I know how the children of Israel felt about manna.

We ate salmon until the sight of it made us cringe. But we did not forget to thank God for healthy food in our time of famine.

Federal Express

One can only handle so much financial stress before it becomes necessary to find supplemental income. The bus driving job was not enough. Federal Express was hiring part-time and offered better pay. I encourage all young Bible College men to get a CDL license while in school and learn to drive the church bus. It can lead to a good part-time job once in ministry.

The FedEx job went from 7 a.m.-to-noon six days a week. It gave us a steady income and health insurance.

Insurance!

From the time we left Bible College until I got a job at FedEx, we did not have health coverage. Other than the time that Micah was in the hospital, we never had any health issues.

I got home from work one afternoon and Kathy seemed to be glowing, "Sit down," she said, "I have some news. I'm pregnant! I know we were not planning on it, but I'm excited!"

It took a moment for me to process the idea of another mouth to feed. "How?" I muttered more from surprise than as a question.

"I guess it's insurance. This is the first month we are eligible at Fed Ex. We haven't had it for two-and-a-half years, but now we do, and I'm pregnant. Aren't you excited? I want a girl!"

"Well," I teased, "I'll just pray for a healthy baby. You can pray for a healthy baby girl."

"Agreed!" Kathy laughed.

Working at Federal Express was taxing, but we finally had financial relief. It allowed us to buy our first home—an old Victorian house in desperate need of updating. Kathy was up to the challenge. Her father was a master craftsman, and she inherited his love of working with her hands.

THOUGHTS
- When you are plagued with financial problems, where do you turn?
- God will supply your needs only when you trust Him first.

CHAPTER NINE

Church Growth

Confess your faults one to another, and pray one for another, that ye may be healed. The effectual fervent prayer of a righteous man availeth much. James 5:16

Baptisms

Renting a facility on Sundays is hard on a baby church. We had no building, no baptistry, and no roots. When Greg got saved, he wanted to get baptized.

I asked the Rec Center if I could use their swimming pool to baptize. They said, "No!" Oak Hills was an affluent area of Portland, and they did not want to ruin their reputation with rumors of a 'cult' in their area.

I asked a few area churches, but one church was remodeling their baptistry. Another did not have hot water. Yet another church just said, "No."

"We're having trouble finding a place to baptize." I said to Greg as I walked into his house, and thanked Glenda for the iced tea. It was a sunny, summer day, so Greg and I took our drinks to the back deck.

As we sat there sipping iced tea, I looked out over their back yard. They had a large, above ground swimming pool. "Hey," I said, "Would you be opposed to being baptized in your swimming pool?"

"Does it count as a baptism if it is not in a church?" Greg asked.

"Jesus was baptized in the Jordan River. The Ethiopian Eunuch saw a pond and asked Philip, 'See, here is water; what doth hinder me to be baptized? And Philip said, If thou believest with all thine heart, thou mayest.'."

Church Growth

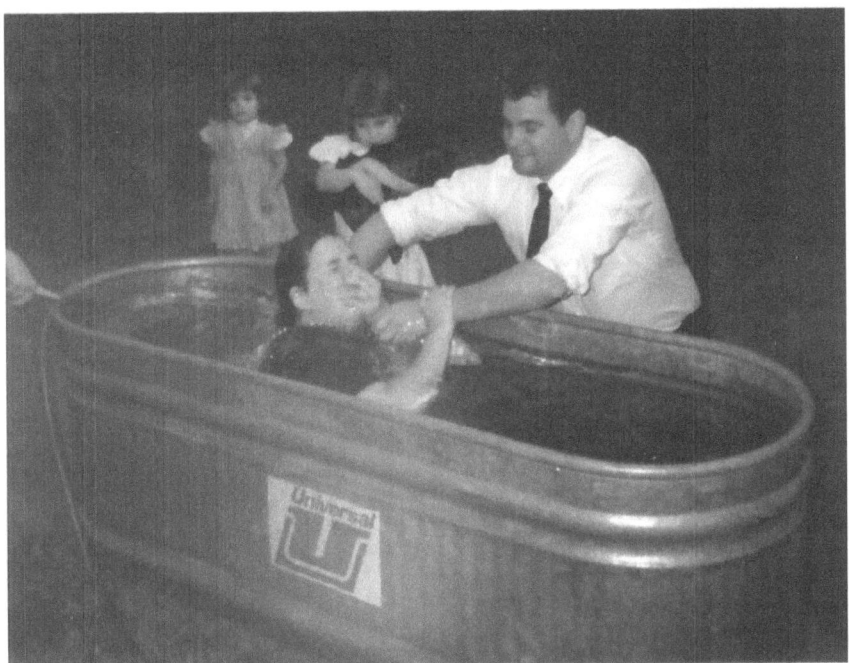

One of our baptisms at Corridor Baptist Church

"So, the only requirement is to believe in Jesus in my heart?"

"Yes." I replied.

"Then I'm ready to get baptized right now."

"Well, let's wait until after church on Sunday so our church family can rejoice with us."

Several people got baptized that Sunday. God was building a church for His Glory.

Door-Knocking Can be Tough

Now that Greg was baptized, he wanted to serve the Lord in every way. He went door knocking with me *once*.

We knocked on an apartment door and a lady in her late 40s answered. "Hi, I'm Pastor Ron and this is Greg. We are from Corridor Baptist Church, and we would like to invite you to our services. Do you have a church home in the area?"

She invited us in. As we sat down on the couch, she spoke, "I used to be a Catholic nun. I left the convent and got married. My husband died mysteriously. He was cut up by yard shears."

Suddenly we heard moaning in the back room. We looked at the lady. She continued, "Oh, pay no attention to that. There is something wrong with my son. Like I was saying, my first husband was killed by

Serving God Behind Enemy Lines

yard shears and can you believe, my second husband suffered the same fate. Both are unsolved murders."

I was concerned.

Greg and I should leave, but I need to witness to her first.

"Ma'am, if you were to die today, do you know for sure you would go to Heaven?"

"I don't know, but I would like to." The lady said with tears in her eyes.

The noise in the back room got louder. We heard a door open, and the son came down the hallway. He had a boombox on his shoulder blaring rock music. He looked at us and began to grunt.

The grunts got louder and louder. The lady yelled at us over the noise, "I think it would be a good idea to leave. My son is upset and it's not good when he gets upset."

She did not have to tell us twice. I left a tract on the coffee table as Greg and I made a quick exit.

Once we were safe in the car, he looked me square in the eye and exclaimed, "I don't think this door knocking thing is for me!" He never went again.

Our First Building

After meeting at the Oak Hills Recreation Center for eight months, we never had anyone from that community visit our church even though I had knocked on every door. If I preached past 12 p.m., the pool outside the Recreation Center opened. It was hard to keep the congregation's attention with bikini-clad women and children screaming on the other side of the windows.

Most of the people attending were from the Hillsboro/Beaverton area. It was time to find a building to rent closer to our congregation where I was not competing for people's attention. Somewhere we could put a sign up and rent fulltime. With our own place, we could have Sunday evening and Wednesday services.

I found an office complex in Hillsboro. They would rent us an 800 square foot office space for $300 a month. I went to the men of the church, "We have opportunity to rent an office space. I think we could make room for a nursery and Sunday School in it as well, but I have no construction skills."

Several men stood up, "No problem, Pastor. It would just be a matter of putting up an interior wall. It won't require any permits and we can do the work in a weekend."

Church Growth

Hallelujah, Corridor Baptist Church had her first building with an auditorium, a classroom, and a nursery.

Though we had no babies for the nursery, Kathy took special care getting it ready. Our little one would be here soon. Joel was four and Micah was three when Keturah Lael was born on September 9, 1988. A girl at last! She was a sweet addition to our family, giving Kathy that much needed female companion that would never forsake her. That is the beauty of a mother/daughter relationship.

Of course, having a new baby in the family created a whole new level of chaos in the Reasoner household. Later, on March 22, 1990, God would add Hannah Beth. Kathy often encourages mothers of three children, "Have as many as you like now. After three children, it is all chaos and another one is hardly noticed."

Greg Graduates

Not long after we moved into the new building, Greg came forward at the invitation. He laid his cigarettes at the altar and never picked them up again. He had smoked since he was 10 years old. Through tears he said, "I've known since I got saved that I needed to quit smoking, but there were some other things I needed to straighten out first. Now I'm ready for God to take my cigarettes." He never had a desire to smoke again after that altar call.

Sadly, smoking for 40 years had already taken its toll on Greg's health. He got sick and Glenda took him to the doctor.

The doctor said, "It is just the flu. Take him home and let him rest."

A week later, Greg could hardly walk. Glenda took him to the doctor again who still insisted, "The flu season is bad this year, take him home and let him rest."

Soon he was almost comatose. Glenda called me. I came over and helped get Greg into the car and took him to the hospital. Again, the doctor said, "It's just the flu."

I spoke up, "It is not just the flu. He is very sick. We are not leaving until you check him out."

The doctor finally ordered a CT scan. Greg's brain and lungs were full of cancer. He fell into a coma for several days.

"What will I do?" Glenda asked, "We are still in our forties! We don't have a will. Oh, Brother Reasoner, pray he wakes back up. I just need one hour of clarity from him to get our will and finances in order. The doctor says his whole brain, except a spot the size of a quarter, is covered in cancer. It will be a miracle if he ever awakens."

"Don't worry," I calmly said, "Our God specializes in miracles."

I gathered the men of the church together. We took olive oil to the hospital, anointed Greg and prayed, "Father God, You promise that where two or more are gathered in Your Name, that You are in the midst of them. You told us to anoint the sick, pray for healing, and trust You to heal them. Glenda needs Greg. She has asked for two hours of clarity and coherency with Greg so they might put their affairs in order. Please, God, answer our prayer of healing."

Within the hour, Greg awakened out of the coma. He was released from the hospital, and they were able to get a will written. Greg said his good-byes to friends and family. He lived for almost a month and then God took him home.

God increased the faith of everyone who was in the hospital room that night, including Glenda, the doctors, and the nurses. He taught us that God still performs miracles when we trust in Him. What a faith building moment that was in all our lives!

When I get discouraged door knocking, I remember people like Greg are in Heaven today because I went door knocking yesterday.

We stayed in the office complex for about two years until a 2,000 square foot ceramic shop in Hillsboro came up for rent. We had four weekends to get the building ready. Finally, three classrooms, a nursery, a church office, and an auditorium were ready for occupancy.

The church grew and many souls were saved in that building. Corridor Baptist Church continued to rent this building even after God called us to Russia. Eventually Corridor moved, and a Hispanic church rented the building.

The 2,000 square foot church building

THOUGHTS
- Do you believe God stills heals people today? Explain.

Chapter Ten

Tires & Splits

Ye are of God, little children, and have overcome them: because greater is he that is in you, than he that is in the world. 1 John 4:4

One Stubborn Tire

After we moved, the church began to grow. In the late 80's and early 90's every successful church had a bus ministry. We needed a bus. A church on the other side of Portland was willing to donate one, but the engine was blown. A mechanic in our church announced, "If you get the money together, I can get a new engine at cost, and I'll install it for free."

But where would we get the money for the engine? I had an idea. I drove past farms every day on my Fed Ex route where old buses just sat in fields. They were broken down and useless. I started asking the farmers if they would be willing to donate their bus. Three farmers said, "Yes." My plan was to scrap them and use that money to buy the engine.

We had a music group spending the week with us, and they volunteered to help us get the buses to the scrap yard. We rented a U-Haul truck, hitched the first bus up, and started our journey to the scrap yard. We took Cornelius Pass Road over the mountain. About halfway down the hill, there is a hairpin turn nestled against a cliff. Twice we braved this route to the scrap yard, almost getting in a wreck both times. We told them we would be back with the third bus in an hour.

I am not sure who had the wild idea—probably me—but we decided to take a different route. German Town Road was the fastest route. We soon discovered it was not the wisest decision. It has switchbacks and hairpin turns. We had the foresight for someone to sit in the bus and steer as we towed it.

However, there were no brakes in the bus. I was driving the U-Haul. At one point I exclaimed, "I don't see the bus in the mirror!"

One of the men looked out his window and screamed, "It is passing us on the right!" The hitch had disconnected, and the bus was being held by the safety chain.

The other man sniffed and proclaimed, "I smell brakes burning. If our brakes go out, we are all dead!"

Only by God's grace did we make it to the scrap yard. However, our adventure was not over. The foreman at the scrap yard took one look at our third bus and said, "You'll have to take those tires off before we weigh it. We took the tires off your other buses. It was hard work, but this bus is older and rustier. Plus, we don't have the right fittings for this bus. You do it."

How hard could it be?

We rented a special tire iron, and I tried to loosen the rusty bolts.

The first three tires came off without too much trouble. The fourth one, even with all four of us standing on the tire iron, would not budge. We needed a plan B. One of the musicians, Jim, had experience with an acetylene torch. He was sure we could cut through the tire. We went back to the rental store and got an acetylene torch.

"I've got this," Jim said, "We'll have this tire off in no time."

This was not a good plan. The wheel caught fire. The smoke rose 30 feet. I am surprised the fire department was not dispatched. We grabbed old blankets to put the fire out. Then, the tire collapsed under the bus. It would be impossible to get it off now.

The foreman approached our group. He did not look happy, "Why do you need this money? What could be worth risking your lives?"

I explained, "I am the pastor of Corridor Baptist Church. We have a bus with a blown engine. We are trying to scrap these old buses so we can buy an engine to take children to church."

The foreman took pity, "Pick up one of the other tires and we'll weigh it. We'll subtract it from the total."

While awaiting the foreman to write the check, we watched as a crane tried to pull the tire off the bus. The entire bus lifted in the air. No success. Next, they put the bus on the conveyor belt for the incinerator. As the tire hit the fire, another smoke cloud wafted high into the air just as the foreman came out with our check. I grabbed the check, "Thank you. God bless you!" We hurried down the steps, into the U-Haul truck, and sped away before the foreman changed his mind!

Once we had a working bus, several of the church families took it upon themselves to start a bus ministry. Soon our small congregation was overrun with bus kids. It was at this time we had an attendance contest with another Independent Baptist Church in Astoria. On our final Sunday of the contest, we had 103 people! The adults felt a little overwhelmed in the close quarters. We decided to have the bus ministry meet in the afternoons so there was ample room for everyone. It was an exciting time of our ministry! Souls were saved every week.

Full-Time at Federal Express

A preacher friend from California came each year to preach for us. He suggested that I go fulltime at Federal Express for one year and set the extra money aside. After that, I would quit and live off the savings while working to grow the church to the next level. Kathy and I prayed about it and decided that we had the self-control to achieve such a goal.

Once I went to work fulltime, I had some clients I delivered to on a regular basis. One particular businessman stopped me as I handed him a package. He said, "You look like a man worthy of good advice. If you have any money to invest in stocks, invest all you can in a company called Microsoft. We will go public next week with a new operating system, and we are confident that our company will be a huge success."

"Oh, I don't dabble in the stock market. I have a young family and we just barely make it from month to month," I responded as he signed for his package.

"Beg, borrow, or steal $1,000. You will not regret it."

"Thank you," I smiled as he handed me back my handheld signature computer.

Of course, we did not invest. That may seem like a lost opportunity. But Kathy and I see it as a miracle! The enemy of our souls has a way of tempting God's children. Had we become millionaires, perhaps we would never have gone to the mission field and thousands would never have heard the Gospel.

During my last year of working at Federal Express, Kathy became pregnant again. On June 26, 1991, Jeremiah Jack was born to complete the Reasoner family lineup. I was able to go on three months of unpaid parental leave. The church was doing great and after much prayer and fasting, we decided that I should not go back to work but become a full-time pastor. We were entering a whole new phase of ministry! And a deepening level of reliance, trust, and faith in our Lord.

Serving God Behind Enemy Lines

Split!

On June 7, 1992, Corridor Baptist Church celebrated five years of ministry. Things were going great. We had about 40 faithful adults and another 40 kids in our afternoon bus ministry. God was growing a church! I was thrilled to see the pews filled on Sunday mornings. The Sunday School classes were bursting at the seams. Life was good and God was showering blessings on us. Oh, the joy of being in the center of God's will!

Just after our fifth church anniversary, we had a church split. It was Sunday morning when the phone rang. That is never a good sign. Kathy answered the phone, "Hello?"

"Umm, we won't be coming to church today. Goodbye."

Kathy turned, "That was weird. It was the wife of our Sunday School Director. She said they won't be in church today. Who will run the afternoon bus ministry? We don't even know the route!"

"Did they say if someone was sick and needed prayer?" I asked confused.

"No. She just said, 'we won't be there' and hung up."

"Wow, I don't need this right before church. But we'll be fine—God's got this. Get the kids into the car. We need to get to church."

I went to visit the Sunday School Director the next day. When his wife opened the door, I smiled, "We missed you in church. Is everyone healthy? Are you all okay?"

"We have decided to leave the church. Your preaching isn't deep enough. Good-bye."

I walked away devastated and confused. I had put years of love and labor into that family only to discover it was not enough.

With him gone, we had a big hole in our Sunday School. He was also the youth director and in charge of the afternoon bus ministry which had to be cancelled. No one else had the time, money, nor talent to continue working the bus ministry.

He also convinced two other families to jump ship and go to another church. Dr. Dennis Brown from Yakima, Washington came down to preach. When he heard the church was having problems, he stood before the people and said, "Everyone who is for Brother Reasoner, sit on this right side of the auditorium." Our elderly folks and young families moved to the right side. When the shuffling was complete, Dr. Brown continued, "All you in the church who are against Brother Reasoner, sit on the left side." Several families stayed where they were seated on the left side. Dr. Brown walked over to the left side, looked them in the eye and sighed,

Tires & Splits

"You that are against him, get up and leave!" We lost a life-long friend and another family.

The next month, our last deacon came to the church office and told me his family was leaving the church. I was devastated, but Kathy would be crushed.

Lord, help me break this to her gently!

I came home to tell her the news, "Sweetheart, could you please sit down? I have some sad news to tell you. Brother Frey came to see me at the church office today."

"Oh, is everything okay? I missed his family this past Sunday."

"He came to tell me they are leaving the church. They have decided that we are too strict in our doctrine. They don't want their children to grow up so sheltered. I'm sorry, I know you really like Mrs. Frey. And our children will miss their children terribly."

Kathy smiled weakly, "Well, they are the last family from that group who came a few years ago. I just pray they don't gossip and take anyone else with them."

I was surprised how well Kathy took it—until we went to bed. When she thought I was asleep, I felt her heaving breath as she began to silently sob. Every few minutes she took a deep, quivering breath and I thought she would explode into a hysterical cry. She did not. She suffered in silence.

That is what pastors' wives do. They suffer in silence and grieve over the loss of a friendship into which they poured their hearts and souls. Yet, they smile at new visitors each week and offer a hand of friendship. Friendships, that they suspect may end with a knife in their back. Perhaps this is what Paul meant in Philippians 3:10:

That I may know him, and the power of his resurrection, and the fellowship of his sufferings, being made conformable unto his death;

God reaches down His hand to man every single day. He is rejected repeatedly, yet He continues to reach down and offer His free gift of salvation and hope. Let me encourage you pastors' wives to just keep reaching out your hand and let God take care of your heart.

Kathy arose in the morning with blood shot eyes and swollen cheeks. It was almost unbearable for me to see her like this, "How did you sleep?"

"I had a little trouble. My mind kept going over all the trials we had endured with the Frey family. The surgeries, the family trials, the financial burdens—we were there for all of it—praying with them that God would show Himself mighty."

"And God always shows Himself Mighty," I said. "Remember that. We work for the Lord, not people. God has promised, 'I will never leave you nor forsake you.' We'll get through this together."

It happens way too often in a minister's family. Tucked away in our homes, we invest hours of prayer for our congregation, begging God to give them wisdom and blessings. Yet, church members are tucked away in their homes, often on their phones with other members, plotting and gossiping against the pastor and his family.

I implore Christians to value their pastor and his family. Most pastors are genuinely striving to serve the Lord and attempting to fulfill God's command in Hebrews 13:17:

Obey them that have the rule over you, and submit yourselves: for they watch for your souls, as they that must give account, that they may do it with joy, and not with grief: for that is unprofitable for you.

Faithful Few

Soon God called away more families. One large family got transferred to Idaho and yet another family retired and moved to the coast. We were left with a handful of people to carry on the work.

Our savings quickly disappeared as we paid both our bills and the debts of the church for several months. It became difficult to make the bills, let alone take any type of salary. We were back to struggling. Had it not been for a few faithful families giving more than their share, we would have lost our house, our car, and our church building. One family in the church owned a Taco Time and let us eat there for free every Sunday afternoon. Often, that was the only meat we ate all week. The rest of the week we ate macaroni and potatoes.

At a fellowship meeting, a preacher friend pulled me aside, "Brother Reasoner, God has put you on my heart and I can't stop praying for you. Is everything okay?"

I grimaced, "Well, we aren't doing so well. We had a split just after our fifth anniversary. We manage to pay our bills, but I have five small mouths to feed. That is a chore."

The preacher gave me a bear hug and said, "At our Wednesday evening service, I will announce that we are having a food drive for the Reasoners who are church planting in Oregon. I'll come down with food for your tribe!"

The next Monday morning, a Ford pickup backed into our driveway. It was full of groceries. Kathy could not hold back the tears as she helped

Tires & Splits

unload boxes and boxes of quality food. "Thank you, Preacher! You have no idea how much this means to me!" She grinned from ear to ear as she wiped tears from her eyes.

The Preacher reached his hand into his coat pocket and pulled out a $200 check, "Someone in the church wanted to give money to help pay bills." It was my turn to wipe away tears.

I pray that if I ever come across a young couple that is struggling like we did, that God would let me know to slip a $100 into their hands. Those missionary handshakes saved our family so many times during the early years of our ministry. We were financially destitute, but our faith meter was growing each time God worked a miracle in our young lives.

Time after time, God came through when we prayed for help. Never get ahead of God. It is dangerous and expensive to leave God out of your plans.

THOUGHTS
- Do you place more value on things or people?
- Does how you live your life, invest your money, and treat other people support or disprove your answer?

CHAPTER ELEVEN

When Thou Vowest a Vow

When thou vowest a vow unto God, defer not to pay it; for he hath no pleasure in fools: pay that which thou hast vowed. Ecclesiastes 5:4

We survived two months on the food and money from my preacher friend. Soon we were back to macaroni and potatoes.

What is happening? Lord, why have You taken Your hand off Corridor Baptist Church?

Kathy and I fell on our faces before God begging Him to reveal what great sin we had committed that He had abandoned us.

Kathy whispered, "I've racked my brain and can't figure out what God is doing. Please Ron, please take me away from this misery. Our children are practically starving. We can't pay our bills." She looked up to Heaven, "Lord, please tell Ron what You want! Please!" She ran into our bedroom, slamming the door. Even through the closed door, I heard her fall on the bed and sob uncontrollably.

One day in 1993, I went to the church office, fell on my knees, begging God to speak to me. I waited for the thunder. Nothing. I listened in the wind. Nothing. Finally, I heard that Still, Small Voice within me.

Missions — remember your promise to Me? You said five years in Oregon and then you would go to the mission field. It has been over five years. The field I have for you is open. You need to go.

At last, the answer! I eagerly surrendered. How would I tell Kathy? I decided to take time to pray and fast before approaching her.

Where are You sending us, God? When do You want us to go? What country was closed six years ago and is now open?

When Thou Vowest a Vow

Just after I surrendered, God sent Dan and Sharon, a young professional couple, to our church. Their tithe saved our church and our home!

One day we invited the couple to our home. Kathy and Sharon prepared lunch while Dan and I went out to knock on doors. After lunch was ready and we still had not returned, Sharon asked Kathy, "With the church so small, how does your family survive?"

Kathy smiled, "By God's grace."

Sharon probed, "Well, so how much is your weekly grocery budget?"

Kathy hesitated before finally saying, "It's $25 a week."

Sharon looked shocked, "You mean per person. So, $175? Right?"

Kathy decided to be honest, "No, $25 a week total for all seven of us, but frankly sometimes we don't even get that. We insist the church pays its bills before it pays us. Sometimes we go without."

Sharon could not contain the tears as she admitted, "My husband and I spend more than that on one meal when we go out! How can you do that?"

Kathy smiled and repeated, "God gives grace."

About that time, Dan and I returned from visitation. We sat down to a meal of soft tacos. Kathy had already fed the children and put them down for a nap. I prayed for lunch, "Lord, we thank You for all You provide. Please bless the doors we knocked on today. May You be glorified. Amen!"

I picked up the flour tortillas to pass them around. Because we were late, they had hardened a bit. I remarked, "Umm, Kathy, these tortillas are a little hard."

Without skipping a beat, Kathy replied, "Ron, you know what the Bible says, 'Endure hardness as a good soldier of Jesus Christ!'"

Dan threw back his head and laughed until tears filled his eyes, "That's a good comeback! I like this family. We all are going to get along great!"

Obviously, Dan was made privy to Sharon's conversation with Kathy because from that day on, this young family gave $150 a week marked 'for Pastor's groceries' over their tithes and faith promise missions giving. To this day, this family is precious to us! They were God's angels sent to keep us fed while God was moving in my heart to ready us for the mission field.

THOUGHTS
- Is there a promise you made to God, but forgot or refused to fulfill?

CHAPTER TWELVE

Called to Russia

The LORD hath appeared of old unto me, saying, Yea, I have loved thee with an everlasting love: therefore with lovingkindness have I drawn thee. Jeremiah 31:3

During the month I prayed about God's next step in our lives, the former Soviet Union occupied my mind. All these countries were open to the Gospel. I had preached hard about someone from our church going to the Former Soviet Republic. Someone needed to go! As I searched for missionaries going to the fields, I found very few Gospel preaching witnesses. My heart was broken. Why were so few surrendering to go? Had God stopped calling or had His children stopped answering?

It was about that time, when Danny Chapman, a boy from our Junior High class at Calvary Baptist Church, called. He was now a college graduate going to Russia as a missionary and wanted to present the field at our church. He had recently been on a survey trip and was overwhelmed with the need for laborers. Much of his presentation centered around the coldness, the darkness, and the hopelessness of this failed country. Danny stuck around an extra day and was eager to go door knocking. While we were out, it started to snow.

"I can't door knock in this weather, Pastor Ron!" Danny said, "I am a Southern California boy and I'm freezing to death!"

Handing Danny my car keys, I said, "Here, go turn the car on and run the heater. I want to finish this street."

As I continued with the rest of the street, the thought entered my mind—

This guy is going to Russia, and he cannot handle the snow? This snow doesn't bother me. Maybe I could be a missionary in Russia!

Called to Russia

I spent hours in prayer and entire afternoons in the library reading newspaper articles and newly published books on the countries of the former Soviet Union. The Iron Curtain was torn down on December 26, 1991. It was now open to missionaries, and I needed more information before approaching Kathy. We were raised during the Cold War. Our mantra was, "I'd rather be dead than Red."

The more I thought about going to Russia the more it became a burden, which became a vision, and then became a calling. I was thrilled, excited, and, yes, I knew God was calling me to Russia. It was time to tell Kathy!

I walked into the living room after Kathy had put the kids to bed. I sat next to her, took her hand, and said, "I know why we have been having so much trouble this year. I promised God that I would take five years to plant a church in Oregon, and this is year six. I forgot my promise to God. Back then, we were not ready to go on the mission field and God led us here. We grew in number, in faith, and in maturity. We are ready and I believe God is calling us."

Kathy chided, "Look around you, Ron. We are in Oregon. We ARE on the mission field!"

"No, I mean to foreign fields!"

Kathy smiled. Visions of palm trees and a tropical paradise filled her mind, "Oh, good. I'm so ready! Where do you think God is calling us?"

Careful! Break this to her gently.

"So, you do agree that God is calling us to the foreign fields?"

"For sure! We've been praying for God to help us understand His next step. I agree He must be calling us somewhere else. I have felt it in my Spirit for a while now. I am battle weary and I need a reprieve. Where do you think God is calling us?"

"Russia. I think He is calling us to Russia."

Kathy's smile vanished, followed by a frown, "Keep praying!"

Help me, Lord! She needs grace!

I took her hand, "Kathy, I've been praying about this for a month. Let's pray together right now."

We bowed our heads, "Lord, we know You are moving in our lives. I believe You had us come to Hillsboro and start this church because we needed the experience and the doors to Russia were not open. I have peace that You are calling us. Please give Kathy that same peace. In Jesus' name, Amen."

Kathy pulled her hand away and clasped them together on her lap. With tears in her eyes she said, "I've seen Russia on the news. They have bread lines a mile long just to get a loaf of bread. We have five children. There is no food in Russia! God wouldn't call us to Russia to starve! We MUST keep praying!"

Lord, help her. We must agree about Your will.

Two weeks later, I approached her again, "Kathy, I can't shake this burden. I KNOW God has called us to Russia."

Tears streamed down her face, "I appreciate your patience, Ron, but you need to pray for me because I don't want to go there." She ran to our room to confront the Lord.

I heard her voice from the other room, "God, I'm tired of being miserable and poor. I know You are moving us, but Russia, really? Help me, God! I want to go where You want us to go, but I don't want to raise a bunch of communist children! I don't want to die in a *Gulag* (forced labor camp). I don't want my children to starve! God? Are You really calling us to Russia?"

Kathy continued to kneel. She had poured out her heart to God, but now it was time to listen for Him to speak. Scriptures about wives obeying and respecting their husbands filled her head. That *Still Small Voice* spoke in her heart, "follow your husband as he follows Me."

Thirty minutes later she came out of our room and stood wringing her hands, "When I was in Bible college, before we married, I walked into our pastor's office. Before I could tell him why I was there, he lectured me. I'll never forget what he said because it was so unrelated to why I was there. He said, 'Kathy, someday you will get married, and you need to follow your husband. Even if he has a successful pastorate where hundreds of souls are being saved each week and one day, he comes to you and says that God is calling him to quit the pastorate and sell hotdogs on a street corner in New York City. He may be totally out of God's will, but you will be totally in God's will by following him.' Until today I never knew why God had him say that. I need to trust you and follow you, even if it is to Russia. I'll go. God says I must go, but I don't want to. My spirit is willing, but my flesh is weak."

I grabbed her hand as I began our family prayer, "Lord, we are Your servants, ready to do Your will. Lead us where You need us until we are home with You."

She said, 'I'll go.' That was good enough for me!

She might have said other stuff too, but she said, 'I'll go!" I began to plan our journey to the mission field.

I wrote a checklist of things that needed to happen before we started deputation.

- ☐ Let the church know God has called us
- ☐ Help the church call a new pastor
- ☐ Put our house on the market
- ☐ Call churches and schedule meetings
- ☐ Get a vehicle for driving around the country to raise support

So much to do! I would need Kathy's full support. Deep within me I began to pray, "God please give my wife a burden for Russia. If she doesn't have one, I know she'll try, but she'll wind up being an anchor if You don't call her."

THOUGHTS
- Has God called you to a ministry?
- Are you fulfilling that call?
- Ladies: Will you anchor your husband's ministry by refusing to step out by faith?

CHAPTER THIRTEEN

Calling a New Pastor

Take heed therefore unto yourselves, and to all the flock, over the which the Holy Ghost hath made you overseers, to feed the church of God, which he hath purchased with his own blood. Acts 20:28

How does a Pastor go about telling his sheep that he is leaving? It was a serious question. If I approached it the wrong way, the church was too fragile to survive another split or disappointment. Some pastors just run away without helping their flock go through the process of finding a new pastor, and the flock ends up with a charlatan. When a pastor loves his sheep, he MUST help them find a new shepherd.

Dan and Sharon joined the church on Sunday morning. Sunday night, I announced God's calling to Russia.

"I have an announcement to make. You all know how I have been preaching on the former Soviet Union for the past year. I kept pushing for someone from our church to go as a missionary there. Well, God has called someone. I am excited to announce that God has called me and my family. Don't worry, I will stay on as Pastor until we vote a new Pastor in. Men of the church, please meet me in my office after services and we will discuss finding a new pastor."

When we gathered in my office, Dan asked, "How do we go about getting a new pastor?"

I replied, "Well, I'll call around to a few pastors I trust and ask if they know anyone with a burden for the Northwest."

"Yes," Dick said, "It must be someone with a burden for the Northwest or they will never stay when the rain starts falling every day. Our weather drives people nuts if they aren't from around here."

Calling a New Pastor

"Let's pray right now for God to give us wisdom and direction." I stood from my chair and prayed, "Father, we love You and want to see this church go forward for You. For that to happen, we need a new pastor. One that You have selected to lead this flock. Guide us, Lord. Lead us to the man You have chosen for this task. In Jesus' name, Amen."

The next week we had a revival scheduled with my pastor from California. He came every year to encourage the flock. I asked, "Pastor, can you think of anyone who can take this little church to the next level. Someone who loves God and will not lead them astray?"

Pastor replied, "Not off the top of my head. I'll have to pray about it."

"What about your intern, Steve House? Isn't he originally from the Northwest?"

Pastor thought for a moment and replied, "Yes, he is from the Seattle area, but he's young. I don't think he's ready to pastor but let me pray about it."

The next day, Pastor approached me, "You know, I think it might be a good thing for Steve House to be a candidate. He and his wife are good people. They just had a baby. I'll have him call you when I get back to California."

Some of the men in the church thought we needed an older pastor with experience. I got a hold of an elderly man from Texas who wanted to be a candidate. He was in his sixties. We paid for his plane ticket, he preached and afterwards we had a time of questions and answers from the congregation. "Do you see yourself as retiring in the Northwest?" Dick asked.

"No, I will retire in Texas. But I still have a good five years of preaching left in me. I will give you five years of solid Bible doctrine."

After the Texan left, the men got together to discuss him. Those who were leaning towards wanting an older pastor started to see the light, "He has moved around a lot in his ministry," one of them said, "Which means he won't stay long."

Another man commented, "Pastor Ron preaches with the passion of youth. I've gotten used to that. Listening to this seasoned veteran was different. I think I like the passion."

"I'm glad to hear you say that" I smiled, "Because I got a call from Pastor's intern, and he would like to come and candidate. He is even younger than me, but he is from the Northwest and desires to be a church planter in the region."

The next Sunday, Steve House flew up. His preaching was concise, passionate, and doctrinally sound. The congregation was impressed.

It was time to vote on the two candidates. Twelve adult voting members gathered to determine the future of Corridor Baptist Church. "What do you all think of the Texan?" I asked.

"He's just too old. We need someone younger," a woman in the congregation advised. Everyone nodded as she spoke. I moved on.

"What do you think of Stephen P. House?" I asked.

"Well, he's young but he seems to have it all together," one person commented.

We had singing evangelist Mark Gray in the services with us that night and he asked if he could speak.

"Yes!" I said, "We need all the wisdom we can get."

"Well," Mark stated, "I'm not a member here so I won't be voting but I would like to shed some light for you. I think you should consider who Steve House is. He is from the Northwest, so he already understands the culture. He is interning under a great man of God that will be available to counsel and guide him when he needs advice. But in addition to that, his father-in-law is Ronald Storz—another great man of God—who will be able to give him guidance and direction. Steve House is a good man. He was saved young and raised in church. He knows Independent Baptist culture and he is surrounded by good men. I think this is important to consider."

Everyone nodded. Dick said, "I move we have a written ballot passed out and filled out by the members of the church."

"I second that motion," Dan said.

I had a prepared ballot. We passed them out and Stephen P. House got 100% of the vote!

I called Steve the next day, "This is Ron Reasoner. I want to let you know that the church voted 100% to call you as our new Pastor."

Steve replied, "Wow! I was praying it would be 100% but I need to take a few days to pray with my wife, Jimna, to confirm it is God's will. I'll call you in a few days."

A few days later, he called me, "Yes. We are excited! It will take a few months for us to get there. Will the church be okay with that?"

I was excited, "Yes, I will stay on until you get here. We don't want any wolves creeping in. It often happens when the flock is left unguarded without a shepherd."

Meanwhile, I needed to find a church to send my family out as missionaries to Russia. I called my Pastor in California, "Pastor, I am

Calling a New Pastor

looking for a sending church. Would Calvary Baptist Church consider taking on this responsibility?"

"Well, Ron, we could. But I think Corridor Baptist Church will really take off under the leadership of Steve House. It would be great if the church you started was also your sending church. Talk to Steve about that first." The Pastor then advised, "He is here in the office right now. I'll transfer you."

"Hello, Brother House." I began, "I was just talking to Pastor about a sending church, and he suggested that I ask you. What do you think?"

"I think it would be great. We probably won't be able to do much in the way of financial support in the beginning, but we will remember to pray for you."

"Well then," I responded, "Let me be the first one to call you Pastor. I look forward to many years of ministry together."

THOUGHTS
- Are you ready to step out of your comfort zone and take on a new ministry to the glory of God no matter where it leads—across the street, across the country, or across the world?

CHAPTER FOURTEEN

God Calls Kathy

For I know the thoughts that I think toward you, saith the LORD, thoughts of peace, and not of evil, to give you an expected end. Jeremiah 29:11

It was a daunting task to uproot a family of seven from the only home we had ever known, and I needed everyone on board.

God, please burden Kathy's heart for the Russian people. She is following with her mind and body, but her heart still lingers in the United States.

Our 10th wedding anniversary was on Friday, July 16, 1993. Someone in the church offered to watch our children so we could celebrate. Kathy bought the morning newspaper, divided it up, and we flipped through the pages. Kathy had the religious section.

I saw her eyes widened as she gasped, "Ron! Look at this! The leading story on the front page of the religious section reads, 'Russia closes its doors to Missionaries.'"

I grabbed the paper and read the story aloud. The Russian Parliament had voted to expel all foreign missionaries and refuse entrance to any new ones planning to enter its borders. The Russian Orthodox Church did not want more evangelistic campaigns nor new variation of churches started. To be Russian is to be Russian Orthodox!

I put the paper down. Horrified and frustrated, I bellowed, "What? This is bad! We just called a new pastor to our church. Our last Sunday is in two days. We have surrendered to be missionaries in Russia and the doors of Russia have closed?"

Kathy broke down in tears. If she thought our lives were unstable before, now it appeared we were going to a closed country! *Gulags* and prisons straight ahead! "We need to pray," she exclaimed and immediately began, "God, what happened? 10,000 Mormons and 10,000 Jehovah Witnesses were waiting at the borders, trained in the language, hoping for Russia to open its doors. They went, but there aren't any independent Baptists that we know of. You opened the door so the Truth of the Gospel could be preached but only the cults went! What happened God? What are You doing?"

Suddenly Kathy stopped praying. I peeked to see what she was doing and saw her turn her head towards Heaven. She seemed to be listening. I wondered if she was hearing the same *Still Small Voice* that had spoken to me. She opened her eyes to see my astonished look. Through her tears, she grabbed my hands and squeezed, "God spoke to my heart about Russia, but I didn't want to go. He closed the door, but if He opens it again, I will be willing to go"

That was on a Friday morning. It was *Duma* (the Russian Parliament) who had passed the law. We spent the weekend wondering what God was doing.

How will You fix this, Lord?

On Sunday, July 18, Pastor House preached his first sermon at Corridor Baptist Church. What a blessing to have a young man of God with a burden for the Northwest to take this church and grow it into the thriving ministry that it is today. Pastor House has been faithful in the good and bad times. Decades later, he is still my pastor, and he is still the senior pastor at Corridor Baptist Church.

What better church to send us into the mission field than the one who taught us to serve and trust the Lord? They continue to support us and keep us in prayer.

On Monday, God showed Himself mighty when President Boris Yeltsin vetoed that law. He said, "We will have religious freedom in Russia. Missionaries are welcome."

This was just one of many laws Parliament passed, and Yeltsin vetoed. *Duma* wanted to go back to Communism, but Yeltsin was committed to bringing Russia into the free world. Communism and freedom cannot co-exist.

A few weeks later, as I watched the news on TV, the Russian White House was surrounded by protestors and military tanks. The newscaster explained, "There is unrest in the streets of Moscow today as the Parliament has barricaded themselves inside the Russian White House in protest of President Yeltsin's social and economic reforms. This conflict has been going on for ten days. It has been the deadliest conflict in Moscow since the 1917 Bolshevik Revolution." The cameras zoomed in on the White House. "You can hear American Rock Music blasting from speakers surrounding the building at the highest volume. Parliament members seem to be miserable from the grueling music, but they refuse to surrender. President Yeltsin disbanded Parliament ten days ago and they refuse to leave."

Suddenly, a tank launched a projectile into the building. Immediately, smoke and flames shot out the broken window. The newscaster cowered in fear, ran a safe distance from the crowd, composed herself, and then brought her microphone back to her mouth, "It looks like a tank has just fired on the White House. The military is storming the building. This appears to be the beginning of the end of Parliament's reign. President Boris Yeltsin has used the military to end this. That's a wrap folks, democracy has prevailed in Russia."

I am sure history will record this event as an attempted political coup, but we know better. It was God calling Kathy to Russia.

THOUGHTS
- When has God worked mightily in your life to show His will?

Chapter Fifteen

Trials of Deputation

And Jesus said unto him, No man, having put his hand to the plow, and looking back, is fit for the kingdom of God. Luke 9:62

My Checklist Was Just Getting Started
- ☑ Let the church know God has called us
- ☑ Help the church call a new pastor
- ☐ Put our house on the market
- ☐ Call churches and schedule meetings
- ☐ Get a vehicle for driving around the country to raise support

Our Home

I mentioned earlier that while I was working at Federal Express, the Lord blessed us with an opportunity to buy an old fixer upper Victorian home for $39,000. It was on a side street bordered on all sides by businesses. It was our first home, and we were excited. It gave the kids a back yard to play in and when the businesses closed in the evening, we let the kids ride their bikes in abandoned parking lots.

We put mostly sweat equity into this home. My in-laws came over several times; once to remodel the kitchen and once to put in a sliding glass door and deck. It was home. Our refuge from trouble.

Now, four years later, Kathy had just finished remodeling the last bedroom, "I'm going to miss this old house," she said as we discussed calling a realtor to put the house on the market.

The realtor came and really liked the house, "I think we can put this home on the market for $89,000. You've done a nice job on the remodel and the market is hungry for 4-bedroom, 2 bath homes. Do you own the house outright?"

"No, we are buying it through an individual."

"Oh—I'll need to look at the contract."

Kathy ran to our bedroom, found the contract, and handed it to the realtor. As she looked it over, the realtor's face went from a smile to a frown, "Oh, this contract does not allow for you to sell without this man's permission. You will have to call him and get back with me."

Holding the contract in my hand, I called the man, "Hi, Mike, this is Ron Reasoner, we are buying the house from you on SE 3rd Ave. in Hillsboro."

"Yes, I know who you are," Mike curtly replied.

"Well, God has called my family to be missionaries in Russia, so we need to sell our house. Can we get your permission to do that?"

"No," Mike snapped, "You make your payment on time. I'm making 10% interest. Our contract is for 10 years. At that time, you can pay off the contract, but not before then. So, no, you can't sell."

"Sir, God has called us to Russia. We can't stay."

"Then I guess you will have to rent it out. Good-bye."

We knew nothing about being landlords. We had always cared for the homes we rented. Surely everyone did that! We asked Dan and Sharon to oversee the home while we were on deputation.

Sadly, we chose a renter from hades. He let homeless teens live with him. We had just finished remodeling and had we been able to sell, we could have made a lot of money. This renter tore the carpet out of one room and put it on the ceiling of another room because the neighbors two streets over complained about the rock band practicing at our house. They painted the walls black. They never took the garbage out.

To show they did not care what the neighbors thought, the rock band got on top of the house and played their music. The police were called, and our home became the go-to place when searching for criminals.

Poor Dan and Sharon! They had to go through the whole process of evicting a gang of criminals. We were on deputation in the Midwest, traveling constantly from church to church and could not get back. In the days before cell phones and the Internet our friends could not contact us.

When the police could not reach us, they called the man who held the contract on our home. Mike decided that he would go and evict the renters. He knocked on the door. The renter answered the door in his underwear, "Who are you, dude?"

Trials of Deputation

Mike was dressed in a suit and expensive leather shoes. He announced, "I am the man who holds the Reasoners' contract on this house. The police have called me to bring order—"

The renter interrupted, "So what? I have nothing to do with you." He proceeded to urinate on Mike's leather shoes.

Mike called Dan to let him know he would be okay with us selling the house if we continued to make our payments, and our buyers would pay us.

Too late Mike, the house was already destroyed.

We learned through this experience that possessions are merely possessions. You can give five years of your life to a project, and it can be destroyed by someone else in a few months.

Things are not important, souls are.

That was a great lesson, because repeatedly on the mission field, we would be defrauded, stolen from, mugged, and discriminated against. We would need to be reminded that stuff is stuff, but souls are forever.

We sold the home for $55,000 because the renters destroyed it. But we sold it, and the burden was lifted.

- ☑ Let the church know God has called us
- ☑ Help the church call a new pastor
- ☑ Put our house on the market
- ☐ Call churches and schedule meetings
- ☐ Get a vehicle for driving around the country to raise support

Calling Churches and Scheduling Meetings

Perhaps there is someone reading this book who does not understand what deputation is. Deputation is the process a missionary goes through to raise support for their calling from God. A family goes from church to church presenting their burden for the mission field, casting that burden to the people, and asking them to partner with them to see souls saved around the world. The partnership is twofold:

- ✓ To promise to pray for us as we descend into the deep.
- ✓ To financially support us monthly to live in a foreign country.

Deputation before cell phones and the Internet was grueling. Most pastors have a system in place to screen phone calls from missionaries. I learned how important it was to be nice to the church secretary! If she liked me, she would let the pastor know I called, and she might even encourage the pastor to call back.

Serving God Behind Enemy Lines

I found that the best place to book meetings was at fellowship gatherings for pastors. Pastors who love missionaries bring their calendars!

Missionaries quickly learn how to jump through hoops. We can walk into a church building and within just a few minutes tell what kind of church it is:

- ✓ Who are the missionaries they support?
- ✓ What version of the Bible do they use?
- ✓ Are the women wearing pants at church activities?
- ✓ What is the subject of their community bulletin board?
- ✓ How happy is the preacher to see us?
- ✓ Are there drums on the platform?

I am not saying any of these things are good or bad. I am saying missionaries need to tread lightly. I am a guest speaker who is to give the people a vision and burden for missions. Christians spend too much time shooting their fellow soldiers in the back and not enough time being burdened for the lost.

After several months and countless hours on the phone, I finally had enough meetings to get started. We would trust God to fill in the gaps of our schedule.

- ☑ Let the church know God has called us
- ☑ Help the church call a new pastor
- ☑ Put our house on the market
- ☑ Call churches and schedule meetings
- ☐ Get a vehicle for driving around the country to raise support

Driving on Fumes

We stepped out by faith and bought a 1978 32-foot Allegro motorhome. We found out it was a gas hog on the way to our first meeting in Southern Oregon.

"Wow," I said as I watched the gas meter continue to rise, "It will take all the money we have left to fill both tanks. Good thing they said there will be a love offering."

Kathy glanced out the window at the meter. "We only have $150 left in our account. Don't let it go past that!"

We gave a sigh of relief when the pump kicked off at $140. "We have $10 to our name!" I smiled, "What do you want to buy?"

Kathy rolled her eyes and answered, "Buy bread, lunch meat, lettuce, and tomatoes for sandwiches. That should feed us until we get to the Southern Oregon Camp Meeting. They are providing meals, aren't they?"

I nodded as I stepped back into the driver's seat and started the engine. Kathy directed the children to take their designated seats and asked Joel, now nine-years old, to pray. "Dear Jesus," he said, "Please help us get to the camp meeting safely. And help us make lots of friends! Amen!"

We had a great week of preaching. I spoke several times and showed our slide presentation. We had excellent food, fellowship and all the children made friends. We were blessed.

As the family loaded up into the motorhome, I went to say good-bye to the host pastor. It was my first church, and I did not know if I should ask for the love offering or just wait for him to give it. I tried several scenarios in my head before settling on, "Thank you Brother for a wonderful week of food, fellowship, and preaching. My family and I are headed out for another church meeting tonight."

I waited for the pastor to hand me an envelope, but he just smiled and said, "Praise God. He is good." After an awkward silence he continued, "Um, I don't have the money to give you for a love offering. I'll mail it. May God bless you on your journey."

I got in the motorhome. Kathy had all the children seated and ready to travel. "Well," she asked, "Did you get our love offering?"

"He said he would send it later. But don't hold your breath. This pastor is struggling just like us and this tent revival cost a lot of money." I sighed, "God will provide. We are in another church tonight. They will surely give us a love offering and we can buy food and gas."

We arrived at the next church and met the pastor. "Brother Reasoner, it's a blessing to have you in our services. We are a young church plant, but God has blessed us, and we are looking for missionaries to support. I'm excited to have a missionary to Russia! Show your slides after the first song, field some questions, and then you will preach after your wife and children sing."

I smiled as Kathy, Joel, and Micah (now eight-years old) recited Romans 1:14-16 and sang *The Church of God is Debtor*. I stood to preach, "Open your Bibles to Jonah, Chapter One. Tonight, I want to preach on the three times the word of the Lord came to Jonah and his three responses. God told Jonah in chapter one to go to Nineveh and he responded in rebellion.

"I understand Jonah's dilemma. He did not want God to show mercy on his enemies. God has called us to go to our former enemies, and learning from Jonah's mistake, we have decided to obey God. In chapter two, after three days and nights in the belly of a great fish, God spoke to

Serving God Behind Enemy Lines

Jonah again. This time he responded in repentance, 'Salvation is of the Lord.'"

I looked at the teenagers in the second row and emphasized, "I love that we serve a God of the second chance. He didn't cast Jonah into the whale's belly and leave him there. When Jonah repented, God forgave him and put him back on the right path. But understand this, teens."

I paused and looked over the small congregation, "Everyone needs to understand this. Sin will take you farther than you ever want to go—Jonah never planned to be in the belly of a whale! Sin will keep you longer than you ever want to stay—Jonah stayed three days in the belly. He had seaweed wrapped around his head and endured the smell of intestinal garbage and stayed there in the puke for three days! And lastly, sin will cost you more than you ever wanted to pay.

"Jonah almost paid with his life! He might have died there in his rebellion if he had not repented. Do you see today that your sins have taken you to places you never wanted to go, it has kept you longer than you ever wanted to stay, and it has cost you more than you ever

Reasoners to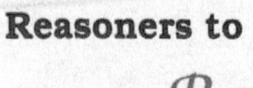

Ron, Kathy, Joel, Micah, Keturah, Hannah, Jeremiah

Missionaries to Russia

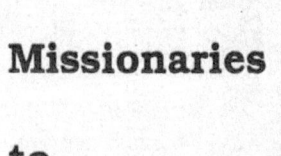

Home Address	Sending Church
BBFI	Corridor Baptist Church
P.O. Box 191	P.O. Box 471
Springfield, MO 65801	Hillsboro, OR 97123

"Finally, Brethren, pray for us, that the word of the Lord may have free course, and be glorified..."
II Thessalonians 3.1

Trials of Deputation

intended to pay? Repent and God will welcome you back with open arms!"

I paused as someone walked into the auditorium and whispered in the Pastor's ear. The pastor turned to his wife and said something before leaving.

I continued, "We all know the story that after Jonah repented, the whale spit him out on dry land. He went and preached in Nineveh an eight-word sermon, 'Yet 40 days and Nineveh shall be overthrown.' The whole town repented. Jonah saw God's mercy, got mad and went outside the city to sulk."

"God spoke to Jonah again in Chapter 3 while Jonah was sitting under the shriveled gourd. Jonah responded with a re-examination of his attitude. God told Jonah to have compassion on the Ninevites, especially the young, innocent children."

I looked at the congregation, and said, "You may be asking yourself tonight, 'Why is this missionary going to preach to our enemies?' I want you to know that God loves the Russian people every bit as much as He loves us. He is their Creator just as He is our Creator. Please join with us in partnership to see Russians saved for Christ!"

I held an invitation and dismissed in prayer. The pastor's wife approached and said, "I'm sorry, my husband had to leave during the services. One of our elderly members died. I'm not prepared to take you out to dinner, and I don't have your love offering check. We will mail it to you. God bless you on your journey."

We arrived back to the Portland area on fumes and pulled the motorhome into the driveway of my parents' farm in Molalla. I directed the children to go into the house to Grandma and Grandpa Reasoner who were lovingly known to the kids as "Grandma and Grandpa with the goats."

I held Kathy back as the children filed out, "Wait a second, I want to talk to you." I waited until the children were gone, and continued, "What are we going to do? We have no money, and we are supposed to drive to Missouri next week for candidate school."

"I wonder if all missionaries experience this kind of poverty. This is taxing on one's faith!" Kathy mumbled, "How much do we need?"

"$600—I just don't see how it will happen." I engulfed Kathy into a hug as I said, "Let's pray for God to help us and then go put on a smile for my parents. 'Father, we have surrendered but I'm wondering what we have surrendered to. We have five children that need food, and we need gas for our journeys. Help us, Lord. Amen!'"

A Little Church

We had one final appointment in Oregon before heading to the Midwest. It was a young church plant on the coast. We drove my mom's car which had a full tank of gas.

As we entered the rented store front, Kathy and I looked at each other in frustration.

Really Lord? We have more people in our family than are in the church.

I preached my heart out, but in the back of my mind, I was thinking, "This is another no love offering church. I have no idea how we will get to Missouri."

At the end of the church service, the six people in the church took up a love offering and gave us $600 — exactly the amount we needed!

The first thing I did with the love offering was buy a 50LB bag of rice and a 50LB bag of beans. I put them in the storage area on top of our motorhome. I told Kathy, "We may eat beans and rice for the next year, but we will not starve."

We never opened either bag and we never went to another church without a love offering. God had tested us one last time to prove Himself faithful regardless of the circumstances and finances.

Clank

We set off for candidate school in Springfield, Missouri. It was a long drive in a motorhome and eventually Kathy got her nerve up to drive. Perhaps it would be more correct to say I got tired enough to let her drive. She did well the first day, but all good things must come to an end.

We were about 50 miles from our destination and Kathy was at the wheel. We had grown low on funds again so I would put the engine in neutral when driving down a steep hill. Kathy decided to give it a try while I was sleeping.

I awakened to a loud, clanking noise. It sounded like the engine had dropped onto the highway. I ran to the front. Kathy was steering the stalled motorhome to the side of the road. "What happened?" I frantically asked.

Kathy burst into tears, "I was trying to save gas, and I missed neutral and put the engine into reverse. I'm so sorry." She thrust the gear shift into park, jumped out of the driver's seat and ran to the back of the motorhome. I later found out she was on her knees begging God to send angels to fix the engine.

All I remember saying is, "$5,000. $5,000. It's going to cost about $5,000 to fix the engine." I sat there for a while and finally worked up the courage to open the door and look at the damage. I expected to see R.V. parts all up and down the highway, but there were none. I looked under the RV. No leaks. No rods through the engine. Umm.

Our motorhome

I decided to give the engine a try. It started. I put it into drive. It moved. We could not believe it. The children cheered in unison. Kathy slowly came back to the front of the motorhome and sat in the passenger's seat. It drove all the way to our destination. Once we were in the parking lot of the missions office, I gathered up the courage to stop the RV and put it in reverse. It worked! God has great angel mechanics!

This was one of many situations when God protected us on deputation and taught us lessons. Here are a few more.

The Middle of Nowhere

One time we drove straight through from Northern New Mexico to Oklahoma City. We needed to drive nonstop to make it to the next meeting on time. I drove all day and Kathy took over for the night shift. My last words before going to sleep were, "Whatever you do, just stay on the freeway."

Kathy drove several hours then pulled off the freeway into a gas station. The gas attendant asked her, "Where are you headed?"

"Oklahoma City."

The attendant smiled, "There is a short cut that will trim off four hours."

"Is it a good road? Can it take the motorhome?"

He answered, "I've never been all the way across it, but a friend of mine said they finished it last year."

Kathy decided to surprise me by being four hours ahead of schedule when I awakened. However, it did not work out that way. About two hours into the trip, the asphalt road became a dirt road. Kathy continued. She did not know that the heat and the jostling of the engine were fusing all the wires together.

Suddenly everything went black, and the engine shut down. Kathy pulled over to the side of the road. I awakened, looked out the window and asked, "Where are we? The middle of nowhere?"

She looked up the road and saw a little café. The name of it was, *The Middle of Nowhere*. "Yep, that's what that sign says, 'The Middle of Nowhere.'" Then she broke down in tears. "I was trying to surprise you with a short cut. The gas station guy said it was a good road!"

I am not a mechanic, but a few days earlier, we were in Walmart, and I happened down the automotive aisle. There was a pack of colorful wires that I just had to have. As I handed them to Kathy, she furrowed her eyebrows and asked, "What are these for? You don't fix cars."

I shrugged, "Just get them. They're cool and I want them."

Now, in *The Middle of Nowhere*, I opened the engine cover to discover that the wires had melted together. My job that night in the freezing cold was to piece the wires back together with my new wire kit.

It took all night, but I did it. The engine finally started, and we hobbled to the next town where I pulled into an auto repair parking lot. I asked the mechanic, "Do you work on motorhomes?"

He smiled a toothless grin and exclaimed, "I've always wanted to. I'll fix all your problems for $200."

I filed our family out of the motorhome and into the waiting room. We caught the attention of a lady picking up her minivan. After she paid, she turned to us and said, "My! What a lovely family. Where are you headed?"

I answered, "Hi, I'm Ron Reasoner. We are missionaries to Russia. Our motorhome needs repairs."

The lady looked at the mechanic and asked, "How long will it take for you to fix it?"

"About five hours I reckon."

The lady turned, "My name is Mrs. Smith and I want to invite your family to my house while John fixes your RV. Five hours is way too long for these children to sit in a waiting room. Besides, where will you eat lunch? I made a pot of stew last night and I need someone to help me eat it." She smiled at Keturah and Hannah as she talked.

Trials of Deputation

I looked at Kathy and she nodded. "Thank you so much," I said, "God bless you for your kindness."

The children enjoyed running and playing with Mrs. Smith's dogs and other farm animals while Kathy and I shared the Gospel with the lady in her living room. She excitedly said, "I am a Christian. I asked Jesus to save me when I was a teenager. I go to church every week and am the president of our missionary society. I can hardly wait to tell them about how I entertained real live missionaries to Russia!"

Four hours later, the mechanic called Mrs. Smith. She drove us back to get our motorhome. We gave her prayer cards for her missionary society. Kathy hugged and thanked her again for her hospitality while I went to pay John $200. He smiled, "The bill has already been taken care of."

I ran back out to thank Mrs. Smith, but she was gone. We loaded up and soon were back on the road. Somehow, we still arrived on time.

Another Repair

Another time our motorhome stopped working outside of St. Louis, Missouri. I pulled it to the side of the road. "Not again!" exclaimed Micah, "I think we spend too much time on the side of the road with this motorhome."

Kathy and I looked at each other. We felt the same way. "Well," Joel said, "Let's pray for another miracle. Dear Jesus, we need help again. Please send someone to help us. In Jesus' name, Amen."

We all repeated, "Amen," and immediately I heard a car door slam. I looked out the window and a man approached our side door.

I got out, "Good afternoon."

"Good afternoon!" the man replied, "I saw you stranded alongside the road and thought I'd stop and see if you needed help."

"Thank you! My name is Ron. We are missionaries to Russia. We are traveling around the country asking churches to pray and support our family to preach the Gospel there."

The man smiled, "My name is Mark. I'm on my way home from a church men's retreat. I just finished praying that God would give me an opportunity to help someone in need and here you are."

Mark called his brother, who owned a towing company. He towed the motorhome to an R.V. mechanic. Mark paid for all the repairs. He took us to a hotel, paid for our room, brought us dinner, and gave us $200 for the road. What a blessing!

As we got back into the repaired motorhome, Micah stated, "God sure has a lot of good people out there to help missionaries in trouble."

I smiled, "You're right, son. Today someone was the answer to our prayers. Perhaps tomorrow, we can be an answer to someone else's prayers. There are always opportunities to serve the Lord if you are willing to listen to His prompting."

Reno, Nevada

A few months later, we were traveling through Nevada to a missions conference in the Los Angeles area. The traffic on the freeway just outside of Reno slowed to a crawl.

"It's Saturday afternoon," Kathy mused, "Why is there so much traffic?"

Joel popped his head up front and answered, "Maybe there's a wreck up ahead. We see a lot of wrecks traveling all the time."

I looked ahead to the left side of the freeway to see a man outside his car, blood dripping down his face and walking aimlessly from the front to the back of his car. Puzzled, I said, "I think that guy needs help. I'm pulling over."

I signaled to get over to the left lane and then pulled ahead of the disabled car. I hopped out of the RV and went to the young man, "Hey, are you okay?"

The young man muttered, "I don't think so. I was driving and a semi-truck just cut me off. His trailer hit my front end and I spun out of control. I don't think the trucker even knew he hit me because he kept going."

I looked at the steam pouring out his engine, "I don't think your car is going anywhere. Would you like me to drop you off somewhere to call for help? I'm Ron, by the way. What is your name?"

The young man struggled to remember. Finally, he said, "I'm Mike. I have a brother in Reno. Could you take me somewhere where I can call him?"

Mike followed me into the motorhome. I introduced him to our family, "This is my wife Kathy and my five kiddos. Guys, this is Mike. He got hit by a semi-trailer and the trucker kept driving. We will take him to Reno and find a payphone."

Kathy walked over to him, "Are you sure you don't need a hospital? That gouge on your head looks awfully deep. Let me get the first-aid kit."

While Kathy headed toward the bathroom, I settled into the driver's seat and invited Mike to sit next to me. I pulled back into traffic and talked as Kathy cleaned his wound, "We are missionaries going to Russia. We are going there to tell the Russian people about Jesus and His death on the cross for their sins. Have you ever asked Jesus to save you from your sins?"

Mike flinched as Kathy put a Band-Aid smothered in Triple Antibiotic cream on his wound. "No, I've never given God any thought, but as I saw that truck coming straight at me, I thought about how I wished I knew where I was going if I died."

I smiled at God's timing, "God brought us to you today. I specialize in telling people about Jesus. God loves you but sinners can't go to Heaven. Are you a sinner, Mike?"

Mike nodded, and I continued, "We all are. God requires perfection to go to Heaven so none of us can go—except God wants us to be with Him in Heaven, so He sent Jesus to earth. Joel, my oldest son, will quote John 3:16 for you."

Joel piped up.

"For God so loved the world, that he gave his only begotten Son, that whosoever believeth in him should not perish, but have everlasting life." (John 3:16)

"Thank you, Joel." I looked back at Mike, "God sent Jesus to be the penalty for our sins. Jesus lived a perfect life so when He died, He wasn't dying for His sins, because He didn't have any, but He died for our sins. Jesus went to Hell for our sins and arose on the third day. Do you believe that Mike?"

Mike thought for a moment and replied, "Yes, I believe."

"Would you like to ask Jesus to forgive your sins and come into your heart to save you?"

Mike smiled, "Very much so. Today I was afraid, and I don't want to be afraid anymore."

I prayed with Mike. Each of the children welcomed him into the family of God as I pulled off the freeway in Reno. I turned to Mike and asked, "Are you sure you don't want to go to the hospital?"

Mike saw a payphone outside a casino and said, "No, please drop me off here so I can call my brother. I hope he's in the phone book, I don't know his number."

I pulled the RV over, turned to Mike, and asked, "Should I wait until you get ahold of him?"

Mike stood, shook my hand, "No, I'll be fine. Thank you so much for helping me."

I handed Mike a prayer card, a tract, and a New Testament. "Now you need to grow in Christ. Find yourself a good independent Baptist Church and become a faithful follower of Jesus."

Serving God Behind Enemy Lines

Mike took the material, "I don't know what I would have done without you. I promise I will look up a good Baptist Church in the phone book and go to church next Sunday. Thank you!"

As I pulled back onto the freeway towards California, Micah came up front and waited for me to acknowledge him. "What Micah?"

He grinned, "I guess we really do sow and reap in life. Sometimes people help us and sometimes it is our turn to help people. Today we helped Mike find eternal life and that's the best gift of all!"

Truly our home on wheels was a mixed blessing on deputation. Despite the problems, it gave our children stability and security during a transitional year in their lives. They were able to get up and walk around during the long hours on the road. It also provided a safe place for my family to stay when I had an opportunity in December 1993 to go on a survey trip to Russia. A survey trip is for prospective missionaries to go to the country they feel called to. It allows them to get a better understanding of the culture, spiritual needs, economics, and living conditions.

- ☑ Let the church know God has called us
- ☑ Help the church call a new pastor
- ☑ Put our house on the market
- ☑ Call churches and schedule meetings
- ☑ Get a vehicle for driving around the country to raise support

THOUGHTS
- When was the last time you stepped off the cliff of faith and Satan tried to convince you that God was not going to catch you?

Chapter Sixteen

The Survey Trip

So, as much as in me is, I am ready to preach the gospel to you that are at Rome also. Romans 1:15

The hum of the jet engine grew louder as I landed at Chicago's O'Hare airport. It was December 1993. We had been on deputation for three months. It had been a long flight, and I was glad this leg was over, but the next would be even longer.

As I walked off the jetway I saw a man nod and walk towards me. I reached out and shook his hand, "Brother Floyd Dorsey, good to finally meet you."

The older man reached down and picked up one of my carry-on bags. "How was your flight?"

I shrugged. "Not too bad. The flight from L.A. to Chicago was a bit bumpy."

He pointed towards the south end of the terminal. "Our Aeroflot flight departs from gate C14."

I shook my head. "I've been praying ever since you faxed me our itinerary. I've heard stories about their safety record."

He scratched his head. "Get used to it. One, if you go through with your plans, you'll be flying Aeroflot a lot; and two, the Russians utilize their best aircraft and crews for international flights. The Communist Party likes the revenue it brings in. I've heard most of the pilots are former military and have thousands of hours flying large aircraft in all kinds of weather and conditions."

An hour later, we boarded our flight and stored our bags in the overhead compartment. I pointed to the window, "They assigned me that seat, but if you'd rather take the window, it's fine with me."

Brother Dorsey smiled and moved towards my seat, "Thanks, I appreciate that."

As I looked out the window, I wondered if perhaps the pioneering spirit ran in my blood. My ancestors had been pioneers seeking religious freedom. They traveled across the dangerous Atlantic Ocean on the Mayflower. Generations later, God was calling me to cross back over the Atlantic Ocean as a pioneer to take the Gospel to unreached peoples.

Lord, please give me wisdom and show me what to do.

The hum of the engine made me drowsy, and I soon drifted off to sleep.

I awoke from a deep slumber six hours later not knowing where I was. As I rubbed my eyes a stewardess came by. She demanded in her broken English, "Quick, give me dishes! We land soon."

I stared at the Russian flag emblazoned on her name tag, then glanced to my right and noticed Brother Dorsey snoring. I leaned over, glanced out as the plane banked and caught a glimpse of endless tall apartment buildings in the distance as far as my eyes could see. I turned back to her and smiled. "Yes, thank you, Tanya." I reached in front of Brother Dorsey and handed his dishes to her.

I looked back out the window at the scene before me. Although it was only 4 p.m. local time, the sun had already set. The lights in the apartment buildings reminded me of huge honeycombs.

Imagine the thousands of souls in those buildings!

Brother Dorsey stirred, stretched, and yawned. "Are we landing already?"

He frowned as we neared the ground. "That's odd, it seems we're flying at an angle."

He shrugged, "So, earlier you were telling me that since you didn't have the money for a survey trip you were going to move your family of seven to Russia on faith?"

I gave my new-found friend a sheepish smile and shrugged. "You see we started part-time deputation in July, although we weren't approved as missionaries until the end of September. By October, word had gotten around that there was a crazy missionary family of seven on their way to Russia. That's when you contacted me. You told me you'd already been to Russia, were going again, and invited me. It was a blessing from the Lord. I have a list of questions a mile long in my wallet that my wife wants answered. What do they sell in the stores? Are the shelves empty like on the news? Do they sell toothpaste? Deodorant?"

The Survey Trip

We raised our heads as the loudspeaker crackled and a voice barked first in Russian and then in English, "You will fasten your seatbelts. We will be making our landing approach into Moscow's Sheremetyevo Airport."

We obeyed and frowned at the same time. I whispered, "He sounds tense." Chuckling a nervous laugh, we stared at the rapidly approaching ground. I turned back to Brother Dorsey and continued, "By the time you contacted me, we were getting enough in love offerings to pay for this trip. I cleared my schedule and found a place for my family to stay while I join you."

He nodded. "Well, when Jeffrey from Revival Fires had a cancellation, I told him about you and here we are."

I pulled a paper out and fanned the cigarette smoke wafting from the seat in front of me. "My wife and I appreciate that. Even though they aren't Baptist, the fact that they want to get Bibles into Russia made an impression. It is okay because you and I are doctrinally like-minded." I looked around to see if any others in our party were paying attention to us.

The passenger in front of us rubbed his cigarette into the ash tray and the air vents pulled the remaining smoke away. I coughed before saying, "We have zero contacts in Russia, and to do this on our own, would have been an enormous undertaking. But Jeffrey seems to have contacts all over; in the Russian military, youth camps, schools, prisons, and hospitals."

Brother Dorsey patted my arm. "It will be my privilege to introduce you to many Russian people."

The plane came in sideways and rapidly dropped. In our experiences, huge planes do not normally drop so quickly. It was like the pilot was on a strafing run. At that moment, the plane's tires screeched on the tarmac; the plane jolted sideways on the ice.

I grabbed the seat as I held back a gasp. Nevertheless, we made it safely onto a frozen taxiway and the plane straightened onto the tarmac. Everyone, including Tanya, cheered, and clapped.

After taxiing to the gate, the crew opened the main door. A cold breeze swept the length of the aircraft. As we retrieved our bags and I stepped back to let someone pass, I commented, "I've gone from sunny southern California, to Chicago, to Moscow's frozen weather." I shivered as another blast of air wafted down the aisle.

We pulled extra clothing from our bags and bundled up. I instantly regretted saving money and buying a synthetic parka. I hoped the expensive ski gloves a church had gifted me would keep my fingers from frost bite.

Ten minutes later we followed the crowd towards passport control. I pointed up at the ceiling decorated with coffee cans.

This reminds me of a scene from a B-rated spy movie.

Nothing was well lit. Police and military guarded every entrance and exit. No matter how much we smiled and waved, they never broke from their scowls, or took their hands off their rifles strapped across their chests.

After making it through passport control and customs, we collected our luggage and boarded the bus rented by Revival Fires. Of course, being in Russia for the first time, I was craning my neck to take it all in. My eyes widened when I saw the giant tank jacks after we left the airport." I pointed to them. "Brother Dorsey, what are they? They look like my daughters' game of jacks."

"Oh, those? They are giant barriers Stalin built to stop the German tanks from entering Moscow during World War II." He tapped my shoulder and pointed to the left side of the bus. "Look, over there, you can see the lights of Moscow and the Stalin Heights skyscrapers. There are seven of them, often called the Seven Sisters."

As we drove to the hotel, we saw an old lady struggling to cross the street, pulling her cart. Everyone on our side of the bus gasped as a *militsiya* hit her with his police car. The impact knocked her through the air into a snowbank. The police officer screeched to a halt, got out of his car, and cursed at her. As she struggled to get up, he got into his car and drove away. By the time our bus started moving, I was encouraged by her resolve as she limped away. Not a sign of an ambulance or even an offer to take her to the hospital. The policeman just left her. Everyone, even the experienced travelers, flinched when they saw the pain on her face.

Brother Dorsey nudged me, "Thankfully she's a tough *babushka* and will live to fight another day." He chuckled at the puzzled look on my face. "A *babushka* is a Russian grandmother. It's a term of endearment." After we moved to Russia permanently, I found out that Russians call these daring *babushkas* who bravely cross the street regardless of traffic flow, 'Russian Matadors.'

We arrived late to the hotel; Brother Dorsey tried to stop the waiter when he insisted on feeding us. The man shook his head and continued serving our group. "It seems they insist on feeding us. I guess they want us to feel welcome."

The Survey Trip

Everyone took a deep breath and moved to sit around several large tables. As we unfolded our napkins, we were served a bowl of sliced up meat. It was cold and looked like sticks of chewing gum.

Brother Dorsey raised a hand to get the waiter's attention. When the man reached his side, Brother Dorsey put both hands on either side of his bowl, shrugged and gave the Russian a questioning look.

The middle-aged waiter, in his broken English, smiled proudly, "That cat tongue, our specialty."

That was all it took; everyone dropped their spoons. Several looked at his face to see if he was joking, but at least on this occasion, the cat did not get our tongues, we got his.

Later that night, I tossed in bed for over an hour. After a while I heard the springs on Brother Dorsey's bed squeak. "You can't sleep either?"

He chuckled, "I'm too excited We've entered a once forbidden country and are about to go around Russia preaching the Gospel. My mind's swimming with the hopes of what we might get to experience." He raised up on his elbow. "The biggest thing on my mind is that just because the national government allows us to preach, doesn't mean the locals won't arrest us."

I sat up and turned on the light. "Add to our excitement a large dose of jetlag." I paused to figure out the time difference from the West Coast in the United States, "It's 11 hours difference for me. No wonder we're lying here staring at the ceiling! Morning can't arrive soon enough."

Brother Dorsey rolled over and put his pillow over his head. "You couldn't be more correct."

THOUGHTS
- What do you suppose is the first thing foreigners notice about your country?

CHAPTER SEVENTEEN

My First Day in Moscow

Have not I commanded thee? Be strong and of a good courage; be not afraid, neither be thou dismayed: for the LORD thy God is with thee whithersoever thou goest. Joshua 1:9

The next morning, Brother Dorsey and I were finishing breakfast when a young man entered the lobby, strode over to us, and stood tall.

He smiled and bowed slightly, "Sirs, Brother Dorsey, it's so good to see you again."

As they shook hands, he turned towards me and said, "I will be your interpreter." As he shook my hand, he smiled, "Brother Reasoner, my name is RoMAN. This is different from how you Americans pronounce it. The stress is on the second syllable. So, again my name is RoMAN." He checked his watch. "I must see to your bags. The bus is coming in 10 minutes." He turned and walked away to complete his duties.

As we rose from our table to retrieve our hats and coats, Brother Dorsey pointed to our fellow believers sitting nearby. "This evening we leave for Smolensk; they have meetings scheduled in Moscow until we head home."

I smiled, "Isn't that the definition of 'Independent Baptist'? We like to do things on our own." I put on my hat and coat as Roman approached the table. "So? What do you have scheduled for us?"

He pulled a notepad from his pocket and thumbed through it. "Ah, here it is." He glanced at Brother Dorsey and me, "There are several army barracks nearby. Revival Fires has you Americans scheduled to cover all of them while on your tour."

He scratched his head under his baseball cap. I asked, "Are you a Chicago White Sox fan?"

Roman was confused until I pointed to his ball cap. He took it off, looked at it and smiled, "It was a gift from another American."

"That's cool."

My Interpreter, Roman

Roman placed it back on his head. "Actually, it is my second one." He lowered his voice, "My first one was stolen by a group of Russian thugs. They surrounded me, beat me unconscious, took my hat and left me to die. I awakened in the hospital two days later."

"Why did they target you?" I asked as we started for the door.

Roman laughed, "Because American items are a rare commodity here. They are literally worth killing for. I was lucky."

I tried to open the glass door in front of me, but it was locked. Roman laughed as he opened the other door, "Here in Russia we have many doors, but only one is unlocked."

I opened my mouth to speak, but Roman waved his hand, "Don't ask. This is Russia. It is our way."

Once outside he paused to pull out a small Moscow map. "We are going to this barracks. We'll distribute the Russian Bibles you brought and walk to the other barracks. In the end we should have time for a late lunch before we board the train to Smolensk."

I looked at Roman. "How did you learn to speak English so well?"

"You see, Grandfather was a communist boss, so my father did not have to join the party due to grandfather's *blot*." He paused and scratched his chin, "In English, this means *clout or influence*. Father insisted from the time I was a little boy that I learn the English language."

He puffed out his chest, "I had to learn 50 words in English each day before I could play." He tapped my KJV Bible. "When I decided to become a better interpreter, I bought an English Bible and read it. Sometimes when I have insomnia, I read it out loud until I fall asleep."

I smiled, "That shows initiative. You should be commended."

He beamed and paused to help me tighten my scarf, "You see, during the Soviet Times, sons and daughters of the Communist Party Elite were taught English and Tennis. Such activities were not available to the common people. My father insisted I excel at them without the help of the Communist party."

Minutes later as we loaded boxes of Bibles into the cargo compartment of what appeared to be an old Greyhound bus, I noticed how Roman constantly surveyed our surroundings and the people walking past. I liked his intensity.

As we drove by Red Square, Brother Dorsey pointed to the Kremlin. "Looks more impressive than the photos on TV, doesn't it? Over there, that beautiful, colorful building is St. Basil's Cathedral. We are approaching it from the south so those are the Kremlin walls just to the west. On the East side is G.U.M. (Government Universal Mall). We'll get a chance to walk through Red Square on our last day."

When we arrived at a Red Army Base outside of Moscow, each of us removed boxes of Bibles from the bus. Brother Dorsey pointed to the sidewalk. "Stack them in that alcove. He chuckled, "The nice thing about nine-month winters is that Russia figured out a long time ago how to keep the sidewalks and streets clear."

As I grabbed a handful of Bibles, Brother Dorsey put a hand on my arm. "Remember the phrase Roman and I taught you?" I nodded. He continued, "Remember it means, 'This is for you, please take it.'" I smiled at my newfound language skill. Brother Dorsey patted me on the back and charged me, "Good. Now go forth and conquer."

Brother Dorsey grabbed an armful of Bibles. "Roman, pass these out to soldiers as they march by."

I stopped a soldier, held a Bible in front of him, and said, "Это для вас, пожалуйста, возьмите её."

My First Day in Moscow

The soldier's eyes widened when he saw the camouflaged cover. He took it and ran his fingers over the cover before gingerly opening it. He looked around suspiciously, then placed his newfound Treasure in his pocket. I will never forget his grateful look. Soon we had handed out all the Bibles.

I pulled my camera from its case and started to take pictures. Roman's eyes bulged as he grabbed it. "Brother Reasoner, no! Be careful where you take pictures. See those men over there?"

I turned my head in the direction Roman indicated and noted two men in heavy winter coats over their business suits, fancy boots, and fedoras. "Yes, what about them?"

He shook his head, "Impetuous American. They're KGB. They're part of the surveillance team that's been tailing us ever since you arrived. If they think you've taken their picture, they will confiscate your camera. If they feel like it, they will arrest you." He slammed the camera back in its case. "Next time, ask!"

I stood still trying to think of what harm a picture could be, then sheepishly put my camera away, and followed them into a restaurant. Brother Dorsey and I laughed as we hung our hats and coats on a hook. "Maybe we can get a bowl of cat tongue."

I put two hands on the back of a little chair and shook it. "I don't know if this will support my weight." I looked around and saw we had the best seats in the place. "At least the Formica isn't peeling." We laughed as we cautiously took our seats.

The waiter arrived and handed us ornate menus. Every time I tried to order something; he shook his head. "I'm sorry we don't have that today."

After four tries, Roman interpreted. "Well, what do you have?"

Since it was the only choice available, I ordered *borscht* (a beet and cabbage-based soup) a staple for Eastern Europeans.

After the waiter left, I pointed to the bare walls and the menus in his hand. "What gives? This is the shabbiest restaurant I've ever been in, and they have the most expensive, elaborate menu."

He winked, "Welcome to Russia. The menus were made during Soviet times when impressing and wowing tourists was important. The ornate menu was just one of the many delusions to show how rich and advanced we were. Over the years, the restaurant has dwindled the menu choices to affordable dishes, but they haven't bothered to print new menus."

Roman reached into his coat pocket and pulled out two envelopes. "Here's your train ticket. The train to Smolensk leaves in three hours."

After 30 minutes I turned to Roman. "Why is it taking so long?"

"Welcome to Russia. The staff doesn't care if we come in or not. They know they will get paid even without customers." He pointed towards the kitchen, "When we ordered, that's when the cook went shopping." He sighed, "It always takes an hour, no matter what you order. That's part of the reason Russians eat at home unless they are traveling."

I pulled out my notepad and made an entry into my journal.

Kathy will want to know about this.

I closed the book and tore a piece of dark rye bread in half from the basket on the table. I pointed it at Roman and Brother Dorsey, "It is hard to explain the spiritual victory one feels giving a copy of God's Word to a Russian soldier."

I munched on the bread and sipped a cup of hot tea. "Bleh! This is the driest, most tasteless bread I've ever had."

Brother Dorsey pointed to the basket in front of us. "Who knows how long that plate of sliced bread has been there. If you don't eat it, they set it on the shelf, and serve it to the next customer."

I gave Roman a questioning look. He nodded. "It's true, they do reserve bread when other diners don't eat it. But it doesn't last long." He sat up straight and bragged, "Russia does not use preservatives or additives. After two days, bread starts to grow penicillin and it must be thrown out."

Puzzled, I looked to Brother Dorsey. He smiled, "I think Roman is trying to say the bread molds after a few days."

I nodded, took a deep breath, and sighed. "Anyway, I was raised during the Cold War. Russia was the enemy that might destroy us. Now, I am in their country giving their soldiers the Gospel of Jesus Christ and telling them how they can be saved. All those millions of prayers for God to open Russia and let the people know Him are being answered before my eyes."

Eventually our food arrived. It was my first bowl of *borscht,* and I devoured it. Roman smiled, "So you like it?"

I shrugged, "Hunger is the best cook—but I think it's pretty good."

On the way to the train station, I remembered a few Bibles in my backpack. I tapped Roman on the shoulder. "I'll catch up." I rushed across the street and approached a *militsiya.* "Это для вас, пожалуйста, возьмите её." The man jumped back and almost dropped his baton. I waited for him to regain his composure and continued holding the Bible for him to take. "Это для вас, пожалуйста, возьмите её."

My First Day in Moscow

The police officer stammered something I couldn't understand and took it. I nodded and waved good-bye.

Five minutes later we crossed a deserted square, Roman asked me to join him in an alcove and politely scolded me. "Brother Reasoner, what on earth were you doing? Don't you know that the *militsiya* are to be avoided. You don't interact with them. If they approach you, you only answer their questions, and don't volunteer anything!" He shook a finger at me like I was a child. "Even if your papers are in order and they want something to do, they can bring you in for questioning! Please don't ever do that again!"

I looked around to see if the *militsiya* were coming to arrest me. When I turned back, I noticed Roman's head bobbing through a crowd a block away and scurried to catch up.

I almost fell as my feet slipped on the slush beneath my feet. The day had warmed above freezing but now as the sun set, the melted mud and snow froze again. It reminded me of a slushy. Suddenly, I craved a root beer float.

This was only the beginning of my journey and already I realized that living in a foreign country would be full of pitfalls. The laws that ensure freedom in America do not protect us once we leave her borders.

THOUGHTS
- What talents have you vigorously developed to be used for God's Service?

Chapter Eighteen

The Train Ride

But sanctify the Lord God in your hearts: and be ready always to give an answer to every man that asketh you a reason of the hope that is in you with meekness and fear: 1 Peter 3:15

As we crossed the street towards the train station, and approached the main entrance, I pointed to the multiple tracks. "How do we know which track is for our train to Smolensk?" Roman pointed to the nearest train track. "See the bluish-green cars with the brackets that are connected to the overhead wires?"

I nodded, and he continued, "They are called *elektrichkas* (local train) lines that go within 100 kilometers of Moscow. We won't be taking one of those because Smolensk is about 400 kilometers from here." He gestured towards the wall. "There, our train track number just appeared on the reader board." He led us toward the middle gate. "Since we're going southwest this is where we go."

"I can't help but admire this magnificent architecture," I exclaimed. We continued to stride towards what I hoped was our train. "Roman, they sure did a wonderful job when they built this."

He turned, beaming a smile, "Yes, we have many good men work on this building."

Moments later we queued up in line.

Whew, I don't understand any Russian. At least I hear the word Smolensk often enough. I'm sure we'll make it.

The female conductor wore her uniform proudly. Each person who moved in front of her seemed to stand erect as if they were before someone of importance. During the 30-minutes we stood in line, it was obvious she enjoyed her power. When it was our turn, I felt more ill at ease than I did

The Train Ride

going through customs at the Moscow airport. Roman handed her all three passports. I stood at attention as he presented our papers. She glared at my picture then held it beside my face. She seemed assured I was the person my papers said I was.

Without looking up she ran a finger down my visa. "Какова цель Вашей поездки в Смоленск?"

Roman stepped forward and answered something in Russian. She folded my papers and handed them back, then focused on the next person in line. "Следующий."

I looked at Roman who nodded toward the wagon steps. I took two bags and marched up the stairs. I then turned around and took the extra ten bags that Roman handed me from the platform. Eventually we got all our luggage on board.

Roman took the lead and found our compartment. We began a chain and passed the boxes one by one to Roman. He stored them under each of the two bottom bunk beds. When he could fit no more, he stacked the remainder in the overhead compartment above the door and hallway. He wiped his forehead with his sleeve. "Whew, that was a workout!"

It was 9 p.m. by the time we got settled. As I sat on the bottom bunk to rest, I asked, "Roman, what did that lady ask when she held our passports in her hands?"

"She wanted to know what business you had going to Smolensk. I told her you were Americans going to see the people there."

I nodded. "What was that last word the lady said when she handed us back our passports? Slee-a-dush-something."

Roman thought for a moment, "Oh Следующий – it means 'next.'"

I took a moment to look around our compartment, "How old are these trains?"

He chuckled, "I think they were new when Stalin took power in 1924."

I stretched my arms out, "This isn't much bigger than my bedroom closet."

Brother Dorsey chuckled, and Roman replied. "It'll seem smaller if the conductor brings another passenger in."

I shook my head and crossed my arms. "No way! We paid for four beds. They can't do that!" I turned to Brother Dorsey, "Can they?"

He nodded. "Yes, it happens all the time. The conductor sees that we aren't using the bed, he finds a stowaway, and most of the time, he'll take a bribe, fill the bed, and pocket the money."

Roman winked. "Welcome to Russia."

We chatted and watched while soldiers, businessmen, oligarchs, and regular civilians struggled with their luggage as they trekked towards their compartments.

As the train lumbered on, we fell asleep. I woke when our compartment door opened, the conductor saw I was awake and slid a bag of walnuts under my seat. "Если кто-то спросит, это ваши грецкие орехи. Вы купили их в Москве и везут к другу," she nodded and slid the door shut.

"What?" I exclaimed, but she was gone.

Roman, who had awakened when the conductor came in, shook his head. "No problem. She would not tell you if you spoke Russian, but I know from experience she is helping a friend smuggle walnuts from Poland. She said, 'If anyone asks, you say I bought these in Moscow and am bringing them to a friend in Smolensk.'"

My eyes widened. Brother Dorsey nodded. Roman pointed out the window and used his favorite phrase. "Welcome to Russia."

"But I cannot lie. I could go to jail," I folded my arms across my chest. "I won't do it."

Roman's eyes widened. "Listen, you naïve American. If you don't lie, we get pulled in for questioning. If we're lucky, I'm the only one who'll be arrested, but then we could all be arrested. Who do you think they will believe? You or the conductor?" He leaned forward and threw a thumb over his shoulder. "Ever been to Siberia? Do you know what Russian prisons are like? Have you ever heard of a *Gulag*?"

He fell back in his seat and gestured towards the walls of our compartment. "They keep eight in this size of a cell. If they could fit more, they would." He sat up straight. "There's no room to sit, they're fed bread and water. You stand or squat for hours until it is your turn to sleep. There are two bunks to a cell. So, when it's your turn to sleep, no matter what time of day, you sleep." He snapped his fingers. "Oh, yes, if you need to use the toilet, you use a bucket in the corner. If you are the last to enter, you stand next to it. And did I mention Russian prisons are overrun with tuberculosis?"

I stared out the window into the night. Lord, how am I going to reach these people? What have I gotten my family into?

Twenty minutes later a *militsiya* entered our compartment and held his hand out. We sat erect and focused on his demeanor. He asked Roman a few questions and examined everyone's papers. I stared straight ahead and breathed a sigh of relief when he left. Thirty minutes later another officer demanded the same information.

The Train Ride

While he talked, I opened my mouth and threw a questioning look at Brother Dorsey. He shook his head. I took the hint and remained silent. When he left, Roman slid our door shut. He nodded to Brother Dorsey, "If he keeps this up, we may not get arrested."

I laughed nervously and pointed towards the front of the train. "What gives with being asked the same questions three times?"

"Welcome to Russia. They hope to trip you up so they can be rewarded for turning you in." He tapped his coat pocket. "That's why you always hope your papers are in order."

I stood and stretched when the train jerked as it moved onto a siding. Both caught me before I stumbled. I thought for a moment and asked, "I understand them checking out our papers because we are American, but why do you even have papers? We aren't crossing a border, why do they need your passport?"

Roman sighed, "Everyone in Russia, both citizens and foreigners, must keep their passports on them. You Americans have visas which gives you permission to be here, I have a прописка (permanent registration). Russians must be registered where they live. We are not free to move around the country without governmental permission."

Picking up Roman's passport laying on the table, I smiled, "You don't look any older than 14 in this picture."

Roman smiled, "I am 14 in that picture." He turned a page and continued, "Here I am 19. Every five years we put a new picture in."

"So, your passport never expires?" I questioned.

"This is my domestic passport. Every Russian citizen gets one when they are 14. It only allows you to travel within Russia. I recently applied for my international passport. I hope to get it soon. Since the fall of the Soviet Union, they are giving more and more international passports out to citizens. Before, only tried and true communist party members could get an international passport."

"They restrict your travel from city to city?" Brother Dorsey asked.

Roman looked shocked and exclaimed, "Of course! It helps to keep track of terrorists."

I caught Roman's sarcasm and smiled, "Like terrorists obey the laws."

Suddenly Roman put his finger to his mouth. Quietly he said, "The walls have ears!" Then loudly announced, "We should not talk against the laws and directives of my great country!"

Trying to take my mind off walnuts and the possibility of a free trip to Siberia, I asked, "When will we get our tickets back? The Conductor took them when we boarded."

Roman laid down, closed his eyes, and sighed, "Tomorrow morning they will be torn in half to prove they were used. She'll grace us with a nice hot cup of tea. It comes with the price of the ticket."

Satisfied my ticket would be returned, I looked again at my return ticket and asked, "Uh, so, Roman, why's Smolensk such an important city?"

He sat up, pulled a brochure from his backpack, spread it out and proudly pointed to a wall on the front page. "Napoléon overthrew the city. It was quite the battle that took place." His finger followed the course of a thick, brick wall across the pamphlet. "This was not able to stop Napoleon. His army was bigger and stronger, and they overtook the city. But his victory was not long endured, for Napoleon could not withstand the Russian winter in Smolensk and soon abandoned the city." He puffed his chest out, "More than once in Russian history, our greatest weapon of war was not a tank or AK-47, but simply Mother Russia's chilling weather."

Three hours later, the rocking of the car kept me awake. I saw Roman and Brother Dorsey sleeping soundly. I put my shoes on and tried to quietly open the door.

I'm starving. Since we're in the last car the food wagon must be this way.

I kept both hands on the walls as I wobbled through the cars. I felt like I was taking my life into my hands. I came upon several passengers smoking in the passageway. "Excuse me." After no response I remembered, "Извините" and resumed my treacherous journey.

Ten minutes later I stood at the food counter. When it came my turn to order, I pointed to the items I wanted. The attendant scowled, "Туристов. Почему они не могут выучить наш язык?" When he saw the blank look on my face, the employee attempted to interpret for me, "Tourist! Learn speak Russian!" I shrugged. After a five-second stare down, he looked away and proceeded to fill my order. He put my food on a plate and shoved it across the counter with disdain. He said something so fast I could not understand a word.

He's probably telling me how much I owe.

I reached into my pocket and pulled out a handful of money. He grabbed two bills and handed me two coins.

I sat down at an empty booth. Within a few moments, a man stood before me, "May I join you?" He asked.

The Train Ride

"Sure. My name is Ron Reasoner."

The man sat across from me, "I'm Volodya Romanovich. Are you American?"

I nodded, "I assume you are Russian?"

He set his glass down, pointed to other businessmen standing and sitting in the restaurant car. "Most of the men you see here are Polish businessmen. Me, I'm from Warsaw." He pulled a business card from his coat pocket. "I sell ball bearings. And what do you do?"

We spent the next 20 minutes discussing how God called me to Russia. I pulled a tract from my shirt pocket. "If you were to die today, do you know for sure you would go to Heaven?"

He looked at his watch and started to rise. I followed him towards the rear of the train. He made the sign of the cross on his chest, "I'm a practicing Catholic." I continued to hold out the pamphlet until he took it. After passing through several wagons, he stopped, nodded a quick good-bye, and entered his compartment quickly shutting the door behind him.

When I reached our berth, I saw my companions standing in the passageway and Roman wiped his forehead. "It's much cooler out here." He stepped aside to make room for me to pass. "I wish you wouldn't go somewhere without telling me." He frowned, "I am responsible for you."

After I finished my tale of the restaurant car, Roman shook his head. "Do you really believe this Volodya guy is who he says he is? Chances are he's KGB and is checking on foreigners. Most Russians wouldn't have a conversation with you otherwise."

I chuckled, "You think everyone is KGB, Roman."

I watched as Roman held his left hand out flat. With his right hand he pulled his pinky finger down, "Here are the facts: One, under communism it was forbidden to become acquainted with Americans." I was intrigued as he pulled down his ring finger, "Two, most Russians are afraid this new freedom won't last long so they are still limiting their contact with Americans." Next Roman pulled down his middle finger, "Three, 100% of people worked for the government under communism." He pushed down his index finger, "And four, private industry is still developing now that Russia is a democracy." He closed his thumb into a fist and concluded, "That leads to number five, most people still work for the government."

I focused back on his words, "Don't you know that they would be heavily rewarded for turning in an American spy? That is what everyone thinks you are—a spy. In a time when most Russians are trying to leave for America, you, an American, are trying to come to Russia. In their

Serving God Behind Enemy Lines

minds, you are either crazy or a spy. We learned in our Soviet history books that sometimes American spies disguise themselves as missionaries of the Gospel. You might as well get used to the fact that Russian people will always question who you really are."

It took me a long time to fall asleep. The wheels on the track made a unique sound. *Da-da-da-dat! da-da-da-dat!* Suddenly, I was awakened by a brisk knock at the door and shouting from the other side. I quickly looked at Roman for guidance.

He mumbled, "The wagon conductor is telling us that we are an hour away from Smolensk. If you need to use the restroom, do it now. They will lock the restroom doors soon."

I was puzzled, "Why?"

Roman laughed. "You haven't used the restroom yet?" I shook my head. He continued, "When you flush the toilet, it spills onto the tracks below. This is not sanitary in the city, so they lock the doors once we get inside city limits."

This I needed to see. I excused myself and waited for my turn to use the restroom. Just as Roman had described, when I flushed the toilet, I saw the train tracks below.

THOUGHTS
- When was the last time you thanked God that you were born in a country where you are free to worship freely and live your life without constant government oversight?

CHAPTER NINETEEN

The Smolensk Campaigns

The Spirit of the Lord is upon me, because he hath anointed me to preach the gospel to the poor; he hath sent me to heal the brokenhearted, to preach deliverance to the captives, and recovering of sight to the blind, to set at liberty them that are bruised, Luke 4:18

Getting Settled

We arrived on the north side of the Smolensk train station around 8 a.m. — two hours before sunrise. As soon as the train pulled into the station, the female conductor whisked the walnuts away from under our bunk. I followed Roman and Brother Dorsey's cue, pretending to not notice her.

Getting off was worse than deplaning from an airliner. Many travelers had multiple huge bags. They were bringing food and gifts from Moscow to their starved relatives in Smolensk. I looked out the window and saw a large crowd.

I set my first load of bags on the ground and stared in awe at the building. I pointed to the blue-green station. "Roman, this is the most magnificent rail terminal I've ever seen."

He set several boxes down. "It's the jewel of Smolensk. Well, this and the Russian Orthodox Church on the hill."

After several trips from our compartment to the platform, we took a deep breath. Roman's scarf was wrapped over his mouth and nose. A cone of ice formed from his breath as he talked. He signaled for a bell hop, who ran over with a large-flat cart and began to load our cargo. Roman led the way toward the street. Brother Dorsey and I followed.

As I reached the first lamp post, I slipped on a patch of black ice. My hand caught hold of a post, which broke my fall. I called out.

The Smolensk Train Station

"Hey guys—my eyelashes keep freezing together." I gently pulled them open.

Roman grabbed my stocking hat and pulled it over my eyebrows, "See, Brother Reasoner, if you pull it down, it'll keep the wind from freezing your eyelashes." He led us to the street and hailed a taxi. He gave the bell hop the equivalent of $1 who brandished a toothless grin and grabbed Roman's hand, "Спасибо! Спасибо! (Thank you! Thank you!)"

That must be a lot of money here.

After the taxi dropped us off at our hotel, it took several trips to get our boxes and luggage from the street into the lobby. We left everything by a post and approached the reception desk. We gave our papers to Roman. He handed them to the clerk. "We have reservations for five days."

The clerk nodded, opened our passports, and entered our information into his log. Moments later after we signed the register, he handed us our room keys, but not our passports, and we proceeded to the elevator.

Three floors up, Brother Dorsey unlocked the door to our room and let us enter first.

I set my suitcase on the bed. Brother Dorsey did the same and gestured towards the front desk. "Roman, how long will it take for them to return our passports?" He unlocked his luggage and pulled a handful

The Smolensk Campaigns

of shirts out. "I know we can't go out in public without them, and I'd like to visit the hall you arranged."

Roman set his dress shoes under his bed. "Oh, three, maybe four hours, but any attempt to speed the process will make them suspicious. They could get mad and take days to finish." He looked at our concerned faces, "Don't worry, we'll have them in due time."

Roman took his empty suitcase and stacked it in a corner of the closet. "And, my fine American friend, don't get caught outside the hotel without your papers. It's against the law." He lowered his voice, "Like I said on the train—even for citizens. That's why the hotel clerk took our documents—to register us with the local government. You need your train ticket, and your passport." He put a hand on my shoulder. "Don't go out on your own."

As we unpacked, I stopped, stretched out my arms and commented. "Hey guys, this room isn't much larger than our train compartment." I resumed putting my clothes in the dresser and grabbed my toilet bag. "I'm going to take a shower. All this smoke, grime, and train smell has got to come off."

I went to the community bathroom to take a hot shower, and soon returned shivering. "Roman? Why can't I get hot water?"

He shrugged, "Didn't you know Russian hotels don't always have hot water." He waved an arm outside, "Each section of a city has its own central boiler. If this area's boiler breaks down, we don't get hot water. It could be days before they get it fixed."

Minus 20 degrees outside and cold showers inside. How much will I be asked to sacrifice for You, Lord?

The phone interrupted my thoughts. A friendly woman's voice said in poor English. "Hello, good Sir. You tired from your trip?"

I sat down on the bed and leaned against the headboard. "Well, yes, it was a long train ride. What can I do for you?"

Her voice cooed. "Well, Sir, as a man, we know you want to relax. We have very nice girls who show you how to enjoy our city. She will be very enthusiastic, and she very beautiful."

The look on my face must have told my companions that something was amiss. "Uh, uh, no thank you. We're not interested." I shook my head as I hung up the phone. "You won't believe this. The hotel wanted to fix me up with a woman!"

Roman, a baby Christian, did not see the problem. "So? It's normal. What's the big deal?"

Serving God Behind Enemy Lines

Brother Dorsey and I sat him down. I pulled out my Bible. "Roman, immorality is a very real problem in any country that attempts to kick God out and stamp out His influence. The offer of prostitutes to 'Holy Men' proves we need to start a church in Smolensk." After our discussion Roman finally understood we were serious about being faithful to our wives.

After lunch, we stopped by the front desk to pick up our passports, then walked to the large hall owned by the Communist Party. It had old-styled theater seats aligned in rows with two aisles down the middle. I excitedly waved at the men cleaning the floors. "Roman? How did you ever get such a large hall?" We started walking to the stage. "I think we can seat over 200!"

He smiled, "Brother Reasoner, we can seat almost 500," As Roman set his backpack on the stage, he continued, "With all the flyers and posters we've distributed, plus the radio and TV ads I was able to secure, there'll be no problem filling this hall. This place doesn't get used often. So, the local party chairman was happy to rent this for only 122,900 rubles a night. He even said he might come to a meeting."

Brother Dorsey smiled, "I wouldn't have expected the party chairman, of all people, to express an interest." He scratched his chin, "Then again, God is in the miracle business."

I was still figuring the exchange rate in my head. Finally, I commented, "That's only $100 a night?"

I motioned for them to go to the rear of the auditorium while I walked up the steps and onto the stage. I moved behind the lectern, smiled, and called out, "Good evening. I'm Brother Ron Reasoner." Brother Dorsey raised a thumb. "The acoustics are excellent, but I'm still glad we asked for a sound system. Who knows how much extra noise there will be with almost 500 people in attendance?"

I jumped off the stage and half-ran to the rear. Brother Dorsey turned and swept the auditorium with his eyes. "If we're going to fill this auditorium for a week, we need more advertising." We grabbed an armload of pamphlets and headed out the door.

Our First Service

That night a pianist played Russian classical music while the people filed in. After he finished, Roman and Brother Dorsey approached the stage. Brother Dorsey adjusted the microphone and set up an easel next to the podium. As Dorsey talked, he drew a picture of a family standing apart from each other. Then he told the story of how they got separated from each other during an earthquake. After 20 minutes he finished and asked for the lights to be dimmed. He pulled a small fluorescent light from his coat pocket and shone it on the paint. An entirely different picture appeared.

The original painting appeared like an earthquake had made a crack in the earth and half of the family was on each side of the crack. When he shone the black light on the painting of the separated family, a cross appeared that bridged the gap over the ravine.

A gasp went from the audience. "Магия!" echoed throughout the hall. In a panic, Roman waved his arms and shouted, "Нет! Нет!" When they quieted, he took a breath and continued. "It's not magic, it's not magic!" He kept pleading. "Please, understand, it's a reaction between the colored chalk and the fluorescent light."

He sighed—relieved—when the crowd calmed down and returned to their seats.

While Brother Dorsey preached, I sat in a chair behind the table full of Russian Bibles we had brought.

I sure hope we have enough.

Brother Dorsey turned his light off as the house lights brightened. I approached the podium, and Brother Dorsey took my seat.

I cleared my throat, "Thank you for coming. I'd like to talk to you today about where you're going." I opened my Bible to Proverbs 16:7.

"When a man's ways please the LORD, he maketh even his enemies to be at peace with him.

"Often in life we mess up. We make wrong decisions that hurt our loved ones. Our friends become our enemies. How can we bridge that gap we have created with our mistakes? We can't, but God can. The first step in making peace with others is to make peace with God."

I moved to the side of the podium, looked over the crowd and asked, "Who is God? He is the Creator, Lord, and Savior of this world. In your heart, you know Who God is. The Bible tells us that nature itself declares God's Glory. You have a beautiful city here in Smolensk. Nature all around you declares God. He is the Almighty, and He wants to have a personal relationship with you." I raised both hands and prepared to continue but noticed Roman nervously interrupting me. I paused and mentally reminded myself to allow Roman time to interpret.

When he nodded, I knew to continue. Shrugging my shoulders, I asked, "How do we make peace with God?" I smiled as I picked up my Bible, "God's Word tells us that we can't, so Jesus Christ did it for us. Colossians 2:14 tells us that Jesus took our offenses and nailed them to the cross with Him. We have come here today to tell you this Good News that God loves you and wants to have a personal relationship with you."

I pointed towards the nearby sports stadium, "You're not going to find happiness in sports, home, or work. I know many of you struggle with poverty, but I assure you, riches will not make you happy. God's Word tells us that only God can make us happy. The Bible offers peace. It offers comfort."

I paused for Roman to interpret and continued, "I want to talk to you about where you're going when you die." Several in the crowd stopped whispering and focused on me. "Would you like to know how to have fellowship with God. Would you like to have fellowship with the Creator of the universe?"

In the next 20 minutes I led them through the plan of salvation, and how to pray. I concluded by inviting all of those who wanted to ask Jesus to save them to come forward. To my amazement, more than half of the crowd stood up and started for the front of the auditorium. Astonished, I waited until all who desired to come forward had filled the front and the aisles.

"Pray after me, 'Dear God, I know I'm a sinner. I cannot make it to Heaven on my own. I know Jesus came to earth to die for my sins. I accept His death on the cross for me. I believe He died, was buried, and rose again. I ask Jesus to come into my heart and life and save me. Thank You, God, for saving me. In Jesus' name, Amen.'"

I looked into the faces of the hundreds of people who had come forward. Some were crying, others were rejoicing. I wiped a tear away, "Now, if you prayed that prayer with me, and were sincere, then you can be assured of eternity." I closed my notebook and smiled at them. "Thank you for being attentive. If you would like a Bible, please come get one from Brother Dorsey, Roman, or myself.

We were unprepared for the onslaught. Even those who did not come forward to repent, now came forward for a Bible. Roman kept sliding boxes to Brother Dorsey and me as we handed Bibles out as fast as we could. When the crowd dwindled down to just a few remaining people, I looked to see if we had enough. Roman handed me the last box and I said, "I think God knew exactly how many we needed tonight. But what will we do tomorrow night?"

Roman smiled, "Tomorrow's train should bring 20 more boxes."

Briefly the question crossed my mind—

Whose compartment would the conductor put our boxes of Bibles in and instruct them to claim them as their own if the police asked?

The Smolensk Campaigns

Visiting the Prison

The next morning, right after breakfast, Roman met us in the lobby of the hotel. He spread a map of Smolensk between us. "When I came down here last week to bring Bibles, arrange the hotel and the communist hall, I also arranged for us to go to the local prisons, schools, hospitals, and orphanages. I've kept all our sites close together. Today we are expected at the regional prison and three orphanages."

He turned to Brother Dorsey, "Did you bring American candy?"

Dorsey opened his backpack and pulled out a large bag of candy, "Yes, I remembered from our last trip."

Roman opened his backpack and pulled out boxes of Russian candy, "We will give these to the directors and pass out the American candy to the prisoners and orphans." He turned to me, "Do you have enough rubles for the 'entrance fees?'"

I sat back, frowned, and folded my arms. "I have a problem with that."

Brother Dorsey was the first to respond. "What?"

I pointed to the candy and pulled a wad of rubles from my pocket, "These...why do we have to offer bribes to preach the Gospel?" I held a finger up as Roman started to interrupt. "No, hear me out. I don't care if it's only a 150-ruble fee." I tapped the table in front of me. "It's still a bribe."

Brother Dorsey sighed. "I agree." He pointed to Roman, "We've had this same discussion. But we're not going to change Russian culture overnight. If you want the opportunity to spread the Gospel, you must pay the warden or administrator the fee they demand." He leaned forward, "Even if it's only the equivalent of two dollars, or coloring books and crayons for their children, these people are dictators within their own kingdom."

Roman leaned an elbow on the table and shook his head. "It's worse than that. All the prosecutors, attorneys, wardens, and guards are all in on the corrupt system. If a prisoner bribes an official and his enemy bribes an official higher up, the one willing to pay the highest price will be rewarded." He pointed one thumb up and one thumb down. He looked at the two of us. "Welcome to Russia."

Twenty minutes later we climbed the steps to the prison and approached a guard. She moved her head back and forth every time Roman translated.

Serving God Behind Enemy Lines

Roman gestured to us. "These Americans have an appointment to speak to the prisoners. Would you inform Warden Balakin we have arrived?"

As the guard dialed, a man approached from a far entrance. He stopped in front of us and stood at attention. "Sirs, I am Assistant Warden Drozdov. I will take you to see the warden." He turned and swiftly stepped away.

We followed and caught up to him as he opened his superior's office door. Warden Balakin sat behind his desk. He kept working after we entered. We stood in awkward silence. Drozdov put a hand to his mouth. "Ahem."

Balakin set the paper in a folder and rose. He pointed to the credenza by the window. "May we offer you tea?" We sat and waited for Drozdov to return with an engraved brass *samovar* (an elaborate teapot) on a cart. A short-uniformed man, whom I assumed was a low-ranking guard, followed with a tray of biscuits, waffle cookies, and chocolate.

The Warden sat and pointed to the Russian tea urn as it was wheeled in. "This belonged to my great-great grandmother." He beamed as he sat back, pulled on his uniform jacket, and pointed again to the shiny brass *samovar*. "I inherited it from my father."

He poured tea for everyone as we said in unison, "It's beautiful!"

I wonder if he's happy we are here.

At that moment, the short guard pulled a tray of small teacups from the bottom shelf of his cart.

That was a quick answer.

Roman had informed me earlier that Russians bring out the large cups for their friends and those they wish to become better acquainted with. They use small cups to encourage people to leave quickly.

Balakin leaned back in his chair and smiled. "It's a pleasure to have you visit my prison." He gestured to the cell blocks behind him, "I am pleased to tell you I have the best run prison in Smolensk," he shrugged, "Maybe in all of Russia."

For the next 20 minutes, he pontificated about how well he treated his prisoners and that his sincere desire was for them to learn their lesson and be released as fully functioning members of Russian society.

When the clock on the wall chimed 10 a.m., he rose and pointed to the door. As we exited his outer office, in a solemn, almost reluctant tone, he said, "I have given permission for you to speak to 50 men." He shook his head, "Some of them are incorrigible and beyond help. I cannot be responsible for your safety."

The Smolensk Campaigns

We reached the hallway and he made sure we were outside his office before he offered to shake our hands. "However, you can be assured my guards will be nearby."

Brother Dorsey was last to shake hands, "Warden Balakin, as we already said, we believe our Lord will protect us. And even if we die, we know we have eternal life."

The warden furrowed his brow. Looking at his assistant, he scratched behind his ear. Both stifled a grin. Roman's eyes shot flames before he quickly looked away. I started to ask, but Roman's quick shake of the head told me to be silent.

Drozdov escorted us through several locked doors. At one door he stopped and let us step inside. "Here's our kitchen. Today is a special day—our meal will assure each prisoner gets one whole potato and one piece of meat." I kept a smile on my face as I inwardly gagged from the smell of rotten meat.

The last door opened into a medium-sized room with 50 men seated on rickety-wooden folding chairs. Guards with AK-47s at the ready were posted every 10 feet. The prisoners' stench reached us as we moved towards the front of the room.

Balakin said they're allowed showers once a week. I wonder if they get soap.

As soon as we entered the room, the chatter went from a loud roar to a slight murmur. Cold dark eyes, set in pale, malnourished faces, worse than pictures I had seen of prisoners in Auschwitz, bored into us, as if daring us to mistreat them more than they obviously already had been. Several had what appeared to be infected, self-applied tattoos on their arms.

Fifty pairs of gaunt eyes stared at us. Brother Dorsey set up his easel, Roman and I set boxes of Bibles on a table.

Lord, I've felt more secure in American prisons. I wonder if the guards are nervous because they fear an uprising.

Brother Dorsey preached first, telling a story of loneliness and abandonment. When he put the black light on his painting, the dark, disturbing forest was flooded with light and comfort. The lonely man Brother Dorsey had painted on a rock, suddenly had the arms of Grace surrounding him. I watched the faces of the prisoners. A few of them looked impressed and touched by the personification of God's comfort to the Believer.

I stood when Brother Dorsey nodded, and we traded places.

Lord, feral dogs look happier than these men.

Serving God Behind Enemy Lines

I put my nervous hands on the podium, mostly to keep the men from seeing how scared I was. "Gentlemen, we were all created to have fellowship with God. He will speak to you wherever you are."

I picked up a Russian Bible from the podium in front of me and held it high. "We have a copy of what He wants you to know—" For the next few moments, I shared:

> *"And ye shall know the truth, and the truth shall make you free… If the Son therefore shall make you free, ye shall be free indeed." (John 8:32,36)*

I leaned forward. "If I were to ask you today what you want more than anything, I would guess that most of you would say, 'To be free.'" I stood erect. "I am here to tell you that you can indeed be free. Not physically, but spiritually and eternally, Christ can set you free. The wonderful thing about this freedom in Christ is that it doesn't depend on your guilt or innocence. In fact, it is understood that we are all guilty before God and need to be set free from the bondage of sin. You have probably only heard of God as a cuss word. He is so much more than that. God is the Creator, the Giver of Life, and the Savior of mankind. Today, we will give each of you a Bible as a gift from Him. This Bible is also called the Word of God because it is God's love letter to you. You can know God and He can set you free."

While I preached, the room became eerily quiet. The buckles on the guard's rifle straps quit rattling as they focused on my every word. Roman kept up a steady pace.

As I finished my sermon, I moved in front of the podium and came within two feet of the meanest looking man in the room. I gestured towards their cell block. "Some of you may have come today to get out of your lockup." I waved my hand around the room. "You may be a guard or a prisoner. The Lord will treat you the same. He loves you and wants you as His child."

When I finished, there was not a dry eye in the room. I was particularly surprised to see Warden Balakin, who had slipped in the back, wiping tears from his eyes. I continued, "If you would like to ask Jesus to set you free, pray with me, "God, I know I'm a sinner. I know I deserve Hell. But You loved me so much, You sent Your only Son, Jesus, to save me. I believe Jesus died on the cross for my sins, was buried and rose the third day for my salvation. I ask You to forgive my sins and come into my heart to save me. I believe in You and Your salvation. In Jesus' name, Amen."

The Smolensk Campaigns

I closed my notebook as Brother Dorsey set Bibles on the table in front of us. I reached down, picked up a handful of books and held them up. "Please come up front, if you want your own copy of the most Precious Gift you could ever be given."

Prisoners stormed the front of the room, guards panicked. Several brought their weapons to the ready, I heard bolts slide home. I felt my heart race as several prisoners rushed towards me.

Lord? What do I do now?

Many knelt and made a profession of faith.

Thank you, Lord. Now I can breathe.

I do not know how many of them who called upon God to save them truly believed. I pray all were sincere.

Roman pointed a finger back towards the prison as we walked to the nearest bus stop, "Do you want to know what will happen to all those Bibles?" He smiled at the astonished look on our faces. "Do you really believe the Balakin will let those men keep them?" He turned towards us. "Listen, a warden in a Russian prison is the supreme dictator. What he says is law."

Our bus arrived and he boarded first to punch our tickets. We sat, and Roman continued, "He'll confiscate as many as he can and give them to family or sell them." He chuckled. "Both of you are naïve." His head bobbled as the bus started to move. He checked his watch. "We get off near the orphanage in 10 minutes. It'll be three more stops."

I gestured back to the prison, "Well, the Gospel is moving, whether it is given away or sold, the Gospel is getting out." I looked Roman in the eye, "Speaking of the warden, what made you so mad in his office?"

He smiled, "You saw that? I hoped I hid it. The warden made fun of you—did you see him scratch behind his ear?"

Brother Dorsey nodded, "So? Did he have fleas?"

"Or head lice?" I interjected.

Roman laughed, "No—scratching behind the ear means he thinks you are naïve. We normally use it when referring to children. He was disrespecting you. That's why I was upset."

Brother Dorsey and I both shrugged as I remarked, "All that really matters is that he heard the Gospel."

Visiting an Orphanage

Two hours later, we exited the second orphanage and took a bus to the third.

The old bus lurched to a stop. Roman gathered the boxes near him and got up. "We need to hurry. I've been on this driver's bus before. He'll close the doors when he thinks you've had enough time; he doesn't care what you're carrying."

Roman was right. The rear bus door caught me right in the head as I exited. I screamed, threw my boxes onto the street, and tried to pry the doors open; everyone, inside and outside the bus, came to my aid, screaming for the driver to open the door. Finally, he obliged, and I fell onto the pavement. I rubbed my head, "That was painful. It's going to leave a mark!" I picked up my scattered boxes and hurried to keep up with Roman as he headed towards the entrance to the South Smolensk Children's Home. Apparently, what had just happened was so common it didn't faze him.

We strode through the entrance into a dark grey hall and waited for our eyes to adjust to the low light. Roman led the way into the administration office. Two women sat behind desks talking on a telephone. As he stepped in front of the nearest desk the woman put up a finger for us to wait. She continued her conversation for five more minutes, unconcerned about our presence. Finally, she hung up the phone and mumbled, "Я слушаю вас"

Roman looked at us and whispered, "She said she's listening to me." He looked at the name plate on her desk. "Tatiana Leonova, I came last week when I was in town. I mentioned I would be bringing some American preachers. We have an appointment with Vera Agapova. Is she available?"

Tatiana pulled her glasses from her forehead to her nose and checked a sheet on the side of her desk. "Yes, she does have you down for today." She rose and walked away. "I will ask if she can see you now."

No sooner did she disappear behind Vera Agapova's office door than she reopened it and nodded. We walked into a plain room. Vera rose from her desk and pointed to the *samovar* on the credenza. "Tanya, serve us tea by the window." In Russia, an employer will often call an employee by their informal name. Vera called Tatiana by her informal name of Tanya.

"Yes, Vera Agapova." As she complied, the four of us sat; Vera Agapova on a Queen Anne chair, us on a well-worn divan. The room was elegant by Russian standards, but far from European or American expectations.

Tatiana carried a platter of small teacups and held it in front of Vera Agapova and then each of us. Before we could thank her, our hostess dismissed her clerk. "You may leave now. Be sure the children are in the hall on time."

The young woman put her hands in front of her; "Yes, Vera Agapova. Right away." She turned and closed the door as she left.

Before her underling had left the room, Mrs. Agapova crossed her arms and frowned. "I want you to know that I oversee this facility. I will not tolerate any violation of my rules." She leaned forward, "I trust that Roman Valerivish has informed you of what we expect?"

Roman nodded. "Yes, Vera Agapova. We will only talk for one hour. We will not give them money. We will not hug or touch them. We will interact with them only in the hall that you have designated."

As he spoke, her eyes roamed between Brother Dorsey and me. We said "Da," with every rule Roman mentioned.

"Good!" She clapped her hands. "I operate an efficient home for my children. I make sure every room is cleaned daily." She sat upright and puffed her chest out, "I'm proud that I've been recognized as the most efficiently run orphanage in Smolensk, maybe in all of Russia."

It was hard to keep a straight face. Where had we heard this before? I wondered if all Russian bureaucrats think this highly of themselves.

Brother Dorsey set his teacup on the coffee table in front of us. "It is obvious that you have a very well-run facility. I commend you for your efforts."

Beaming at the compliment, Vera Agapova rose as she checked the watch inside a brooch on her chest, "It is time for your meeting." She gestured towards the door, "Shall we go?"

She led us down a hall. The spackled walls were chalky and unpainted, the windows were grimy. The staff in the hall avoided her gaze. As we neared what turned out to be the dining hall, we heard a cacophony of voices. As soon as the head mistress entered, the noise quickly diminished into complete silence.

Roman translated as she introduced us. "Today we have two visitors from America." She paused and pointed to us sitting behind her. "Mr. Floyd Dorsey is from South Carolina and Mr. Ronald Reasoner is from Oregon."

She peered over her glasses at the children. "You will give them your full attention." She stepped aside and gestured for one of us to come to the podium. Her parting glance at the audience said: "Is that understood?"

"Da, Vera Agapova," and nodding heads responded from everyone in the crowd. Children and staff alike.

Brother Dorsey rose, took his Bible from the table beside him and stepped towards Roman. Brother Dorsey smiled at the children as he picked up his chalk and began to draw while addressing his audience, "I want to talk to you today about Someone Who wants to help you. He has a plan for your life."

He drew a beautiful forest scene of evergreens and animals. He continued to talk as he drew, "God is the Creator of Heaven and Earth. He made the mountains and streams and all the wonderful animals in this world." Dorsey paused as he turned his attention from the forest to the sky in his painting. "God made the sun, the moon, the stars, and all the amazing galaxies science is continually discovering. God is big, much bigger than you or I can think or imagine. Yet, this Great Creator wants to be your Friend. He wrote you a love Letter. Today we will give you a copy of that Love Letter known as the Bible. In this Book, you will find all the answers to your problems and anxieties."

Brother Dorsey stopped drawing and motioned for the lights to be turned off as he turned on his black light. Suddenly a brilliant, shining path appeared throughout the forest that climbed the mountain and continued as a staircase up into the Heaven. Gasps and comments of awe and wonder filled the room. "See, God has a plan for you!" He motioned for the lights to be turned on, closed his Bible, and pointed to me. "Brother Reasoner will come and tell you about a little boy who was able to do wonderful things for his country and fulfill God's plan for his life."

As I walked across the platform, I looked at the crowd.

Lord, I see so many hard faces, so many innocent ones. Help me to reach them.

I opened my Bible and started telling them the story of David starting with 1 Samuel 16. "Here is a boy, maybe 14 or 15 years old. He was just a shepherd boy that no one paid any attention to, yet God had a plan for him."

I told about Samuel anointing David to be king and David killing Goliath in the Name of the Lord. When I finished with David being crowned king of all Israel, many of the children smiled. I paused, raised my eyebrows for effect, and told that God promised to send the Messiah through the children that David would someday have.

"God can make a beautiful painting of your life that will end in Heaven, if you will respond to His call to you. The Messiah was sacrificed for all of us, whether we are from America, Russia, or wherever. God loved us so much; He sent His only Son to die for us. Jesus lived a perfect life, was crucified for our sins, and rose again the third day to conquer death."

I looked behind me and saw, while I had been preaching, Brother Dorsey had laid out Bibles on a table.

As I finished my message, I picked up a Russian Bible and held it high. "Here is a copy of that Love Letter Brother Dorsey talked about from the God of the Universe Who has a plan for you." For a few moments, I made the usual altar call I had been making all day. "So, if you want to know more about Jesus, if you want a Bible, please come up now."

At first none of the children moved. A few of the older ones gave furtive glances at the staff and Mrs. Agapova. After they were given a nod, the children rushed towards the front. Many little ones hugged our legs and called out, "Конфеты!"

In response, the three of us reached into our pockets and handed one piece of candy to each waiting hand. Just as it was at the other two orphanages we had visited; it took over 30 minutes to pass out the candy and Bibles.

Later at dinner I pointed a fork at Roman. "Be honest with me. Did my eyes deceive me or did I see staff members taking Bibles away from the children?"

He sighed. "Yes, I guess you didn't notice it at the first two orphanages. Just like at the prison, the staff will take the Bibles for their family or themselves." He shrugged, "Some might even try to sell them." He tapped his finger on the table, "Don't be surprised. Some of these people are truly hungry for the Gospel. Others are looking for a way to make money. Most Russians must sell their personal belongings to make ends meet. Often government employees go months without a paycheck. Unlike your American government who just prints more money, ours simply does not pay its people if they don't have the money."

I saw something in Roman's eyes that told me he spoke from personal experience. "How does your family survive?"

He hesitated and looked out the window. Finally, he nodded and returned his gaze to us. "I will tell you a story I have never told anyone. It was about 1984. I was 11 years old and still in grammar school. My father was working in Kazakhstan. He only came home for a few days every two months. My mother worked as an accountant, but she had not been paid for several months. While I was gone to school one day, she cleaned off her beautiful patent leather shoes. The few times she had worn them to office parties, her co-corkers were green with envy. She hardly wore them, so they looked brand new. Momma knew she had to sell the shoes to buy food. She took the day off work and stood all day on the street corner, trying to sell her prized possession. No one bought them. She picked me up after school and made me stand with her. Finally, someone took pity on us and paid half the price Momma was asking. We took the money and bought food."

"I'm sorry you had to go through that." Brother Dorsey said.

"Life was, and still is hard for my people." Roman gathered and stacked the remaining dishes on our table. "You've done a good thing. You've given many of these children hope. When a child reaches the age of four, they know they won't be adopted. I know of one widower who drops his children off every Monday morning and picks them up every Friday night just because he doesn't have any one to care for them. So, some of these children aren't orphans. Their parents just can't afford to care for them while they work. Perhaps those children will be able to take a Bible home with them this weekend."

Brother Dorsey finished chewing his food and shook his head, "Well, at least we got the Gospel out. I wish there was a way we could get the Word of God into the hands of people who really want it."

Roman spread his hands, "I can see that both of you are very disturbed." He looked down and then back into our eyes. "You don't know how bad it is in these homes. At least you've given them some hope. I think some will be able to keep the Bible and grow in His Word." A tear slid down his cheek.

Both of us responded at the same time. "And the others?"

Tearfully, the young Russian said, "Only a few of these children will get a good education. Once they reach puberty most girls are forced into prostitution. The boys see drug running for the Russian Mafia as a good career path."

I put my hands to my face and sobbed. Roman reached over and touched my arm, "You must realize, these children have no hope. They see that lifestyle as their only choice."

I pulled out my journal and wrote furiously. Our best calculation from the number of hands raised during the invitations, was 100 from the three orphanages were saved—not only children, but also workers and directors who also gladly received the Word of God.

Visiting the Hospital

Early the next morning, still basking in the blessings of the previous evening when 206 people came forward at our meeting, we met for breakfast in the hotel café. Roman pulled out his map, "Today, we will visit two hospitals. One is for terminally ill people—cancer, T.B. and such.

The Smolensk Campaigns

The other is a mental hospital. Then we will squeeze in a government school after lunch."

Brother Dorsey and I stared at Roman, processing the plan. Finally, I asked, "When you say, 'mental hospital', what does that mean exactly? Are these people capable of understanding the Gospel?"

Roman smiled, "Our mental hospitals are made up of people who had a nervous breakdown or are recovering from some sort of addiction. I am sure a few of them will not be able to understand, but the doctors probably won't even let them come to the meeting."

Brother Dorsey addressed our other concern, "And the TB patients? Will we be exposed?"

"How big is your God?" Roman chided, "Is He not able to protect you?"

Embarrassed, Brother Dorsey and I nodded. In unison we proclaimed, "He is able."

We met with the administrators of both hospitals, had tea, and thanked them for the opportunity to see their great establishments. We preached and gave Bibles at both hospitals. Again, we were overwhelmed by the substandard facilities; dried blood on the floors, cracked tiles, filthy bathrooms, and dirty sheets on the beds that looked as if they had not been changed since Stalin built the buildings.

As we exited the second hospital, I turned to Roman and sighed, "These hospitals have no medicine nor modern equipment. How can they hope to heal their patients?"

Roman looked back at the cold, crumbling structure, "Now you can understand the Russian saying, 'I will go to the hospital to die.'"

Brother Dorsey and I looked at each other in silence. Brother Dorsey touched Roman's shoulder and said, "Someday I will take you to America for a visit. You can see our hospitals and understand why we are burdened and saddened by the conditions in Russia."

Roman bowed his head and mumbled, "Our government put all our money into the military to try and outdo America. We, the people, starved and suffered so this could happen. Some people called Gorbachev a traitor when he broke the Soviet Union. Others called him a hero, because he saw people suffering and said, 'No more!'"

I made a mental note to tell Kathy about Russian hospitals. As missionaries, we will be at the mercy of their doctors and healthcare system.

God, I know You will protect us, but it wasn't comforting visiting those hospitals and seeing how bad they are.

Visiting the School

We arrived at a small café for lunch near the school we were to visit. The menu had *borscht* and dumplings. As we ate, Roman warned us, "The school we are about to visit is considered the premier school in Smolensk. The teacher insisted we allow a question-and-answer time at the end of our lesson."

"This should be interesting," I said as I sipped the last of my tea. I watched as Brother Dorsey forced down his tea. I could not help but tease him a bit, "Do you miss your coffee?"

Brother Dorsey looked at Roman, "What's the deal with that, Roman? Why don't any of the cafes serve coffee?"

Roman nodded as he translated the question in his head and then responded, "Tea is cheap and available to everyone. Coffee is expensive and only the Communist bosses had the money to buy it. I think I saw a jar of instant coffee in a kiosk the other day. It was $15 for 100 grams. Do you want to buy some?"

Brother Dorsey quickly figured out that was less than four ounces, "That would be about $6 for a cup of black, instant coffee—no thank you!"

The school building was nothing special. It was grey and dilapidated like all the other buildings we visited. We were escorted into a classroom of ninth graders. While we waited for the teacher to finish her geography lesson, Roman whispered, "This is the last year of school for most of these students. The smartest will go on to 10th and 11th grade before entering the university. The rest will enter a trade school this fall. We call it college."

The teacher nodded for Roman to bring us to the front of the class. After we were introduced, Brother Dorsey and I gave our testimonies of salvation. The teacher had warned us not to preach but would allow us to talk about our American life. Since God was the center of our lives, we figured that our testimony would be a great way to witness without preaching.

The teacher came forward as I finished my testimony and said, "Now we want to ask questions about America!"

"Please do. We would be honored to answer them as best we can." I cheerfully replied.

Anton stood and Roman translated as he asked, "Are most people homeless? I saw on the Russian news that many people live under bridges in cardboard boxes in America."

Brother Dorsey and I caught our laughter before it escaped our lips. He stood to give the answer, "No, most Americans live in nice homes.

They work hard and make enough money to pay their bills and eat three meals a day. We do have homeless people and some of them do live under bridges in our large cities, but we have homeless shelters for those who want help."

Nina asked the next question. She looked at me and asked, "Are there a lot of cannibals in America like Jeffery Dahmer?

Again, I fought the urge to laugh. Instead, I answered as seriously as I could, "Um, no. Jeffery Dahmer was a crazy man who did crazy things. He is the only American I have ever heard or read about that did such hideous things."

"Have you ever been shot at by black gangsters?"

"Why do they call downtown LA, the jungle? Is it because wild people live there?"

Eventually, the questions became a little more normal: "How do you celebrate New Year's?" "Why are Americans so proud?" One young girl laughed as she asked, "Will you take me to America with you?"

After passing out Bibles and candy to the students, we were escorted out of the room and politely shown to the front door. I do not know who was happier about our departure, us or them.

At the bus stop, I looked Roman up and down. Finally, I said, "What was that? Why such weird questions about cannibals and homeless people?"

Roman smirked, "Have you ever heard the word, 'propaganda'?"

"Of course."

"Those students have been told their whole lives that all Americans are homeless, cannibals, running from the mob, and living in a jungle with wild people. That was all part of our government brainwashing program about America."

"Wow! I can't believe it." Brother Dorsey exclaimed.

Roman smiled, "I'll tell you a joke—Once a first-grade teacher gave a lesson on why Russia is so much better than America. She said, 'In America, there are no pets, people are sad, they are homeless or live in tiny apartments. They work hard and get very little money. The children are sad and hungry.' The teacher paused for dramatic effect, 'Isn't that terrible? BUT thankfully, there is a country where people are happy, have plenty to eat, live in big houses, and have more than one pet. That country is Russia!' The teacher saw a little girl burst into tears as she raised her hand. 'Yes Jenna?' the teacher asked. Jenna exclaimed, "We must live in America—I want to go to Russia!'"

It took a moment before I processed and understood the joke. Brother Dorsey and I both let out a groan. I thought for a moment, "I'm trying to think of what propaganda America has told about Russia. All I can think of is that the people were not allowed to prosper, and they were forbidden to worship God freely."

Roman smiled, "That's not propaganda, that's truth."

I laughed as I continued, "Well, I can think of another thing—we were taught that all Russian women are named Olga and weigh 200 pounds but from the short time you took us on the metro to the train station, I saw nothing but thin and beautiful young Russian women on the subway. Even the orphans and hospital patients had beautiful facial features. However, I'm not sure if that propaganda is from America. Perhaps Russia is just trying to hide their beauty queens from the world."

We arrived back at the hotel, changed into our suits, and headed over to the communist hall for another night of evangelistic meetings. As I walked into the hall and saw hundreds of people already waiting for the meeting to start, I stepped behind the curtain and fell to my knees praying.

God, You are doing something great here. Hundreds, perhaps thousands of souls have been saved in Smolensk this week. Please hide me behind Your Cross and shield me from any sin of pride or self-edifying that might cause You to withdraw Your Holy Spirit from this work. Please don't let me get in Your Way. Thank You, God, for allowing me to witness Your Great Grace and Harvest this week.

THOUGHTS

- When you pray for your missionaries, pray for their safety as they are behind enemy lines preaching the Gospel.
- What risks have you taken lately for the sake of Christ?

CHAPTER TWENTY

The Decision

Trust in the LORD with all thine heart; and lean not unto thine own understanding. In all thy ways acknowledge him, and he shall direct thy paths. Proverbs 3:5-6

On our final day in Smolensk, I woke at 3 a.m.
Lord, I've been tossing and turning all night. I believe You've called me to preach to these people. I see the hunger in their eyes. Give me strength to bring my family to this place.
I slid from under the covers, grabbed my pants and put them on. I snatched my Bible and headed to the lobby. For two hours I poured through Proverbs and Psalms. My note pad was covered with scribbles I call handwriting. I flipped through the pages and smiled.
Okay, that settles it.
Friday afternoon we rented the local swimming pool. Brother Dorsey and I felt that we must start a church in Smolensk. To have members, the saved must be baptized. Roman and another young lady were ready to be baptized. Others came to watch but were not ready to commit. Roman went first and gave his testimony, "Two years ago, I made the decision to get a job translating for Americans. I was able to buy an English translation of the Bible and read it from cover to cover. While reading the Gospel of John I realized I needed Jesus as my Savior. After spending the week with Brother Dorsey and Ron Reasoner, I realize I need to be baptized."
Brother Dorsey put his hand over Roman's mouth and nose, "Upon your profession of faith, I baptize you, my brother, in the name of the Father, and of the Son and of the Holy Ghost," and as he immersed Roman in the water, "Buried in the likeness of His death and raised in the likeness

of His resurrection." After Brother Dorsey raised Roman up, I handed each of them a towel.

I then got into the water to baptize Tanya, who also gave a sound profession of faith in Jesus Christ. Thus, began Bible Baptist Church of Smolensk, with my sending church in America as the mother church. Though there were only two baptized members, over 100 others filled out visitor's cards and committed to attending on a weekly basis if Roman came from Moscow to preach. When I returned to the United States, I sent Roman weekly sermons via fax machine.

On this last evening of the Smolensk revival, I looked at the audience of about 300. "Before we close, I have an announcement."

Everyone stopped fidgeting. I had their undivided attention. "As you know, tomorrow Brother Dorsey and I leave for Moscow. From there we leave back to America."

I leaned forward into the microphone, "Today is December 12, 1993. I stand before you and promise I will return to pastor this church in September 1994."

I saw a spectrum of looks in the audience: excitement, disbelief, and confusion. Later as I shook hands with parishioners, a burly railroad worker, shook his head, "I do not understand. Americans come, stay for a week, and go home." He scratched his beard as Roman translated. "Why do you want to come back here? All of us would love to escape to America."

I smiled and waved an arm around the hall. "God has called me to love the Russian people. Just because our governments don't get along doesn't mean that God doesn't want Russians to hear about Jesus."

Several bystanders nodded, clutched their new Russian Bibles, and shouted, "Thank You, Lord."

On the way to dinner Brother Dorsey gave me a questioning look. "You are taking a risk." He gestured in the direction of the hall we'd just left. "What if you don't raise your support?" He sighed, "There will be a lot of disappointed Russians. Did you think of how difficult it'll be for the missionary the Lord does decide to call to this city?"

"Brother Dorsey, I felt the same way about accepting the call to Russia as I do about telling them I would be back in a year. God is able! I remember quite well Professor Baskin in Bible College telling us time and again, 'Set a date, not a dollar' amount for getting to the mission field. God will provide!"

Our bus arrived at our hotel, and we got off. "God knows better than anyone else how much support I need."

The Decision

I waved behind us. "We've had over a thousand decisions for Christ. We can't leave these new-born believers for the Mormons and Jehovah Witnesses."

Brother Dorsey gave me a puzzled look, but conceded my point, "Well, Amen to that!"

THOUGHTS

- Have you set a dollar amount instead of a date on your ministry?
- Are you waiting for God to give you stable finances before you serve Him faithfully?

Chapter Twenty-One

Meeting the General

Wherefore he is able also to save them to the uttermost that come unto God by him, seeing he ever liveth to make intercession for them. Hebrews 7:25

Later that evening, we boarded the train and arrived in Moscow at 8 a.m. the next morning. We checked into our hotel and immediately met up with the Revival Fires team. We drove to a Red Army base outside of Moscow. A soldier entered the bus to examine everyone's papers, I gave Roman a puzzled look. "You're telling me that some high-ranking Russian general wants us to preach to his men?" I shook my head. "Really? I'll believe it when I see it."

The soldier exited the bus and strode to the guard shack to make a call. With permission granted, the bus crossed the base. We gawked at the soldiers marching in perfect ranks. In one building, we admired hundreds of guns, cannons, tanks, and nuclear weapons in flawless rows. We were surprised that they would show all these things to Americans.

The bus was met by a four-star general and his entourage. As we dismounted, I turned to Roman and Brother Dorsey. "Okay, now I believe it." I stopped and pointed at a large red star near the building's entrance. "Will you look at that! It's impressive—the Red Star of Russia."

We were escorted down a long hallway and into a conference room. Soon we were seated around a large table with the general's staff, wearing their immaculate dress uniforms and accoutrements, on one side, and all of us on the other. Young, enlisted soldiers entered and poured tea.

When everyone was served, General Igor Fedorov rose, which brought the room to complete silence. "To my new American friends." He waved his hands towards us. "Welcome! As a Christian, I look forward to the message you have for us and pray that my men will be inspired by your sermon. First, we will eat, then we will gather in the meeting hall for your message, and then we will tour our great and modern military base."

He gestured towards his staff. "I have before you the most excellent staff any officer could ask for. They have developed the best trained force in all of Russia, and maybe the world. There will be nothing you will not be allowed to see."

The General then led us into a large dining hall where we had a lunch of salmon, caviar, and *borscht*. The Revival Fires director raised his water glass. As he spoke, his interpreter translated. "My newfound friends. Thank you for your hospitality. Here's to a strong friendship between us and our countries."

As we exited the dining hall, we followed the soldiers to a large assembly room where our director preached, and we handed out Bibles to each of the soldiers present. On cue, the soldiers held their Bibles up and yelled, "Слава Богу!"

Giving Bibles to the soldiers at the base

I turned to Roman, "What did they just say?"

Roman smiled, "They said, 'praise God'." He glanced at me sideways, "It's a good phrase to know — you should learn."

From the assembly room, we were escorted by Lieutenant Kalashnik to tour the base, "Welcome to the Underwater Research Facility. It will be my pleasure to answer questions." He nodded and we took the cue to follow him.

Serving God Behind Enemy Lines

As we walked across the base to Lieutenant Kalashnik's company headquarters, he proudly pointed out several features of the base. He led us to a large, gated motor pool. "You will please come in and I will show you something fantastic." For the next hour we walked through rows upon rows of Russian T-14 battle tanks.

I ran my hand over the side of one and caught Brother Dorsey's eye. He nodded.

He agrees, their technology can't produce a smooth hull. What other shortcuts have they taken?

The Lieutenant noticed my hand lingering on a raised rivet. "I see you notice the hull is not smooth." He came to my side. "You may have better technology, but my men fight for Mother Russia. Your men will run at the first sign of difficulty. My men will fight to the end."

As a guest in their country, I simply nodded and kept my mouth shut. I was learning they will do and say things I find awkward or know to be untrue, but I must be respectful for the sake of the Gospel. If I get expelled, who will finish the work God has started with me?

Me with General Federov

Meeting the General

As we exited, I noticed that the Russians were stepping all over themselves to not shake hands with us in the doorways. As we waited our turn to leave, I leaned and whispered to Roman, "What gives with not shaking hands over the threshold?"

His eyes widened. "Oh no, Brother Reasoner. You never shake hands over a threshold. If you do, you will become enemies within a year. You don't want to start World War III, do you?"

That night in our hotel room, I remarked: "I wonder if the entire event at the Army base was staged? It seemed surreal." Years later I found out that General Fedorov had immigrated to America and traveled around sharing his testimony and preaching.

The next day, we went sightseeing on Red Square and boarded a plane that evening for America. What stories I had to tell! I had video of all that God had done. Kathy would want to know every detail. Deputation became a time of excitement and anticipation to get back to Russia.

THOUGHTS
- Millions of people prayed for over 70 years for God to open Russia.
- What country are you praying for that God would tear down their walls and give free access to the Gospel?

CHAPTER TWENTY-TWO

Blessings of Deputation

Finally, brethren, pray for us, that the word of the Lord may have free course, and be glorified, even as it is with you: 2 Thessalonians 3:1

As my plane touched down at Los Angeles International Airport, I was glad to be home and excited at all the things I would tell Kathy and the kids. The trip to Russia had taught me a lot about their culture and desperate need for the Gospel. While I was in Russia, Kathy and the children stayed in the motorhome in a church parking lot in Porterville, CA. We were so thankful for the many churches who installed full motorhome hookups for traveling evangelists and missionaries. It helped us many times.

When I arrived at the motorhome, I told my family bits and pieces of the trip. It took weeks to tell the whole story. I was overwhelmed with how God worked. But, that night, I called the children together, "Let's have a family talk! Everyone gets to talk about what they did while I was gone."

Jeremiah, now two years old, piped up, "Mommy almost burnt the motorhome down!"

I twisted my neck to look at Kathy. Before I could even ask, she answered, "Well, it got cold one night. I decided to plug in two space heaters. It was too much for the extension cord and it burned up. Thankfully, Keturah smelled the cord smoldering and asked what that funny smell was. I found the cord smoking and unplugged it. We were cold without two heaters, but we are still alive."

Micah was next, "The pastor at this church has four boys. We had a great time playing football after school. I was the best player."

Blessings of Deputation

I smiled at Micah's excitement and nodded for Joel to tell a story, "We went to this church and there was a girl who kept smiling at me. I got her address so we can write each other."

I looked sternly at Joel, "Son, you seem to find girlfriends at every church. How are you going to write to all of them? It's not proper to tell someone you will write to them and then not do it."

Joel looked down and answered, "Yes, sir. I'll stop asking for addresses of girls I never plan to write."

Keturah raised her hand. "My turn! After I saved the family—" she looked around to insure everyone was listening and acknowledging her heroic feat, "We went to dinner one night with a family from this church. I love being a missionary. Everyone is so kind."

Hannah took over, "Someone asked me at church on Sunday if my parents were missionaries. I looked at her like she was stupid and replied, 'We are all missionaries!'"

At one of the many churches we visited

Kathy stifled a laugh and reprimanded Hannah, "Hannah, we must not be disrespectful to adults, and we do NOT use the word 'stupid' in this home!"

"Sorry." Hannah replied as she stuck out her lower lip, "But I'm a missionary too!"

"You are right, Hannah. We are all missionaries in this family." I glanced slowly from child to child. Finally, I announced, "It sounds like you had a good time while I was away. Mom tells me you were all well behaved, so I have a surprise."

The children gasped and looked at me with great anticipation. "A church across town called and asked if they could pay for our family to go to Magic Mountain Amusement Park."

The children yelled together, "Yippee!" They jumped up and down in glee. Jeremiah stopped jumping and asked, "What is Magic Mountain?"

Joel answered, "Don't you remember passing that park with all kinds of roller coasters and rides before Daddy went to Russia? That was Magic Mountain!"

What a blessing when churches offered to treat our family to a day of fun. We also went to Disneyland, Knott's Berry Farm, Six Flags over Texas, and Six Flags St. Louis. Some churches took the children to museums, zoos, and historical sites. The children still talk of these wonderful times.

Prayer Partners

Another blessing of deputation was the prayer partners we met. I am convinced that when we get to Heaven, we will be surprised that the Christians with the most crowns and rewards will be the prayer warriors.

On one occasion, I remember turning and hearing, "Hello, Brother Reasoner," an elderly lady said as she looked at our display board. "I have prayed for many years that God would open the doors of Russia for the Gospel. I was so excited when Pastor announced we would be having a missionary to Russia in our services. I want you to know that when I prayed, I asked God to open the doors for just a little while. I should have had more faith and asked for more, but I believe you will only have a little while. Go quickly!"

I smiled and answered, "Thank you for praying. Please take a prayer card and pray for us."

She pulled something from her Bible. It was a folding photo album. She carefully unfolded the plastic pages and pointed to our prayer card, "I already got one and promise to pray every day." I wanted to hug her.

I had no idea what our family would face in Russia, but I was blessed that many committed to daily bring our names before the Throne of Grace.

Missions Conferences

A big part of being on deputation and going on furlough is the Missions Conferences. This should be the yearly highlight of every church. During a Missions Conference, a church decides the fate of millions of souls around the world. If God's people do not give, missionaries cannot go. It

Blessings of Deputation

is the responsibility of the missionary to place a burden on the heart of God's people. It is the responsibility of God's people to commit their finances and time unto the Lord.

On one occasion, I remember Kathy talking with the children as I drove toward Oklahoma City. "There will be 15 different missionary families at this conference! We got a brochure in the mail from Southwest Baptist Church. It has pictures of all the families." She turned a page, "See, here is our photo. Who wants to look at the other missionary families?"

The children answered in unison, "I do!"

Kathy handed the brochure to Joel, "Oldest to youngest. Pass it to Micah when you finish." For the next hour, we heard the children chatter about the missionary children they would meet.

Missionary kids, known as MKs, have a special bond that others cannot understand. They follow their parents to the uttermost parts of the earth, forsaking grandparents, friends, their native tongue, and their native home. Often, they are referred to as third culture kids—children who are raised in a country different from their country of citizenship. They face prejudice and ridicule that most American children never know.

Adult missionaries are also encouraged by other missionaries. If they are in the same country, they become a great source of ideas and wisdom. If they are from different countries, they can offer new and interesting ways to share the Gospel in countries where few have heard the name of Jesus Christ.

Missions Conferences are also a place to raise funds for special needs, such as a washer and dryer, a car to get around, and tuition for language school. We had all these needs, plus we needed to ship a container to Russia. It would be full of Russian Bibles and personal belongings. When God's people work together, they can accomplish great things for Christ.

As we loaded our motorhome after a great week at Southwest Baptist Church, five-year-old Keturah started to cry. I sat down at the kitchen nook, pulled her on my lap and asked, "What's wrong, honey?"

She sniffled, "I'm always saying goodbye. We go to a church, I make friends, and then I have to say goodbye. Will we ever see them again, Daddy?"

"I think so, Honey," I said as I stroked Keturah's long hair and patted her back. "Every four years we will come back to America and report to the churches who have helped us get to Russia. We ask people in the churches to pray for us, but we also should pray for the churches—that the people will remain faithful and still be there when we come again in four years. Won't that be fun to see how your friends have grown?"

She nodded as I took her off my lap, "Now, go get in your seat. Mommy has everything packed and we need to get on the road. We are going to another Missions Conference where you will meet new friends."

Surrendered Lives

Perhaps the best and most eternal blessing of deputation is when people of all ages understand that this earthly life is not about accumulating stuff, but about seeing souls eternally saved through the preaching of God's Word. The next step after understanding that their life is not about them, is to surrender their life to whatever God may call them to do. It is scary to step out by faith and yield one's life to whatever God would have them do.

"What will you do in Russia?" A man asked me during one Missions Committee meeting.

"I will plant churches. On my survey trip, I saw the enormous need for Gospel-preaching churches. The Russian people have been deprived of the Word of God for 70 years. They were brainwashed that God is not real. Those who refused to bow to the government as their god, were imprisoned and even killed for believing in the True and Living God. I saw hopelessness and emptiness in their faces. Only God can help them, but someone must go and tell them of God's great love for them."

The man furled his brow and harshly asked, "Will you be arrested? What will happen to your family? Aren't you afraid you could die?"

"I died when I surrendered my life to Christ and confirmed that when I surrendered to go to Russia. If His will is my death on the foreign field, then I pray many souls will be saved by the testimony of my sacrifice."

Finally, the interview with the missions committee was over and the man approached me, "I didn't mean to come off as crass, but God was tugging on my heart as you spoke. I believe God is calling me and my family to Russia!"

"Amen!" I replied, "I look forward to seeing you there. May God give us both many years of ministry in Russia."

During deputation, five men surrendered to become missionaries under my preaching. Praise God for His calling on their lives! Some of them are still on the mission field to this day.

THOUGHTS

- Have you surrendered your life to missions?
- Not every Christian is called to be a missionary, but every Christian should be surrendered to go.

CHAPTER TWENTY-THREE

The End of Deputation

But they that wait upon the LORD shall renew their strength; they shall mount up with wings as eagles; they shall run, and not be weary; and they shall walk, and not faint. Isaiah 40:31

A Test

In April 1994, a man called while I was staying at a church in the Midwest. Pastor Jones and I were talking in his office when the phone rang. He answered it, and soon handed the phone to me, "It's for you."

I took the receiver, "Hello? This is Missionary Ron Reasoner."

"Brother Reasoner, allow me to introduce myself. My name is Joe Smith, and I am a member at Sauk Trail Baptist Temple in Richton Park, Illinois. I read an article about you in the Baptist Tribune."

"Yes, I really enjoyed writing about my survey trip to Russia. God blessed and it was humbling to be used in such a great way." I shot a confused look at Pastor Jones and shrugged, "What can I do for you Mr. Smith?"

"Well, to get to the point, I'd like to know a little more about you."

At that moment, Pastor Jones' chair squeaked as he rose and mouthed. "I'll be in the sanctuary. Take as long as you need."

I nodded as Smith continued. Twenty minutes later the tone of his voice dropped. "Well, that's about it. The main thing I was interested in is that you're a King James only preacher, that you're supported by your local church, and that you're not going to Russia for a vacation but to plant churches and staff them with Russian ministers that you've trained." He coughed. "Is that a good summary?"

"Yes, sir. We have about 4-5 months to go before we plan to depart."

"Hmm, interesting. Well, I need to attend a meeting. I hope to talk with you soon. Where are you going next?"

I pulled out my planner and gave him my itinerary. "Brother Smith, thank you for calling, I look forward to meeting you sometime."

After two months of phone calls where Mr. Smith called me every week or so, he finally said, "I want to support you, but my pastor is against it."

I swallowed hard, but I knew how I had to respond, "I believe in the authority of the local church. If your pastor says it's not a good idea, then it's not a good idea."

I could hear the smile in his voice as when he replied, "That is the answer I wanted. I would not support you if you accepted my offer without my pastor's approval. I feel there is an urgency about you getting to Russia. I also feel I can only support someone who truly believes in the authority of the local church. When I read your article in the Baptist Tribune, I knew the Lord wanted me to support you. I had to ensure that you were the man of God I hoped you were. I will commit to supporting you for two years at $800 a month. My pastor agrees with this, and it will be processed through my local church."

"I don't know what to say, except Praise the Lord. We are going to Russia in September and trusting God to give us whatever funds He knows we need. Thank you for being sensitive to the Holy Spirit's moving."

Finishing Deputation

In July 1994, I entered my brother's kitchen. Kathy gave me a hug and the children gathered around. After taking time to kiss every skinned knee and scratch; and act as judge for every squabble, Kathy handed me several notes with a smile. "Honey, these pastors want to confirm that you really want to cancel. I assured them that their secretary copied our message correctly. They still want to hear it from you."

I gave her a kiss, took the papers, loosened my tie, and tossed my briefcase in a corner. "I told them when they insisted that I schedule with them that I had no intention of being in America in September. Now I must call and remind them that we put a date, not a dollar amount on our departure."

I pulled out my calling card and 45 minutes later was talking with the last pastor on my list. "Dr. Walls, my wife and I appreciate the prayers and the opportunity you've given us to speak at your Missions Conference."

The End of Deputation

I listened to him for a few moments and interrupted, "No, you do not understand, I'm calling to cancel my visit. All along our prayer has been to raise our support in 10 months. No one knows how much missionaries need to survive in Moscow, because no Independent Baptists have gone. We have asked God to give us what we need, and we believe He has done just that!"

I laughed. "Yes, we're overjoyed too. God is moving! Thanks again, Dr. Walls. Please give whatever funds you had for us to another missionary. I would appreciate if your church would keep us in your prayers. Good-bye."

I rushed out of the bedroom and gave Kathy a hug. I took a deep breath. "Now we take the big step and make travel arrangements." I checked my watch. "Good, I can still call the travel agency." I rushed to the phone and punched the number in.

Travel Plans

In moments, I was talking to an agent. I dropped my pen at his response. "What? We're ready to go. What do you mean we shouldn't buy our tickets until our visa work has been submitted? It's no problem. I have a group who promised visa support. I'll call you back as soon as our paperwork is submitted."

I hung up and immediately called Revival Fires, "Umm, yes, this is Ron Reasoner. I went on your trip to Russia last December. I talked to Mr. Carter about visa support as missionaries in Russia. Whom do I talk to about this?"

The lady on the other end connected me with Mr. Carter's secretary. I repeated the question to her. She replied, "Oh, Ron, I'm so sorry, but we checked into visa support for one-year visas and the requirements are beyond what we will be able to do. Again, I'm sorry."

I sat down, shoulders slumped, and head hung low. I don't know how long I sat there. Eventually Kathy came in, "Ron, I've been calling you. Dinner's rea—" She rushed to my side. "Honey, what's wrong?"

"Revival Fires can't give us visa support. I don't know how or where we will get it.".

Suddenly she smiled, "I read about this travel agency in a Christian magazine that offers visa support." She ran out and soon returned. I grabbed the advertisement from her and immediately dialed the agency.

After 10 minutes on the phone, I had secured one-way tickets for far less than the other organization had offered. I had a list of items I needed to FedEx to complete the visa process. We pulled everything together and spent a fortune on fees.

Serving God Behind Enemy Lines

The agent warned me it would take at least 20 working days for the visas to be processed once all the documents were submitted to the Russian Consulate. Twenty working days would be cutting it close. Now all we could do was wait and pray.

A few days before we were scheduled to leave for Russia, I was attempting to herd the children through the foyer of Tri-City Baptist Temple in Gladstone, Oregon. I felt a hand on my shoulder. I turned and held out my hand, "Pastor McCormick, I was hoping to see you before we left. Thank you for your hospitality."

He took me to the missionary prayer board and pointed to a prayer letter from Mark Morrissey, "Did you know that he is spending the summer in Russia? He is a chalk artist and is returning soon." As I read the prayer letter, Pastor McCormick pointed to the bottom, "Here's his phone number in Russia. Maybe he can help you find an apartment."

The next morning, I called Mike as soon as I woke up. In moments, the ringing stopped. "Привет, Майк здесь."

I chuckled to myself.

He's in Moscow, of course he'd answer the phone in Russian.

"This is Pastor Ron Reasoner in America. Do you remember me, Brother Morrisey?"

Immediately he switched to English. "Hello Pastor Ron. I haven't seen you in years. I think the last time was when I helped you with a Vacation Bible School at Corridor Baptist Church. How are you doing? What can I do for you?"

In a few short minutes I gave him a summary of our call to Russia. "I heard you're returning to the states in a few days."

"Yes, my wife and I fly out on September 6th."

"Well, could you help us find an apartment? I was planning on staying in a hotel for the short time we need to find a place."

Mike laughed. "Since I'm leaving soon after you arrive, I'll come pick you up at the airport, but we fly out early the next morning. By the way, it's very difficult to find a place to rent. Would you like me to ask my landlord if she would rent to you?"

"That would be a huge blessing!"

He hung up and called me back an hour later. "My landlord is happy to oblige. I'll give you the keys and she will meet you the day after you arrive, so you can pay the first month's rent."

God, You worked out the final details that we did not even know were important. We have a place to live! We have no idea how much You are doing for us behind the scenes. Lord, You are amazing beyond our understanding.

The End of Deputation

There was one hurdle left. Two days before our scheduled departure, our visas had still not arrived. After breakfast I gathered the family into my brother's living room to pray. Nine-year old Micah started to bow his head with everyone else, then raised his head. "Dad, how come we have to pray every day?"

Kathy handed me my Bible. I opened it up and placed my finger on the page so he could follow along as I read 1 Thessalonians 5:17,

"Pray without ceasing."

I set the Book aside. "You see Micah, sometimes the Lord chooses to not answer our prayer the first time we pray. He tells us to keep praying." I looked into the eyes of my children and nodded. "The Lord has answered all of our prayers, hasn't He?"

Each child nodded. "Well, then we—". I pointed to everyone, "Will keep praying. The Lord knows we can't go without visas. If he chooses that they don't come, He has a better plan."

Later that day, while Kathy was preparing lunch the phone rang, "Ron, can you get the phone?"

I sighed and grabbed the receiver. Mom said, "Ron, you have a package from Federal Express here at my house. It looks like the passports and visa things you have been stressing about."

"Let's go!" I shouted, "We need to go to Grandma with the goat's house. She has our visas!"

We drove to Molalla. Mom handed me the package. Under the watchful eyes of my family, I pulled out our visas. After checking the spelling on everyone's papers, I shoved everything back into the package and handed it to Kathy, "You oversee these things. They are our life's blood in a Russia."

God had answered every prayer! The visas arrived on Saturday afternoon. Our plane flight was scheduled for Monday morning!

THOUGHTS
- Can you recall a time in your life where God waited until the last minute to answer your prayers?
- Did you falter or were you faithful?

CHAPTER TWENTY-FOUR

Saying Goodbye

The LORD bless thee, and keep thee: The LORD make his face shine upon thee, and be gracious unto thee: The LORD lift up his countenance upon thee, and give thee peace.
Numbers 6:24-26

Labor Day, September 5, 1994, finally arrived. Both sets of parents and my older brother's family drove to Sea-Tac the night before our early morning flight. We booked rooms at the Motel 6 in Fife. Everyone helped transport our 14 bags and 7 carry-ons.

Sunday evening was spent in the various motel rooms reminiscing about the past and speculating about our future. Mom's career as a teacher was evident as she told the children, "I'm so excited for you. You will grow up in a different culture, know two languages, and see parts of the world few Americans have ever seen. What an educational experience!" My dad just nodded.

We hugged my parents good night, and I moved the gang on to my brother, Rob's room. Over the years, Rob and I had learned to navigate through our differences. Having an adult relationship with Rob is a perfect example of learning to get along with people who believe differently. He was a Pentecostal Pastor and I an Independent Baptist. We had all the arguments and discussions about our beliefs, and it only caused bitterness and anger. We learned to focus our common beliefs, and to love and respect one another despite our doctrinal differences.

I knew saying good-bye to Rob and his wife, Audrey, would be difficult for Kathy and the kids.

Give us strength, Lord!

Saying Goodbye

Audrey opened the door in tears, "I was just thinking about all the nights we spent playing games and fellowshipping about the goodness of God." She turned to Kathy and grabbed her arm, "You are my best friend! I will miss you terribly! Who will go shopping with me at all hours of the night and make a midnight Taco Bell run?" She burst into a new round of tears, "I'm going to miss you all so much!"

Hannah squeezed around me and grabbed Audrey's legs, "You're the bestest aunt in the whole world! I will miss you so much!" More tears.

Keturah moved closer to Judi, Rob and Audrey's daughter, "Why don't you come with us?" she asked.

Judi was smart for her eight years, "I don't have a plane ticket, or that visa thingy Uncle Ron has talked about nonstop for the past two weeks." She grabbed Keturah and continued, "But, I'll miss you. You can draw me pictures and Aunt Kathy can send them with the letters she writes to my mom."

We moved onto Kathy's parents' room. As they opened the door, Joel ran in first and grabbed Kathy's dad, "Grandpa Ben, I'm going to miss you the most. I'll miss our snowmobile rides, the four-wheeler rides, and feeding the Koi in your pond. Take good care of the fish you named Joel!"

Micah, not to be outdone by his older brother, piped up, "And Grandma Judy, I'll miss your chicken and dumplings, scalloped potatoes, and your snorting laugh."

Kathy grabbed Micah and scolded, "Micah! That's not nice to make fun of someone's laugh! Apologize to Grandma!"

Grabbing Grandma Judy around the waist, Micah said, "I'm sorry Grandma, I didn't mean to offend you. I wasn't making fun of you; I love your laugh. It makes me smile!"

Grandma Judy turned to look at Kathy, "I can't believe this day has finally come. When you called me last year and told me you had something important to tell me, I thought you were pregnant again."

Kathy smiled at the memory, "And when I told you God had called us to Russia, you said, 'I think I'd rather you be pregnant.'"

Grandma Judy sighed, "And to think when you met Ron, I was excited to hear he was from Oregon, only eight hours from Boise, Idaho. I was worried you would marry someone from Florida, and I'd rarely see you. Now you are going halfway around the world."

I saw the conversation going off the rails and needed to turn it into a positive spin, "God will take care of us. You do not need to worry." Grandma Judy and Grandpa Ben frowned but nodded.

Jeremiah let out a loud, long yawn. "I guess that is our cue to get to bed," I said. "We'll talk more in the morning." Kathy hugged her mother and we headed towards our room. We put the kids to bed and soon we heard five heavy breaths of sleeping children. Just as I expected, however, neither Kathy nor I got much sleep. The excitement and anticipation were just too much.

As our family of seven got in the station wagon one last time, I asked Kathy, "Did you get all the plane tickets, visas and passports?"

"I've got them right here. And I've got five children buckled in and ready to go. I feel like I'm missing something. I keep telling myself as long as I have seven passports, seven visas, seven plane tickets and seven people, that is all that really matters."

"Let's pray for safety. Father, we embark on a new journey today. I'm excited and optimistic but I'm also a little nervous. Lord, I believe. Help Thou, my unbelief. Amen."

We drove to the airport in a caravan of four vehicles.

Everyone gathered the bags as Kathy herded the kids to the inside ticket agents. After what seemed forever, we finally checked our bags and got our 21 boarding passes. The flight was from Seattle-Boston-Amsterdam-Moscow.

Lord, give us strength!

Our entourage hurried through security. The gate agents saw us coming, "Reasoners?"

"Yes." I said, "Are we late?"

"You are the last ones, where are your tickets? Let's get them scanned!"

No time for final words of comfort and encouragement. We quickly hugged our families good-bye. Kathy's mom began to cry uncontrollably. I had never seen her get emotional before. I heard her tell Kathy, "I love you. I hope I will see you again!"

Now everyone was crying. I think my mother-in-law's fear suddenly hit everyone between the eyes. Would we be exiled to a Russian *Gulag* for preaching the Gospel? Worse yet, would we be killed as martyrs? It all became real.

I hurried the family onto the jetway. Everyone looked back and waved to our loved ones who were now buried in each other's arms sobbing and moaning.

Surely God will bring us back together!

I was the first to board. The other passengers glared. Written on their faces was, "Here comes the jerk holding up the plane." Their looks of

Saying Goodbye

disgust turned to horror as child after child boarded. No one enjoys children on a plane! Kathy boarded last and surmised the situation. She flashed a smile and said to no one in particular, "Oh, sorry! This is our first time flying as a family and we didn't realize how long it would take to get checked in." As if on cue, the children flashed their missionary smiles as they strolled down the aisle to our seats. Suddenly all was right in the world and the passengers smiled back.

The flight attendant directed me to our row. Our 10:30 a.m. flight left at 10:35 a.m. We watched as the great Northwest got smaller and smaller until it disappeared through the clouds. I could not decide if my heart hurt because I was leaving my homeland or if it was about to explode with excitement over our upcoming adventures.

As we landed in Boston and gathered our things, one passenger leaned over to me and said, "Your children are very well behaved. I was pleasantly surprised."

Another passenger joined the conversation, "Is Boston your final destination?"

"No, we are headed to Moscow, Russia."

"Where? What for? Do you have family there?"

"No," I replied, "We are moving there as missionaries. We will start churches and preach the Gospel to people who haven't had opportunity to hear in over 70 years."

Both were speechless. Their eyes bulged as they looked at each other, then to our children. One managed to mutter, "Good luck. You are crazy."

Our flight from Boston to Amsterdam was on time and we had to run across the airport. Again, we were some of the last to board and endured the disappointed looks. At nine and a half hours, this was the longest leg of the journey.

This plane was huge. It had ten seats across. Kathy sat in the front row of the economy mid-section with three kids, and I sitting right behind with the other two. It was our first experience flying internationally with the children. We were terrified we might misplace a kid.

Once in the air, I noticed Kathy crying. I leaned over and touched her arm, "What's wrong?"

"I just mentally said good-bye to America—the only home I have ever known. I'm going to a new country, and if I embrace Russia as I should, it will become my home and America will never be home for me again. That's a sad thought."

"We'll go back to visit. Our family is still there. Don't worry, Kathy. God will take care of us." I smiled and added, "I know you said you wanted to keep a journal of what a missionary wife goes through. Perhaps now would be a good time to start."

Kathy made sure all the children were busy coloring. Some had already fallen asleep. She pulled a small notebook out of her purse and began to write. Her journals of our life on the mission field would become a source of history, documentation, daily struggles, victories, defeats, and refuge in times of sorrow about our life and ministry in Russia. Those journals are a continual cultural lesson of life in Russia and contributed greatly to the writing of this book.

Several hours into the flight, a group of teenagers in business class started to make a ruckus. They were excited to be going home. They chattered gleefully. Kathy nudged Joel and said, "Walk over near that group and see if you can figure out what language they are speaking."

Joel returned a few minutes later and said, "Mom, I think they are speaking English, but they have a terrible accent."

Kathy motioned for me to listen to the group, "What language are they speaking?" she asked.

I listened for a moment and then chuckled, "They are Brits, Kathy. They are speaking the King's English. We are the ones with terrible accents!"

We arrived in Amsterdam and went straight to our next gate. We had a two hour lay-over. It was a challenge to keep five, excited kids in check. They were hungry, grouchy, and jetlagged. We must have done a good job because a man walked over to me, "Are all these children yours?" he asked.

"Yes sir."

"They are so well behaved. I don't think I've ever seen such well-mannered children. Where are you going with such a large family?"

"We are going to Moscow, Russia as missionaries."

"Wow! My wife and I are from Amsterdam. We are awaiting a flight to Paris. I thought we were going on a great adventure, but ours will be nothing compared to yours! You are a much braver man than I am. Good luck."

Finally, they called for our flight. We stood with the children in a line. I went first, Kathy last. All our ducks were in a row. As I handed the agent all our passports, she immediately handed them to another agent who pulled our family aside. "We must check your visas for errors. Russian border patrol will not let you enter Russia if even one number or letter is out of place."

Saying Goodbye

We waited for our passports and visas to be verified. The agent handed me the passports and we were on our way, walking down the jetway on the final leg of our incredible journey.

We settled the children into their seats. It was a KLM flight. The flight attendants were attentive to our children, giving them a gift pack with coloring books, crayons, candy, a small airplane, and a flight wings pendant. It was a three-hour flight and the children fell asleep just as we prepared to land into the great unknown—Moscow, Russia.

Let the adventures begin!

All my siblings and their children in 1993

THOUGHTS

- When you set out on a journey, are you excited about what God will do, or are you fearful what might happen?

CHAPTER TWENTY-FIVE

Russia, At Last!

Whither shall I go from thy spirit? or whither shall I flee from thy presence? If I ascend up into heaven, thou art there: if I make my bed in hell, behold, thou art there. Psalm 139:7-8

International Travelers

Twelve time zones later, and almost 24-hours of flying from Seattle to Boston to Amsterdam to Moscow, we finally landed. It was Tuesday, September 6, 1994. Have I mentioned the age of our five children? They were ten, nine, five, four, and three years old. The journey was exhausting to say the least. The layovers were more taxing than I ever imagined.

When we arrived on Russian soil, our first hurdle was to get through passport control. This time around, it didn't seem as hectic. I was more nervous about keeping everyone close together.

The line was long and slow. Passport control in Russia is like nowhere else in the world. They assume everyone is a criminal. They interrogate and stare you down before stamping your passport. There were over 200 people in front of us. I strained to hear some of the questions being asked.

Lord, give me wisdom to answer correctly.

Kathy seemed as exhausted as I was. She stopped to readjust a strap on her backpack. I focused on getting our herd towards the bureaucratic labyrinth ahead. More than once, our children stopped to wave at the Russian border guards who blocked all the exits with machine guns and frowns. Not one of the soldiers responded to their smiles. Jeremiah, the youngest, was tired from the long flight and struggled to keep up.

A Russian border guard rushed towards us.

Russia, At Last!

Oh no! Lord, we're in trouble already and we haven't even officially entered Russia.

I whispered out of the corner of my mouth, "Kathy! Keep the children close!"

The guard, his jaw firmly set, stuck his hand out, pointed to our passports in Kathy's hand, and waved for us to follow.

All kinds of scenarios raced through my head, not the least of which was the *Gulags*. Did they know we were missionaries come to preach the Gospel? Were we being arrested? Why had he singled us out? If we're arrested, who will take care of the children? Surely they wouldn't lock them up. How am I going to protect my family against the guards and machine guns? What would I do if we got separated?

The guard took us to the front of the line and motioned towards the next available passport agent. The blonde female officer stared with her mouth gaped open. Finally, she composed herself and took our passports from under the bullet proof glass. She held each passport in front of the owner's face and frowned.

Her broken English was difficult to understand. "Where you come from?"

I looked her in the eye and smiled, "Oregon; it's north of California."

Her mouth was the only part of her face that moved. "Why you here?"

I never took my eyes off her. "I'm going to Pastor a church in Moscow and Smolensk."

She frowned. "How long you stay?"

I pointed to our passports and visas, "Our visas are good for three months, but I hope to get them extended."

She tapped a finger on our documents. "Where you live?"

"We have rented an apartment in Moscow."

Her eyes wandered over the gaggle of children nervously standing around Kathy and me. "Are all these yours?"

I rose to my full height and nodded, "Yes, Ma'am."

The whole process seemed like an eternity. We visibly sighed and smiled when she slipped everything under the glass. I took our documents and Kathy herded the children through the turnstile. We were finally in Russia!

While we waited at baggage claim, I pointed to Heaven. "The Lord sure worked a miracle."

A man in a business suit standing next to me turned and smiled. "Excuse me, my name is Jonathan McMasters. I couldn't help but notice your family as you went through passport control. I can explain something about Russian culture."

The carousel started to move, I held a hand up and tapped Joel and Micah on the shoulder. "You boys stay with me and help with our bags." I caught Kathy's eye and pointed to a wall. "Take the youngest and wait over there." She nodded and rolled our carry-on bags towards the wall.

I extended my arm and shook Jonathan's hand. "Pleased to meet you. I'm a missionary from the States. I thought we'd just been blessed with a miracle."

He smiled. "Children are a great commodity. Most couples have only one or two. Anyone with three or more is considered a hero and those who have five are given a medal of honor. This allows them to cut to the front of any line." He reached down and retrieved the last of his bags and set it on a cart. "Well, maybe it was a miracle, maybe not. Either way, it saved you at least an hour."

I pointed to the cart. "How much does it cost to rent one of those. With all our family's gear I sure could use a couple."

Jonathan chuckled. "This isn't the States. The carts are free."

As he walked away, I turned to Joel and Micah, "I still think it was a miracle." I pointed to a row of luggage carts lined up by a post, "Each of you bring a cart."

Ten minutes later, after collecting half of our bags, I realized the rest were not on the stalled carousel. All of us approached the lost luggage counter. "Excuse me." I said.

The clerk looked up from his paperwork and stared wide-eyed at us. I placed the claim checks for the missing suitcases in front of him.

He examined each ticket and handed me a form. He tried to explain how to fill it out. Praise God we had the information needed to give to the clerk and he filled out the papers. In horribly broken English, he explained that they would deliver the bags that evening.

Our First Russian Home

We went through customs and Mike Morrissey was there waiting. Short, stocky, and in his fifties, he was a sight for sore eyes. I hugged him with vigor. "Brother Morrissey, with all the delays I was worried you would give up."

Brother Morrisey laughed and took a cart from Kathy. Our entourage, complete with a train of luggage carts, headed for the exit.

We loaded what luggage we had into a dark green, military looking van he had hired. I commented, "Wow, it is a good thing half of the luggage got lost. There wouldn't be room in this van for us and all the luggage."

I paid the driver $100, which is more expensive than I would pay later, but Russian taxi drivers at that time did not trust Americans so the cost was higher.

The ride through Moscow was as eventful as the one I took on my survey trip. I watched everyone lean to the left or right as the crazy driver weaved in and out of traffic. Apparently, lane markings, stop lights, and the common courtesy we are used to in America did not mean the same in Russia.

Our van was bigger than the Ladas and Volgas on the road. The one lesson I learned from the last visit was that the biggest vehicle has the right-of-way.

I watched the children squeal with glee every time we slid around a corner. When I noticed Kathy's white knuckles, I put my arm around her and shouted, "It's okay. We'll be to our new home soon."

The driver raced along at incredible speeds and ran red lights when he saw no one was coming from the other direction. We screamed when he jumped a curb and drove onto the sidewalk because traffic was stopped. He wanted to get around it and the sidewalk was available with just a handful of people who had to jump out of our way.

After 20 minutes we drove past Red Square. It was 3:30 p.m. Sun rays danced across the Kremlin walls. I leaned towards Kathy and shouted over the gleeful children. "It's amazing to see it again."

Kathy, tired and frazzled after our long day, shouted back, "There's just something about seeing the Kremlin walls and St. Basil's Cathedral with your own eyes." She raised her arm and pinched herself. "Am I dreaming?"

I laughed and whispered, "With this man's driving and our jetlag kicking in, you might be having a nightmare."

The driver brought the van to a screeching halt in front of our apartment complex and unloaded our bags. Brother Morrisey picked up the two heaviest pieces and started for the entrance. The two oldest boys each picked one. Kathy slung Jeremiah on her hip and picked up another. I put a fist through the straps on two bags and struggled to catch up.

As he walked up to the door, Brother Morrisey set one bag down, pulled a keychain out of his pocket and held a fob to a panel. "This is called a *domophone*. It opens the security door. I'll give this fob to you before we leave. You can't get into the building without it unless you call someone to ring you in."

He held the red door open. "Let's take the elevator. Unless you want to carry these up to the 16th floor."

Everyone shouted; "ELEVATOR!"

Seconds later we were doubting the wisdom of our decision. The elevator creaked and smelled of a combination of burnt oil and urine. I quickly instructed the boys, "Don't put the luggage on the floor! Hold it." I then turned to Brother Morrisey and commented, "Is it even safe? The button for our floor doesn't light up."

He laughed, "According to some neighbors, it hasn't worked in years. I'm pretty sure it's burned out."

I pointed to scorch marks on the elevator panel.

Brother Morrisey shrugged. "Don't worry, it's been like that for weeks. It's okay. If it doesn't stop at 16, we'll go to 17, and walk down."

Exiting the elevator, Brother Morrisey pulled the keychain out and opened a second security door. He turned and said, "Behind this locked door are four apartments. We share this security door with them."

We walked down the hallway. Brother Morrisey unlocked another metal door and immediately moved to unlock a fourth metal door."

I could no longer keep silent, despite my fear of scaring Kathy and the children, "Did we just open four metal security doors to get into this apartment? Why so many?"

Brother Morrisey turned and said, "When the Soviet Union fell, people lost their bank accounts overnight. They lost their jobs, and they lost the Cold War. Everyone was destitute and without hope. Many began to ransack apartments even if the owners were home. The goal of every apartment owner became 'make your apartment harder to get into than your neighbor's.'"

Brother Morrisey continued through the last door, and we followed him into the 650 square foot apartment. His wife, Sister Anna, smiled as we entered. "I'm so glad you made it. It was a hard flight for us when we came three months ago, and you had five extra hours of flying with five children."

Still pondering the dangers if robbers knew where we lived, I was pulled from my thoughts. "What's all this stuff?", Kathy exclaimed as she pointed to the fully furnished living room.

Before Brother Morrisey could answer, she started exploring and gave him a questioning look. "I'm surprised it's completely furnished." She pointed to a closet. "The landlord's things are still here! Look at that bookshelf. It runs the length of the living room. It's full of books and trinkets. Where will we put our stuff?"

Sensing the need to get involved I stepped forward. "Um, Brother Morrisey, when will the landlord take her things?"

He gave me a surprised look. "Oh, no. They are living with their parents so they can rent this out. They don't have any place to store this. You'll just have to learn how to move around it. Don't touch it! They'll be very offended. It's hard to find a place to rent in Moscow so I suggest you learn to get along with Olga, your landlord. The Soviet Union has fallen apart, and Russia blames America. Years ago, the communist government gave her this apartment. You won't find many people willing to entrust their most sacred possession to an American."

I could tell how exasperated Kathy was. I pleaded, "We have a container coming in a few months. I have no idea where we will put everything!"

Kathy took a deep breath. I could tell she was gathering all the resolve she could muster. "I guess we'll cross that bridge when we come to it." She reached out to Brother Morrisey, "Thank you so much for helping us out and getting us this place. We had no idea it was so difficult to find a place to live in Moscow. We are tired. With you and your wife spending the night in this apartment, where will everyone sleep?"

Brother Morrisey opened the futon in the living room. "One bedroom has two beds for the five children."

Kathy, the trooper she is, sighed, "We will learn to make it work."

Sister Anna took Kathy by the arm and gave her a tour of our new home while Brother Morrisey and I went onto the balcony and gazed at the city below. He leaned with his back on the railing. "While they're gone, I'll show you how to hook up the washer."

I followed him to the bathroom. He chuckled. "If you do it wrong, the drain will overflow into the apartment below. Make sure the drain is hanging on the bathtub wall." When he finished, he raised his head, "Simple isn't it?" He chuckled, "Do it right every time, or you'll flood at least the apartment below, if not several floors of apartments. A Russian acquaintance told me he just finished paying for repairs of the four apartments below him when his flooded."

While the women were talking, Joel and Micah put everyone's luggage near the bed they were going to sleep in, and Keturah helped her younger siblings with their pajamas.

As we walked down the hall, Brother Morrisey reached into the master bedroom and grabbed two suitcases. He handed the small one to me and wheeled the larger one down the hall. "Everything we need for tomorrow morning is in our backpacks." He set his load by the door. "I have 150,000 rubles. Can you buy them from me?"

I did the math in my head. I reached into my wallet and pulled out several bills. "Sure, I have $120. That'll make it easier for me to go shopping."

He pulled his coat from the chair, put it on, and moved towards the door. "Now I'll take you to a few local stores and try to explain how to shop. It will be overwhelming but at least I can share what I've learned the past few months."

I said good-bye to Kathy and the kids and promised to return with special prizes.

Learning How to Shop

Back on the elevator, we descended to the first floor and out onto the street. We rounded the corner of our apartment building and came to a store. Brother Morrisey said, "We won't buy anything here today. I want to take you downtown to the Irish House. It is the only foreign food store that I have found but this store is much closer so you might find yourself shopping here quite a bit. Notice the three separate lines. The first for ordering, the second for paying and the third for picking up your order. Don't forget that or there will be a lot of yelling."

Brother Morrisey turned and directed me to walk toward a pedestrian bridge over a set of train tracks. "We cross this bridge, walk up that hill and catch a bus to the metro. Any bus will take you to the metro station."

The bus arrived and it was already full. "Shall we wait for the next one?" I asked, "This one is awfully crowded."

Brother Morrisey laughed as he squeezed onto the bus, "They are all this full. Hurry! Get on!" Brother Morrisey took something out of his pocket and passed it to someone standing by a pole.

The man placed it in a hole punch and then handed them back. "I'm getting our tickets validated," Brother Morrisey explained

We arrived at the metro station and Brother Morrisey handed me a green token, "This is your metro ticket. Put it in the slot next to the turnstile and then quickly walk through. If you aren't fast enough, the gates will close on you."

I took the token, placed it in the slot and walked through.

Something was wrong—I felt someone extra close to me.

I turned and saw a young man following me through my turnstile. I looked at Brother Morrisey. He smiled, "He's a jack rabbit—that's what

Russia, At Last!

they call people who board a bus or walk through a metro turnstile without paying."

We stood behind the solid white line near the track, waiting for a train. "Notice the mirror?" Brother Morrisey pointed to the front of the platform. "That is how you know which direction the train is coming from. The mirror is the front of the train. Here comes our train. Get ready to push your way on."

The train came to a stop. I quickly noticed that everyone waiting to board the train moved to the side of the doors, providing an open path for people exiting. A stream of people spilled out. The race began to get on the train before the doors closed. It was crowded. My personal space was violated!

"Five stops on the green line and then transfer to the blue line." Brother Morrisey instructed. "If you take the wrong escalator at the transfer station, you will have to exit the station and pay to get in again."

The walk between lines took five minutes.

I looked around the metro train car, which was less crowded. At our stop, Brother Morrisey led the way, "Now we walk about a mile and come to the Irish House. This is the only place I trust to buy meat and vegetables. Last week a thousand people died by eating bad meat from one of the open marketplaces."

At Brother Morrisey's suggestion, I bought sandwich meat, bread, and two 2-liter jugs of water. It was a workout to haul them down the street, onto the metro, transfer stations, walk to the bus stop, board the bus, and walk the half mile back to our apartment.

As we walked into our new home, Sister Anna called from the kitchen. "I know it's late, but I made some tea and chocolate. Would anyone care for some?"

Kathy put a piece of chocolate on a napkin for each child. Sister Anna poured the tea and we all sat down.

Kathy pointed outside; "What time do the stores open? We need to get something for breakfast."

Sister Anna's chair screeched on the floor as she pushed her chair back. "Oh, I forgot to tell you. I have 10 eggs, 2 liters of milk, and cheese. You can use that for breakfast."

Kathy exclaimed, "Yes, definitely. Thank you!"

Anna yawned, "I guess we should say our goodbyes. We leave at 4 a.m. We'll try to be quiet."

After an awkward silence, I asked, "Do we need to get up with you to let you out?"

Brother Morrisey held out his hand, "We can lock the doors without using a key. We will let ourselves out."

I took his hand and gave him a half-hug, "Thank you so much for all your help. Everything you did for us is a huge blessing."

Kathy moved to hug Sister Anna, then held her hand out to Brother Morrisey. The children waved goodnight and we took them to their room for evening prayers. By the time we got them tucked in, the Morriseys had gone to bed.

We fell asleep to the faint smell and sounds of the heavy traffic outside our 16th story window. Tomorrow would be a busy day and we needed to rest.

THOUGHTS
- Have you ever been someplace where everything was new and unfamiliar?
- How long did it take you to become comfortable?

Chapter Twenty-Six

First Day in Russia

I will instruct thee and teach thee in the way which thou shalt go: I will guide thee with mine eye. Psalm 32:8

I woke to the smell of meat, eggs, and tea. *Where am I?* I opened my eyes, saw the loud, obnoxious wallpaper, and remembered. I slung my feet over the side of the bed and rubbed my eyes.

The bedroom door opened, and Jeremiah peeked in. He ran back into the kitchen yelling. "Mommy, Daddy's up! Daddy's up!"

I stood, put on my pants and suddenly the three youngest entered and tackled me. We flopped on the bed, and I lost the impromptu wrestling match. Kathy stuck her head in. "Good, you're almost dressed." She pointed a spatula towards the door. "I need you to find a store and buy groceries. I started a list." She sniffed the air and ran back to the stove.

I tucked my shirt in as I walked down the hallway and into the kitchen. Keturah jumped up as soon as she saw me, "Mommy says you need to go shopping. Can I go?"

"No, honey. I will go alone. I need to focus on where I am going and what I am doing. I can't be worried about children too."

Five sullen faces fell. I held a hand up. "Don't worry, we'll get this shopping thing figured out and then we will take turns." I glanced at Kathy, and she gave me an 'I do not think that helped' look.

Then she smiled, "But good news! While you were sleeping, the airport called and said they were on the way. At 3 a.m., the rest of our bags were delivered!" She gestured towards the living room. "Now you have toys." She nodded and the children ran out of the kitchen.

I smiled. "Thank you for doing that. I must have slept right through everything."

Serving God Behind Enemy Lines

When we finished eating Kathy picked up her shopping list and set it in front of me. "You don't have to get everything, but it would help if you got as much as you could."

I read the list, "Let's see, butter, bread, eggs, cheese, four pounds of meat—" I paused and looked up, "Any particular cut or type?"

She shook her head. "Anything to help tide us over for a few days."

I nodded and continued, "Vegetables, cookies, and a cake mix." I looked at Keturah who had returned to the kitchen with a doll under her arm. I gave Keturah a pat on the head, "I bet I know who the cake mix is for! Your birthday is only two days away!" Keturah beamed. I folded the list and put it in my shirt pocket.

Our Attempts to Buy Food

Fifteen minutes later I walked into what I assumed was a grocery store. As my eyes adjusted, I noticed it was not much bigger than a 7-11. There were three lines. I stood in the shortest.

Immediately a store clerk yelled and pointed at the longest line. Several customers scowled and frowned. My Russian was limited, so I obeyed. About the time I reach the head of the line I remembered the reason for the three lines. The longest was for placing orders. The line by the cashier was for paying. The last was for picking up the order.

Oh yeah, Brother Morrisey told me that. I should have remembered! I must be jet-lagging worse than I thought!

I took my list and handed it to the clerk. She looked at it, handed it back and said something I could not decipher.

Lord, help me. Obviously, she doesn't read English. We need food.

At that moment I noticed shelves behind the counter and pointed to what looked like canned meat. I held up four fingers; "I'll have those four cans." I leaned over the counter to see if any of the other items Kathy wanted were available.

At that moment, several people behind me started grumbling. "Торопитесь! Если вы не понимаете наш язык, почему вы ходите по магазинам?" I did not understand a single word.

In exasperation I folded the list and pulled out my wallet.

From behind I heard, "Нет, нет, Вы платите там."

More unintelligible words, but the salesclerk pointed towards the cashier line. I kept my wallet in my hand and moved to where she pointed. I turned back when I heard her grunt. She handed me a piece of paper. I grabbed it and headed for the next line. Several people pointed to the end of the line. I felt their eyes on me until they were sure I was complying.

First Day in Russia

I turned toward home with a heavy heart.

Some provider I was.

I walked in the door to eager, hungry faces. Kathy came out of the kitchen wiping her hands on a towel. "Well, what did you buy?"

Joel walked behind me and looked out the door. "I was hoping you'd left the rest of the groceries outside."

I handed the cans of meat to Kathy and removed my coat and hat. "Talk about an experience. It's not like home."

"How will we open it?" Kathy asked.

Joel rummaged through the kitchen drawers, found an old fashion can opener, and handed it to me. "This is all I could find."

I picked a can up and rotated it in my hand. "Hmm, I can't read Russian, and there isn't a picture telling us what type of meat it contains." I shrugged and punched triangles into the top of the can.

Keturah stuck her head under my arm, "What kind of meat is it, Daddy?"

I shrugged, "Don't know, Sweetheart, we'll find out soon enough." I soon had the top off and the rank smell permeated through the apartment.

Joel held his nose. "Yuck, it smells like dog food."

Micah added. "Do we have to eat that?"

Kathy leaned forward, "Looks like Spam." She picked up the two other cans. "Hum. They're all the same. Sister Anna left some ketchup, maybe that will help. Open the other cans." She tapped Micah on the head. "After your father opens the cans put the meat in the pot on the stove."

Micah took a knife and worked chunks of meat from under the triangles I'd made in the can. "Good idea. We don't want to waste any of God's blessings." I smiled, "Hey guys, can't we have fun no matter what the Lord sends our way?"

Moments later we all stared at our unfinished bowls of mystery meat. Kathy pursed her lips and put her fork down. "Joel, get your coat." She pointed to Micah, "Help your father clean this up." She pointed to me, "This time I'm going shopping."

I went to the closet and pulled out her coat. "I hope you have better luck." She grabbed her purse. "Remember, Brother Morrisey said that every few apartment buildings have stores. Maybe you can find another store that has a better selection. And don't forget the landlord is coming over at a 5 p.m. to get the first month's rent."

Kathy looked at her watch, "It's only 11 a.m. Do you think I'll be gone that long?"

I kissed her cheek as she opened the door, "I hope not!"

Locking the door behind them, I turned, walked towards the kids' bedroom, and rubbed my hands together as I moved down the hall. "Okay, kids, let's surprise Mommy, and do a load of wash before she gets back. Everyone bring your clothes you wore on the airplane."

All four children ran and started piling their dirty clothes on the bathroom floor. In moments, the first load was in, and the machine chugged along. I double-checked the hookup as Brother Morrissey had instructed. With a satisfied smile, I called out, "Okay, kids, set up the game of Sorry."

Towards the end of the first game Micah rolled a six and smiled. "Sorry!" Before his left hand could move my marker, we heard banging from the bathroom.

I sprinted down the hall and saw the washer bouncing up and down. I pulled the plug out of the wall and wiped my forehead.

Lord, I thought I'd balanced the load.

I adjusted the clothes and plugged it back in. The dance resumed. I unplugged it, opened the lid, and looked around. Nothing. I closed the lid, picked up the first two children I saw and placed them on the lid to keep the washer from walking across the room. I reinserted the plug and the machine hardly wobbled.

"Micah, bring the game. We'll play in here."

Two hours later I heard a key turning the lock on our front door. Kathy and Joel came in carrying two bags. The look in her eyes told me she had not fared any better. The four younger children scurried around them. "What did you get? Did you get cereal? How about a chocolate cake?"

Kathy slumped in a chair, removed her shoes, and rubbed her feet. "I'm glad you told me about the different lines, or it would've taken longer."

I helped her with her coat and hung it on a doorknob. "Now I don't feel as bad." I sat next to her. "Tell me about it."

She put her head in her hands and sighed. "The only thing they had a lot of was vodka. It was cheaper than bottled water. After an hour of walking aimlessly, I remembered to pray and ask God for help."

Joel held the bag in his hand high and smiled. "At least we found Pepsi!"

She smiled a wan smile and continued, "It took another hour for me to find our way through the maze of 40 high-rise apartment buildings. We went to four stores." Her shoulders slumped. She opened the first bag and pulled out the two 2-liter bottles of Pepsi. Joel unloaded the other package

First Day in Russia

and revealed two unwrapped and uncut loaves of bread. Kathy sighed; "I think shopping will be a daily chore."

I looked at the pile of MRE (Meal Ready to Eat) packages Kathy had stuffed into our luggage at the last minute. Would they keep us from starving until we figured out how to shop?

Wow, God, just wow!

I focused on my family sitting at the kitchen table and staring at the bread and Pepsi. Finally, I pulled Keturah close and whispered, "You may not get a birthday cake this year since there are no cake mixes here and Mom's cookbooks are in the container. But you'll get plenty of love and Mom did remember to pack a few presents. Living in Russia is going to require sacrifices from all of us." I looked into Keturah's disappointed eyes, touched her cheek, and continued, "But with sacrifice comes God's blessings. So, hold on to your hats, we are about to get blessed!"

Meeting Olga

That evening at 5 p.m., we sat on the couch waiting for Olga. Suddenly, we heard a strange song playing. I answered the telephone, but there was only a dial tone. The song continued. Joel jumped off the couch and ran to the front door. He picked up a phone on the wall, "Hello?" He paused and then said, "I'll open," and pushed a button.

"What did you just do?" I asked.

"Brother Morrisey showed this to me while you were in the kitchen with Sister Anna. He said it would sing if someone was calling from downstairs."

Soon the doorbell rang. I opened the first and second entry doors to find a short, plump violet haired lady. She spoke in broken English, "I Olga. You Ron?"

I moved aside to invite her in, "Yes, I'm Ron. Please come in and meet my family. This is my wife, Kathy." The children had already lined up according to birth order so I could quickly rattle off their names, "This is Joel, Micah, Keturah, Hannah, and Jeremiah. Please come in and have a seat."

Olga removed her coat and hung it on the rack. She took her shoes off and grabbed a pair of slippers. Stopping to look in the mirror, fluff her hair and smack her lips, Olga then proceeded to the living room. She sat in an armchair. We crowded onto the couch. "I hope you like my house."

I answered, "Yes. Thank you, Olga, for allowing us to rent your home. We will take good care of it."

Olga paused to look at each of the children, "My childs are old- 12 and 16 years. The money to help them go to university."

Serving God Behind Enemy Lines

At the mention of money, Kathy stood, walked to the desk, opened the top drawer, and handed me an envelope of cash. I held it out to Olga, "Here is the first month's rent."

Olga stared at the envelope in horror.

What did I do wrong, Lord?

Finally, she sighed, took the envelope, and stuffed it in her bag.

"I would like you to count it, before you leave, Olga. I want us to have an honest relationship."

Olga retrieved the envelope, opened it, and counted out six $100 bills, "Good. I want US dollars. I come first day of month for money, okay?"

"That sounds good. Again, thank you for trusting us with your home."

Olga stood, "I must to get coat from bedroom. May I?"

Kathy walked into the hallway and opened the master bedroom door, "Please."

Olga opened several closet doors before finding her winter coat and hat. Satisfied, she walked toward the front door, "I must to go. I come again first of month."

We stood in a line to say goodbye as she put on her shoes and coat. She stuffed her winter coat into a large bag she brought with her. Olga nodded and said, "Goodbye."

After I locked the entry doors, I found the family in the kitchen. Kathy was cutting up bread and the sandwich meat from the Irish House. "She seemed nice enough."

I nodded, "I wonder why she was horrified when I handed her the envelope?"

Kathy shrugged her shoulders, "Who knows. It's probably some Russian custom we are violating. If you ever get a hold of Roman, we can ask him."

Olga continued to come on the first of each month to get her payment. One month she sent her daughter but when she got the money home, $100 was mysteriously missing. Olga called to ask if we both had counted the money. When I said, "yes," she hung up and came herself to get the money from then on. We rented the apartment for two years until our first furlough.

THOUGHTS

- Learning a new culture is terrifying.
- When was the last time you helped an immigrant maneuver through our cultural nuances?

CHAPTER TWENTY-SEVEN

Finding Roman

Wherefore I put thee in remembrance that thou stir up the gift of God, which is in thee by the putting on of my hands. For God hath not given us the spirit of fear; but of power, and of love, and of a sound mind. 2 Timothy 1:6-7

Friday was Keturah's birthday. After family devotions, I closed my Bible and sighed, "Joel, Micah, both of you are old enough to understand prayer." I looked at Keturah and the two toddlers.

The youngest will have to learn by osmosis.

"Here's something we need to pray about. Last year, on my survey trip a young man named Roman was my interpreter. From what I saw he was the best." I tapped my Bible, "I believe he's the man the Lord wants me to work with." My voice cracked. "I have tried to get in touch with him for months and again this week, but no one answers."

As I talked, Kathy put her arm around me. "Children, you've seen how hard it is to shop for food." She pointed towards the street below. "If we knew how to speak Russian it would be easier," she chuckled, "We might even know what we're eating." She squeezed my hand, "Think of Daddy trying to tell people about Jesus when he can't speak their language."

I scratched my head. "In Russia the phone numbers are permanently assigned to an apartment. If he moved, I assume the new resident would at least answer."

Joel sat up, "Daddy, why don't you just get another interpreter?"

I patted him on the knee. "Yes, I've considered that, but he's the man I really feel a connection with. If it's God's will, I'll accept another."

I shook my head. "Most adults make $60 a month. I'll be paying him a lot more," I moaned. "Roman and I got along so well. I felt as if we became friends during the time we worked together."

Maybe he got into an accident? Maybe a family emergency forced him to move.

I looked at Kathy. "Besides, if he can help improve our language skills, we really might find out what the mystery meat was."

I clapped my hands. "So, just like we've done every time we've had a crisis, we're going to have family prayer." I looked into each child's eyes. "The Lord will answer our prayer!"

I folded my hands and before I closed my eyes, I nodded to Jeremiah to do the same. "Most gracious Heavenly Father, You've brought us to the ends of the earth. We need Roman. Please, please, let me find him and let him be willing to work for You with me." I opened my eyes to see all five children staring at me. "Amen."

I picked the receiver up and dialed Roman's phone one more time. A Russian woman's voice answered." я слушаю вас".

"Is Roman home?"

"Что? Кто это?"

I slapped my forehead.

Russian, Ron, speak Russian!

Then using the best Russian I could, I stammered, "Роман дома?"

Lord, please help her understand what I said.

"О, Роман! Да, он здесь." I heard the receiver bang against something.

In moments Roman's voice boomed from the speaker, "Hello?"

I spoke quickly, "Roman! It's Ron Reasoner! How are you? It's good to hear your voice. I tried calling you from America. I've been in Moscow for three days! I called every day but there was no answer."

"Brother Reasoner, I'm pleased to hear from you. You are in Moscow now?"

I tapped Kathy on the shoulder and waved for her to take the children into another room. "Yes. We arrived on Tuesday. Roman! I've been praying I would get in touch with you. Your phone hasn't worked in months. I didn't know what to expect."

Lord, I need him. Has he been preaching even though I wasn't able to send him sermons? Have I offended him?

As he talked, I paced as far as the cord allowed. I could feel his smile through the phone line. "Yes, my Brother. My phone has not been working. I get them to fix it, and it breaks again."

Hallelujah!

"Roman, I was concerned you wouldn't want to work with me." I sat on the futon and leaned back.

I heard rustling on his end and assumed he was sitting down. "Oh no, Brother Reasoner, it is an honor for a Russian to work with an American. Even though we've only known each other a short time, I feel like you're a friend."

The line when silent. "Roman, are you still there?"

"Sorry, Brother Reasoner, my mother asked if I am having lunch at home. Perhaps we should meet in Red Square?"

I checked the time on my watch. "I'd like that. Can we meet at 1 o'clock in front of St. Basil's Cathedral?" I stood and walked towards the end table where we kept the phone. "I'm looking forward to seeing you."

I left the apartment and followed the crowd to the bus stop. I hopped on the bus I hoped would take me to a metro station. It did. I then scratched my head.

Lord, was I supposed to take the metro train six stops. Or was it five?

I could not remember what Brother Morrissey instructed. I asked several people where Red Square was. They shrugged and turned away.

Finally, a middle-aged lady took me by the hand as I exited the train. She was silent as we walked to Red Square. I offered her money, but she said in broken English, "Welcome to Russia," and walked away.

Roman arrived twenty minutes late. I soon learned twenty minutes late was on time for young Russians. We walked to a McDonald's and ordered two Big Macs, two large fries, and two large drinks.

Roman set his food on the table and grimaced, "I can't work with you. Moscow is big city. Since you already have apartment, probably too far from my home. I would go to university classes and then your side of town. It's not possible! Where do you live?"

I cringed, "I do not know my address. It's a building with a fox on it. The street is called Cow-something."

Roman thought for a minute and then asked, "Kashirskoe street?"

"Yeah, that's it."

"I live near that street, but it is long. After we eat let's go see where you live."

We got back on the metro and exited at Kashirskya station. Roman directed us to a bus that would go the length of Kashirskoe street. I was proud when I remembered which stop was ours. Roman was in shock, "Your apartment is right across from mine."

I smiled, "Perhaps God would have us to work together after all."

Lord, forgive me for doubting.

Roman came up to meet the family. Kathy described our shopping escapades. "Joel saved one of those cans. He's hoping someone will tell us what the foul-smelling meat is."

As soon as Joel heard his name, he jumped up and ran into the kitchen. He returned with his trophy. Roman ran a finger across the label. "This is canned pork. It's not the best but is edible."

Everyone shook their heads and said, "Welcome to Russia."

Roman laughed at our antics. "How about I take you shopping?"

Kathy nodded. Micah picked up the pork can and started towards the trash, "Hallelujah!"

"Next," Kathy sighed, "We have a question about something that happened with our landlord. Ron tried to give her an envelope with our rent money in it, and it upset her. Why?"

Roman laughed, "I think you need more than shopping lessons. You need cultural lessons as well. See, you never pass money from your hand to someone else. That is the definition of a bribe, 'from hand to hand'. Instead, you put the envelope on a table or chair and the person will pick it up."

I smiled, "Knowing is half the battle."

Over the next several weeks, Roman took us shopping at the more 'modern' stores where we bought fresh meat and vegetables.

Roman taught us Russian from the books we brought. Joel picked it up quickly and within six months was able to shop and interpret for Kathy.

It was not long before we noticed that most trucks in Russia had a special plate on their bumper, "T.I.R." We often mused what it meant. We decided it stood for, "This Is Russia."

Whenever we encountered a new cultural experience that confused us, we said, "T.I.R." It was not for us to question the ways and thoughts of the Russian people. We would remind visitors that just because someone does something different does not make it wrong. It means they learned life differently than we did. T.I.R. — deal with it!

THOUGHTS
- Describe a time God made a divine appointment for you.

Chapter Twenty-Eight

Surveillance

See then that ye walk circumspectly, not as fools, but as wise, Redeeming the time, because the days are evil. Ephesians 5:15-16

We had been in Russia a month when my mom unexpectedly called. She began with, "Ron, I have something I need to tell you."

"Mom!" I interrupted, "It's great to hear from you! Why do you sound so nervous?"

Kathy gathered the children around to say hello to Grandma Reasoner. Sensing something was wrong, I put my hand up and motioned for them to be quiet. Kathy led the children to the kitchen so I could concentrate.

"I just got off the phone with Jeff." She lowered her voice, "You know he is stationed in England, with Air Force Intelligence, right?"

"Yes, we are talking about taking a vacation there next summer."

"Don't!" Mom screamed. She lowered her voice, "He was detained. They took him to a basement and shined a light in his face while interrogating him about why you are in Russia."

"Wait! You are saying he's in trouble because of me? Why?"

"I guess when you registered with the American Embassy in Moscow, your name got flagged because Jeff has a high security clearance. They suspect you are collaborating to sell State secrets."

"You've got to be kidding!" I replied, "We registered with the Embassy so they can tell us to leave should the Cold War start again. Why would I do that if I were a spy? That's crazy."

"I know!" Mom whispered, "But they have protocols in place to prevent treasonous acts. He endured 24 hours of continual questions. Jeff kept repeating over and over, 'My brother is a Jesus Freak—he went to Russia to preach about God. I don't have any contact with him.' They finally let him go. Jeff insisted I call you. You must have NO contact with him while you live in Russia and he is active military."

"Wow!" I sat down on the couch, "The U.S. Government forbids brothers from talking to each other?"

I paused to think about the gravity of the situation and finally answered, "This is weird, but I get it. I won't contact him."

I heard my mother let out a long sigh. She took a deep breath, "Also, Jeff said to warn you that you will have people watching you from both sides. American spies will be following you and the KGB is already following you."

I stretched my legs and chuckled, "Yeah, we've recognized a few KGB spies following us on the metros and buses. Some are easy to spot. The other day, a man was jogging in the park near our family outing. He was wearing a polyester jogging suit and running around in large circles. That's normal American behavior, but Russians don't do that. They walk everywhere they go—they don't need to go jogging in the park for exercise."

Mom nervously laughed, "Well, now you can play the game of 'who is the American spy in the crowd.' I'd better get off the phone. This costs $10 a minute and we've been talking for five minutes. I love you, Son, be careful."

"I love you too, Mom. Give my best to Dad and the rest of the family. Let Jeff know I will not contact him."

That afternoon, Roman came over to teach our Russian lessons. I started to tell Roman about the strange conversation with Mom. He immediately gave me a dirty look, put his finger to his lips, cleared his throat and opened our language book, "Joel, count to fifty in Russian as quickly and loudly as you can."

Joel smiled, "Раз. Два. Три. Четыры—"

As Joel counted, Roman whispered, "My Uncle is KGB, and I am in the military reserves. If I continue my university education, I won't have to actively serve. You must not discuss such things with me. It is dangerous."

My eyes widened, "You are in the military and your uncle is a KGB agent? Should you be my interpreter?"

Roman put his finger to his lips and sheepishly said, "It is okay, don't worry."

I nodded and joined Joel as he counted.

Surveillance

Halfway through our language lessons, our doorbell rang. "Roman, will you answer that? Everyone we know in this country who speaks English is in this room. Our Russian was still beginner level—we won't understand." Roman rose to answer the doorbell receiver, listened for a few seconds, then said "Спасибо!" and hung up.

"Who was that and what was it about?" I asked.

Roman smiled, "Follow me." He opened the bedroom door where the four youngest were supposed to be playing. I stepped in to see Jeremiah on Joel's top bunk. He had the small window open, throwing Joel's toys out the window. Roman pointed to Jeremiah and said, "Someone called to say a child was throwing toys out this 16th story window. It is very dangerous. Someone could be seriously injured by a toy falling from this height. Or worse yet, Jeremiah could fall out."

I grabbed Jeremiah off the bed, spanked and chided him, "Jeremiah! What were you thinking? You could have fallen out and died. You better pray you haven't hurt someone with your carelessness!"

Jeremiah buried his head in my shoulder and sobbed, "Joel promised to play with me today and he didn't, so I threw his toys out the window."

Joel ran to his bed, took a quick inventory, and proclaimed, "Jeremiah! You threw out my erector set and my teddy bear! How could you?"

"I'm sorry, Joel. You said you would play with me."

Joel walked over, took Jeremiah from my arms, gave him a hug, and said, "I forgive you. I doubt I'll ever get my toys back, but I forgive you."

Later that evening, Micah called from the living room, "Hey, Dad, that new phone machine you bought is making funny noises." Kathy shot a questioning look as I rose from the kitchen table and ran into the living room. We gathered around the fax machine, waiting for the message. The humming and zagging of the machine droned on and on. Finally, it spit out the paper. To my horror, the message read, "I will pay you for this new information. Meet me at our regular spot."

I looked at Kathy who shared my look of shock and confusion. "What is this?" I asked under my breath.

"Wow! First a phone call from your mom and now this—what's going on?" Kathy whispered.

I looked at my watch and then at the children. "It's bedtime—get your jammies on and brush your teeth. We need to pray and get you all in bed. Hurry up!"

The children scrambled in different directions, the girls to get their jammies on and the boys to brush their teeth. They passed each other in

Serving God Behind Enemy Lines

the hall as they switched tasks. Kathy and I tucked the children into bed and returned to the doorway, "Let's pray. God, we know that You have called us here to preach the Gospel. We have no desire to become involved in politics. Give us wisdom to deal with this situation with my brother and the fax we just received. Protect us, lead us, and may You be glorified in our little family."

I closed the kids' bedroom door and directed Kathy to the living room couch. I took her hand and whispered, "I don't think we should leave the house tomorrow. We will still have language lessons with Roman, but we better keep a low profile for the next few days. I don't know what's going on."

What is going on, Lord?

Neither of us got much sleep that night. As I lay in bed the next morning, worrying about what the day might hold, Kathy stirred. "Are you awake?" I asked.

"I barely slept."

"Do we have enough food for three meals today? I don't want anyone to go outside."

"Hmmmm," Kathy mumbled, "We have eggs, milk, and toast for breakfast. I bought all the ingredients for stew yesterday. We can have that for lunch and sandwiches for dinner. We're okay."

I stood to get dressed as I continued to troubleshoot our day, "I know you like to take the children outside after they finish their school, but not today. We need to keep both metal doors locked. We are safest inside."

Kathy looked towards the front door, "I hope no one rings the doorbell. I don't want to answer the door."

I rubbed my chin.

Should I tell her? Probably—

I looked at Kathy, "I need to tell you something. Remember when I had lunch with the newest missionary, Brother Fran?"

"Yes, you helped his family move in and showed a few places to shop."

"Brother Fran told me while he was out shopping, the police came to their apartment. They banged on the door, screaming 'Police—Open!' continually until Mrs. Fran opened the door. Three policemen burst in and started tearing the house apart. Mrs. Fran gathered their seven children into the kitchen and sat in the corner crying. She's six months pregnant, but the *militsiya* didn't care."

Kathy gasped, "What happened? Did Brother Fran come home to rescue them?"

I shook my head, "The police asked her for the passports. She handed them over, and they left with them. Brother Fran didn't get home for several hours. He had to hire a lawyer to find their passports. No one told them to register with the police. They paid a fine and then received the passports back."

Kathy sighed, "Now I'm definitely not answering the door!" Her face paled as she asked, "Are our passports registered?"

I smiled, "Yes, Sergey, the contact Brother Morrisey gave me, helped me register the second day we were here but I had no idea it was so important. Otherwise, I would have warned him."

The rest of the day was spent in prayer, Bible study and schooling. Kathy and I gave each other fearful looks whenever we heard police sirens on the street. From time to time one of us would venture onto the balcony to see if the *militsiya* was coming.

When Roman arrived that evening, the fax was laying on the dining table where we had language lessons. Roman picked up the fax and nonchalantly remarked, "Oh, I see you got my fax."

Kathy jumped up putting a finger in Roman's face, "That is from you? We were so nervous all day! How could you be so mean?"

I joined in the scolding, "Roman! What were you thinking? We spent the day cooped up in this tiny apartment fearing for our lives!"

Seeing his prank was not kindly received, Roman wiped the grin off his face and defensively declared, "I thought you Americans loved to joke. It was a joke."

THOUGHTS
- Have you ever been stalked or bullied by someone?
- How did it change your plans, actions, and feelings of security?

CHAPTER TWENTY-NINE

Tears for Babushka's Bible

And the child Samuel ministered unto the LORD before Eli. And the word of the LORD was precious in those days; there was no open vision. 1 Samuel 3:1

In early November, the day finally arrived when our much-anticipated container was delivered. We had spent two months dreaming of unpacking the Bibles, clothes for the kids, furniture, peanut butter, peanut M&Ms, washer & dryer, toilet paper, schoolbooks, commentaries, and many other things. After spending days clearing customs, it got loaded onto a flatbed and driven to our apartment.

People gathered along the narrow road staring as their "American family" unloaded their belongings. I quickly understood that Kathy would have to 'stay by the stuff' in the container while Roman, the kids and I carted box after box into the apartment. I thanked God for the afterthought of packing a hand truck in the container.

We frantically tried to get everything unloaded before Roman and I left on our next trip that evening. As I stood to admire the 100 boxes of Bibles stacked in our hallway, I turned to Roman, "I'm glad you agreed to help. It was supposed to arrive this morning but came this afternoon. The driver gave us four hours to empty it. We couldn't have handled it without you."

I set the hand truck against the wall. "If the container hadn't arrived, we would have run out of Bibles in Smolensk. Will you stay for dinner?"

We walked into our apartment and felt the cool breeze from an open window. Roman smiled and jerked a thumb over his shoulder towards Kathy in the kitchen, "Do you think I'd pass up her cooking? My parents told me not to get used to meals with all these spices, but I've come to love Kathy's Mexican food."

Tears for Babushka's Bible

We struggled to lift our heavy television and carried it into the living room. We set it on a stand. Wiping sweat off my brow, I turned the TV to face the futon.

Hannah's pigtails flopped as she called out. "Oh goodie, now I can watch my TV!" She scurried and sat on the futon trying to be patient as I hooked it up. She grabbed the remote and frantically pushed the buttons from channel to channel. She paused as each station's program appeared and spoke Russian. She came back to the first channel, stomped her foot, and pouted, "We bought this TV in America! Why does it speak Russian?"

I could not contain my laughter as I knelt beside Hannah, "Honey, TVs work with satellites, airwaves, and local channels. American channels can't reach all the way to Russia. I'm sorry."

Hannah frowned, "I don't understand you. I'll go ask Mom."

Smolensk Revival

Two nights later we stood in front of a crowd of 300 in Smolensk. I was my usual animated self as I preached, both hands waving.

Lord, this crowd is even more enthusiastic than last night.

I paused, put both hands on either side of the lectern and leaned forward. "So, if you want the peace that passes all understanding that I've talked about tonight, please pray with me." I folded my hands and looked at Roman out of the corner of my eye.

Good, he's keeping up.

I moved from the platform and stood in front of the crowd. "Let's pray. Lord Jesus, I know I have sinned and cannot save myself. I repent of my sins. I surrender my life to You. I gratefully accept Your gift of salvation that you purchased on the cross. Amen."

I opened my eyes and panicked.

Lord, where can I go?

A sea of Russians stormed the aisle and surrounded me.

They are going to trample me!

I yelled, "Please, be patient. I have some information to give you that will help you read your Bible." The first wave jostled us. They were pulling Bibles from our hands. Tracts littered the floor.

My voice drowned in the commotion. They did not wait for us to turn and pick up Bibles from the table. Many reached around us. I gritted my teeth when one man crawled through my legs to grab a Bible. A woman tore my shirt as she grabbed one I was handing to another lady.

Both Roman and I were bleeding from fingernail scratches. It took over 30 minutes before the crowd thinned.

Serving God Behind Enemy Lines

I then noticed an old woman hugging a Bible with part of my sleeve hanging from it. She approached us. We could barely understand as she cried. Roman calmed her down and translated. She nodded and kept kissing my hand.

"Brother Reasoner, she's telling me a story I've heard many times." He pointed and we moved towards a few chairs by the wall. "For over 70 years, under communism, they were forbidden to read this Book.

"She says, 'My grandmother had a Bible and loved it dearly. She kept it hidden and I never knew where. She told me it was for my safety. As I grew up and moved away, I often thought of the words she read to me, and I wondered what happened to that Precious Book. I wanted one. I prayed for years, and today you gave me one. Thank you! Thank you!'"

As Roman finished, she kept saying "Спасибо". She lunged and almost knocked me out of my chair as she hugged me. The elderly woman kissed her new prized Bible and walked away.

Next, an old man came and sat beside us. He talked so fast, Roman could not keep up, so he summarized. "For 70 years, we came to this hall to hear Soviet propaganda and lies. Now, we come to hear the Truth of God's Word and His great love for us." The man kissed his Bible and left.

I could not hold back the tears of gratitude to God for allowing me to be a part of His work in Russia. I came from a land where the Gospel is freely preached on the TV, radio, and in local churches. God brought me to a land famished for the Word of God.

What an awesome privilege given by God! Romans 15:20-21 came alive to me that night:

> *Yea, so have I strived to preach the gospel, not where Christ was named, lest I should build upon another man's foundation: But as it is written, To whom he was not spoken of, they shall see: and they that have not heard shall understand.*

More Decisions to Make

Our original plan when we got to Russia was to stay in Moscow until our container arrived and then move to Smolensk where we already had a church started from my survey trip.

One evening, we invited Roman over to discuss the idea. "Brother Ron, I don't think you have considered all the problems involved with moving to Smolensk. First, no one will rent their apartment to an American. Secondly, since going to Smolensk each week, I've learned that they don't have a good hospital—I thought Moscow hospitals were bad, but Smolensk is worse. You have five children to consider."

Tears for Babushka's Bible

Kathy interrupted, "But God is able to protect our children."

Roman rubbed his cheek, "Also, their soil is nuclear contaminated, and their water has too much iron and other minerals that can't be filtered out." He looked at me, "Haven't you noticed the gold teeth of the people there? Their teeth rot before they graduate from high school."

I echoed Kathy, "But God is able."

Roman sighed, "What about my people here in Moscow? There are 11 million people in this city and not one Gospel preaching Church."

I felt a dagger go through my heart.

I saw a concerned look on Kathy's face as she said, "I know you want the church in Smolensk to be strong before you give it over to the Russian pastor, but if we continue to live in Moscow, the children and I need a church. I do a Bible lesson while you are gone but we need preaching."

Lord, she is right. I need to decide.

I looked at Roman, "Perhaps we can find a strong Christian to preach every other week. I will rotate preaching in Moscow and Smolensk."

In the weeks that followed, we found a communist hall in our Moscow apartment complex to have Sunday services for $100 a week. We had 13 people our first service: our family, Roman, his mom and dad, Roman's best friend, and two girls from the playground.

The children sang *Jesus Loves Me* in English and Russian. I preached on the universal love of God. At the invitation, Roman's friend, Alexei came forward for salvation.

Roman's dad, Valerry, came up after the services. He spoke tolerable English, "Ron Reasoner, I want to tell you that I am already a Christian. When you came last year and Roman got baptized, he explained salvation and I repented. Roman baptized me."

Lord, let's leave the doctrine of the local church as the only institution with the authority to baptize for another time.

I asked, "Is your wife a Christian?"

Valerry lowered his voice, "No. She is not ready to admit God is real. I have always known Someone was watching over me. I refused to join the communist party because I knew they were wrong about God. I didn't know who God was until Roman told me about the Bible. He gave me one from your campaign and I read it through twice already."

Pastor Jerry Scheidbach Visits

In early December, three months after our arrival, Pastor Jerry Scheidbach came to Moscow. Before we left the States, Jerry and I had discussed starting a Bible Institute. The purpose of this trip was to do evangelistic meetings and to bring over the Bible Institute material.

Roman and I found a theatre in Moscow with a seating capacity of 300. I gave him a $200 budget for advertising. He purchased TV and radio time, and printed flyers to stick on light poles. We were blessed to now have a church to invite people to after revival meetings.

Roman put his hand on my shoulder as I taped up yet another flyer, "I am not sure how these meetings will go in Moscow. We have only had them in Smolensk. This might be a mistake."

I turned to Roman, "We must trust God. He works in people's hearts everywhere. We must pray; they will respond."

Lord, something else is bothering Roman. He has been distracted today.

"Roman, is something bothering you?"

He shuffled his feet in the newly fallen snow, "It's my dad. He has a large bump on his lower back. He went to the doctor, and they said it is cancer. They told him he will die in four months if they don't operate. Then he will be in the hospital for six months for chemotherapy."

"But—" I interjected, "why the doubtful tone? You don't think the doctors are right?"

"Brother Ron, we have a phrase in Russia, 'you go to the hospital to die.' Our medical care is so bad that no one goes to the hospital until there is no hope."

"What? Russia competed against America during the Cold War on all fronts, not just the space race, right?"

Roman fell silent. He sighed and looked away. I waited. He looked back with tears in his eyes, "I love my country, but it has many problems. One of them is our health care system. No one wants to be a doctor because they get the same salary as a factory worker, yet they work around blood and are responsible for people's lives. Imagine trying to save someone's life when you don't have the necessary medicine or instruments. Our government put all its money into the space race. There wasn't anything left for food or health care. Often the worst students become doctors."

"Wow! Doctors in America are the smartest, most educated, and best paid. They are expensive because we understand the importance of good health." I snapped my fingers, "Roman, I know an American Missionary Doctor in Moscow. He sees Russians and Americans for $25. I'll pay for your dad to get a second opinion."

The next day, we entered the small office where the doctor greeted us, "This must be Valerry. I'm glad you called. Come into the examination room and we'll have a look at your tumor."

Tears for Babushka's Bible

Five minutes later, the doctor slipped out. He smiled as he called me over, "Valerry has an ingrown hair that festered and got infected. I've numbed the area and am waiting for the local anesthesia to take affect before I dig it out. I just thought you would like to know the good news."

As Valerry and I walked back to the metro station, he could not stop smiling, "Brother Ron, thank you for saving my life! Who knows what might have happened in the Russian hospital! I might have gotten tuberculosis or some other deadly disease and died."

I smiled, "I'm just glad God allowed us to get into the doctor right away and he was able to correctly diagnose you. Praise the Lord!"

"Yes! Praise the Lord. I am going to be faithful to Him! I'll help you with the evangelistic meetings. I owe my life to God!"

We opened the first night of the revival with Pastor Scheidbach playing his banjo. He was the perfect stereotype of an American with his cowboy hat and boots. The Russian people loved it. There were 200 people on the first night. About 50% came forward at the invitation to pray the sinner's prayer.

In each Bible, we put a tract with the address of our Moscow Church. As we prepared to pass out Bibles after the service, I warned Pastor Scheidbach, "When you hand out Bibles, be quick to pull your arms back." He did not understand the importance of my instructions and almost lost his shirt.

As a result of the Moscow campaign, over 250 people got saved, and the Moscow Bible Baptist Church started to grow.

On one occasion, Roman pulled me aside after a service, "This is Sheriee Vladamirovna. She came to our evangelistic meeting and would like to tell her testimony."

I smiled and encouraged the short middle-aged woman to speak, "I am from small village in Central Russia. My parents were Christians." She paused for Roman to interpret, then continued, "We suffered great persecution. My father went to prison for preaching the Gospel. Often my teacher put me in front of my class and told the children to ridicule and tease me because I was seen going into a Baptist Church. I had no friends, but I knew God loved me."

Tears came to her eyes as she pulled a piece of paper from her pocket, "This is the only page of God's Word we had in my family. It is from the book of First John."

Valerry stood beside me and interjected, "I have heard that under communism only handwritten copies of God's Word were allowed."

I glanced at the paper in Sheriee's hand. Tears came to my eyes as she picked up the Bible we gave her. She kissed it and said, "I want to thank you for coming to Russia and giving me a complete Bible. This is a dream come true! I never thought I would have one." She took my hand and kissed it.

"Thank you for sharing your story," I said, "You are a blessing!"

On another occasion, Roman pulled me aside again and introduced Galena Sergeiovna. She also had a story, "My husband left 10 years ago for the war in Afghanistan, but never came home. My son is now 18 and cannot remember his father. The government refuses to tell us if he died in action or if he simply went elsewhere to start a new life. I went through a difficult time this past year. I was ready to end my life, but I saw your flyer about God. I came to your meeting and God saved me! Now I have real purpose in life! I read the Bible you gave me and sing the songs I remember from our church services. I have hope! Thank you for coming to Russia."

I looked for a hymnal through my tears and handed it to her, "Here, I want you to have this so you can remember the songs and learn new ones." Galena hugged me and kissed the tattered hymnal.

With the growth of the Moscow Church and people getting saved, it was time to have our first baptism. Roman secured a swimming pool in downtown Moscow. The day before the baptism, Valerry called. I could hardly understand him through his excitement, "Brother Ron, my wife and my brother asked Jesus to save them last night! After your sermon on Sunday, they asked me to explain salvation. They repented. Can they be baptized?"

I smiled, "Of course, if they believe in their hearts and have repented of their sins."

Roman could not miss his classes at the university, but they had a bomb threat that day. He arrived just in time to see his father, mother, uncle, and best friend be baptized into our local New Testament church.

What a blessing to be a missionary! I think of Charles Spurgeon who said, "If God has called you to be His servant, why stoop to be a King?"

THOUGHTS

- Imagine for a moment that you only had one handwritten page from the Bible.
- How would you feel when someone placed a complete copy of God's Word into your hands?

CHAPTER THIRTY

Raising Children in Russia

Train up a child in the way he should go: and when he is old, he will not depart from it. Proverbs 22:6

Helping on the Mission Field

"Joel!" I called, as I tied Jeremiah's shoes and tugged on his coat. "Tell your mother I have her coat and hat ready." I checked my watch, "It's time to leave for the evangelistic service."

My oldest turned his head and yelled, "Mom! Dad says it's time to leave."

I nudged him towards our bedroom. "I could've yelled myself. Go and tell her."

At that moment, Kathy stuck her head out of the kitchen, the two barrettes in her mouth bobbling up and down. "Almost ready. Finishing Hannah's hair." She waved a hairbrush at the rest of us lined up at the door. "Good, Keturah, you look precious in your dress. You and Hannah look like twins in your matching outfits." She waved the brush again, "Did you all brush your teeth?"

She grabbed a handful of Hannah's hair and deftly wove it into two pigtails. "Make sure they have their heavy coats."

I knelt and examined each of the boys. "These guys look sharp in their dark pants, white shirts and ties." I pointed towards the closet, "Go get your coats."

Ten minutes later we rode the elevator down to the street. Joel held the door open and let everyone exit. "Dad, can we do this every week?"

Micah and Keturah both nodded. All three chimed in. "We like helping with the service."

Serving God Behind Enemy Lines

I patted Joel on the head as we walked to the bus stop. "We'll see how the Russians like what we do. If it works, we'll try it again. If it doesn't, we'll try something else."

Roman met us at the third transfer on the way to Odintsovo, a suburb of Moscow. We climbed the stairs to the local train station. I bought eight tickets, stuffed them in my pocket, and directed everyone to board the waiting train.

After four stops, Roman lifted his backpack from between his legs, "This is our stop." Once we were off and counted heads, Roman and I took the lead. Kathy made sure the children kept up.

I raised a hand, "Over here kids, the Odintsovo Cultural Hall is this way." We walked through fresh snow as they followed me up the stairs and into the massive brick building.

Joel and Micah pushed hand carts across the floor and unloaded boxes of Bibles we brought with us. After Kathy fussed with Hannah's hair; she turned her attention to Jeremiah. She checked his face, pulled out a handkerchief and licked it with her tongue, "I don't know how one boy can find so much dirt in such a small amount of time." She finished, called out, "Okay, everyone, get on the stage."

Joel put the last box on the table and moved the cart alongside a wall. The three children ran to join Hannah and Jeremiah on the platform for a brief rehearsal.

As people started coming in, Roman and I mingled among them. We moved to the podium at 7 p.m., as Kathy and the children took their seats in the front row.

After a few announcements, I nodded and Kathy led the children, oldest to youngest, onto the platform. While she adjusted Joel's tie, I moved a hand towards them. "I thought it would be nice to have our children sing their favorite song for you." I lowered the microphone to the children's height. Roman and I stepped back to make room for them.

Kathy played the piano as the children sang *Jesus Loves Me*:

Иисус любит Он меня,Это твордо знаю я.
Jesus loves me! This I Know. For the Bible tells me so;
Он дети Себе берёт, И за Руки их видёт.
Little ones to Him belong; They are weak, but He is strong.
Да, Иисус любит Любит Он меня
Yes, Jesus loves me! Yes, Jesus loves me!
Да, Иисус любит Говорит мне Библия.
Yes, Jesus loves me! The Bible tells me so.

Raising Children in Russia

The Russians smiled, pointed, and clapped as the children sang. Kathy moved to the bottom of the stairs and led the children to their seats. I placed my Bible and notes on the lectern. It warmed my heart to see the approval on the faces of so many.

The children settled in their seats and Kathy passed out paper and pencils for them to "take notes." My desk was covered with pictures of me preaching.

Fifteen minutes after I finished, Roman, Kathy, and the children were surrounded by Russians fawning over them.

Lord, that Joel is amazing, it looks like he is not waiting for Roman to translate, he's conversing with that man in fluent Russian.

Evidently someone requested the children to sing again as the sound of their voices reverberated through the hall. I was hemmed in by the usual clamor for Bibles.

Bullies in the Park

Though Russian adults fawned over our children, some Russian youth preferred to bully them—especially targeting Joel and Micah. On one occasion, I took the children to the park on a Saturday morning, while Kathy and Roman went grocery shopping. I removed my jacket to play catch with our youngest, Jeremiah. He was doing well keeping up the Reasoner tradition of being baseball players. I reached for my jacket.

It only took a moment, but when I turned back around, I noticed a small gang approaching Joel and Micah on the swing.

They probably just want to take the swing from the boys.

But the gang was not interested in the swing. They were after my sons. They formed a wedge, splitting them up. The biggest boy in each group started hitting them.

Micah shouted, "Что ты делаешь? Ты с ума сошел?"

Lord, which do I help first?

Since Micah was closer and the boy attacking him was bigger, I focused on him. Out of the corner of my eye I saw Joel in a shoving match with his attackers. I heard him yell, "Вы ищете, чтобы получить травму?" but my Russian skills had vanished. It took a split second to realize that Joel was speaking in formal Russian while Micah was using street slang. *How fitting of their personalities.*

One boy raised his fist to hit Micah a second time when he saw me approaching and yelled, "Он с ними, пошли!"

As they ran off. I turned towards Micah. He had a fat lip.

Lord, what about the other children?

Serving God Behind Enemy Lines

I looked around and saw them hiding under a bench. I waved them over.

They lined up in birth order. I gave the boys a once over for any real damage. I looked at Joel, then went back to check Micah's lip. I dabbed the blood with my handkerchief. "What made them run away?"

Micah yelled, "Ouch," grabbed the handkerchief from my hand and was gentler with his wound than I had been. He applied more pressure and looked in the direction the gang had gone. "Dad, your leather jacket is what scared them. I heard them yell something about the Mafia as they ran off."

Keturah, Hannah, and Jeremiah were trembling as I knelt by their brothers.

I stared at Joel. "What did you say to those boys?"

Taking the children to the Russian Circus

He laughed, "The big guy pushed me, I pushed back. In the past six months I learned enough Russian to stand up to him. I told him: 'If you want a fight, both of us will get hurt. There will be a lot of blood. One or both of us will be in the hospital, probably you. Let's avoid all that and just be friends.'" He took a deep breath, "That's when I heard the guy beating up on Micah yell out 'Mafia."

Micah hugged Joel, "I don't know if it was your bravery or Dad's coat, but the Lord protected us!"

Hannah looked at her brothers. She walked over, grabbed Joel's hand, and reached up to stroke Micah's cheek. Finally, she turned to me with tears in her eyes and asked, "Why did they do that to Joel and Micah?"

I smiled and said, "I guess they heard us speaking English and they were afraid. Fear causes people to react strangely when they don't understand. It's called prejudice. Let's pray that God will help these kids understand that we are here to help them, not hurt them."

Hannah was shaking. She understood what I said but was still upset. Finally, she spoke, "Daddy, when we save all the Russians, can we go home?"

Baseball

One day in March of 1998, Kathy ran into the living room holding a copy of *The Moscow Times,* a free copy of an English newspaper distributed through the western stores. "Look! —it's a signup sheet for American Baseball. For all ages! Our kids can play! It starts this Saturday. Should I call and sign them up?"

I drew my attention away from my Bible study and took the paper from her, looking at the full-page advertisement. "Yeah—call them! It would do our kids good to interact with other Americans."

We left early that Saturday for Moscow State University, Moscow's only baseball field. We walked to the metro and switched lines several times. Two *militsiya* approached Joel and Micah as we awaited the next train. I quickly stood between them and my boys.

"Documents please!" the older policeman asked me in Russian. I pulled my passport out of my pocket and handed it to him. Upon seeing the American Eagle on the front cover, both policemen's eyes grew big. The older policeman pointed to my boys and in broken English asked, "What sticks for?"

It took me a moment to understand the question, but finally I replied in English, "These are baseball bats, and we are going to the baseball field at Moscow State University." I held up my baseball mitt as I spoke. It was obvious they could not understand me. Joel stepped forward and translated in perfect Russian.

After looking through the pages of my passport, the police nodded, handed it back and mumbled, "All the best," as they walked away. I turned to Kathy and smiled, "That was unnerving."

She laughed and pointed to the approaching train, "Keep moving— nothing to see here—just another day in Moscow."

We exited the metro at University Station. Kathy pulled the map out of her backpack, "It looks like the baseball field is across the street, through that park and down a side street." She spied the underground walkway and led the way as I took up the rear. We were quite the sight—each child carried their baseball mitt from the States. Joel and Micah had mitts in one hand and baseball bats slung over their shoulders.

As we entered the stadium, we were inundated with conversations in English. We had stepped into Little America smack dab in the middle of Moscow, Russia. I walked over to the registration table and introduced myself, "Hi, I'm Ron Reasoner. We called earlier this week and signed our children up."

The man sitting at the table jumped up and introduced himself, "Hi, I'm Dean and this is my wife, Jessie. Fill out these forms, pay up, and we'll help you get your kids to the right tryouts. I'm glad you came."

Dean's quick smile to his wife, did not escape me, but I ignored it. "Should we pay in rubles or dollars?" I asked.

"Either is fine," Dean answered grabbing the stack of rubles I held out. He handed it to Jessie, then led us to the various tryouts. Kathy stayed with Jeremiah and Hannah who were trying out for t-ball, while I went with Keturah for coach-pitch baseball. Dean took Joel and Micah to try out for Little League Baseball.

Eventually Dean circled back to me, "You have several children the same age as mine. My wife and I work at the Embassy. We have reserved the American Embassy *Dacha* (vacation home) next Monday and Tuesday. Would you like to join our family for some R&R?"

"I didn't even know the American Embassy had a *Dacha*. Is it far?"

"It is nearby on the shore of the Moscow River. I can give you the address. Bring your tennis racket—it has a tennis court. The kids should have fun with the American TV channels and the game room."

I smiled as Kathy approached, "Honey, Dean and his wife would like to invite us to the American Embassy *Dacha* next week. Do we have any other plans?"

Kathy tilted her head and tapped her finger on her chin, "Let me think—no—not anything that comes to mind."

I looked back at Dean, "It sounds like a plan! What can we bring?"

Dean smiled, "Don't worry about bringing anything, we have access to the commissary at the Embassy. It is I who should be asking you what you like. Root beer? Dr. Pepper? Perhaps an American beer?"

Kathy and I both lit up, "Root beer!" I exclaimed.

Equally excited, Kathy jumped up and down, "Dr. Pepper! Dr. Pepper!"

Dean laughed at our excitement and lowered his voice a bit, "I suppose you wouldn't be opposed if I brought a couple extra six packs for you to take home. What if I bring a few jars of peanut butter as well?"

Kathy grinned from ear to ear, "Oh my goodness! That would be a huge blessing! My kids miss peanut butter and jelly sandwiches so much!"

Dean smiled, "I'll see what other American food we can muster up from the commissary as well."

Monday morning, we piled into our Skoda Felicia hatchback. Joel and Micah sat in the baggage area while the three youngest sat in the backseat. Kathy pulled out her trusty Moscow map book and navigated me through the streets of Moscow until we finally reached the *Dacha*.

Dean, Jessie, and their boys greeted us in the driveway as we exited the car. Kathy was the first to speak, "I didn't know this kind of place existed. I was told there are no individual homes in Moscow proper."

Jessie smiled, "We are on an island called Serebryany Bor. It's not in the city limits."

Kathy grinned, "It's beautiful. Thank you so much for inviting us. We look forward to the peace and quiet away from the city life."

Their boys took our children inside. Soon Jeremiah came back out, "There's a foosball table and lots of toys. This place is cool."

I unpacked our tennis rackets and turned to Dean, "Are you ready to get beaten?" Dean smiled and led the way to the tennis court.

Jessie hollered sarcastically after us, "Don't worry about us! We'll bring in the bags and get lunch started."

Dean looked at me and smiled, "Did you hear something?"

I smiled back, "I believe we are already out of earshot."

Moments later, Kathy came out of the house carrying a root beer in one hand and an open Dr. Pepper in the other. I stopped mid-serve, dropped my racket, and ran off the court. I turned back to Dean who was still waiting for my serve, "Sorry, I see root beer!"

Dean followed me as I explained, "When we got to Russia, we missed our favorite drinks; mine is root beer, Kathy's is Dr. Pepper. We decided to pray for God to bring them to Russia. We joke that whoever gets their drink first is more spiritual. Little did we know both were available in Russia all this time!"

I took the can of root beer from Kathy, opened it, and took a big swig, drinking half the can. I pulled it from my mouth, burped, and gave a big smile, "Excuse me, but this is so good!"

Over the years, a great friendship developed between our family and the Martins. Our boys babysat their boys several times and our whole family was invited multiple times to have dinner in the American Embassy Compound. We saw a side of diplomatic life we otherwise would never have seen. The Embassy compound is a walled American City in downtown Moscow. We loved visiting there.

Joel & Micah are in the front row — me in the back as coach
Moscow State University in the background

On one occasion, I noticed a brick sitting on Dean's fireplace mantle, "What's with the brick?" I asked.

"That is from an Embassy project during the Cold War. We hired a Russian company to build an office building. When it was halfway completed, a group of American engineers came to inspect it. They discovered that every other brick had hidden listening devices. We tore the whole thing down and brought over American workers to build our new Embassy."

"Wow!" I said, "So cloak and dagger—but hey, we are in Russia. I guess no one can be too careful."

Dean cleared his throat and leaned forward, "Speaking of cloak and dagger, I have something I need to tell you."

I put my root beer down on the coffee table and leaned forward as well, "Why so serious?"

Dean half smiled and admitted, "When your family signed up for Baseball, I was assigned to befriend you. We know your brother is in military intelligence."

I interrupted Dean, "How?"

Dean put his hand up, "Let me finish. I was assigned to find out if your Russian was good enough to become a double agent. I want to let you know that I filed my report last week."

Trying to hide my disappointment and feelings of betrayal, I sighed, "Well, what did you say?"

Dean smiled, "I concluded that our government need not worry about you being a double agent—you will never speak Russian well enough AND you invite me to church and preach to me about God and salvation every time we are together. You really are a missionary trying to win souls!"

Well Lord, at least we are deemed faithful witnesses for You!

THOUGHTS

- When is the last time you prayed for the protection of missionary children that your church supports?
- Children are a vital part of ministering on the field.
- Missionary children are the best source of future missionaries because they already know the language and culture of their field.

Chapter Thirty-One

2,000 Churches by 2000

Wherefore come out from among them, and be ye separate, saith the Lord, and touch not the unclean thing; and I will receive you. And will be a Father unto you, and ye shall be my sons and daughters, saith the Lord Almighty.
2 Corinthians 6:17-18

In 1996, we traveled back to the States to raise funds for buying a house in Russia. During that time, Roman transitioned to another church where his girlfriend attended. We didn't see much of him when we got back from furlough. We also moved into a new apartment in the Marino neighborhood of Moscow. It was a busy time and the next two years flew by quickly.

In 1998, we celebrated four years in Russia. The Moscow Church was growing. The Smolensk Church merged with another Independent Baptist Church and was growing.

One day, Joel and Micah burst through the front door. At 14 and 13 respectively, they could go outside and roller blade with their Russian friends if they checked back in every hour. I heard them talking excitedly as they opened the front door, "Dad, guess what?"

I met them in the hallway and took the bait, "What?"

Joel raced to tell before Micah could, "There are a bunch of Americans passing out free Russian Bibles near the metro station."

Micah injected, "Yeah, Dad, you should go and see who they are. Maybe you know them."

Kathy laughed, "You boys have been around the world. You know how big it is. It's a slim to none chance we know them." She turned and continued, "But, I need to get sour cream and mayonnaise for the beef stroganoff tonight. Maybe we should go together."

The children singing at Corridor Baptist Church while on furlough in 1996 —From left to right: Joel, Micah, Keturah, Hannah & Jeremiah

I looked at Joel, "You are in charge while your mom and I are gone. Don't go outside with the kids. Watch a movie until we return."

Kathy and I locked the door as we left. "I think it is a bunch of neo-evangelicals. What's your bet?" Kathy asked as I pushed the button for the first floor.

"I'm going with Pentecostal. There seem to be a lot of them in this area." We exited onto the street and walked toward the metro station. There were a few people in line to get Bibles, but nothing like the crowds of the early 90's. Moscow had a prosperous, thriving economy now and few people seemed to need or care about God. They sought the almighty American dollar.

Serving God Behind Enemy Lines

As we approached the front of the line, I did a double take. I grabbed Kathy's arm, "Hey, don't we know that guy? Isn't that Bob Valles from Pacific Coast Baptist Bible College?"

Kathy strained her neck around the lady in front of her. Finally, she confirmed, "It sure looks like him. Go introduce yourself."

I slipped out of line and walked behind the table, "Excuse me. My name is Ron Reasoner."

Bob's eyes lit up as he grabbed me in a big bear hug, "Ron, It's me—Bob Valles. Fancy meeting you in Russia. What are you doing here? I haven't seen you since I graduated from Bible College. Are you with the '2,000 churches by 2000 Campaign' also?"

I shrugged, "I have no idea what you are talking about. After college, I started a church in Hillsboro, Oregon. When the doors of Russia opened, God called us here." I grabbed Kathy's hand as she approached, "Remember my wife, Kathy? We've been in Russia four years. We live in that building over there." I asked, "What are you doing here?"

Bob smiled, "When you and Kathy got together at Bible College, I knew you two were going to do great things." He gestured towards the middle of the square. "I'm the assistant pastor of an Independent Baptist church in New Philadelphia, Ohio. There are 105 men from our church here helping Missionary Medford start a new church. Do you know Brother Medford from Belarus?"

"I've heard the name. I'm not sure we have ever met."

"Come, I'll introduce you to my pastor."

Kathy spoke up, "I'm going to the store and then heading home. We have five children and even though the eldest is 14, I can't leave them long before World War III starts. I hope we talk again soon, Bob. It was great to see you."

I followed Bob into a tent near a makeshift stage. "Hey, everyone, look who I found on the streets—an old college mate. This is Ron Reasoner. He is a missionary here. Ron, this is my Pastor, Mark, and this is Missionary Medford."

Missionary Medford looked at me with squinted eyes and an obvious frown. Finally, he stood and shook my hand, "Ron Reasoner. I've heard your name before. How long have you been in Russia?"

"Going on five years next month," I replied, "We started an Independent Fundamental Baptist Church right here in Marino."

Pastor Mark stood up and shook my hand, "You may be the answers to our prayers. We are holding an evangelistic campaign. I was just telling Brother Medford that I hate to start a church and leave it for the wolves to feast on. Surely, we can just feed the people who get saved into your church. Doesn't that sound great, Brother Medford?"

A hint of anger crossed Brother Medford's face before he composed himself and motioned for me to take a seat, "I'd like to share my vision for '2,000 churches in Russia by the year 2000'." He leaned forward, "That is if you have a few moments."

I listened for 20 minutes as he elaborated on his vision. "You see, Brother Ron, we blitz a community, find believers, convert many, the Lord provides leaders for each church, then we move on to the next town." He reached over and picked up a water bottle from a bucket on the table. "So, what do you think? Will you consider joining us? If so, we'll feed all the converts we get in this district to your ministry."

My stomach rumbled.

Lord, what he says is impressive. But is this part of Your plan for my ministry? Is he legitimate?

I motioned towards his people wandering the square, talking to Russians, some with an interpreter, while others evidently with some Russian language skills, were conversing one-on-one with passersby. "Pastor, I need to ask a few questions. I'm impressed with the coordination it took to get an event such as this into Russia." I pointed to him and then myself, "I can only assume that since we're both Independent Fundamental Baptists that we're pretty close on our doctrine." I leaned forward, "Let me pray about it. I'll come to your open-air meeting tomorrow and hopefully by then, God will give me peace one way or the other."

I stood to leave, shook hands with the three men and headed home.

As I entered the apartment, Joel and Micah met me in the hall. Joel had a mischievous look on his face. Together he and Micah broke out in a chorus of, *It's a small world after all—*

I smiled, "It is indeed. Mom must have told you that we met someone from college, didn't she?"

That evening, after the children were in bed, Kathy dried while I put away the dishes. She handed me a plate, "What's your take on this, Brother Medford?"

I frowned. "I can't put my finger on it. He seems more interested in what we can do for him, not what he can do for the Kingdom of God. I feel he doesn't like that we're here and he needs us. Pastor Mark's church gave him a lot of money for this campaign. Now they want converts fed into our church when Brother Medford wanted to start his own."

My wife grabbed two cups and tea bags from the cupboard. She took a breath as she poured water. "Do you think he will just report that he started our church and call it one of his 2,000?"

"I don't know. I wouldn't put it past him. But honestly, it is God's Church, not ours and it won't matter in eternity who started it. All that matters is that souls were saved."

"You are right. How will our working with him help the Kingdom?" She brought the cups to the table, and I pulled our chairs out for us to sit.

I pulled a pad of paper and pen from my shirt pocket. I wrote "pros" on the left side of the sheet. "On the plus side they do have a good discipleship program. Pastor Mark offered to fly me to the States, so I can attend a training session on the program."

Kathy set her cup on its saucer. "Did he give you a copy of the material? How's it laid out? Is it something you think we will use here with the Russian people?" She tapped my arm. "Even if he pays your expenses, if it's not a viable program for us, it's a waste of his time and ours."

"That is a good point. We have been praying for a discipleship program to use here. Maybe this is the answer to our prayer." I wrote this down under the "pro" side. I set the pen down, "On the negative side, Missionary Medford comes across as a glory-seeker." I wrote that under the "Cons".

Kathy mused, "I wonder where he gets the helpers. Maybe he works with the Russian Baptists."

I wrote that down under "cons."

"I have no interest in working with the Russian Baptists. You know they don't believe in eternal security, and they don't believe in the autonomy of the local New Testament Church. Not to mention they use real wine and leavened bread in their Lord's Supper."

Kathy interrupted, "You definitely need to know if working with him means working with the Russian Baptists."

Thirty minutes and two cups of tea later, I pushed the paper in front of her. "Well, that's it; ten pros and ten cons." I closed the pad. "Thanks for your help. We should pray. I need to get back to him tomorrow. They are having a concert and then preaching in our little community square at 2 p.m. We'll go and see what God does."

We spent the next hour on our knees before the Lord.

The next morning revealed a beautiful summer day. We put Joel in charge so Kathy and I could go to the concert and service. I went straight to the tent, got a handful of Russian Bibles, and began passing them out.

Almost immediately, a tall, dark headed Russian approached me, "Who you and what you do?" he asked in broken English.

"I'm Ron Reasoner and I'm a missionary telling the Russian people about Jesus. Have you ever asked Jesus to save you?"

The tall Russian smiled and said, "I'm Andre. I am Christian. I help with this meeting, and I must make sure you are not a Jehovah's Witness or a Mormon. Are you a Baptist?"

I smiled, "Yes, Andre. It is nice to make your acquaintance. We have a church here in Marino, and we would love to have you visit." I pulled a tract from my jacket pocket and handed it to him. I turned to Kathy and introduced her, "Andre, this is my wife, Kathy. We have five children."

"Wow! Five children! You are rich!" Andre grinned.

I smiled, "Yes, I am rich in blessings from the Lord. God is good."

Andre replied, "I have a wife and daughter. They spend the summer in Ukraine but will come back in two weeks. She is English teacher and will be very welcome to meet Americans. I come to your church."

I wanted to check Andre's testimony, so I asked, "Andre, how long have you been a Christian?"

"I became Christian in university. I study to be pilot, but I did not finish all years. I only now, two years ago, began to live for Christ. I go to Central Baptist Church in downtown Moscow since my family move here six months ago from Ukraine."

Andre helped us pass out tracts and interpreted when I could not fully understand.

Suddenly a microphone began to screech and loud, rock music began to play over the loudspeakers on the makeshift stage. A group came onstage and introduced themselves as the Christian Band, "Agape."

A husky Russian voice started singing, I felt my blood pressure rise as I heard the words. I handed the remaining two Bibles in my hand to Kathy, then moved to where I could see the platform. She followed.

I was irate, "Honey, this is ridiculous. That band says they're Christians, but the words don't have any scriptural significance." I shook my head and frowned. "What solid Christian organization would hire a band that doesn't play Christian music?" I glanced up as a rather long riff belched from the speakers. "I bind Satan from this square. I pray that some good will come from all this."

I saw Bob in the crowd and hurried over to him. His smile turned to a frown and then a scowl as I pointed towards the screeches emanating from the other side of the square. "Are you responsible for that?"

He took a deep breath and sighed. "Unfortunately, yes. Missionary Medford contracted a Russian church to provide Christian music. He trusted them to hire a 'Christian' band."

Bob craned his neck and peered through the crowd. "Come with me."

We entered the tent where Brother Medford was calmly drinking a soda. I walked up to him and demanded, "Do you approve of this music? I need an answer before I spend any more time with you."

The startled look on his face told me he was not used to being confronted.

Lord, give me strength to stand strong.

Medford's eyes bulged, his jaw clenched, then relaxed. "Okay, that's a fair question." He tilted his head towards the band. "I'm upset as well. Our advance team contracted with the Central Baptist Church to provide music. They got the permits. I assumed that since the band leader called himself a Christian that they assumed the band members were also Christians."

He crossed his legs and clasped his hands over a knee. "Believe me, I agree. We will not use this band again. I will personally instruct the Russian Baptists on what is acceptable as to what type of music we utilize."

He rose and extended his hand. "Please come to our meeting tonight. Maybe we can work together and bring the Gospel to the Russians. We have rented a room in the Marino Mall. Perhaps your church can meet there as well if we decide to work together."

Bob walked out with me, "Ron, I have talked with men in our church, and we want all the people that get saved from this campaign to go to your church. Brother Medford has reluctantly agreed."

"Why is there any question? We are both Independent Baptists!"

"I'm afraid he might be a little too ambitious about getting those 2,000 churches by the year 2000." Bob chuckled, "I wouldn't doubt it if he goes back to America and reports that he started your church."

I stopped to face Bob, "It's not my church. Only God builds the church so if someone else wants to take credit for work I have done, I'm not worried about it. God knows the truth."

"Come to the meeting. We will be going over the first discipleship lesson."

"Who wrote the discipleship lessons? I won't have anything to do with the Russian Baptist doctrines."

Bob smiled, "No, we brought this book over from America. We use it in our church."

The next evening, Kathy and I went to the discipleship meeting. There were about 20 people from the community who were interested. A woman clutched my arm then released her grip, pointing to the back of the hall. I turned and saw a Russian Orthodox Bishop, in full regalia, with a priest at his side standing at the back of the room.

What's going on?

Brother Medford broke away from the crowd and rushed to meet the cleric. Immediately upon reaching him, the bishop extended his hand. Brother Medford knelt and kissed the ring on the bishop's right hand and said a few words.

I could not hear what the bishop said before he turned and exited the building. Bob and several others stood beside me as Brother Medford approached. "What was that?" I asked.

A look of surprise came across his face, and he smiled. "Why, Brother Reasoner, the Lord set up a divine appointment. The local bishop just told me he approved our meeting. He gave us permission to preach." He straightened up, "I have found it is best to keep good relations with the Orthodox Church."

"I disagree," I challenged.

Brother Medford puffed his chest out, "I did my research. If you'd done the same, you would know the Russian Mafia and the Russian Orthodox Church will harm or even kill those who oppose the church. You can thank me later when you don't have any problems with the Orthodox church in the future! At least now we don't have to worry about the bishop or mafia hurting us."

I frowned and shook my head, "We bow to no one but Christ."

Brother Medford's cold stare sent chills down my spine. He turned and walked away.

Bob came up to stand by me, "We leave tomorrow morning, but from what I saw here today, we want to work with you."

I shook my head, "I want to make it clear that Brother Medford has no authority over the Marino Church. We are sent from our home church in Oregon, but the head of our church is Jesus Christ, and I am the under shepherd here. I answer to only Christ and my sending pastor. We will be happy to accept any new converts into our church, baptize and disciple them, but understand they will be taught local church authority."

Pastor Mark, who was standing behind me, tapped me on the shoulder, "We wouldn't want it any other way."

Serving God Behind Enemy Lines

A few weeks later Andre met me at the Moscow airport baggage claim carousel. He loaded my bags onto a cart and pointed to the nearest exit. "I parked out this way." Soon we were driving towards our home. "How was your trip to America, Brother Ron? What did you think of discipleship program?"

I tapped my briefcase. "It's very good. I have a floppy drive containing the entire 16-week course. I already have a Russian man working on a translation." I leaned back in my seat and rubbed my eyes. "It's good to be home. I'm so tired."

The streetlights flickered through the car windows as we passed them. "Tell me, Andre, what's new with the ministry? Has your family returned yet from Ukraine?"

His hands whipped the steering wheel around as he turned a corner. "The '2,000 by 2000' people have moved on." He tapped his chest with a finger, "I don't have a job anymore. They'll hire other Russians in the next town." He turned onto the highway towards Marino; "Tomorrow I start a new job at a book publisher. They pay $200 a month. That will not pay rent and buy food for my small family."

I pulled my notepad from my shirt pocket and opened it to the third page. I scribbled, 'Good paying job for Andre' on my daily prayer page and then put the pad away. "I'll be praying you'll find better work soon."

He pulled off the highway and headed down our street. "Oh yes. I want to work in the aviation industry." He pulled the car to a stop in front of our apartment building.

THOUGHTS

- How much are you willing to compromise to get the Gospel out?
- Do you have a warning system in place to stop you from slipping into the world's methods?

CHAPTER THIRTY-TWO

Buying a Home in Russia

And every one that hath forsaken houses, or brethren, or sisters, or father, or mother, or wife, or children, or lands, for my name's sake, shall receive a hundredfold, and shall inherit everlasting life. Matthew 19:29

"Joel, Micah, Keturah, Hannah, Jeremiah, come in here NOW. I won't tell you again!" We had an important decision to make. My wife and I sat at opposite ends of the kitchen table. She pursed her lips then stuck her head into the hallway.

We heard rapid footsteps as they ran and slid down the hall, pulled their chairs out, and sat with their hands angelically folded. Kathy pointed to Micah. "I told you 15 minutes ago to get the others—that it's time for our family talk."

I pointed to Kathy, "Why can't you children listen and obey? Your mother and I have told you many times when we call—you come. Stop what you're doing—and come." I nodded to Kathy. "Mother, please read the scripture we chose, and then pray."

Kathy flipped through her Bible until she came to the correct page, "Philippians 4:6-7,

"Be careful for nothing; but in every thing by prayer and supplication with thanksgiving let your requests be made known unto God. And the peace of God, which passeth all understanding, shall keep your hearts and minds through Christ Jesus."

She closed her Bible, folded her hands, then looked at her children as they did the same. She bowed her head. "Heavenly Father, we thank You for this opportunity to show the children Your mercy and blessings—that

You do answer prayer. Give us wisdom and help us trust You. In Jesus name we ask and pray, Amen."

I leaned forward; "This is going to be a long family talk. I had an appointment with Dr. Jones today."

Keturah's eyes widened. "Are you going to die?"

Kathy gave Keturah her 'think before you speak look' as I reached across the table and put my hand on her forearm. "No, but he told me my coughing won't get any better if we continue to live in Moscow." A collective sigh came from the children. "We have to make changes."

I looked at the concern in each of their faces and continued, "Like your mom just prayed, we need direction from God. Where do we move? We want to stay in Russia, in the Moscow area even. But how large of a home do we buy? Will the government allow us to buy a home in Russia? Where will we get the money?"

Hands went up around the table. It seemed they all had an idea. I held my hand up and everyone quieted down. I took a deep breath. "Now, first off, Doc says I'm getting what's called black lung disease. Russians who survive the early stages build up a tolerance for the pollution that has accumulated in their lungs. In my case he feels it would be best for us to move back to the States or at least to the outskirts of Moscow where the air is cleaner."

House Hunting

Thus began our quest to find a home outside the pollution zone. We had been looking for houses for six months when the Russian economy collapsed on August 17, 1998. Hyperinflation became rampant. Banks went defunct, businesses closed, and many people lost their jobs.

While it was difficult to see the poverty and desperation of the early 1990s return, it changed the housing market overnight and suddenly we could afford a much nicer house with our American dollars.

One day in February 1999, we opened a local paper, *From Hand to Hand,* and laid it in front of us. Kathy sighed, "We have seen many houses, but nothing fits us." She pointed to the paper. "What about this property about 20 kilometers—12.42 miles, from here." My eyes fixated on the advertisement. Kathy's finger slid on the paper as she read and translated the ad:

"For Sale large 1,000 square meter house on 15 Sotoks (land size)
30,000 US Dollars"

She tapped a finger on the advertisement. "For this price it must be a misprint. It's probably only 100 square meters which is about the size of this apartment."

Buying a Home in Russia

"Or—" I interjected, "it's a rundown shack. Worse yet, it might be a scam."

I reached across the table; she slid the paper towards me. "I think we should look at it anyway." I copied the phone number onto the pad in front of me. "I'll call tomorrow. Maybe we can look at it in the afternoon."

Kathy smiled, "Perhaps we should have our interpreter call. When the seller hears your accent, the price will double."

Lord, I know I'm being optimistic, but house prices have dropped since the Russian economy collapsed. Maybe the price really is $30,000.

On a cold February afternoon, I parked our Skoda where it would not get stuck in the snow. We stared at the house. Kathy pointed to what appeared to be a garage. "It'll be expensive to finish the roof on that." I removed the keys from the ignition and opened the door. Kathy continued her assessment, "This house is more than 100 square meters. This location would be perfect for us. Look at the forest. That's exactly what the doctor ordered."

Our feet sunk two feet into the snowy driveway. Kathy pointed to the house. "I don't know what the inside is like but look at the windows!"

My eyes were drawn to the window openings, "What windows?"

"Exactly!" Kathy replied, "There aren't any! This is just bricks with a roof on top. If the inside is like the outside, who knows how much it's going to cost to make it livable."

"I agree, and if we wipe out the building fund to buy this place, how will we pay to remodel it?"

I pointed to a man by the front door in a large overcoat standing next to a young Russian soldier. I waved to the man. Then whispered out of the side of my mouth. "Wait here; I'll see if that's the owner."

Lord? Who is this guy? Why does he need a guard to sell a house?

He turned as I approached. I smiled, nodded, and in Russian said, "Добрый день. Я Рон Ризонер. Мы приехали чтобы посмотреть на вашего дома."

"I am General Dobrow." He smiled, "Da, Da, you come and look at house." He led the way to the front of the house. I turned and motioned to Kathy.

The four of us entered the front door and stepped into a large living room. "How big is your home?"

He replied, "1,000 square meters—it has a dance floor and many large rooms." He waited for Kathy to finish looking into several of the large side rooms. I could tell by the look on her face something was wrong.

"Why is there no floor in that room? It's just dirt." Kathy asked.

Serving God Behind Enemy Lines

The General waved his hand and replied, "It's a simple fix."

I moved towards a wall and ran a hand over a windowsill. Immediately the General remarked, "The exterior walls are a full meter thick. My house is like a fortress."

I turned to the two men, "General, I have to be honest with you. I wonder why you are only asking 30,000 American dollars."

His face turned white. "Oh no! Who gave you that price? I must have $189,000."

I pulled the paper from my pocket and showed the General the advertisement. He snarled, "That must have been my assistant! He is a fool. You must continue to look at my beautiful home. Maybe we can make a deal. I owe money to the Russian Mafia. If I don't pay, even my soldiers can't protect me."

We moved through the debris-laden floor towards a plank that led upstairs. I started up, then turned back to hold Kathy's right hand as she put her left hand on the wall to steady herself. We walked into a huge room, large enough for a church auditorium.

This must be the dance hall.

I grabbed Kathy's hand again as we jumped across a two-feet wide chasm. It went all the way to the basement 25 feet below. Kathy gasped, "Look down! There is one solid block of ice. It looks deep."

I stopped the General and asked, "Why is there ice in the basement?"

The General frowned, "This subdivision is built on a swamp. This house has been vacant for six years because I do not have money to finish it. The snow melts into the basement and makes a lake. You will need several sump pumps to keep the basement dry. This house is just a box and comes as is—no lights, no water, no plumbing; none of it is done yet."

We walked up a plank to yet another level. Kathy whispered, "There are seven levels in this home if we count the basement. This is too much for us. I want a home where each child has their own room, and you can have an office. If this is the place God has for us, He has much greater plans than I do."

I smiled and whispered back,

"For as the heavens are higher than the earth, so are my ways higher than your ways, and my thoughts than your thoughts." (Isaiah 55:9)

As we reached the top level, I began to imagine it as our personal living quarters.

Lord, this is perfect! We'll have a lot of work to do, but for the right price we—I mean YOU can handle it.

Buying a Home in Russia

"General, your house is beautiful. I like that it's not finished so we can remodel to suit us."

His eyes widened and he said something so fast I did not understand a word. After an awkward silence and observing the blank look on my face, he slowly repeated himself, "If you like, I sell you all this for $189,000. I spent more than $180,000 on the bricks to build this structure."

Kathy and I frowned. I held my hands out. "General, I love your house. It would be perfect, but we don't have that kind of money. We thought the ad in the paper was a misprint. I guess this was a mistake." I took Kathy's hand and started back down the planks. I turned back and said, "Thank you for your time."

As we got into the car to leave, I turned to Kathy, "I really liked this house. It is like the ministry compound of Hudson Taylor or Adoniram Judson. Too bad the ad was a mistake."

Kathy sighed, "Stop by a newspaper kiosk on our way home. I'll get the latest ads. I guess God has something else." She frowned, "It would have been so perfect."

"I'm tired of looking. We've seen so many over the past six months."

Kathy took in a deep breath, "I wonder how many more we will see before God gives us the right one."

Four months later we pulled our Skoda into the driveway of General Dobrow's house. I stared at the huge edifice, "This is by far my favorite home. I was surprised when General Dobrow asked us to come see it again."

Kathy tilted her head sideways, "You haven't been scared away by the other missionaries laughing at you for trying to buy a house?"

I opened my car door, "No, and I'm not frightened by Valerry's horror stories of people being stabbed and murdered because they have a large home." I pulled the keys from the ignition and continued, "We are doing God's work. He knows what we need. He knows my health problems. I'm trusting Him."

Kathy opened the passenger door. "Amen."

We walked along the mud path to the main entrance of the house where General Dobrow was waiting. He smiled, "Today is the day, I know today is the day you will buy my beautiful home."

Kathy's hand found mine as I greeted him, "I was surprised when you called. You said you have a lower offer. What is it?"

The General walked into the house toward the basement opening, "See! The ice has melted, and I pumped all the water out."

We followed and investigated the basement, "That's wonderful General. As I told you before, we love your home, but we are missionaries and don't have a lot of money. What is your new price?"

Front of the Compound — Notice no windows, missing parts of the roofing, and it is overgrown with bushes

He grinned, "I must have money soon. I will sell you my home for $75,000."

Kathy and I both sighed in unison. I turned to face the front door, "General, I'm sorry, but that is still too much. It will take a lot to finish this home. We don't have that kind of money."

The General pursed his lips, his eyebrows furrowed, and he kept crossing and uncrossing his arms. He started to talk several times, but the words did not come out. Finally, he let loose a torrent of Russian.

While he talked, Kathy and I moved where the last vestiges of sunlight poured through an opening of a window. I whispered, "Dear, look at that sunset, if we could buy this, we could view the sun setting over the trees every night. It's beautiful. Lord, I pray we can make a deal." Grabbing her hand, I began our family prayer, "Lord, we are Your servants, ready to do Your will. Lead us where You need us until we are home with You."

Kathy nodded to the Russians as they came across the room. She whispered, "Amen, let it be so Lord."

The General stopped in front of me, "I need to sell this home for a very low price. I cannot afford to finish the work. No other Russians want to buy it because the house is too big and too expensive to finish." He paused, shuffled his feet, then looked me in the eye, "The Russian Mafia told me today they want their money before Constitution Day on June 13th or else—" He slid a finger across his neck, shuddered, and continued, "I will sell you the house for 75,000 US dollars."

"I'm sorry, General. We don't have that much."

I saw the anger and disappointment on his face before he turned towards the front entry to leave, "I will find another buyer!" he yelled over his shoulder.

That evening I looked up as Kathy came into the kitchen from putting the younger children to bed. "I still think the General's house is the best we've seen." I picked up the latest financial statement of our monthly support. "The money's just not there."

Kathy sighed, "It would be so perfect. A dormitory above the garage, a church auditorium in the dance hall. Imagine the souls that would be saved in that building!"

I grimaced, "I like your idea of a dormitory. We just don't have that much money." I put her hands in mine. "We don't believe in the prosperity gospel. We will offer the money we have. We will not offer more and expect the Lord to fill in the gap." I put my head in my hands. "Lord, I don't know where else to look. Every other place we've looked at doesn't compare to the General's."

She put her hand on mine, "We've fasted and prayed several times about this. Maybe the Lord is telling us to keep looking."

I tapped my fingers on the tabletop. "Maybe it's for the best. The General's house has no plumbing, electricity, no heating system, the walls need to be plastered, and the window package alone will be over $10,000. I can't even begin to estimate what it will cost to make it livable."

Kathy frowned, "Well, it's 9 p.m. and it's your turn to pray with the older children."

I steadied myself at the door as a coughing fit overcame me. Joel rose on one elbow, "Dad, I know the Lord's going to answer our prayers. We're going to move where it'll be healthier for you. Micah and I were just praying that it would be big enough for us to even have church services on our property."

I patted them on the head. "That's a good prayer." I took a deep labored breath. "We'll have to—"

Serving God Behind Enemy Lines

I stopped as I heard Kathy pick up the phone. "Yes, General, he's right here."

The boys' eyes widened as we heard Kathy rush down the hall and whisper, "The General's on the phone."

I gave her a quick hug. "You pray with them while I see what's on his mind."

She nodded and went into their room.

I picked up the receiver. "Good evening, General."

"Are you still interested in buying my wonderful house?"

Movement down the hall caught my eye. I turned and saw Kathy and the boys watching me. I gave them a thumbs up.

Focus! Lord, help me focus.

"General, I would be honored to buy your beautiful house but I'm a missionary and don't have $75,000.

The General sighed, "What about $45,000? Would you buy it for $45,000?"

Lord, help me be firm. Don't let me mess this up.

"You know I love your home, but I don't have $45,000."

The General gruffly replied, "How much do you have?"

I meekly said, "$30,000 is all I can scrape together."

There was silence, and I heard muffled voices, then the General said, "Okay, you come tomorrow and sign papers for $30,000."

I dropped the receiver into its cradle and yelled, "HALLELUJAH." Keturah and Hannah came out of their room. "Daddy, what's wrong?"

"Nothing, Sweethearts. Absolutely nothing!"

The next morning, Kathy replaced a broken rubber band as she counted stacks of 100-dollar bills and placed them in my briefcase. "One, two, three, four, five, six, seven, eight, nine, ten—Here's another $1,000. Could you put the rubber band on it?" She straightened a stack that had fallen with one hand and reached for another handful of bills. "I don't feel comfortable carrying all this cash on the street." She resumed counting.

I continued rubber banding the bills in stacks of 10. "I don't either, but God has brought us this far. He will see us through it." I shoved another pile of bills towards her side of the table.

She paused and looked at me, "I hope we aren't walking into an ambush. I just keep seeing AK-47's pointed at our heads. Are we fools?"

I grunted and took the pile of cash, "That's it. 30 stacks of 10, 100-dollar bills, is 30,000 in US dollars."

Buying a Home in Russia

Kathy filled the briefcase, snapped it shut and pushed it to me, "I know Pastor Igor is going to be there in the background as a witness, but the General has guards. We'll be no match."

I spun the combination lock and set it on the floor next to the window. "We have to remember; we've prayed about this. Remember in 2 Kings 6:15-16; Elijah's servant was afraid of the army that had come to kill Elijah?"

She nodded. "That's right, his answer was—

"Fear not: for they that be with us are more than they that be with them."

The next morning, on June 29th, 1999, Kathy got the kids started on school. I looked at my watch, "We will be late if we don't leave now!" I grabbed my leather coat. "I'll get the car from the guarded parking lot. Meet me downstairs in 15 minutes."

Kathy was waiting when I pulled up. She jumped in and we rehearsed the plan, "Remember, first we go and get the paperwork done for the house and land to be in our name. THEN we come home, get the money, and go to Cber Bank. We're doing the exchange of the legal documents for the $30,000 in front of the ATM. All ATMs have cameras. That way if something goes wrong, we have proof."

We picked up our Ukrainian Pastor friend, Igor, who had offered the use of his lawyer, Tanya, and their legal knowledge of purchasing a home in Russia. I drove towards the resort where General Dobrow was now the Administrator. They took Kathy's passport, then Pastor Igor, our lawyer and General Dobrow got in a car to go to the Land Registration building. They thought it best we Americans stayed behind.

"I think it is a good idea we decided to put the house in my name," Kathy said, as we sat on a park bench at the resort, "We know when the Russian government wants to get rid of an American family, they revoke the man's visa knowing his family will not stay in Russia without him."

I nodded, "As we discussed, if I get kicked out, you can return to sell the house. It's a good plan."

Not 30 minutes later, the car drove back. Pastor Igor, the lawyer, the General and the Soldier piled out of the car and called us over. Tanya spoke up, "There is a new law that foreigners cannot own land. We cannot put the land in your name." She turned and pointed, "We can put it in Pastor Igor's name and perhaps in the future, the law will change. As far as the house goes, it is not complete enough for the Land Registration office to give us a deed for the house. They said when you finish the house, it can be in your name, but not the land. We can have a private contract between you and Pastor Igor that says you own the land."

Kathy and I stared at each other. I asked, "Pastor Igor, would it be a problem for the land to be in your name?"

Pastor Igor smiled, "I would be honored to help a brother in Christ."

Our lawyer gave Kathy her passport. Tanya turned to me, "We will return again shortly when I have confirmed that the papers will be completed today."

They piled into the General's Mercedes and sped away. An hour later, they returned with completed documents. The General handed them to me to examine. Then he took them and said, "Now we go to the bank, and you give me money and I give you documents."

We agreed to meet at the Cber Bank in one hour. We drove home to pick up the money.

As we arrived at the Bank, we saw several black cars with tinted windows. I looked at Kathy, Pastor Igor, and our lawyer, "Do you still think this is safe? Are those documents genuine? Do we really own that property?"

The Lawyer nodded, "Yes, I was there to make sure it was real. All that is left is for you to give him the money and get the documents."

I stepped across a few puddles and moved onto the sidewalk with Pastor Igor at my side. "I don't see the General. Maybe he's inside."

Pastor Igor pointed to a young man standing by the bank's front door. "You must be right, there's one of his men."

The Soldier was peering down the street, he turned and waved when he saw us. A car door opened across the street. General Dobrow exited, swishing his head, and checking the crowd.

The General stepped up to me. "Thank you for buying my house. It's good to see it go to someone who can appreciate it."

I moved slightly to where the ATM camera would get a better picture. I placed my briefcase on a small shelf then spun the dials on the lock.

The General picked up several bundles and fanned them to verify the bills. Satisfied, he nodded to a soldier who transferred the bundles from my suitcase to the General's, counting and fanning the stacks as he worked. After the General's case was secured, he pulled out the legal documents. He set them on top of my briefcase.

Lord, this seems like a scene from a 1930's gangster movie.

We shook hands, nodded goodbye and retreated to our vehicles. I sat in the driver's seat of our Skoda with my heart pounding and hands

Buying a Home in Russia

shaking. I turned to Pastor Igor, Tanya, and Kathy. "Praise the Lord! He did it!"

The back of the compound from the Birch Forest
Two of the children exploring

THOUGHTS
- Have you ever been so convinced that something was God's will, you fasted and prayed and did everything necessary to make it a reality?

CHAPTER THIRTY-THREE

The Uphill Battle

Rejoicing in hope; patient in tribulation; continuing instant in prayer; Romans 12:12

On the first day of remodeling our missionary compound, we arrived early and walked through a steady drizzle up the driveway towards the house. I silently prayed,

Lord, what are our priorities? We need a place to live. Which of the rooms would be best to live in while we work on the property? Are we all going to sleep in one room while working?

Mud and clay oozed over the top of my boots. I tried to lift my left leg and the mud held the boot.

Kathy let out a laugh, "Are you stuck?"

I grimaced and replied, "I was just praying that God would give us wisdom on where and how to start this project. I think this is His way of telling us to get gravel on the driveway and sidewalks first!"

Kathy nodded, "It makes sense to do outside work in the summer and focus on the inside when it gets cold."

A rumbling from the street broke into our conversation. An old gray van pulled up. Pastor Igor and a short, stocky man exited. Three other Russian men came out the rear door.

Suddenly the muck released first one and then the other boot. I met them at the corner of the house as Kathy followed close behind. Pastor Igor reached out and shook my hand, "Доброе утро, Brother Reasoner,"

I nodded and replied in English, "Good morning, Pastor Igor."

Igor gestured to the man next to him, "This is Anton Medvedov." The man thrust out a hand and gave a firm handshake. I expected nothing less from a man whose last name means 'bear'. While Pastor Igor and I

The Uphill Battle

talked, Bear walked back to the vehicle, took off his jacket, then set it on the passenger seat.

When he returned, I led the five of them to the front entrance. I began a running commentary, "We need doors and windows. I'll order those. Meanwhile, you can put up a blanket over this front doorway."

The men muttered and grumbled between themselves. They spoke Ukrainian, so I only caught about every third word. Igor saw my confusion and said, "I will order a truckload of lumber and the men will make doors and bunk beds for themselves."

I nodded and pointed to the floor. "Our home was the neighborhood homeless camp for the past six years. I need all the trash brought into the back yard and burned this afternoon."

Bear shook his head. He pointed to all four workers and held up two fingers, "It will take two days with all of us working."

Kathy and I could clean this mess up in just a few hours. I need to take control immediately!

In the best Russian I could muster, I emphasized, "No, if you work hard and don't take long breaks, it can be done today."

The four men began whispering in Ukrainian. I stared undaunted at the small group. Finally, Bear nodded and began to delegate. Two workers brought their few tools from the truck and placed them in a corner. My attention focused on the small pile of tools, "Where are your power tools?"

Bear grunted, "You supply tools. I write list of tools we need."

"We'll talk about it later." I replied looking at Kathy as I raised my eyebrows and frowned.

The big man, evidently not used to having someone stand up to him, stood with his mouth open. I motioned for Igor to follow me. We slipped and sloshed across the driveway to the garage. "Pastor Igor, like I told them, the first project is getting rid of this garbage. Then have them spread gravel." I tried to size up the amount of gravel needed. Igor followed my finger as I pointed the length of the driveway. "How many tons of gravel? Six?"

He nodded and spoke in his normal mixed English and Russian. "Da, six tons good. We put it down, maybe add some after next rain. Maybe three, four seasons we have enough."

We walked back into the house where Bear and his co-workers leaned on their shovels. The shortest, an older man with a full grey beard, came towards me.

I stretched out my hand, "Я Рон Reasoner."

"Я Vlad." He took my hand, "We good work!"

I released the handshake and smiled, "I look forward to a great relationship. You are Christians, I am Christian. We will glorify God together in this building. We plan to have a church, a Bible Institute, a home for my family, and a guest house for visiting missionaries. We are doing God's work and seek His praise."

Since the men were not working anyway, I decided to finish our tour of the home and what we wanted to have done. I pointed to the first room on the left of the living room. "You will use this room to live and sleep in. Keep your stuff in here."

They dropped their gear inside the big room. Kathy spoke up this time, "This room is too big for our purposes. We would like to divide the room in half, make the first half a mud room and the second room will be our guest room."

The men looked at me. I saw the need to validate Kathy's instructions. I almost shouted, "Kathy will be heading up a lot of the project ideas around here. We have an American saying, "If Momma ain't happy, ain't no one happy." Together Kathy and I tried to think of an equivalent Russian saying.

Vlad seemed to understand a little English and smiled as he turned to the other men and uttered the Russian phrase, "Man is the head of his home, but his wife is the neck that turns the head." All the men winked at me. They understood.

Kathy continued taking them through the compound, detailing our plans for each room. As we finished the grand tour of the 11,000 square foot building, we made it back to the living room. I checked my watch and tapped Igor on the shoulder. "I need you to arrange for the gravel to be delivered. In the meantime, have them move all the garbage to the firepit. We are off to City Hall. Apparently, there are a lot of stamps and signatures I need to make this home legal."

Igor nodded, "Buy several wheelbarrows and shovels while you are out. I will work on the equipment list with Bear."

With great effort, we slogged to our Skoda. I opened Kathy's door and marveled at her nearly clean shoes. I walked to my side and sat with my mud-clogged boots in a puddle. I grabbed a stick from the ground and scraped mud and clay from the soles as I prayed.

Lord this took two hours longer than I thought it should. Maybe we can be back after lunch to make sure they are moving the garbage.

I finished with the right boot, tossed it onto the floor in back and put on my loafer. When I finished the left boot, I tossed it next to its twin just as a man came out of the woods about 10 yards away.

The Uphill Battle

I stepped out of the car onto a flat rock to greet him as he came straight towards me and extended his hand. In broken English he called out, "Hello there, you be American spy who buy General Dobrov's home."

I shook my head, "No, I'm not a spy. I'm a Pastor from America. I came to preach the Gospel of Jesus Christ to the Russian people." I reached into the car and pulled out a tract. "Here, I'd like to invite you to our services." I turned the pamphlet over and pointed to the address on the back. "We start at 1 p.m. on Sunday afternoon. Please come."

The man chuckled, "I see, that makes good cover. I worked for KGB at UN in New York City until 1985." He pointed to a roof sticking out from the tree line a half block away, and chuckled. "That my house. I'm retired now, but I served 35 years. Being Communist, I could never use missionary cover."

I continued shaking my head as he talked, he slapped my shoulder and winked. "That's okay, your secret's safe."

I pointed to Igor directing his crew. "No, I'm not a spy. See that man over there? That's Igor, he's a pastor friend from the Ukraine. He found these workers to help us remodel our house."

Igor waved when he noticed our attention was focused on him. I waved back, then turned to my new-found KGB neighbor. "I'm sorry, I should've introduced myself right away. My name is Ron Reasoner." I pointed to Kathy who peered through the window. "This is my wife, Kathy. I am starting a church in Moscow, but the Moscow pollution has forced us to move here."

The gregarious agent reached out and vigorously shook my hand. "My name Ivan Mikhailov." He chuckled, "Your handler did good job picking this home for you." He smiled as I continued to protest. "Don't lie. Why else would American buy property in the middle of KGB retirement community?" He checked his watch, "Oh my how time runs. I must be going; I have tennis game in 30 minutes."

I watched him leave.

Lord, how can I get him to believe I'm not a spy?

I returned to the car and smiled at Kathy. Through her giggles she said, "Will the Russian people ever stop thinking we are spies and start believing that we are here on God's business, not the U.S. Government's business?"

I started the car and commented, "Working for the government would probably be a lot more profitable financially but we aren't here to make money, we are here to lead souls into the Kingdom of God." I put the Skoda into first gear and headed to City Hall.

Serving God Behind Enemy Lines

Five weeks later as I drove past Lenin's statue once again on my way back from City Hall, I pondered the situation.

Lord, I can't do this much longer. It's been a little more than a month and I only have six stamps on three permits.

I turned a corner, sped onto the highway, and switched the wipers on high when it started to pour.

Lord, I feel as if I'm wasting time and money.

I raised my eyes to the sky.

It's like You said in Luke 16:13:

No servant can serve two masters: for either he will hate the one, and love the other; or else he will hold to the one, and despise the other. Ye cannot serve God and mammon.

I pulled into our driveway and parked on the newly laid gravel.

Lord, if I spend too much time here, I run the risk of running afoul of the law. If I spend all day at city hall, I run the risk of wasting Your money and my time—all the while neglecting my family and Your ministry.

I sighed as I saw the trench around the perimeter of the property was not much further along. I bellowed, "BEAR, where are you!"

He stuck his head out from their window. "А вот и Вы. Наконец-то вы опоздали."

I'm late? What were they doing while I was gone? What is their excuse this time? Lord, give me wisdom!

The four men caught up to me as I finished walking the perimeter. I faced Bear, stood as straight as I could, and crossed my arms. I waited a full minute while they shuffled their feet and stared at the ground. "Well? What's the problem this time?"

Bear spoke up, "Брат Reasoner, when we got up this morning, we noticed that two wheelbarrows were stolen last night." The others nodded.

In my frustration, I did not even try to speak in Russian. I held five fingers up, "Again? That makes three wheelbarrows that have been stolen in the five weeks you've been here."

They did not even need the translation as I yelled, "Why don't you just pile the dirt away from the trench." I pointed to my watch, "The cement trucks will be here in two days. You don't even have the trench dug, let alone the rebar and forms ready."

Bear shook his head, "We need another wheelbarrow to move the dirt."

Lord, why do I have to put up with these guys? If I didn't know better, I'd think they are stealing my tools and sandbagging me.

The Uphill Battle

I felt a calming spirit come over me. I took a breath, "I'll get two more wheelbarrows today. Just dig!"

They nodded and led me to the back end of the fence line. Bear explained their problem with the electric welder, which I had bought at their request.

Lord, give me strength. As an experienced welder he should know the answer to his questions. Why can't he figure things out for himself? Maybe I should get another crew.

I tried to refocus on Bear's babbling, "And so I told her I would send the owner over next time I saw you."

"Repeat that please!" I said in Russian.

I listened carefully as Bear talked about the neighbor lady who had come to complain. "She had guests over to watch the tennis national championship on their big screen television and our welder messed with her television reception. She was angry!"

"Okay, we will take care of it!" I said, "I'm off to gather more stamps on our house papers."

Lord, what shall we do about the complaining neighbor? Well, she's a lady, I'll see if Kathy will take care of it.

A Family Meeting

Three nights later I nodded to Kathy as the children started to clear the dinner table. "All right, kids, let's get the dishes done before we have a family talk."

Joel stacked dishes while Keturah and Hannah consolidated leftovers. "Dad, I have something I'd like to bring up. Can I go first?"

I took a sip of my tea. "Sure Son." I looked around the table. "We'll go around the horn starting from oldest to youngest tonight."

From the look on their faces, I assumed Joel was going to be their spokesman. They cleared the table in record time.

Lord, I haven't seen them this excited about a family talk in a long time. I wonder what they want.

Kathy took her seat across from me, and we opened our binders. I nodded to Joel, "You seem to have been chosen to speak for the others. Am I right?"

"Yessir."

"Okay, after we pray, you can have the floor." We bowed our heads, "Heavenly Father, we thank You for this day and for another day to serve You. We pray for wisdom as we share our thoughts and plans for the future of our family." I raised my head, "Amen."

Joel stirred in his seat. "Uh, Dad," he looked from Kathy to me, then to his siblings, "We've been praying to God and talking." In one breath, he said, "Why can't we have more time together as a family like we used to?"

Kathy and I glanced between each other and the children. The five of them sat, lips trembling.

Joel's voice quivered as he blurted out as fast as he could, "We haven't had a family game night in months. You still pray with us, but they sure are quick." He let his breath out, leaned back in his chair. "There, I said it."

The younger children had been focusing on Joel as he gave his speech. Evidently, he had rehearsed it with them because they lip-synced his speech.

Kathy and I put our hands onto the middle of the table. The children did the same as I spoke, "For the last few weeks, we've been concerned about the same thing." I leaned back in my chair. "But it goes deeper than that."

I held up my left hand and counted off. "One—
- ✓ "Our family time hasn't been consistent, in quantity or quality.
- ✓ "I haven't been preaching as strongly as I know I can.
- ✓ "I'm not making much progress in getting the permits.
- ✓ "We're spending too much time and money on the remodeling project.
- ✓ "This makes for a poor testimony with our neighbors, our church family, and our fellow missionaries."

I put an elbow on the table and my chin in my left hand. "So," I pointed to Kathy, "We've been praying for a solution." I pointed to them. "I'm proud of you for noticing the problem and doing the same."

Kathy and I were both smiling as I explained, "Last week I talked to a neighbor who's trying to get their project through the building department."

As I talked the children were filled with anticipation. "Anyway, my friend Nikita has seen me almost every day for the past three weeks. He asked me why I did not find a Russian who could act for me. All I have to do is give them what's called 'Power of Attorney.'"

Each of them had a puzzled look. I opened a folder and pulled out a form. "See, I fill this out with someone's name."

I tilted my head, "Now it must be someone I trust. Then they can go to city hall for me. If he can, he will make a commitment that I have to abide by. If not, he must find me."

Joel and Micah nodded they understood. The three youngest still looked puzzled.

Kathy reached over and patted them on the shoulder. "All you need to know is that Daddy will be home more, and we'll spend more time with him."

"Yeah! Hallelujah!" All five clapped.

We let them enjoy the moment, then I folded my hands and bowed my head. The children did the same. "Father, it's no coincidence Your Holy Spirit was working on everyone's heart with the same goal. We pray for You to provide someone whom we can trust to represent us; Lord, whoever we find will also represent You and will be tasked with completing Your compound."

THOUGHTS
- Do you have family altar time with your family?
- How often?
- How important is it to you?

CHAPTER THIRTY-FOUR

Andre & Gala

And the things that thou hast heard of me among many witnesses, the same commit thou to faithful men, who shall be able to teach others also. 2 Timothy 2:2

One Sunday, Andre, who had attended our church since the 2000 Churches Campaign, came with his wife, Gala, and daughter, Masha. They sat in the first row. Immediately after the altar call, he approached me.

Lord, I sense this man will be an asset to our ministry. Please give me wisdom as to how You want to use him. Can I trust him with 'Power of Attorney?' He may not speak perfect English, but between my poor Russian and his English, maybe we can succeed.

Andre stopped a few feet from me as I continued to deal with my new interpreter, "Vladimir, let me get this straight. After last week's sermon from Acts 19 where Paul condemned the making and worshipping of idols, you went home and told your parents?"

"Yes, Mr. Ron. I told them how you said such things can cause problems in your family and your children could be influenced by the evil in the home."

I nodded, "And they got angry?"

Vladimir bowed his head, "Yes sir, they told me I had to quit working for you. This is my last Sunday."

"Why?"

"Because my parents are artists. They make icons for the Patriarch and one of their icons hangs in the Vatican. You have spoken against their livelihood."

Andre & Gala

"But do you understand that God's way is always the right way? If God's Word speaks against something, it is wrong. It doesn't depend on our life or our feelings, it depends on what God's Word says."

"Mr. Ron, thank you for helping improve my English-speaking skills, but I choose my parents over God's Word. They pay for my university, my food, my clothes—everything. I'm sorry, but I will not be back. I hope you can find another interpreter." Vladimir grabbed his backpack and ran out the door.

Andre approached, and we sat down, "That's my third interpreter this year. Since Roman got married and went to serve in his wife's church, I haven't been able to find a faithful Christian man who believes and lives the Word of God."

Andre put an arm on the back of the chair next to me. "Sorry, Brother Ron, but I overheard what that young man was talking to you about. Take comfort that you suffer persecution in the same manner that the Apostle Paul did when he preached against idol worship."

I waved my hand in dismissal of the topic, "God has given us several good interpreters. I just pray that Vladimir will someday believe in the truth of God's Word. Now, what would you like to talk about?"

He folded his hands on his lap, scratched his head, then rubbed his chin. "Uh, you see I've been praying about what the Lord would have me do." He seemed to get over his nervousness and pointed towards the front door. "I still want to get a job in the aviation industry, but that will be my vocation. I want to do something as a lay person for the cause of Christ."

Lord, could he be the one?

I carefully asked, "Tell me, where do you work now?"

He shook his head. "I work as a print editor. Tomorrow I'm going to the *reenok*," he paused and thought of the correct English word, "Uh, I'm going to the open marketplace to look for work. I need extra money; I only make $200 a month. I may have to get a laborer's job in the evenings."

Kathy came down the aisle, holding Jeremiah's hand; Andre's wife and daughter, walked beside her. "Good afternoon, Andre. Good to see you again." She turned to me. "Honey, why don't we invite them for dinner? I have plenty of chicken."

Andre and Gala nodded. The mention of food made their eyes widen as he grinned. "Da, da. We come."

We headed towards the exit. I locked up our little store front we rented in the mall for church services. Kathy herded the kids, and we walked out together. I glanced at Andre, "We live across the street. We'll

Serving God Behind Enemy Lines

have plenty of food and we could talk about a job I might have for you." Gala's glance at Andre told me to be careful.

After dinner, the adults sat at the kitchen table while the children laughed and played in the living room.

I pointed to Gala, "Andre tells me you're an atheist. Is that true?" I raised an eyebrow, "Why?" Kathy filled everyone's teacup; Andre and I opened another teabag and dipped it in the fresh water.

The Ukrainian woman waved a hand towards the kitchen window. "I see so much evil out there." She sighed. "How can there be a God?"

Andre started to speak, "I th—"

Gala cut him off. "I've heard your point of view. I want to hear from the holy man." Kathy reached behind her and pulled two Russian Bibles from a shelf and handed them to our friends.

For the next hour Kathy and I laid out the scriptures for her. Finally, I closed my Bible. "So, when God created the world, it was perfect. When He created man, He gave humanity the choice of whether to love Him. Love demands you let the other person choose to love you. Adam and Eve chose sin over God. He allowed but didn't create sin."

I pointed out the kitchen window in the direction she had pointed earlier, "It's man's inhumanity to man that causes the world's problems."

She shook her head. "That's similar to what my husband said." She crossed her arms. "I'm not convinced."

Kathy tapped the Bible in front of Gala. "You can keep this. We have plenty. If you read it, you will find the answers you're looking for."

Gala pushed the Bible to the side. "I won't make any promises." She fiddled with a napkin and sighed. "You might be offended, but I don't want to disappoint my parents."

Andre leaned forward. "They're high-ranking members of the Ukrainian Communist Party. It would bring shame on them and hurt their status if Gala became a Christian."

Lord, help this to come across the right way. I don't want to appear to be insensitive.

I took a sip of my tea and raised the cup towards her. "Gala, I understand how you feel. You see I was raised a Catholic, like the Russian Orthodox Church." I pointed to a picture of my parents on the wall. "They were upset when I started attending Baptist services. After all these years, we still get along, we just agree to disagree."

I pointed to her and then to the sky. "That's a decision between you and the Lord." I glanced over at her husband and added, "If and when you do accept Jesus Christ you will be guaranteed eternal life. You won't ever lose it."

At this point Andre interjected, "I disagree with you there. My church believes that you can lose your salva—"

Gala raised her voice, "Oh Andre—not that again!"

Kathy and I flitted back and forth as they debated. Finally, Gala slapped a hand on the tabletop. "Andre, be realistic. If this God of yours is Who He says He is, if He's as perfect as you say, and loves you like you claim, then eternal life is guaranteed. I love our daughter, Masha. Nothing she will ever do will make me disown her. Do I love my daughter more than your God loves you?"

Kathy and I let the awkward silence linger as Andre sat with his mouth wide open. The silence was broken when a burst of children's laughter came from the living room. Gala pulled out a handkerchief and wiped tears from her eyes. Kathy put a hand on her new friend's forearm. "What's wrong? Can I get you anything?"

Gala blew her nose and said, "It's not often our daughter has fun playing with other children. To hear her laugh, it—" She stopped and sobbed some more.

Andre scooted nearer to his wife and squeezed her shoulder. He looked at both of us sitting across from them. "Most children tease Masha because of her cleft palate." He pointed to the living room. "We've heard nothing but laughter and acceptance from your children." He stopped and wiped a tear off his cheek. "That means a lot."

Kathy scooted her chair, "How about Gala and I serve ice cream?" I nodded and my wife motioned for Gala to come to the refrigerator. "Does Masha like ice cream?"

I reached over and retrieved my briefcase. As I opened it, I called out, "Just one scoop for me, chocolate."

I took out the Power of Attorney document and passed it to Andre, "I've had a problem with getting permits from the Domodedovo City Hall. After two months, I still don't know if I'm getting the right permits and how many more I need. I'm afraid I'll inadvertently break the law."

I shook my head. "That would be a poor testimony. I'm spending so much time there I don't have time to—". I pointed to the living room, "spend with them, supervise the remodeling, and I don't have enough time to invest in the ministry."

I leaned forward, "Andre, if you agree, tomorrow we can go together to a notary and fill this out. After we both sign, you can represent me at city hall. I want us to meet every day and make sure we do everything that's required."

Our wives returned from serving the children. Gala sat at the table and asked Andre what we were talking about. After they had spoken for a few minutes she frowned, shook her head. "Nyet!" and immediately began yelling in Russian.

Andre sighed and turned. "She says, no. She doesn't want me doing ministry work. She married a pilot. I have a job. It's tight, and we are constantly borrowing money from friends and family." He lowered his head. "I'm sorry, I really would like to help."

I loosened my tie and smiled as I tapped the table between us, "Gala, I appreciate your concern. Currently, I don't need your husband to help in ministry. I need him to help me get building permits from City Hall."

"No! Andre has a good job now. To give it up in this economy would be foolish."

I turned the pad to face them. "Gala, if Andre works for me, I will pay him," I tapped the amount I'd written, "$400 a month. That's twice what he's making now."

Her hand went to her mouth, and she started to sob. Kathy handed her the box of tissues.

The next morning, Andre arrived at our apartment early. Kathy, Andre, and I climbed into our Skoda and headed for the compound. I concentrated on driving while Kathy and Andre chatted about the project and what she hoped to accomplish, "One of the first things we need to deal with is the neighbor lady. She keeps complaining to our workers about the welder messing with her TV reception. I need to go apologize and see if we can make friends."

I drove into the driveway and smiled, "I'll get the tea started while you and Kathy go meet the neighbor."

An hour later, I was still waiting. I went out to the dirt road and looked down the way. I was happy to see them walking toward me. I practically shouted, "I thought I might have to rescue you. What took so long?"

Andre and Kathy looked at each other and burst into laughter. Kathy explained, "It was an ordeal. The lady was drunk, kept repeating herself, was very forgetful of who we were, and gave us the grand tour of her home several times."

Andre finished the story, "As we were leaving, Ludmilla told us to never hesitate if we needed help with anything." He turned and pointed down the road, "She said her husband is the Chief of Police in Vednoe, which is an affluent area. That might prove useful in the future if we have any problems with permits and stamps at city hall."

I smiled. "Well, we need to get over to the city notary and get these papers signed, so you can get to work on those stamps and permits."

Several weeks passed. One day Andre came dragging his feet into my office. I immediately thought there was something wrong with our documents. "Andre! What happened? Is everything okay with the house documents?"

Andre managed a weak smile, "Oh yes. Brother Ron. Everything is going well with the house."

"Why the long face?"

"It's Gala. She is very sick. Ever since we moved into our new apartment, she has boils. More and more each day. I took her to the doctor, but I'm confused."

"What did the doctor say?"

"He said her blood has quit circulating throughout her body. As a result, these boils are forming in the areas that have no circulation. Does that sound like a good diagnosis?"

"Andre, is her heart beating?"

"Of course!"

"Then her blood is circulating. The boils are probably a result of some bacteria she encountered in your new home. I warned you that building was old and dilapidated."

"Old and what? I don't know this word—decapitated?"

I stifled a laugh, "No—dilapidated—it means falling apart. What did the doctor prescribe as the treatment for her boils?"

Andre folded his hands behind his back, "He wants her to come into the hospital every day for two weeks. He will draw blood out of her arm in a large vial. He will reinsert the needle on her backside. He says after doing that for two weeks, she will be healed. It doesn't sound right."

"But—it's dangerous! What if air bubbles get into her blood? She could die."

"I know. I asked her not to do it, but she insists. I'm already looking for a new place to live."

I put a hand on his shoulder, "Let's pray—for God to protect Gala and for you to find a safer home." The Lord soon answered both prayers.

One September afternoon, a week after the footing for the fence was poured, I was working on a sermon while sitting at my makeshift desk in what would become my office. We had been remodeling the new house for three months. I suddenly looked up when I heard a truck pull into the compound. I set my books aside and before I reached the window, I heard Bear calling, "Brother Reasoner, bricks are here."

By the time I reached the driveway, Igor had parked his car and was directing the driver to back up to where the bricks would be stored. The other workers came from the other side of the compound. Bear climbed into the back of the truck and helped the crane driver attach the hook to a chain around a stack of bricks.

After working with Igor for months, he and I worked quite well in understanding the butchering of the other's mother tongue. I unfolded the paper, "Pastor Igor, this looks in order. Thank you for getting such a good price."

He smirked and pointed to the bricks. "I found a friend from the Ukraine who was selling these at the *reenok*. He gave us a good price."

The short worker looked startled when he overheard Igor's comment.

Igor and I went to the other side of the truck. I picked up a brick and tossed it from hand to hand.

Lord, I'm not an expert on bricks. Give me wisdom.

I tossed the brick to Bear to set on top of the pile.

Igor scanned the property and pointed to a section of unfinished welding. "We should be finished with this by 5 p.m. Then we'll have a solid stairway out the back door." He turned and pointed to the pallets of brick 100 feet away, "They can start laying bricks Monday morning. We should have a front fence in no time."

I mused, "Perhaps people will stop walking through our property as a shortcut to the forest. I thank you again for the good deal on the bricks, Igor."

Igor smiled and then cleared his throat, "Yes, I'm leaving now for Kiev. I'm preaching there this weekend; tonight, I'll stay with my sister in Tula."

"Why don't you fly? Isn't it safer and cheaper?'

Igor's eyes opened wide, "Oh no! I will not fly domestic flights in Russia. It is too dangerous."

I pondered, "But Ukraine is a separate country. Isn't that considered an international flight?"

Igor smiled, "Technically, yes, but Russia considers all the former Soviet Republics domestic flights and uses the old Soviet planes for these routes."

I remembered my fear of flying Aeroflot on my survey trip and replied, "I've flown Aeroflot several times and never had any problems."

Igor sat down on the front porch and motioned for me to do the same, "Twenty years ago, I tried to take a plane from Moscow to Kiev. Just before takeoff, as our plane approached the runway, one of the wheels fell off. Thankfully, it was going slow enough that the plane just fell to one side, scraped its wing, and screeched to a stop."

He shook his head at the memory, "We filed off the plane and were directed to another plane. We were nervous but decided it was a fluke. Surely the next plane would be fine. As the next plane approached the runway, the right engine caught on fire. The plane squealed to a halt and emergency procedures were executed. All the doors were opened, and it was a free-for-all to get off the plane."

I gasped, "Is this a true story, Igor?"

Offended, Igor furrowed his brow and narrowed his eyes, "Yes! They offered to put us on another plane, but most of us left the airport and took a train. I now take the train. This time I have a lot of food and supplies to take to my family, so I am driving."

Ten minutes later we waved goodbye, and I walked back to my sermon preparation. When I reached the front door, I passed the short worker who had kneeled to re-tie his boot. The man stood, noticed I was staring at him and looked away.

Lord, he knows something I don't.

As he started to walk back to his welding, I put a hand on his shoulder and asked him in Russian, "Tell me, why were you so startled when you heard me thank Pastor Igor for the bricks?"

He started to back away. Suspiciously I said. "I want an answer—one Christian to another."

He looked down at his feet and spoke softly. "You are a Holy man, I can't lie. I am from Ukraine, I know the man who makes these bricks, they are not good." He looked up at me, "Pastor Igor did not pay much for them—much less than you paid him."

I patted him on the shoulder. "Okay, thank you, go back to work."

Lord, so that's it. And I thought I could trust Igor. What am I to do? I can't afford more bricks.

I walked back to the driveway and ran my hands on the top of one pallet.

Lord, this is bad. If I confront Igor, his name is on the deed. He could take the house from me.

I shuddered at the thought of losing the house.

Lord, I need to make some decisions fast. Send someone to help me! I beg You.

A car horn snapped me out of my thoughts. I turned and saw Andre getting out of his Lada. I checked my watch.

Was it time for our daily meeting already?

I double-checked my watch.

Hmm, so it was.

We met half-way between his car and the front door. I led him up the stairs and into my office. I went over to the teapot and poured him a large cup of his favorite tea and then one for myself.

He took his cup and doctored it up. We spent the next 45 minutes discussing the day's successes and failures. Andre spoke casually, "We need six more stamps before we can legally hook up to the electric grid, 25 smoke detectors—one for each room—a visit from the gas company, the fire department, and the city sewer commissioner before they will even start their stamp and permit processes. That's just our next few steps."

After he drained the dregs from his third cup of tea, he set it down. "So, there you have it. We're not bad off."

I finished scribbling notes from our conversation and tossed my pen aside. "Andre my friend, I need advice." He listened intently while I explained Igor's indiscretion.

Andre checked his watch and rose. "Let's go, I have an idea, we have just enough time." As we walked towards the stairs he pointed to his car and my Skoda. "Mine or yours?"

I pointed. "Yours, I'm too distracted and upset. I don't want to get behind a wheel. Besides, you know where you want to go."

We fastened our seatbelts. Before long we were speeding through the town. After he had turned several corners, I questioned him, "Are you going to keep me in suspense? Where are we going?"

"Oh, I'm sorry, I think we should talk to the person who sold Igor the bricks." He pulled into the first parking spot he found on the street outside the *reenok* and opened his door. I did the same and exited. Andre continued, "I'm thinking that since this guy doesn't know either of us, we ask questions—"

By the time we traversed the labyrinth of stalls at the marketplace we had our plan.

Lord, help us pull this off.

A stocky, olive-skinned man rose as we entered his booth. Andre took the lead and did all the talking. I watched the man's body language and listened to the tone of his voice. They conversed happily in Ukrainian.

Andre & Gala

Suddenly Andre switched to Russian so I could understand, "I'm helping a friend build a fence. What type of brick would you recommend?"

The man pulled a pad of paper and took notes as he asked questions. Twenty minutes later we strolled back to Andre's car.

I buckled the seat belt and shook my head. "Andre, you're a genius."

As we headed back to the compound Andre explained. "I think his answers have made it clear what you must do." He stopped at a traffic light and looked at me. "Igor bought substandard bricks and charged you double. Though he is a brother in Christ and a fellow Ukrainian, I do not trust him. You cannot have him manage your project any longer. Remember, if you handle this wrong and he gets mad, he holds the deed for the property."

Andre & Gale with their two children. Circa 2003

THOUGHTS
- Have you ever been in a situation where someone betrayed you?
- How did you handle it?

Chapter Thirty-Five

Moving Forward

And whatsoever ye do, do it heartily, as to the Lord, and not unto men; Knowing that of the Lord ye shall receive the reward of the inheritance; for ye serve the Lord Christ. Colossians 3:23-24

That night after dinner, Kathy came into the kitchen and sat down. "The kids are asleep. I shut all the doors. If we don't talk loudly, they won't hear a thing." She accepted the teacup I set in front of her. "Well, how are you going to do this?"

A chill came over me. "The more I think about it, the more anxious I get." I pointed to the notes I'd taken after Andre and I left the *reenok*. "According to the salesman the bricks should've cost $1,000." I tapped Igor's receipt. "Igor charged me $2,000."

She took the paper out of my hand and read my scribbling. "You mean they will write the receipt for whatever amount the customer tells them?" I nodded. She continued, "Igor paid him the correct amount and you paid Igor an inflated price."

"Yep!" I pointed to the next line. "On top of that, the salesman told me we didn't get quality bricks. We got the cheapest." I shrugged, "He estimates that in this climate they may last 10 years. Better quality bricks last 40."

Three days later, at 10:30 p.m. we were sitting at the same table. I opened my Bible and looked at Kathy. "I've fasted and prayed since Andre, and I went to the *reenok*. I still don't have peace." I looked down and laughed.

Kathy leaned forward, read the scripture I pointed to while it was upside down and laughed harder than I did.

We recited it from memory:

> *"Have not I commanded thee? Be strong and of a good courage; be not afraid, neither be thou dismayed: for the LORD thy God is with thee whithersoever thou goest. Joshua 1:9"*

I closed my Bible. "That's it. I feel the peace I've wanted for the past three days. The Lord knows what He's going to do. I must trust Him." I raised my head and looked at the kitchen clock. "It's too late to call Pastor Igor. I'll do it tomorrow."

Domodedovo Compound in winter using the bricks Igor bought

The next morning right after the children started their coursework, Kathy sat next to me at the table, she folded her hands and prayed as I made the call. Igor picked up the phone on the third ring.

Lord, I haven't rehearsed what I'm going to say. Like You did with the prophets of old, put the words You want in my mouth.

A groggy voice answered the phone, "Allo?"

I've awakened him. This is not good.

I cleared my throat and forged ahead, "Brother Igor, this is Ron Reasoner."

I heard a commotion in the background before he said, "Brother Reasoner, so good to hear from you. Tell me, how were last Sunday's services?"

Kathy stopped praying and brought me a glass of water.

"Very well, Brother, very well."

Okay, Lord, here goes.

"Brother Igor, when I hired Andre, it freed me up to put my focus back on where it should've been all along." I took a sip of ice water. "In the past month or so attendance has increased, and more people are in our discipleship program than ever." I put an elbow on the table and leaned on it. "Tell me, how are your services going?"

I could sense sadness in his voice. "Oh, Brother Reasoner, attendance is down, and my Deacons are fighting. I don't know what to do. Would you please pray for me?"

Thank You, Lord, that's it!

"Igor, I think we both have our priorities upside down." He started to interrupt, "No, hear me out. You've been traveling back and forth every week to help me. It's probably taken time from your sermon preparation, your visitation, and most importantly, your time with the Lord."

I raised the mouthpiece over my head and kept the earpiece in place. I mouthed to my wife, "Praise the Lord!" Kathy reached over and squeezed my hand.

"But, Brother Reasoner, you don't have anyone else. What are you going to do? You can't do it all."

"Brother Igor, I'm forever indebted to you. If you hadn't agreed to hold the deed, I wouldn't own this property. God has given me Andre as a helper. I think he can handle getting permits and the needed materials. God wants pastors to concentrate on building His kingdom. We must trust Him."

I heard a big sigh. "Okay, I'll trust the Lord to help me; the same as you are trusting the Lord to help you."

I hung up the phone and both Kathy and I shouted, "PRAISE THE LORD."

Immediately the children came running. Micah was the first to reach the kitchen. "What's happened? Why're you guys so happy?"

After we explained the situation and how the Lord had put words in my mouth, we all jumped up, "PRAISE THE LORD."

Then Joel shook his head. "Dad, you forgot one thing."

Everyone turned.

He pointed out the window to the south. "Those lazy workers we've been praying about are still working for you. I don't think we should be rejoicing until that prayer's answered also."

There was silence as Kathy and I realized the impact of our young man's insight. I turned to Joel, "We will have to keep these workers on until I can find replacements. They have started working harder since I changed their payment from a daily amount to each individual job."

Kathy added, "And when we brought over those two American missionaries from Belgium and Germany who plumbed the entire house in one week—that motivated the Ukrainian workers. They saw what quality and speed we expect."

Micah, longing to be a part of the conversation added, "Remember when Grandpa Ben came over from America to install the kitchen, pantry, laundry, and guest room off the kitchen? EVERYONE was surprised how quickly and efficiently Grandpa worked and he's old! In 10 days, he completed the kitchen. The Ukrainians said it would take them two months with a team of four people."

I smiled at the memories and then turned back to Joel, "Let's keep praying about the workers. They will go home for Christmas and New Year's. Pray we can find new workers by then and I won't invite them back."

Reward for Faithfulness

Three days later, just before quitting time I was giving my friend Nito a tour of the property. "So, my friend, what do you think of my project now?"

"Brother Ron, we fellow missionaries gave you a hard time about buying this compound, but it might work out after all. However, you are still in a precarious position. Igor could come back at any time; you don't know what the General might pull," he shrugged, "Who knows what friends he has in high places."

At that moment Andre's Lada pulled into our driveway. He walked up and handed me a stack of papers. "Four more stamps today. Tomorrow I'm praying for six."

"Andre, you remember Brother Nito, don't you? He preached for us a few months ago."

They shook hands and I led them inside to my office. As soon as we entered, I filled three cups with water from the ever-present kettle.

I pointed my cup to Nito, "Andre, this isn't a chance meeting. I asked Nito here so we could present a gift to you."

Nito leaned forward, put his hands on the table and smiled. "Andre, Brother Reasoner has told me about your daughter's cleft palate. He also told me how you have asked every hospital in Moscow for help. None of them will do the operation for free even though they are legally obligated." He pointed to me, then back to himself. "Both of our ministries have a special fund to help in these cases."

Andre looked at Nito and then back to me. I patted him on the forearm. "Yes, it's true. Our ministries have teamed up to pay for Masha's surgery to fix her palate."

Andre's eyes widened, his hands trembled, and tears started to flow. "I don't know what to say. I don't know if I can accept charity."

I smiled. "No, my friend, don't think of it as charity. Think of it as a bonus for all the hard work that you've done." I rose, "Now, I think you need to go home and call the Canadian Hospital that offered to do the surgery for $600. Get an appointment and tell your family about Masha's date with her new life."

Domodedovo Compound after replacing the cheap bricks Igor had bought with a new fence that stands to this day.

Andre stood and whispered, "Praise God!"

I put a hand on his shoulder. "God answers prayers. You make the appointment, tell me when, and I'll go with your family to the hospital. I'll pay them in cash for everything."

THOUGHTS
- Does your work ethic speak to the glory of God?
- When others watch you work, do they understand that you work heartily as unto the Lord?
- If not, why not?

CHAPTER THIRTY-SIX

Eur-Asia Baptist Bible College

Ask of me, and I shall give thee the heathen for thine inheritance, and the uttermost parts of the earth for thy possession. Psalm 2:8

We had been remodeling the compound for several months, and orientation of the Fall 1999 term was about to start. Here was yet another class of eager students. Eight men and women sat around our living room table. Most were students from local universities; two came from Moldovia.

I smiled. "Welcome to Eur-Asia Baptist Bible College. With so many people accepting the sacrifice Christ made on the cross; we need to plant churches; the newly saved need their faith strengthened. To plant churches, one must have trained men to pastor those churches. We've already graduated five men who are serving the Lord around Russia and the Ukraine."

I slid a transparency of myself and another man on to the overhead projector. "This is my friend Jerry Scheidbach from America. He came to Russia in 1994 to do evangelistic meetings and brought the materials you see today. It was his vision to start this Bible Institute." I replaced our picture with a slide showing the logo for EABBC. "It's our goal to teach Christians to share the Gospel with the Russian people." I pointed to them as they avoided making eye contact. "You need to consider accepting God's call."

Yuri, a short stocky man from Moldovia raised his hand. I nodded and he stood. He looked at me while my latest interpreter, Olga, translated. "Are you expecting us to do this full time? Or as a vocation?"

Serving God Behind Enemy Lines

I tapped the Bible in front of me. "My job is to give you the tools to do the work God's called you to. If He wants you to be a physicist and lead Bible Studies for your neighbors or to pastor your own church, it's between you and God."

As I talked and Olga translated, we passed out notebooks. "This will be a two-year course." I held up and opened a copy of the binder, flipping through it so they could see inside. "We cover Baptist history, English, Church Polity, and Missions. Every Saturday when you arrive, we will have another section of material for you. Take it home, study the Bible references we give you and answer the questions."

Some Eur-Asia Baptist Bible College students inside the compound From top to bottom: Vlad (not in this book), Me, Dimitre, Glenn, Oleg, Argum & Yakov

"Will there be tests?" one student asked.

I nodded. "Yes, and term papers as well. To graduate and fulfill your calling—whether you pastor a church, or lead a Bible study, you need to demonstrate you know and understand what the Bible teaches. Sound doctrine is important for the Gospel to flourish."

I reached between a man and a woman, picked up a Bible and held it high. "All of you need to know this. Read and study it. Get to know who God really is. It will change your life and how you minister to others."

I stood behind the podium and pointed to a map of the world.

Lord, this is going well, I pray some will be willing to accept Your call.

"Today we begin studying missions." I opened my Bible. "Our class verse will be Isaiah 6:8:

"Also I heard the voice of the Lord, saying, Whom shall I send, and who will go for us? Then said I, Here am I; send me.

"God is looking for spiritual soldiers to go forth and conquer this world for the Lord Jesus Christ. The question you must answer in this class is, 'Am I willing to say, 'Here am I; send me?''"

I paused for dramatic effect so God could work on their hearts. I looked each of them in the eye as they pondered this question. Finally, I continued, "Turn to Mark 16:15-16." I waited for them to find the Scripture.

Thank you, Lord. Some of them are really getting good at finding verses in their Bibles.

"And he said unto them, Go ye into all the world, and preach the gospel to every creature. He that believeth and is baptized shall be saved; but he that believeth not shall be damned."

I closed my Bible, "Think about this," I tapped the shoulder of the man next to me, "As Russians, you can easily get into countries such as Iran, Iraq, China, and the former Soviet countries that Americans can't. Those countries welcome Russians because of the friendship between their governments, but they deny access to Americans because of the unstable political relationship with America."

Oleg stood, "Missionary, you talk of going to another country but there are so many unreached right here. I know of a nomadic group called the Reindeer People that wander in the Arctic North." He paused, glanced at his classmates and then back at me. "Why don't you go up there and preach the Gospel to them? Then we will pray about going to other countries."

I looked at him.

Serving God Behind Enemy Lines

Lord, I gave up my homeland. I left my family and my mother tongue. I came to Russia with my wife and five children where I had to learn a new culture and language. Haven't I sacrificed enough?

All eyes were on me as I contemplated how I would reply.

Haven't I done enough for You, Lord?

I heard the *Still Small Voice* within me say, "I gave My Son to die for you. Can you ever do enough?"

I cleared my throat and forced myself to say, "I'll pray about it and if God wants me to go to the Reindeer People, I'll go. Who will go with me?"

Dimitre, the Ukrainian, stood up, "I lived in Labytnangi near the Arctic Circle for several years. Reindeer People sometimes came through our town. One even came to our church and became a Christian."

Dimitre scanned the room as he spoke, "He was running from the Shaman in his village who had commanded him to kill his brother because the Shaman had seen it in a dream. The young man killed his brother, then the Shaman told another brave to kill him. He ran away from his family, his tribe, and the only life he had ever known."

Dimitre focused back on me and finished, "I want nothing to do with Reindeer People and Shamanism. It is too dangerous!"

As he sat down, I sensed fear had come over everyone. Some shook their heads, others folded their arms and looked away. Complete silence.

No one, including me, wants to go. Problem solved!

I dismissed the class and hoped the topic didn't come up again.

Plans

The next day, I stood in the foyer after service, Andre came up and extended his hand, "Missionary, I'll go with you to the Reindeer People."

Okay, Lord.

As Andre and I walked out the door with our families close behind us, we headed for the exit of the mall. I touched his elbow. "If you have time this evening, come over for dinner. We can start planning."

What am I saying, Lord? I don't even want to go on a Reindeer trip!

Kathy spoke up. "Andre, please come. I'm making spaghetti and meatballs."

He turned to Gala, "Is that okay with you?"

Gala smiled and replied, "Certainly, may we bring something?"

Everyone stopped at a crosswalk, and Kathy answered, "You can bring a loaf of bread."

With that, we parted ways.

Eur-Asia Baptist Bible College

Later that evening I leaned forward, "Andre, there are so many unknowns. Kathy and I have never thought about taking trips to faraway places within Russia."

Andre excitedly interrupted, "When we first met, you said your plan was to start churches in and around Moscow, start a Bible Institute, and send native missionaries to surrounding countries."

I scratched my head, "One reason why is that we believe native speakers can do a better job." After a long silence, I sighed. "Now we are considering a trip deep into Siberia to reach a nomadic people who will be difficult to find."

He interrupted, "Pastor, you and the Lord are causing my faith to grow. We can do this! I know somebody in the town of Karaul who can help."

The Lord was working on my heart as Andre expressed his passion. *Maybe the Lord is growing us and expanding our outreach.*

"Let's pray about this."

Andre slowly sipped his tea "Well, we cannot go now because it is too cold, but we have time to plan."

The Internet & Putin

December 1999 arrived in full force. Snow covered the ground and temperatures consistently dipped below 15-degrees Fahrenheit. Most important to us, the Internet came to Moscow, and I was able to get dial-up in our apartment.

"Kathy, come here! I want to read you this article about Y2K. Have you heard of it?"

She came into the living room holding one of my shirts she was ironing. "Something about computers crashing and all the nuclear bombs going off?" She asked.

I smiled, "Something like that. This article from *USA Today* says Russia will be the most dangerous place to be if the computers mess up."

Kathy snapped her finger, left the room, and returned with the latest copy of *The Moscow Times*. "I just read an editorial mocking that idea."

I took the paper and scanned the article. Throwing back my head, I laughed, "According to this article, Russia's nuclear codes aren't even attached to a computer. They must be manually entered."

Kathy turned to go back to her ironing. Over her shoulder she remarked, "Perhaps Russia is the safest place to be for Y2K."

A few days later, I again called Kathy into the living room, "Did you see the news?"

"No, what?"

"President Yeltsin has resigned! His Prime Minister, Vladimir Putin will be sworn in as the new president tomorrow!"

Kathy read over my shoulder. She sighed, "I've said a hundred times—you couldn't pay me a billion dollars to be the president of Russia. The elderly people place their every hope on the leader. They worship him like a god and expect him to supply their needs. They are starving to death, and the youth are ashamed to be Russian. Everyone is broken."

I nodded, "I agree, but perhaps this Putin character can pull Russia out of its economic slump, bring it into the 21st century with the rest of Europe and return national pride to the people of Russia."

We shook our heads and said together, "I'll believe it when I see it."

On December 31, 1999, Vladimir Putin was sworn in as president.

Reindeer Plans

Eight months later, I scribbled my last note on a pad of paper and slid it across to Andre. "Okay, here's what I have: we will fly to Norilsk. Hopefully, the Reindeer People will be in the area. If not, we will contact your acquaintance who lives there. All the details will be left to God."

Andre looked at the map and ran a finger down the page. "Yes, it's a six-hour flight. Bring warm clothes. Even in the summer, the temperature could get below zero."

I touched Andre's arm and waited for him to look me in the eye, "What do you know about Norilsk?"

Andre thought for a moment, "It's Northeast of Moscow in the Arctic Circle in the permanent permafrost zone. In high school geography class, they bragged that it produces a large amount of several natural resources that fuels Russia's economy. It has a highly desired job market because people get paid up to three times a normal Moscow salary to work there."

"Well, I'll buy the tickets next week for our trip. Let's pray and ask God to guide us, 'Lord, we feel You are leading us on an incredible journey. We don't know what lies ahead, but You do. Give us faith and courage to trust You. Please keep us safe as we serve You. In Christ's name, Amen.'"

THOUGHTS

- Jesus sent them out two by two.
- Do you have a friend with whom you can go soulwinning, and serve the Lord with?
- If not, who can you pray about partnering with?

CHAPTER THIRTY-SEVEN

Heading North

For unto you it is given in the behalf of Christ, not only to believe on him, but also to suffer for his sake; Philippians 1:29

In July 2000, I hugged and kissed each of my children as I made my way through the gauntlet towards the front door of our new home. It had been a year since we purchased the Compound. After months of work, it was now livable. I stopped at Joel. "Remember, make sure the others mind your mother."

The children have grown so quickly these last six years in Russia. Joel is now 15, Micah 14, Keturah 11, Hannah 10, and little Jeremiah 9. I am leaving them to find an unreached people group. Lord, please be with them and keep them all safe.

I walked over to Kathy, "I feel bad about leaving you here with all these unpacked boxes and so much to do."

Kathy smiled, "Don't worry! We didn't know when you were planning this trip that the electricity, plumbing and several bedrooms would be done enough to move in. I'll work the kids to death. We'll be moved in, and half the house finished by the time you return."

Always the trooper.

I kissed Kathy goodbye and turned to leave.

She stopped me, reached into my coat pocket, and retrieved an envelope. "Good, you have your tickets to Norilsk, your passport, and your papers. I'm not sure how you will keep track of all this without me, but God is with you." She tilted her head towards the children, "We'll be praying for you every day."

Micah tapped my forearm. "Dad, can we pray before you go?"

Kathy and I smiled, "Sure, son. Why don't you lead us?"

He cleared his throat, "Dear Jesus, Dad's going on a trip. He needs You to help him. Keep him from bad men. Bring him home safe. Help him preach Your Gospel to the Reindeer People. Amen."

As soon as he said 'amen', Keturah started crying. I stroked her long, dark hair, "What's wrong Sweetheart?"

She wrapped her arms around me and squeezed. "I'll miss you. But what if bad men get you?"

I put a hand on her shoulder. "I go on trips as God directs and I always come back." I caught Hannah and Jeremiah out of the corner of my eye. I winked at them. "You don't want me to go either do you?" Both nodded and rushed to my side.

Everyone gathered for a group hug. Finally, I pulled away, kissed Kathy on the cheek, and pointed for the older boys to take the boxes to the waiting taxi.

At the Domodedovo Airport, the taxi driver unloaded my luggage and held his hand out. "Это будет 1,000 рублей."

Let's see, he wants 1,000 rubles.

I rubbed my chin.

At 28 rubles to the dollar, that's $35.

His eyes widened as I handed him two $20 bills and a Russian tract. "Keep the change." I leaned through the open passenger window and tapped the Bible I had given him and told him in the best Russian I could muster. "Обратитесь к Богу. Он поможет вам (Turn to God. He will help you)."

The driver took the money and scratched his stubby beard. "Okay, maybe I come to church."

Andre was nowhere to be found. I saw a cart nearby and loaded the boxes and luggage.

Still no Andre.

I paced back and forth along the unloading zone.

Still no Andre.

I checked my watch.

We're going to be late! Lord, help Andre get here!

Finally, I felt a hand on my shoulder, "Brother Ron! Sorry I'm late. The local train broke down and we had to wait for another one."

Frustrated, I turned to face Andre, "We better hurry or we will miss our flight."

We pushed the loaded cart to the Siberian Airline counter and handed our passports and papers to the agent. The attendant processed our tags and placed everything on the conveyor belt. Her hands moved

Heading North

quickly as she stamped and shuffled our papers. She gathered them up into two piles and handed each of us an envelope. "You need to hurry—it's boarding soon."

We took our envelopes, grabbed our bags, and rushed towards our gate. "Lord, help us make it!" I whispered as we ran.

Andre pointed to a sign. "Look, Missionary, there's our gate. It does not look like they've started boarding yet."

We stopped at the end of a long line of passengers and caught our breath. Andre smiled, "God must love you very much. He answers all your prayers."

I glanced upwards.

Lord, I sure hope so. By the way, I've got a few more. If it wouldn't be too much trouble, can we please meet with a lot of Reindeer People?

After boarding we found our seats and stowed our carry-ons. As we sat, Andre pulled out a piece of paper. "Missionary, I have prayed for us to find a good place to stay." He tapped a finger on the paper. "I want to show many Reindeer People about Jesus." He pointed a finger to the ceiling. "I want to please Him."

He turned his paper over. "I have phone number of Russian Christians in Karaul. If we go to that village, I pray they let us stay." He turned and looked out the window and sighed. "In small villages there are no hotels. If we no find someone to give us a room, we must sleep on street."

I tapped the phone number we had, "It's essential you keep this contact. If we venture outside of Norilsk to find Reindeer People, we'll need it." I shuddered; "I don't want to sleep on the streets in the Arctic Circle. I don't care if it's summer. I have a feeling it still gets cold at night."

I reclined my seat and stretched. "I'm excited about getting to Norilsk. I read that several Reindeer Tribes summer there." With that, I dozed off.

After the plane landed in Norilsk some 1,800 miles northeast of Moscow, we gathered our belongings and walked across the tarmac to the terminal. We were immediately surrounded by *militsiya*. The biggest took my arm and directed me down a different hall away from Andre. I glanced back to see Andre being paraded into another room.

The door closed behind us; the police officer pulled out a chair and forced me to sit. We sat in silence for several minutes.

Lord, how can I get out of this if I can't get anyone to pay attention to me?

I tapped my foot to make a noise. "Excuse me, I would like to make a call to the embassy."

The police officer laughed and jabbed his friend, then shook his head. "You are not in America, there is 'no phone call.'"

My eyes widened as the meanest-looking Russian I'd ever seen entered. With my limited Russian I asked: "What have I done wrong?"

Instead of answering, he jabbered away in Russian so fast I could barely understand him.

Lord, I'm only comprehending a quarter of what he's saying, I think he believes I'm a spy.

I took a Russian Bible and tract from my coat. I handed them to the interrogators.

Lord, if they're going to keep me, I may as well start my prison ministry.

I began to nervously preach in broken Russian about God's love and how Jesus came to die for their sins.

After 20 minutes, the first interrogators left. Another man came in. I did not completely understand the questions he asked either. After a few attempts to unsuccessfully answer what I thought he was asking, I handed him a Bible.

Lord, help me to speak Russian well enough to give him the Gospel.

"Jesus loves us so much that He died on the cross for our sins." He listened for about a half hour and left.

I sat alone until another policeman came into the room. This time I immediately answered their questions with my Bible and the Gospel story. He listened for 15 minutes then left.

This continued several more times. Each time an officer of higher rank came in. Finally, after two-and-one-half hours, the head policeman walked in with an interpreter. He did not speak English any better than I spoke Russian.

"You American. Norilsk closed to Americans. You come; you spy." The senior officer jabbered something so fast I gave a questioning look to the interpreter. In a menacing tone he scowled, "Why you here?"

Closed? Lord, I never thought of researching about this town being closed to Americans.

I took another Russian Bible from my coat, opened it to John 3:16. I ran my finger across the page as I read the passage upside down.

"Ибо так возлюбил Бог мир, что отдал Сына Своего единородного, дабы всякий верующий в Него, не погиб, но имел жизнь вечную."

Heading North

I closed the Bible and slid it across the table. "You see, God loved you so much that He was willing to sacrifice His Son for you. I am here to preach the Gospel to the Reindeer People." I looked the Chief of Police in the eye, "Did you know that you can have fellowship with God—the Creator of all the universe?" For the next 15 minutes I shared the Gospel.

I paused to catch my breath and gather my thoughts. I started to quote Mark 16:15 when the Chief put his hand up for me to stop. He pulled a box from his pocket. The interpreter's face flashed a look of shock and awe.

I focused on the officer-in-charge as he spoke, "I do not care about your religion. I only care about spies. I know you are not a spy. No spy can preach for two-and-a-half hours! I am giving you permission to be in our city for one week."

He took my passport, stamped it, and handed it to me. "Here," he said, "Now go."

THOUGHTS
- Are you willing to go to jail for your faith?
- Would you be bold enough to preach to the prison guards?

Chapter Thirty-Eight

Norilsk

But none of these things move me, neither count I my life dear unto myself, so that I might finish my course with joy, and the ministry, which I have received of the Lord Jesus, to testify the gospel of the grace of God. Acts 20:24

I was overjoyed to see Andre slumped on a bench. Amazingly, our bags and boxes were at his feet. I called out, "Andre, my friend, I didn't think I'd ever see you again!"

He jumped up and started to speak. I put a finger to my lips. "Shhhhh, not here." We glanced over our shoulders to see if any *militsiya* were following.

We walked out of the airport into bright, green sunlight. Andre pointed at a bus pulling up across the street. "We need to take that Автобус to the center of Norilsk." He looked into my eyes and said, "They were convinced that because you're an American you must be a spy."

He took out a handkerchief and wiped his brow. "I told them that in the two years I have known you I have never heard you talk about anything but your family and your faith."

We dropped our stuff at the curb near the bus stop. Andre sighed, "I spent the past several hours trying to secure your release. I talked to every person in uniform I saw. I don't know if it helped."

We boarded the bus and exited three stops later. We found ourselves in a dense cloud of green smog. After walking a few blocks, we saw a man sitting on a bench.

Andre asked, "Excuse me, we just flew in from Moscow. Why is there so much green in the air?"

Norilsk

The man's brow furrowed. "Это от никеля и нефтеперерабатывающих заводов."

Andre nodded, "Спасибо." As we walked away, he mused, "So that's why Norilsk is a closed city." Andre set his luggage down, knelt and retied a shoe. "It seems the pollution from the copper and nickel mines creates all this. This area of Russia is rich with natural minerals and oil."

Lord, you know that as a child I suffered from bronchitis. You know pollution is toxic to me. You know that's why we had to move from Moscow to Domodedovo! Stop it, Ron! I trust You, Lord.

"We're here. No matter what difficulties this creates, we're going to make the best of it. Let's drop our luggage off at the hotel and then evangelize."

We spent the rest of the afternoon passing out tracts and visiting hospitals. While touring one hospital, I approached a nurse and Andre translated. "Why are there so many cancer patients in this city?"

The old nurse waved an arm towards the window. "The average citizen gets cancer after seven years." She shrugged. "We don't know why but some are immune. Those who are immune can make a great living. Otherwise, people only come here for two-three years, make big money, and then leave before it affects their health."

An orderly walked by and said, "The city is a forgotten prison colony left over from the Stalin era. The descendants remained, and it has grown to a city of 175,000 people."

Thankful for the friendliness of the hospital employees, I asked, "We heard there are Reindeer People in Norilsk. Do you know where we can find them?"

The nurse furled her brow and replied, "I haven't seen any of them around town. Perhaps they haven't arrived yet. We had an unusually long winter."

"Where will we find them?" Andre asked.

Both the nurse and orderly shook their heads and walked away.

As we headed down another street passing out tracts, I commented, "You know, I've been in Russia more than seven years. I love how most Russians are willing to take a tract."

I pointed to a kiosk, stopped to buy some drinks, and held up my bottle of Sprite. "Imagine, in this forgotten city, way up in the Arctic North, Coca-Cola is marketing its products."

I handed a Sprite to Andre and continued, "If only we Christians could get the Gospel to the world as well as Coca-Cola markets its products. Nearly everyone in the world would have access to the Gospel!"

The next morning as we left the hotel, I stopped at a bench. "I feel like my chest is going to explode, my throat is constricted." I hacked and coughed and could hardly talk.

Lord, I need relief. What can I do? It's just not safe for me here. I feel Job's verse today—

Though he slay me, yet will I trust in him. (Job 13:15a)

I pointed to a mountaintop peeking over a roof. "Let's climb that mountain. I need fresh air." Andre hailed a taxi and said to the driver, "Take us to the foot of that mountain."

On the road to the mountain

He gave us a strange look before heading towards the mountain. At the trailhead, we paid him and hiked a few minutes before we ran into a guard. She looked at us strangely when we said we wanted to climb her mountain. "I need to clear my lungs from the green smog," I explained.

She and Andre talked back and forth; he handed her a tract. He took his camera out, "She has never met an American before, she said you can take a picture with her."

Armed with another Sprite, we continued to the top. I felt my lungs clear; the fresh air was so good!

"Andre, come over here!" I pointed towards the city below, "Isn't that a wonderful example of God's creation?"

"Indeed, God is an Artist! The green gas below gives a mystical feel." With that, Andre turned, took off his shirt, and jumped into the icy cold pond. "Join me, Brother Ron! The water is clean and gives me energy!"

I took a moment to think of the English word Andre was attempting to describe—*invigorating*. "No thanks. I'll take the photos."

I managed one photo before Andre jumped out laughing, "That pond is colder than jumping into the snow after sweating in a *banya* (sauna)!"

With the guard on the mountain

I smiled as Andre quickly redressed. I sat on a rock as he lay in the sun to dry off. "This fresh air feels good! I think it is clearing both my mind and my lungs."

Back down in the city, we again passed out tracts. While conversing with an old man, I said, "You should climb that mountain over there. The air is so fresh!"

His eyes widened, "Oh I would never climb that mountain!"

"Why not?"

He smirked as if we were fools, "It's nuclear radiated."

We gasped as we stared at the mountain. I mused "So, we came down from the mountain glowing—but not like Moses!"

Andre laughed as he shook his head, "I think the guard was posted to ward off trespassers. She either wanted us to be radiated or she thought Americans were immune to nuclear radiation!" He sighed, "But, I'm not American."

That night, after dinner, as we drank our tea, I set my cup down. "Andre, while it is interesting witnessing to people in this former Stalin concentration camp, I know God wants us to get the Gospel to the

Reindeer People. Where can we find them? Call your contact in Karaul. Ask him if he knows where to find Reindeer People."

Andre stepped out into the hallway to make the call. He returned a few minutes later, "I've got two good news and one bad news."

"Sandwich it for me." I instructed.

"I didn't buy bread—do you want me to go to the market?" Andre asked confused.

I laughed, "No—sandwich the bad news; start with good news, then the bad and then more good news."

"Oh! Got it. So good news is we may stay with the Christian couple in Karaul. The bad news is to get to Karaul, we first must get to Dudinka and take a boat upriver. My friend says there are no Reindeer People in either town right now."

"That is bad news—what's the other good news?"

"He heard there is a Reindeer festival coming to his town of Karaul. Karaul is the Reindeer word for *Hello*. They hold a yearly Reindeer festival there."

The next morning, after breakfast, I asked our waiter. "Where can we buy a ticket for the train to Dudinka?"

"No train." He shook his head, "Maybe taxi."

We left the restaurant wondering how we could get to Dudinka, 50 miles west of Norilsk. Andre approached several townsfolk to confirm what we had been told. "Missionary, most of them do not know where the Reindeer People are. They are nomadic. The elders often live next to the river to fish with homemade nets."

He pointed to an old man. "He said even they don't know how long or where their relatives and friends stay in each place. They go where the reindeer lead them. Every year is different." His saddened face told me everything. "The train works no more."

Talking and walking only made my lungs hurt more, so while I rested, Andre continued to inquire about transportation. He came back just before lunch. "Missionary, train tracks are now a gravel road." At that moment, an old beat-up car of indiscriminate make and model pulled up. He waved at the driver and shook hands with him. "He agreed to take us until his car can't make it any farther."

But Lord, what about when the driver won't take us farther?

The driver put our luggage in the trunk.

Lord, my faith is stretched. I'll go but we need a ride the whole way!

I moved to the front passenger seat and Andre squeezed into the rear. After driving four hours the driver stopped. I climbed out and gazed at

Norilsk

the mountains. The air was fresh, and I took several deep breaths. "I'm glad we stopped for a break; my legs are cramped. I need to stretch."

I turned when I heard a door slam and saw the driver unloading our gear.

Lord, what's going on? We need a way to go the last ten miles. And it looks worse than the last forty.

I pointed to the driver. "Wait a minute! You can't leave us."

At that moment I heard a diesel engine. Before long, an old tractor pulling a flatbed trailer came around a corner. Andre and the driver waved and shouted.

I approached from behind and tapped Andre on a shoulder. "Would you please tell me what the commotion's about?"

Andre pointed to the tractor driver. "This is the taxi driver's cousin. He will take us the rest of the way, but we must pay him."

I pulled out my wallet and walked up to the tractor, "I'll pay you 20 American dollars," I snapped my fingers, rushed to my bags, and pulled out a Russian Bible. "And I'll throw in this."

The man's eyes bulged when he saw the Bible. This time I understood every word the man said. His cousin leaned towards him and interjected, "It's the same Bible that grandmother read to us. It's yours if you take him to Dudinka."

The tractor driver hugged the Bible, then put it in a box behind his seat. The two Russians loaded our luggage onto the trailer and in moments we were on our way. I looked around at the seemingly endless tundra.

Thank You, Lord for the clean air and for a ride to Dudinka.

After the bone-rattling tractor ride, we unloaded our luggage in front of the port authority building. When I reached the front of the line, I said in Russian, "I need two tickets to the town of Karaul."

The clerk shook his head, "У вас нет разрешения."

Lord, what does he mean I don't have permission to go there?

I stared at the clerk in disbelief. "I need to get up North to the town of Hello. My documents say I'm free to travel in this district!" I waited for Andre to translate.

The clerk shook his head. "You don't have authorization to enter a restricted military zone."

Lord, there must be a way. I've been arrested at the airport and interrogated for hours. I've exposed my lungs to perilous green gas, and I've been nuclear radiated. Surely these trials were not in vain! I must go North to the Reindeer People. Please show me what to do.

I sighed and maintained eye contact with the clerk, "Isn't there anyone in authority I can appeal to?"

The man laughed and pointed across the way, "There's a General in that tower who could give you permission." The smirk on the clerk's face told me there was little to no chance, but I had to try.

Riding on the tractor trailer — Andre is on the right

THOUGHTS
- What obstacles have you overcome to share the Gospel?

Chapter Thirty-Nine

Dudinka

I had fainted, unless I had believed to see the goodness of the LORD in the land of the living. Wait on the LORD: be of good courage, and he shall strengthen thine heart: wait, I say, on the LORD. Psalm 27:13-14

As I walked across the gravel lane towards the military base, I shivered, and not just from the cold. There was an eerie silence across the tundra. The only sound was our footsteps as the wind blew wisps of charcoal-colored dust in our faces.

Why am I doing this? I'm walking into a trap! Russians this far North are still bitter about losing the Cold War. As an American, I am still their enemy.

Townsfolk watched from a safe distance as this crazy American and his interpreter approached the military gate. The entrance to the base was heavily guarded with razor-sharp fences, machine guns, and German Shepherd/wolf guard dogs. The dogs went livid as I drew near. Even from behind the fence, they were violently trying to attack. It seemed obvious that they had been trained on American meat and I was the only American within a thousand miles! I felt intimidated.

Lord, give me strength. I can do all things through Christ which strengtheneth me.

The highest-ranking soldier pursed his lips and pointed his weapon at me. "What do you want?"

I was tired and suffering from sleep deprivation. It seemed as if every step of our journey was met with one more roadblock. Perhaps the machine gun pointed at my head clouded my judgement. My mouth was not working in Russian like I wanted. I did not wait for my interpreter and demanded in Russian: "Take me to your leader!"

What? Was I crazy?

I swallowed hard and softened my voice. "I mean, can I please talk to someone about getting permission to go up North?" The guard yanked the passport out of my hand and zeroed in on the USA emblem. The look on their faces told me what they were thinking, "What was an American doing this far North in the Russian tundra?"

The guard disappeared up the steep metal stairs to the tower. He soon returned, restrained the dogs, and opened the gate. Despite the near freezing temperature, sweat dripped from my brow. I walked up the steps to a large set of doors. A tall soldier scowled as I walked past. I was between two burly soldiers. The clomping of their boots and my soft footfall told me I was no match.

But like David when he went against Goliath, they are no match for my God.

The guards guided me into an office. "Wait for our commander." They then left with Andre.

I waited in the small office. My mind began to panic.

I am in the middle of the Russian Arctic North, inside a secret military base. No one, not even my wife knows where I am. This could be where my journey ends. They could keep me, and the American Embassy would have no idea where to find me. Where did they take Andre?

With each passing minute my fear of joining the unnamed political prisoners of the Cold War grew exponentially. Finally, I heard someone coming up the steps.

Clunk! Clunk! Clunk!

The door opened. A huge man, roughly 300 pounds and six feet five inches tall, lowered his head to walk through the door. My eyes were drawn to my passport in his hand. He paused just inside the doorway and waited for me to acknowledge him. He towered over me as our eyes locked, and said, "Now that I've got an American, I think I'll keep you."

Lord, he can keep me here forever, no one will ever find me.

"What do you want?" He demanded.

I squirmed, "We need clearance to go North. I am a missionary. My friend Andre and I want to preach the Gospel to the Reindeer People. We have permission from the police to be in Norilsk, but I need your approval to go North."

Dudinka

He frowned as he picked up Andre's passport from the desk. He looked at it and replied, "Do you know if Andre served in the Russian military?"

I nodded.

"Then I might give him permission, but why should I give it to you? Perhaps you are a spy."

Lord, we can handle this.

I took out a Bible and a tract and set them on his desk. I began to tell him about God and Jesus' death on the cross.

Tears came to his eyes as he said, "My grandmother told me this story as a child. I am almost ready to accept what you say. My heart tells me it is Truth."

Surprised at this response, I opened my Russian Bible to the Gospel of John. Heavy footsteps could be heard coming up the stairs. The General took out a handkerchief, blew his nose and said, "I'll think about what you said."

He quickly stamped our passports and gave us permission to go North! He shoved them at me and nervously stared at the door. "Now go; get out before something bad happens."

He did not have to tell me twice. My chair screeched on the linoleum floor as I pushed it back. I ran towards the door. The cold Arctic breeze hit me in the face and I fled, taking the stairs two at a time. Andre was at the bottom under the watchful eyes of two guards. I gave him his passport and motioned for him to follow me. The guards blocked us until the General ordered, "Let them go. I have no further need of them."

It was euphoric to now be outside the razor wire! Freedom never tasted so good! After saying a prayer of thanks to God, we went back to the Port Authority.

The same clerk was on duty. I proudly displayed our permission stamp. "Two tickets to the town of Hello." I did not mention why we wanted to go North. I had learned in Russia; you only give as much information as needed.

"You are in luck!" said the ticket salesman, "There is a boat coming tomorrow morning at 8 a.m."

I pocketed our tickets as Andre and I walked out onto the street. I opened the departure schedule and ran a finger down the middle column. "It seems the boat comes once a week, and we only have permission to be there for three days." I sighed. "It was the hand of God that brought us here at the perfect time."

We floated on air as we went to find lodging. We booked a room in a primitive hostel near the river.

7 a.m. the next morning we stood in a line with almost 100 people waiting for the boat. Most of the passengers had spent the night on the riverbank. We passed out tracts and shared the Gospel with those waiting with us.

8 a.m. came and went with no boat. No big deal—maybe it was late. 9 a.m. came and went. 10 a.m. and 11 a.m. came and went. Finally, at noon, we went back into the Port Authority.

The bespectacled clerk never glanced up from his desk: "It came last night and was already full, so it kept going." He never stopped shuffling paperwork and stamping tickets.

Lord! You led us to the Reindeer People. This was our last chance.

I felt my face flush and as calmly as possible said, "When will the next boat come?"

"Seven days."

I have never felt as low or as much of a failure as I did at that moment. I was completely deflated.

Lord, we only have permission to be up North for three days. We cannot wait another week.

We walked to a pier with a dilapidated boat. I caught the attention of a man I assumed was the captain. Andre called out and I nodded in agreement even though I did not understand most of it.

Lord I'm going to trust You. I don't know everything he's saying, or what the captain's response is, but please Lord. I want to go to Hello.

For the next hour we went from boat to boat along the river asking fishing boats to take us to Karaul. We heard the same words every time. "У меня нет разрешения (I don't have permission to go there)."

With each denial, Andre pulled out our papers and pointed to the stamps of approval. After a few rejections, I did not need his translation.

Lord, I can't blame them; they don't want to risk going without permission and they refuse to meet the General in the tower.

We sat on a log and Andre frowned. "Missionary, I never see you so depressed. Why? Do you not have faith?"

I took a deep breath and caught myself as the pain racked my lungs. Even though we were miles from Norilsk and the green gas, my lungs still had not recovered. I glanced at Andre and contemplated our situation, "I'm human. I get discouraged too. This is one of those times. I can't believe we aren't going to preach to the Reindeer People."

Dudinka

God, did You send me here to fail? I've been arrested, interrogated, filled with poisonous gas, nuclear radiated, a military prisoner, and got my hopes up for a boat trip, only to have missed the boat. Why did You let me get this close only to be unsuccessful? What are You doing? How are You working?

I looked over at my companion.

Lord, I'm out on a limb here. Think of this man's faith! If I fail, how can he be inspired to answer Your call?

I stood and picked up our bags. "Let's go back to the Port Authority one more time. If nothing else, maybe they will give us our money back."

Again, I caught the clerk's attention and Andre translated, "Are you sure there are no more boats going North? We've asked all the fishing boats, none of them have permission."

From the back of the room, we heard a man say, "Tell them about the other boat."

"What boat?" we eagerly asked.

"Never mind," said the clerk, "You don't want to get on that boat."

I leaned on the counter, "Why not?"

"No self-respecting Russian would ever get on that boat."

It was Andre's turn to ask, "Why not?"

"Because" the ticket salesman growled looking at us as if we were idiots, "It's filled with Reindeer People. Who wants to travel with those smelly barbarians?"

"Give us two tickets, PLEASE!" we said, grinning from ear to ear.

That evening we boarded the boat. It was filled with 150 Reindeer People. They were the teachers, guardians and children of tribal leaders returning from summer camp where they studied the Russian language! It was the time of the White Nights when the sun never set. We stood on boxes on either end of the deck and preached all night to as many people as would gather. We preached of the True and Living God Who created the sun and everything it shines upon. We told of Jesus, His Son, Who died on the cross for our sins.

After we finished speaking, we gave out Bibles and tracts, and were able to get God's Word into the hands of all the tribes represented on that boat.

Never doubt God—He always has a plan.

THOUGHTS
- Can you think of a time when you thought God had failed you only to see how He was working out a great plan for His glory?

CHAPTER FORTY

The Town of Hello

Distributing to the necessity of saints; given to hospitality.
Romans 12:13

"Andre, we could have traveled for years in the Northern tundra and never met as many Reindeer Tribal leaders as we did on this boat."

I moved as more tribespeople pushed us aside on the gang plank. "God appointed this meeting with the Reindeer People from the foundations of the earth. This miracle was scheduled even while I was complaining and doubting!"

Our first meeting of the Reindeer People on the boat

A clock struck 8 a.m. in the distance. It had been a long all-night journey up the Yenisei River. "Andre, find a phone to call your friend."

The Town of Hello

I knelt to open my backpack. "I'll pass out tracts."

Twenty minutes later he came back. "Vlad will meet us at the port in 30 minutes."

I looked back at the dock. "Sounds good. Let's keep passing out tracts as we walk back." Many people took a tract.

Lord, bless these tracts and put it in their hearts to read them.

As I finished praying, I heard Andre call my name. I looked to see him standing with a short middle-aged man. I walked over to them.

"Brother Ron, this is Vlad." I reached out my hand and Vlad took it. "Nice to meet you." He said in heavily accented English.

I smiled at the friendly man, "Nice to meet you too."

Vlad turned to Andre and speaking in Russian invited us to his home. Andre walked between us as Vlad led the way. He stopped at a small shack, opened the door, and motioned for us to enter. Adjusting my eyes to the darkness, I saw a woman and two young girls seated at a small table. The woman jumped up and said in Russian, "Please sit down. I'll get you some bread and tea."

Vlad closed the door and walked into the tiny kitchen. "This is my wife, Tanya, and my two daughters, Nastya and Alena." Pointing to us, he continued the introductions, "Dear, this is Brother Ron and Andre. Please sit down."

Vlad turned to the older daughter, "Nastya, did you find out from your Reindeer friend if they will be holding a festival tonight?"

Nastya sat up straight, "Yes, Papa. They will begin the festival at 6 p.m. in the town square."

I smiled at Andre across the table and pointed to Heaven. Andre nodded and spoke in Russian to the family, "God brought us here at the right time."

After a breakfast of bread, salami, and cucumbers, Vlad pushed back his chair. "Come, you must be tired from preaching on the boat. You must sleep. When you awaken, I will take you fishing. I think God will bless if a holy man is with me. We will eat fish for dinner and go to the festival. My family will help you pass out your brochures about Jesus."

We slept for three hours, ate a quick lunch, and then Vlad took us fishing on a small canoe. It only took us an hour to catch three large fish. Vlad was ecstatic, "I usually only catch one after fishing for three hours. God indeed has blessed us."

We returned to the shack and took a photo with the fish. Tanya fried the fish, serving them with rice and bread. I thanked her for the delicious meal and hospitality as the girls cleaned up the table.

As we approached the town square, I could hear music playing and someone singing in Nenets. There was a semi-circle of Reindeer People standing around a dance floor. I peered above the crowd to see their colorful attire as they performed a traditional Reindeer dance. The dancers acted out the song as the woman sang. It was beautiful.

I turned to Andre, "This is great. It looks like everyone in the village is here." I gave a handful of tracts to Vlad's family, and we all passed them out to those in attendance.

Only eternity will reveal how many souls were saved from the plowing of the fields in the town of Hello—Karaul.

The fish we caught in Hello — Vlad, me & Andre

THOUGHTS
- Are you given to hospitality?
- Have you opened your home to a traveling preacher or missionary?

CHAPTER FORTY-ONE

Rehearsing All That God Did

And when they were come, and had gathered the church together, they rehearsed all that God had done with them, and how he had opened the door of faith unto the Gentiles.
Acts 14:27

Back at the Norilsk airport, I saw several of our "friends" who had arrested us days earlier. I smiled and waved. They just stared stone-faced. As we handed our tickets to the airline attendant, I looked back one last time toward the *militsiya*. I waved good-bye. They nodded in acknowledgment and looked relieved that we were no longer their responsibility.

Andre and I could barely keep our eyes open on the flight back to Moscow

Sometime later Andre whispered, "Brother Ron, are you awake?"

I rubbed my eyes and nodded, "I am now."

Andre continued, "I'm sorry to awaken you but I am so excited about all that God did. I can hardly wait to tell Gala. Perhaps she will see God's hand as I saw it throughout this trip. Hopefully she will come to know our Great God Who loves to the uttermost parts of the earth."

I sat up and smiled, "God is good, Andre. He always has a plan, and His plan is always the best."

"I agree! I have seen this truth and I believe!"

We fastened our seat belt as the pilot announced our descent into Domodedovo Airport. We hurried through the airport, found our baggage, and hailed a taxi. I was excited to go home and tell my family of all the Great and Mighty things God had done.

I opened our front door at the compound to see six lovely faces gathered at the entrance. "You're home!" they all cried in unison.

Joel grabbed my coat while Micah took my luggage. Kathy hugged me first, but it soon turned into a group hug. "Let's go into the living room! I have stories to tell!"

Six glowing faces listened as I recalled the arrest, the green gas, and the nuclear mountain. Looks of astonishment turned to amazement as I told of the tractor ride, the military general almost getting saved, and then the miraculous boat of Reindeer People.

Kathy could see the look of fatigue on my face as I struggled to tell more. Finally, she interrupted, "Okay, kids, it's late. Let Daddy rest. It was a long trip, and he needs to sleep. Brush your teeth, get your jammies on, and get to bed. Joel, pray and thank God for Daddy's safe return."

Joel stood, "Father, we thank You for how You worked in Dad's life. Thank You for leading him where You wanted him to go. Help us all sleep well, knowing You are guiding and protecting us each step of every day. In Jesus' name, Amen."

I slept eight hours straight and awakened to the children whispering "Be quiet! You'll wake Daddy! He's had a big adventure and needs to rest."

I dragged myself out of bed and downstairs to the kitchen table. Kathy set a plate of eggs, bacon, and toast in front of me. I reached up, kissed her cheek, and said, "You have no idea how great it is to be home. Two weeks without a home cooked American meal was rough! I don't think I can eat another bowl of buckwheat!"

Kathy sat down and smiled, "I can't imagine how difficult it was. Unfortunately, it's Saturday and you have two sermons to prepare for tomorrow. The kids and I will walk to Baskin Robbins this afternoon so you can study."

After they left, I soon fell back to sleep.

The next morning, I stood before the church. Most of the Bible College students were present. Some had arrived early, hoping to get the scoop on the Reindeer adventure. Yakov and Sada, the Armenian couple, continued to jabber their questions: "What did you enjoy the most? Were you ever scared? Did the Lord do any miracles?"

"Wait for the sermon!" I told them with a grin.

We sang a few hymns, did the announcements and then I stood, "Before I preach, I know everyone is excited to hear about our trip." I paused.

Rehearsing All That God Did

Lord, please let Andre's words inspire them to take a more active part in missions. Maybe even come along on the next trip.

"Andre, please say a few words."

He made his way to the front, clasping and unclasping his hands as he talked. "At first, I did not want to go. But somehow, I felt the Lord tell me to go."

He paused and pointed to me. "Brother Reasoner told me he would pay for everything."

Everyone's eyes widened as he told them of the green nuclear mist we walked through. He stopped as if he'd lost his train of thought.

I stood to help him, "He talks about my faith," I chuckled. "I watched his faith grow in the 10 days we traveled together."

Andre took a step forward having regained his composure. He pointed to me. "I went with him and preached to many Russians and Reindeer People."

Andre concluded, "I saw him taken away by the FSB. My faith grew as I prayed during my interrogation. After I was released, I prayed until he was freed." He shook his head. "In 10 days, I preached many times. Sometimes from memory, sometimes from notes." He pointed to me, "I saw him in despair, then he prayed, and God answered his prayer." He tapped his chest. "I felt my faith grow because of him. I'm glad I went to visit the Reindeer People." He paused, nodded, and went back to his seat.

I wiped a tear from my eye as I stood behind the podium. I opened my Bible and said, "Stand with me as we read Jeremiah 33:3,

"Call unto me, and I will answer thee, and show thee great and mighty things, which thou knowest not.

"Most of you know this is my life verse. I have claimed it and prayed it almost every day of my Christian life. On this trip, that's exactly what God did!"

I spent the next 30 minutes rehearsing the miracles of our Reindeer trip, proclaiming the grace of God in every trial and His divine guidance each step of the way. I lowered my voice and announced to the group, "I think God would have us go again."

Immediately six Bible College students jumped up. One called out, "I want to go!"

Another bowed his head and prayed, "Here am I, Lord, send me."

The others also joined in agreement, "We ALL want to go!"

Well, Lord, they say that success breeds success.

I held up my hand, "Okay, now that you've seen what the Lord can do, I'm pleased so many of you want to go. The only time we can go is between June and September. I'm scheduled to be in the States next Summer."

They plopped back into their seats disappointed.

"Don't despair. I can't guarantee that we'll be able to take everyone. I may not have enough money." I passed my hand over them, "Some of you are excited now, but your interest may fade. When I return from America, we'll see what the budget is and how many are still interested. I'd like to go again in 2002."

THOUGHTS

- In your spiritual walk, who has been a source of encouragement to press toward the mark for the prize of the high calling of God in Christ Jesus?
- Does your life encourage others to press on for that same high calling?

CHAPTER FORTY-TWO

Preparing for the 2nd Trip

For I rejoiced greatly, when the brethren came and testified of the truth that is in thee, even as thou walkest in the truth.
3 John 1:3

Back in the United States

During the next eight months we had classes every Saturday at the Bible Institute, Andre continued getting permits for the compound, and I supervised the remodeling. It was a blessing to no longer commute from Moscow to Domodedovo. Living onsite gave me ample opportunity to see how hard the workers labored each day.

It worked out as I had planned. When the Ukrainian Baptist workers went home for Christmas, I never invited them back. I now employed two brothers, also Ukrainians, who were finishing the compound. In addition to the remodeling, I was preaching in three churches each week.

Joel, now 17, graduated from High School in May 2001. We returned as a family to the USA for a furlough. I needed to raise funds to finish the compound and Joel needed to seek God's will about which Bible College to attend. He knew he was called to Russia as a missionary, but he needed a degree. He was also looking for a wife who was surrendered to God's will and would join him on the mission field.

We were in America when the Twin Towers in New York City, and the Pentagon in Washington, DC were attacked on 9/11/2001. Who can forget that day? It had a profound impact upon the whole world. It is hard to fathom the evil that Satan plants in the hearts of people. It is his plan to destroy God's creation and to stop the spread of the Gospel.

As it happened, Kathy took a short trip to Russia at the end of September 2001 just three weeks after 9/11 to sign some house papers.

Serving God Behind Enemy Lines

Russian law had changed, and we were able to get the land officially in Kathy's name. Our Russian email inbox was full of warnings—about a month old—from the USA embassy in Moscow saying that there was chatter of something huge about to happen in the world; stay low and avoid large public gatherings. Intelligence knew something was going to happen, they just did not know what or how awful it would be.

In January 2002, I preached at a small church near the naval station in Arlington, Washington. Several young sailors were in attendance, and I felt God would call one of them. I preached fervently about the need for helpers. I begged, "This is a Macedonian call for help. Come over and help us!"

At the invitation, I waited for one of the young men to surrender to God for missions. Instead, an elderly couple shuffled down the aisle. Brother Glenn Sanders grabbed my hand, "Brother Reasoner, I have a full pension. We are ready to go to Russia."

I remembered meeting Glenn and Winnie Sanders at a missionary retreat in Romania several years earlier. They were a blessing to the missionary there. I asked, "Why did you leave Romania?"

Glenn answered, "My diabetes was out of control and my health was bad, but we've gotten that straightened out. The missionary in Romania replaced us with another couple so we are free to come help you."

Really God? I was looking for a young helper! Are You seriously sending me Brother Sanders?

I smiled, "Let's go out to dinner and talk."

Two months later, we met the Sanders at the Seattle airport to fly back to Russia. While waiting for them to arrive, Joel asked, "Dad, I know when you were preaching that night in Arlington you wanted a young man to surrender, but God called Brother Sanders instead. Why?"

I looked all my children in the eye, "People fear the unknown. Some spend their whole lives wondering if they step off the cliff of faith, will God catch them? They never step off because they fear the fall. Glenn and Winnie Sanders have jumped off the cliff so many times, they know God will catch them, so they continue to jump."

Back in Russia

Upon our return, I called each of the Bible College students and asked them about the summer plans for our next Reindeer trip. Despite my fears of their interest waning, they remained solid in both their faith and desire to visit the Reindeer People.

One morning Kathy called out from our bedroom, "Ron!"

Preparing for the 2nd Trip

I stuck my head out the bathroom door, a razor in one hand and shaving cream in the other, "Yes?"

"Winnie's on the phone. She wants to go on the trip, but at her age she can't do much." Kathy held the phone next to her chest and walked into the bathroom. "Glenn really wants to go too. Even though he's 74, he feels the Lord has things for him to do on the mission field."

I squirted shaving cream on my fingers and patted my face, "I don't know. She's not in the best of health, and with his diabetes, it is too risky."

Kathy signed and continued, "She thought that's what you'd say. She wants to watch everyone's luggage at the base camp and be a prayer warrior." Kathy put the phone to her ear. "Winnie, Ron says he'll think about it. But what about your husband's diabetes?"

My eyes bulged out and I started to speak. She held a hand up and continued, "Winnie, Glenn can talk to Ron this afternoon. We'll see if they can come to an agreement." She put the cordless phone back on the receiver in the bedroom and stared at me, "Ron, don't look at me like that. I agree with you about Glenn's health. But that's his decision."

I scraped the blade across my day-old stubble as she talked. I shook the razor at her and scolded. "Listen, I'm the one who will be out there with six rookies, Joel, and two elderly retirees;" I pointed a finger at her. "Not you."

Undaunted, she handed me a towel, "You missed a dollop of shaving cream."

I wiped my neck and hung the towel up. She followed me as I walked down the stairs to breakfast.

"And—" Kathy continued, "Don't act like I'm refusing to go on this trip. You know I'd love to go, but someone must stay home with the children. They are my first responsibility after you, and I am tasked with watching Yakov and Sada's daughter so they can go." She paused the conversation and poured me a cup of tea. She placed it on the table and continued, "Besides, I need to make sure we invest time each day in prayer for the success of this trip."

Keturah and Hannah had just finished setting the table. Joel was teasing Jeremiah, and Micah was filling platters with food from the stove. Their heads swiveled from Kathy and me as we continued.

We sat at either end of the table. Once the children were seated, I nodded to 16-year-old Micah. "I think it's your turn to say the blessing."

We held hands and he started. "Lord, we thank You for this food and the bounty You've blessed us with." He paused and looked at us then bowed his head, "Lord, help Mom and Dad to settle their argument." He let go of Hannah's and Keturah's hands. "Amen."

Everyone reached for a different dish and ladled food onto their plates. Kathy poured juice and passed the glasses around. I scooped out some scrambled eggs, then pointed the spoon at her. "I know, I'm sorry it sounded like I faulted you for not going. I'm worried about Glenn. I've been with him when he's had an episode. It's not pretty. It's too much of a risk."

Kathy cut her ham with a fork. "That was three months ago. He's been watching his diet, he's lost 30 pounds, and hasn't had another episode." She put a piece of ham to her mouth. "Besides, they've been great helpers since coming here in March. They deserve to go and he's willing to split the expenses 50/50."

At 2 p.m., Glenn came into my office. He set his briefcase next to his customary chair, went to the teapot and poured his usual cup. He stirred sugar and cream as he sat. "Winnie said you don't want me going on the Reindeer trip." He took a quick sip of the scalding brew. "I think I deserve to go." He held up a finger and started to count off his reasons:

"1. I've worked with you on this remodeling project, and I haven't charged you one thin dime."

He sat back and held up another finger, "2. You're going to mention my diabetes, but I've lost weight, I'm watching my sugar, I eat right."

He leaned forward, "3. You need another strong Christian to help shepherd this large group through the unknown."

He took a deep breath, "4. I really feel the Lord wants me to go."

He tapped his thumb on my desk, "5. Winnie agrees with me; you know what a prayer warrior she is. She has a special pipeline to God."

He tapped his back pocket, "Lastly, 6. It won't cost you a penny for us. We'll pay our own way and share half the cost of all the others."

I shook my head. "I know, my friend, but—"

He shook his head in return. "No, you wait a minute. We've been over your itinerary. We'll be on a train, at a hotel or some sort of lodging, or transportation." He shrugged his shoulders. "With the Lord on our side, what could go wrong?"

I sipped my tea as my friend made his case.

Lord, but what if? What if he forgets to take his pills? What if he doesn't eat right? We'll be in the Arctic Circle and no way to get help.

My shoulders slumped. "Okay, I give in. If God tells you to go, how can I tell you to stay home?"

Preparing for the 2nd Trip

On Saturday, May 25, 2002, the team met for an overview on what to expect. I sat on a stool and pointed. "You all know Glenn and Winnie. They are helping in the ministry, and have asked to go on the Reindeer trip."

I sighed, "National Geographic spends millions of dollars in their attempts to locate Reindeer tribes in the Arctic North. My budget is $212."

Glenn interrupted, "With my portion, that's $424."

I continued, "Everyone needs to be prepared to give a short testimony of how they came to Christ." I pointed to them. "Why did you become a Christian? How has it changed your life?"

I looked around before saying, "Joel, you go first."

"Yes, sir." He rose, shuffled his feet, and took a deep breath, "I accepted Jesus as my Savior as a little boy. I fought with my brothers all the time, and realized I was a sinner and needed real forgiveness."

As he talked, he gained confidence and waved his arms for emphasis. "Four years ago, I told my parents that I wanted to be a doctor, but one day my brother Micah and I were coming home from school and a gang of boys beat us up. It was then I realized the need for more missionaries in Russia, and I surrendered to God's calling. I've been serving with my dad since I began leading songs at age six, but I want to do more! That is why I want to go on this trip." He returned to his seat.

Wow! That's my boy.

I pointed to Oleg. "It's your turn. I want you to tell us about your walk with the Lord and what you will be doing on the trip. Why do you want to go?"

The stocky Moldovan and the petite woman sitting beside him stood. "I'm Oleg Turcan. This is my lovely wife, Annya. I grew up in an orphanage. When I turned 16, they cast me into the streets." He scratched his chin as he pondered. "I got a job with the Russian Mafia. I did odd jobs for the bosses. One day the head man's son got caught breaking a man's legs for not paying protection money. Boss man told me to confess, and I would be taken care of when I got out of prison." He shrugged, "So, I confessed."

Oleg paused to formulate his thoughts, "In prison, I met a pastor who told me about Jesus and that I needed to ask Him to forgive my sins. That's when I became a Christian. I was in prison for three years when that happened. Then two years later I was set free when a friend bribed a government official."

I almost fell out of my chair.

Lord, help me to know how to disciple him to become the Christian You want him to be.

Oleg took out a handkerchief and blew his nose. "I want to tell people that if Jesus can help me, He can help them."

I stood and pointed to Yakov. "I'd like to hear from you next."

He stood, "I am Yakov" He put his hand on his wife's shoulder. "This is my wife, Sada. We come from Armenia. I met my wife when I was a New Age religious instructor. The more I studied, the more I became convinced that the earth was not created by accident. There had to be Intelligent Design. I asked a friend many questions. He told me about Jesus' salvation. I became a Christian and Sada followed me."

He sat and I pointed to Dimitre. He strutted to the front and stood tall. He waited until everyone's eyes were on him, "I have friends at the Church in Labytnangi. I called them and because of my friendship, we can stay in their dormitory for free." He rubbed his chin, "I want to go on this trip so I can learn how to preach better. Brother Reasoner is helping me start a church in Moscow. It is going great."

I sat in the back with crossed arms.

Lord, why is he so arrogant? Give me patience and wisdom to deal with him.

As Dimitre returned to his seat I moved towards the window and leaned on the windowsill. "Dimitre, you need to tell us when you realized you were a sinner and how you came to Christ." I pointed to each of them. "That goes for all of you. Make sure they understand why you felt the need for a Savior."

Dimitre shifted in his seat, then raised a hand.

I nodded, "Yes?"

"Brother Reasoner, you tell us we're going to be on this train for 48 hours." He spread his hands, "What are we going to be doing during that time?"

I pointed to everyone sitting around the table. "I expect everyone," I tapped my chest, and pointed to Joel, "Myself and my son included, to walk the aisles and share our faith with fellow passengers. We are perhaps the only born-again Christians they will ever meet. We must redeem the time."

I pointed to Joel, "Please close us in prayer."

Joel stood, "Father, thank You for the opportunity. Thank You for everyone who has surrendered to go. From the youngest to the oldest, use us to spread Your Word among the Reindeer People."

Preparing for the 2nd Trip

I pointed to several boxes of tracts sitting in the corner. "Everyone will have an ample supply of material to pass out. You have three weeks to rehearse your testimonies and be able to give it no matter how many times I interrupt you with questions."

I moved to the front. "That's the only homework you have between now and the trip."

I nodded, "See you next week."

THOUGHTS
- Do you ever feel too old or too sick to serve the Lord?
- Find Scriptures supporting how God used a variety of people—regardless of age, ability, and status!

Chapter Forty-Three

Leaving on the 2nd Trip

And the lord said unto the servant, Go out into the highways and hedges, and compel them to come in, that my house may be filled. Luke 14:23

The Team

- ✓ Joel — My Oldest Son
- ✓ Yakov & Sada — The Armenians
- ✓ Nina — The Syrian
- ✓ Dimitre — The Ukrainian
- ✓ Glenn & Winnie — The Elderly Americans
- ✓ Oleg — The Moldovan
- ✓ Annya — Oleg's Wife & a Muscovite
- ✓ Myself

On July 14, 2002, we arrived at the Moscow Yaroslavsky Train Station. We talked in small groups while we waited to board the Polar Arrow Train for the 1200-mile ride to Labytnangi.

I cautioned the team one more time. "Remember what I told you. The FSB will have agents roaming the train and the stations. Even more, understand that some vendors are informers who want to gain favor with the *militsiya* by turning you in for some infraction. It may be legal now in Russia to preach the Gospel, but there are plenty of laws we break unintentionally every day."

Joel interrupted, "Like the time you got a ticket for a dirty car."

I nodded, "When the train pulls out of the station, you are to pair up with your partner. The first team will take the first two cars, the second the next two, the third will take the two cars behind us, and the fourth will

Leaving on the 2nd Trip

take the next two." I held up a copy of the tract I had chosen for the trip, *You Are Special*. "If you need more, there are plenty."

I pointed to Glenn, "He and I will stay in our seats and watch the luggage." I checked my watch, "Every couple of hours we'll send out teams. Except for sleeping and eating we need to focus on passing out tracts. As for Bibles, we only have a few for the train. Give them only to people you believe are sincere."

Joel cinched the straps on his backpack. "Dad, I'm glad you insisted on getting here early. It looks like the train will be full."

I looked up and down the platform at the crowds milling around. "Not to mention being able to get all of our luggage stowed together."

It took over 30 minutes for us to pass through the usual gauntlet of *militsiya* and security. Somehow, we made it into our car in the middle of the train. I surveyed as everyone found their assigned bunk. The beds were three high. I had a middle bunk.

Thank You, Lord, I could not have made it to the third level.

When I bought the tickets, all the bottom beds were sold. I was forced to buy second and third level bunks as near to each other as possible. When people on the bottom bunk saw that Glenn and Winnie were assigned second level beds, they offered to switch places.

We settled in, placed our bags on the bunks and the large luggage under the bottom bunks. During the day, the middle bed was folded up against the wall so people could sit comfortably on the bottom one without hitting their head. We offered to let the kind-hearted Russians sit on the bottom bunk they had surrendered to our elderly couple.

Forty-five minutes later the train started with a jerk. I was proud of Dimitre when he tapped the man sitting next to him. Soon several passengers were listening, "Do you want peace and eternal life?"

The man frowned, "Go away, not interested."

The gregarious Ukrainian stood, moved across the aisle, sat next to a man with a beard. "What about you? Do you want peace and eternal life?"

The man shrugged, "Who wouldn't?" He scratched his chin. "There are no guarantees."

Dimitre stood where he could be heard by everyone, held a pole, and swayed as the train moved down the track.

Joel and I strained to listen as he talked. "I was a drunkard and had a hard time keeping a job. My wife and daughter left me. Then one day, someone asked me if I wanted to find peace and eternal life." The sunlight vanished as the train entered a tunnel. When we came out the other side, he finished his testimony, "My life was just like going through that tunnel;

dark and lonely. It wasn't until I saw the Light of Christ that I realized I could have eternal life. I asked Jesus to save me, and He did. God put my life in order, and my wife and daughter returned to me." He paused and waved a hand at his audience, "You too can know Jesus and He will set you free—right now if you want."

The bearded man nodded.

Dimitre's eyes widened nervously, "Well, then, ah," He took a deep breath and pursed his lips. "All you have to do is repeat as I pray." He folded his hands and bowed his head, "Lord Jesus, I thank You for dying for me and paying the price for my sins. I admit I am a sinner; I accept Your salvation and ask You to help me to grow in my faith." He opened his eyes, raised his head. "Amen."

As soon as Dimitre finished, Joel and I joined him in passing out tracts to nearby passengers. The bearded man, excited about his newfound faith in Christ, reached for his copy of the New Testament.

Encouraged by Dimitre's success, Winnie and Annya picked up their purses and went into the next car. Joel and Oleg walked the other direction. The rest of the team dispersed to their assigned cars.

Lord, I pray that Joel will work well with these people. If he wants to serve them, this is the best way to learn.

I scratched my chin, as I looked at the team.

How well have they learned their lessons? Will they become discouraged when rejected? What else could I have done to prepare them?

I folded my hands in prayer and nodded to Glenn. He winked and I caught the attention of the man who had rebuffed Dimitre earlier. "Are you going all the way to Labytnangi??"

He gave me a questioning look. "No." He picked up a book and started to read.

Lord, he looks troubled. Please give me an opportunity.

I leaned forward and read the title of the book. I pointed to it, "*War and Peace*. While I was in college, I read it in English. Just last year I attempted to read it in Russian."

He turned towards me, and with a thick Romanian accent snarled. "Oh, really? What do you think of Tolstoy?"

"I find Tolstoy to be a profound thinker—one of the greatest authors to have ever lived."

He closed his book and nodded.

Well, Lord, I have his attention. Maybe I can reach him, You use different people to reach different people. Lord, help me to remember all the Russian I need to show him the way.

Leaving on the 2nd Trip

I leaned back and folded my hands over a knee.

We talked about Tolstoy and Russian literature until some of the others returned. I tapped my knee, "Leo Tolstoy was a deeply religious man who believed in the sovereignty of God. Tell me Boris, do you think of Jesus as a Spiritual or Historical Figure?"

He pursed his lips. "Well, Mr. Holy Man, let me tell you. I have studied history for years. I know Jesus once lived." He shook his head, "But I don't believe in spiritual beings."

I nodded, "I can respect your opinion—from what you've said, you've studied a lot." I leaned over and lowered my head to look out the window. "But tell me," I waved my hand towards the tundra outside. "Do you think all this happened by accident?"

As I sat back, I continued, "I think the Supreme God, the Creator of the universe provided all this for us to enjoy—for us to have fellowship with Him."

He chuckled. "You must be crazy. Science has proven it's taken billions of years for the earth to evolve." He leaned back against the wall and folded his arms. "What do you have to say about that?"

I noticed two ladies seating across the aisle putting together a jigsaw puzzle. I smiled as I turned back to Boris, "Let me ask you something. If I were to take the puzzle pieces those ladies are putting together, put them into a box and shake it furiously, how long do you think it would take before the puzzle put itself together?"

Boris snorted, "That's ridiculous! Everyone knows a puzzle must be assembled by people!"

I smiled, "I agree Boris, that puzzle can't put itself together. You easily understand that, but you think the world put itself together." Boris cocked his head and fell into deep thought.

We continued talking for two hours. As the train pulled into his station, he rose and pulled his luggage from the shelf. I followed him to the platform, looked him in the eye and handed him a Russian Bible. "Remember the puzzle, Boris. Take this Bible. When you feel like your life is falling apart, you can find what you need in here." I opened it to the Gospel of John and inserted a tract. "I suggest you start on this page."

Boris held the Bible. "Okay, Holy Man, I will keep this. But I don't need help." He unzipped his backpack and stuffed it inside.

"Boris, I'm praying you will understand that God loves you and wants to save you. С Богом! (Go with God)."

Lord, save this man's soul. I will never see him again, but You are with him always.

Glenn and the others disembarked with me, and we purchased *butterbrat* (sandwiches) for 50 cents from locals on the side of the track. While we waited for our food, Joel and Oleg joined us and told us their experiences.

I motioned for everyone to come closer. "You did well. Tell me, did everyone accept tracts? Did you get any rejections?"

Winnie nodded. "I don't understand it. These people have been oppressed for so long and some of them still aren't interested."

The others nodded as they listened to Winnie. Not every witnessing opportunity had been successful.

"You must realize that not everyone's going to accept what you say. Remember Mark 4:14-20. Sometimes you plant the seeds of faith, someone else waters it, and finally someone else reaps the harvest."

Passengers started to reboard. We queued up as well. Joel touched my arm. "Dad, it was great. I saw a couple of boys and said a quick prayer for boldness. I asked them if they had ever heard of Jesus Christ." He shook his head and continued. "The biggest one told me: 'only as a swear word.'" Joel tapped the tracts sticking from his shirt pocket, "I gave each a tract, and told them where I come from and why I am going to the Arctic. In the end both accepted Jesus Christ as their Savior." The smile on his face told me he was gaining confidence in sharing the Gospel.

I put an arm around his shoulders and squeezed. "Good job, son, good job."

Lord, this is starting off well. We have had several great witnessing experiences and we still have 40 hours to go. I pray that these converts are sincere, and that Satan does not snatch them away.

During the train ride we looked for more opportunities to share the Gospel. Many people accepted Christ as their Savior on the train. What a great way to start our journey!

THOUGHTS

- How persistent are you in your soulwinning?
- If a friend or family member rejects Christ, do you continue to pray and pursue them with the Gospel?

CHAPTER FORTY-FOUR

Labytnangi & Salekhard

And they, when they had testified and preached the word of the Lord, returned to Jerusalem, and preached the gospel in many villages of the Samaritans. Acts 8:25

Our train car master moved past our cubical announcing the arrival in Labytnangi, "Bathrooms are closing in 20 minutes. We will reach Labytnangi in one hour. It is the end of the tracks. Gather your sheets and teacups. Return them to my office."

Nina took my sheets. Everyone piled theirs on her arms as well. Annya gathered our teacups. Together they took off for the office. I turned to the team, "We are almost there. Let's get our luggage out and get ready to disembark."

Dimitre moved in front of me, "I lived and worked in Labytnangi for several years at the local church. I have arranged for us to stay in the church dormitory. It is within walking distance from the station. You should follow me."

Lord, he is taking control. I know he struggles with pride, and I do not want to feed his ego, but he knows where he is going. Please keep him in check.

I peered out the window as we approached the platform. The train station was in the shape of a half circle. Glenn stood next to me and noticed the unique architecture, "It's a funny looking building but having a curved roof makes sense considering the amount of snowfall this place gets."

Winnie stood on the other side of Glenn and smiled, "Hallelujah! Our feet will soon be on solid ground. Forty-eight hours on a train has been quite the experience. I am ready for it to be over!"

We grabbed our backpacks, slung them over our shoulders, and grabbed a suitcase in each hand. I noticed Joel helping Winnie get her backpack on and then put on his own. He picked up several suitcases, weighed them and handed the lightest to Winnie.

Good job, Son, you make me proud.

Dimitre took a bag in each hand and pushed his way to the front, "Single file now, follow me!" He stepped off the train onto the platform and took off.

"Slow down!" I called out, "Wait for the rest of us to get off and arrange our bags!" He looked back, frowned, returned, and helped the ladies get their luggage off the train. Once everyone disembarked and settled, he started again. I was close enough to hear him sigh under his breath, "Let's try this again."

The church was centrally located. The pastor met us inside. After exchanging pleasantries, he showed us to the dormitory. It was the size of a small apartment—two bedrooms with bunkbeds lining the walls, a kitchen, and a bathroom. Annya was the first to say what we all were thinking, "Is there hot water for a shower?"

The Pastor frowned, "We are happy to offer you indoor plumbing, but we have no hot water."

Annya would not be deterred, "I will take the first shower and then go to the market for vegetables and meat to make *borscht* while the rest of you settle in." With that, she ran to the girls' room, grabbed her toiletries, and scurried to the shower. Three days on a stuffy train and no chance to shower left us smelling pretty rank.

I turned to the Pastor, "Tell me about your city."

He sat at the kitchen table, and I joined him. Winnie pulled a liter of water out of her backpack, went to the stove, filled the kettle, and began a pot of tea.

Winnie, ever the servant, what a blessing!

The pastor smiled as he watched the elderly lady start to work, then turned his attention back to me, "Labytnangi is on the edge of the Arctic Circle. It was built in the 1950s by *Gulag* inmates. We have grown over the years to a town of about 30,000." He stopped, winked, and added, "We don't get a lot of tourists here. Thank you for coming."

"Dimitre tells me several Reindeer tribes summer here. Have you seen any yet?"

I caught a glimpse of disdain in the pastor's eyes as he looked at Dimitre.

Oh, does this pastor have an issue with him too?

Labytnangi & Salekhard

He answered, "We had a bad winter. Not all the snow and ice has melted yet on the tundra. Perhaps the Reindeer People will come soon. Their festival is not until the end of July. You are early."

Dimitre told me it was the middle of July.

I sighed and asked, "Do you know where any might be?"

The Pastor paused a moment to take a cup of hot tea from Winnie, "There are some in Novyy Port year around."

"How do we get there? Train? Bus? Boat?" I asked.

"Only by helicopter. It will be easy to get a ride there but getting back can be difficult. No one wants to go to Novyy Port, but everyone wants to come back, and helicopter is the only way."

Dimitre entered the conversation, "What about Salekhard? Do you know if there are any there yet?"

The pastor nodded, "Perhaps a few." He shook his head, "But no guarantees. You should go. If nothing else, you will enjoy the Reindeer Museum and they also have an exhibit of the wooly mammoths."

"How do we get there?" Joel asked.

The pastor turned to acknowledge Joel for the first time, "Your Russian is excellent! Are you Russian?"

Joel blushed, "No, I'm Brother Ron's eldest son. We came to Russia when I was 10 years old."

The pastor turned back to me, "He must make you proud!"

I opened my mouth to respond, but he continued, "You have to cross the Obe River to get to Salekhard. The quickest way is to take the ferry. It's a beautiful ride and the ferry crosses several times a day during the summer. We have a man in the church who owns a van. You could rent it. He will meet you as you get off the ferry and drive you wherever you want to go."

"That sounds like a plan." I said to everyone. "Let's rest today, and tomorrow we will go to Salekhard."

With that, the pastor arose, "Well then, I'll leave you to it. Ummm, Brother Ron, could you follow me outside?"

Once we were out of earshot of the others, he mumbled, "Dimitre mentioned you were willing to pay for the use of our facilities—you know, for the water and electricity, and cleaning." Even though Dimitre had said our lodging would be free, I had budgeted for this because nothing is free in Russia.

I pulled out my wallet and handed him a $100 bill, "Will this be enough?" The pastor's eyes lit up as he walked over to a bench, looked at me, then the money and then the bench. I remembered the Russian custom

Serving God Behind Enemy Lines

of not passing money from hand to hand. I put the bill on the bench and the pastor swiftly picked it up, put it in his pocket and left.

I awakened the next morning to the smell of eggs, and toast. As I walked into the kitchen, Winnie was cooking, "Good Morning, Winnie, I see you have been busy."

She smiled, "I asked Annya to buy 20 eggs, bread, butter, and meat when she went shopping. I gave her the money."

I approached the stove and looked at the sausages in the fry pan. Before I could ask, Winnie gleefully replied, "It's reindeer meat. It was the cheapest meat at the market; she bought two kilograms. I've already sampled it." Winnie kissed the tips of her fingers like a gourmet chef, "Delicious!"

By now, the rest of the team was stirring. The smells brought everyone to the kitchen. We ate in shifts. Within the hour, the team was fed, dressed, and ready for adventure.

As I locked the front door, I heard Winnie whisper to Glenn, "Do you have your pills to take with lunch and dinner?" Glenn shook his head and touched my shoulder, "Brother Reasoner, I need to go back inside. I forgot my pills." We patiently waited until Glenn came outside. I locked the door and Dimitre led us to the ferry on the shores of the Obe River.

Yakov was the first to notice the gigantic Wooly Mammoth monument overlooking the Obe River. Everyone snapped photos—the beauty of digital photography! Winnie handed me her camera, "Can you get a photo of Glenn and me together with the Wooly Mammoth? This is something you don't see every day!" After a few shots I handed it back. She looked through them, and smiled, "Thank you!"

When we disembarked at Salekhard, an army green van was waiting. Dimitre rushed to take the front passenger's seat. The rest of us climbed in the side door. As we settled in, the driver introduced himself in Russian, "I'm Anton, I'll be your tour guide today. Our first stop will be the Reindeer Museum."

That said, Anton, took off like a firetruck going to a fire. Those of us in the back scrambled to buckle up and find something to hang on to. Winnie tapped me on the shoulder, "Why are we taking a military van?"

I turned around and asked, "Why do you think it is military?"

Winnie replied, "It is army green. I've never seen a car this color."

I smiled, "I asked that same question many years ago and a Russian man said the colors of the cars are according to the year they were manufactured. They don't change anything on the design of their vehicles, but you can tell what year a car was manufactured by its color!"

Labytnangi & Salekhard

As we pulled up, Anton pointed to a winding sidewalk, "That way to the Reindeer Museum. Follow the path to the *chum* (teepee) display and the gift shop is on the other end. I'll just wait here until you are done."

We enjoyed the exhibit. It was another great photo opportunity with teepees, Reindeer clothing to put on, and even a live reindeer to pet. Eventually we made it to the gift shop. Yakov walked beside me as I commented, "Perhaps someone here will know if any tribes are in town."

The man working at the museum gave us bad news, "No Reindeer tribes have arrived yet. They aren't expected for another two weeks." Seeing our disappointment, he added, "But I have a geologist friend who works in the village of Polyarnyy Ural. I talked to him earlier. He said there are several groups camped about five hours from the village. Do you want to talk to him?" I nodded as he removed a satellite phone from its charger and dialed. He smiled when his friend answered, "Hey, Victor, there is someone here who wants to ask about Reindeer People sightings."

Dimitre grabbed the phone. We listened to the conversation. The geologist had spotted a tribe just that morning. Yes, there was a place to stay in the village—a hunting lodge that charged $3.00 a night per head. The geologist would let the lodge owner know we were coming.

We decided to divide and conquer. Joel, Glenn, and Oleg would leave on the early morning 185-mile Northeast helicopter ride from Salekhard to Novyy Port. Winnie would stay at base camp in Labytnangi as our prayer warrior, and I would take the remaining six on a 3-hour train ride from Labytnangi to Polyarnyy Ural.

It was barely noon by the time we had seen both museums. My heart became burdened for the people in this Northern Region. How many missionaries came here to preach the Gospel? What of the surrounding villages? I returned to the van and sat beside Anton. I looked him in the eye and asked, "Do you know of a village nearby where they don't have Bibles or a Gospel witness?

Anton smiled, "A real Holy man who loves God and would rather tell others about Jesus than anything else!"

Anton rubbed his chin. Finally, he snapped his fingers, "My relatives live about 15 kilometers away. No one has ever visited their village."

I called out to the others, "We are done sightseeing. It's time to be about our Father's business. Let's go share the Good News."

"Amen!" Yakov said as he took Sada's hand and headed for the van. The others nodded and fell in step.

Before we entered the first village, Anton pulled to the side of the road, "If you need to take care of business, now is the time. There are several trees for privacy. The village does not have indoor plumbing. Anton pulled out a leafy branch from under his seat. Seeing my confusion, he said, "This is to ward off the mosquitoes. They are extra-large here."

I pulled a can of Deet from my backpack and stepped out of the van. I quickly and lavishly sprayed myself and handed it to Yakov, "Spray yourself and pass this around."

Yakov immediately passed it to Sada, "Oh, Brother Ron, I don't need it. Mosquitoes don't like me."

The men headed one direction; the ladies went the other. Anton, Dimitre, Oleg, Joel, and I soon returned, and the ladies came back a few minutes later. Sada looked around and asked, "Where is Yakov?"

Just then we heard screaming. We turned to see Yakov struggling to latch his belt with one hand, while hitting himself with the other. He was jumping around like a mad man. "Help me! Help me!" He screamed. Sada ran to his side and started hitting his back. He was covered in mosquitoes. Blood streamed down his face and neck. He had taken his coat off, and mosquitoes covered his arms. Blood was everywhere.

From the safety of the van, we yelled, "Get them all off before you get in!" Yakov swung his coat across his body—first one direction and then another, still screaming. I jumped out of the van, sprayed Deet on him and then shoved him inside. Sada jumped in as well and I yanked the door closed. I leapt into the passenger seat. We all stared in amazement as mosquitoes attacked the van. Unfazed, Anton started the engine and pulled back onto the gravel highway.

For the next two hours, the men paired off to go door to door. The women walked around town and into the local shops handing out tracts and giving New Testaments to those who repented. When we met back at the cultural house, everyone was grinning from ear to ear. We hopped in the van and drove to another village. After three villages, we were out of tracts and New Testaments. God blessed and 35 people prayed the sinner's prayer. Tears of praise and gratitude filled our eyes as we thanked God for the privilege to witness for Him.

We returned to Salekhard and purchased helicopter tickets for the early morning flight to Novyy Port. There were no return tickets available, but Joel and the Novyy Port team wanted to go and trust God to provide.

I then purchased six tickets to Polyarnyy Ural, and we spent the rest of the evening in prayer and packing. Early the next morning, I prayed with Joel's team. They were packed and ready to leave. Winnie kissed Glenn good-bye. I hugged Joel and gave him final instructions. Oleg kissed his wife, Annya. We agreed to meet back at base camp in four days.

"Well!" I sighed after the three amigos left, "We have two hours before our train leaves. God blessed us with souls on the train, souls in the villages, and now let's pray for souls in the tundra."

I opened my Bible to Philippians 4:6-8 and asked Yakov to read.

"Be careful for nothing; but in every thing by prayer and supplication with thanksgiving let your requests be made known unto God. And the peace of God, which passeth all understanding, shall keep your hearts and minds through Christ Jesus. Finally, brethren, whatsoever things are true, whatsoever things are honest, whatsoever things are just, whatsoever things are pure, whatsoever things are lovely, whatsoever things are of good report; if there be any virtue, and if there be any praise, think on these things."

"Thank you, Yakov. I'll close in prayer.

"Dear Father, we know You want to see the Reindeer People saved more than we do. We need Your help. Please protect Joel and his team as they travel to Novyy Port and bless their time there. May Your Name be glorified. Now Lord, I ask that You bless our trip as well. Help us keep our thoughts pure and concentrated on You. God, use us to see Reindeer People saved for You. In Christ's name and for His sake, we ask it, Amen."

THOUGHTS
- Can you think of a time when someone's misinformation cost you time, money, and/or resources?
- How did you deal with the loss?

CHAPTER FORTY-FIVE

The Value of One

Likewise, I say unto you, there is joy in the presence of the angels of God over one sinner that repenteth. Luke 15:10

As my team traveled to the train station, this verse kept reeling in my mind:

Be careful for nothing; but in every thing by prayer and supplication with thanksgiving let your requests be made known unto God. (Philippians 4:6)

Lord, when I chose that verse, I had no idea how much we would need it!

Our tickets were in the fourth-class seating section. We found our car and stood in line. When it was our turn to board, I put my hand on Yakov's shoulder, "Ask the conductor to tell us when our stop is. Remember, it's Polyarnyy Ural."

Yakov smiled as he handed our tickets to the conductor, "We are going to Polyarnyy Ural. Could you please tell us about five minutes before we arrive so we can get ready to disembark?"

The conductor frowned, "Which Polyarnyy Ural? There are two. One in Asia and one in Europe." Looking back, the conductor should have known, but information is power, and I did not offer him any money for his information.

Dimitre popped his head between Yakov and the conductor, "Europe!"

We loaded our bags, set them in a corner near the door, and took our seats among the passengers. We spent the next two hours passing out tracts. Finally, the conductor came through our wagon. He approached Yakov, "We just passed Polyarnyy Ural, Asia. The next stop is Polyarnyy

The Value of One

Ural, Europe. You will only have two minutes to disembark." He gave each of us a strange look, then walked away.

Yakov, Dimitre, and I took the heavy bags. Sada, Annya, and Nina took the backpacks and shoulder bags. When the train stopped and the door opened, I almost stepped into thin air. I barely caught myself. "There is no platform! This is impossible!" My mind kicked into overdrive, and I dropped my bags. "Yakov, I'll get down. You throw me the bags!"

We got everyone and everything off just as the whistle blew and the train powered up its engines. Huffing and puffing, we watched the train leave. Only then did we survey our surroundings. All was deathly silent.

I looked at the frozen tundra and the foothills leading to the Ural Mountains in the distance. As the train faded out of sight, I turned to see the team glaring at me. The area seemed deserted. Obviously, a village used to be here. Where houses once stood, were piles of cement rubble.

The train master said there were two Polyarnyy Ural stops. Was I wrong to trust Dimitre? Did we pick the wrong one?

I checked my watch.

Lord, it's not even 9 a.m.; we are far enough North, and the sun will not completely set tonight. Darkness will not be a problem, but fatigue and cold might kill us! It's early, we are excited, and adrenaline is powering us. So, we—no, You, have time. I feel the weight of these souls You've blessed me with. Please, Lord, show me what to do.

Yakov moved in front of me, stomped to warm his feet and shouted over the howling wind. "Where are we?"

Annya tripped over a cement block and landed on all fours. I reached down to help her up. "Are you okay?"

She brushed the mud from her knees and looked at me, "Where's the hunting lodge? I'm cold!" She wrapped her arms around herself.

One by one each of them stared expectantly at me.

Lord, they have every right to be upset. But what's the answer? I've sensed Your Holy Spirit for years; I recognized Your voice. Where did I go wrong?

I moved in front of them and shouted. "Listen, we're in Polyarnyy Ural, Europe. I'm sure this is where the Lord wants us to be." I put a hand on Dimitre's shoulder. "This is the type of situation I told you about during training," I glanced at the others. "The Lord's schedule isn't the same as ours. We need to walk in His Spirit, not ours."

Nina and Sada shook their heads. Nina shouted, "You never told us it would be this bad."

"Is it starting to rain? I feel drops," Dimitre muttered as he dropped his suitcase of Bibles on the ground and pulled his scarf tighter.

Annya cried, "That is not rain! That is snow! We have no place to stay. Are we going to die?"

Everyone was giving me that 'I trusted you—look what you've done' stare.

"Missionary, I think you made a big mistake! There is no one in this village. It's a ghost town. Why did we get off here?" complained Dimitre. It seemed lost on him that he had chosen this stop.

I reached down, picked up my gear and motioned for everyone to follow. "Let's look around,"

I bowed my head. "But first, let's take a moment to pray.

"'Lord, we thank You that we made it off the train safely. We ask for Your guidance. Amen.'"

I raised my head and pointed towards some piles of rubble. "Perhaps we'll find someone who can help."

Lord, it's just You and me. Let's go.

Finally, 30 minutes later in the very back, I saw two concrete slabs leaning against each other with a blanket over the front. There was a pinprick of light and a stream of smoke billowing from a crack at the top.

"Follow me! I found someone." I looked towards the Heavens.

Thank You for answering my prayer.

We trudged another 100 yards and I pulled the blanket back. A man with a long scraggly beard, dressed in an old army jacket and leggings sat in front of a small fire. He looked like a mountain man from the old American West. I gagged from his body odor. He motioned me in.

He studied me before asking, "What are you doing here?"

I took a breath. "I'm a missionary from America. I came to Russia to tell people about Jesus Christ." I motioned for Yakov to join me.

The mountain man's eyes watered, and a tear trickled down his cheek. He set cups down in front of us and wiped his cheeks with the back of his hand. "I've been waiting for you. What took you so long? My grandfather told me someday a Holy Man would come and tell me about a Holy Book." He wiped a sleeve across his nose. "When the government moved our town to another continent, I volunteered to stay and maintain the railroad tracks. I've waited 40 years for you."

I reached into my bag, pulled out a loaf of bread and set it on the makeshift table. "Do you live alone?"

"I am a hermit. I seek peace."

I could hear Nina, Sada, and Dimitre shuffling their feet outside.

The Value of One

They were in a hurry to leave. I frowned, "Do you know where the hunting lodge is? I booked rooms over the phone. They said it was in the city of Polyarnyy Ural. Isn't this Polyarnyy Ural?"

The man threw back his head and laughed, his toothless mouth flapped open and shut several times.

"What's so funny?" I asked.

He howled, "You're in the wrong continent! This is Polyarnyy Ural, Europe and the Polyarnyy Ural with a hunting lodge is back in Asia. You passed it on the way here."

I heard murmuring outside.

Lord, I need to regain control. No, please, Lord, let me sense You are in control. You tell me what to do.

"When does the next train arrive?"

Again, he laughed, "It only comes once a day. It won't be here until tomorrow. It's a 16 kilometer walk to the Asian Polyarnyy Ural." He shrugged. "If you leave now and follow the tracks, you might make it before the freezing temperatures."

Suddenly there was a commotion outside. When Dimitre heard that it was 10 miles back to the Asian Polyarnyy Ural, he jumped up, grabbed his personal gear, and ran towards the tracks shouting, "I'm leaving now!"

Nina called after him. "Hey, come back and get your bags!"

I sighed.

We need to get moving. But how many Christians will this man meet? How will my family take it if I die in the Arctic? And how will Joel get home?

I had to take the time to witness to my new friend. I opened a Russian Bible to the Gospel of John, "This is the Peace you seek." His eyes widened when I handed him a Bible. He motioned for me to sit next to him.

He took the book from my hand and followed my finger as I read John 3:16 aloud in Russian. When I finished, he took the Bible from me. "Now, Mr. Holy Man, what do I have to do to have this Peace? The Peace my grandfather told me to wait for?"

I pulled a tract from my backpack, and we read the Scriptures together. I pointed to the prayer on the final page, "If you repeat this prayer with me; and are sincere in accepting the sacrifice Jesus made on the cross, you will have eternal life, and the peace you seek."

This time tears flowed; he made no attempt to wipe them away. "Yes, I want to pray. Teach me."

I bowed my head; I tapped him on the knee, "Repeat after me, 'Dear Lord, I know I am a sinner. Thank You for sending Your Son to die for my sin. I accept His sacrifice on the cross in payment for my sins.'"

I opened my eyes and saw movement as he tapped his chest. "I feel different. I do not know how to say it." He paused. "I feel clean. Like I have never felt before."

I put my arm around him.

Lord, I must leave him now. How can he grow as a Christian with no one to disciple him?

"You are a new believer in Christ." I tapped the Bible he cradled on his knee. "Read this every day and Christ will teach you how to live for Him." I reached into my backpack for one of the discipleship books I had added to my baggage at the last minute, "This is a book for new believers. It will help you understand your Bible and how to fellowship with God."

My eyes widened as he closed the Bible and kissed it.

That's it, Lord. If You can guide me from Oregon to the Arctic and have me preach Your Word to him, You can disciple him.

With tears running down his face, he said, "Thank you for coming." He pointed towards the horizon. "Follow the train tracks. It will be snowing in the mountain pass so be vigilant. Stay on the tracks and you won't get lost."

I shook the hermit's hand, then Yakov and I joined the others outside. Everyone grabbed their gear. Nina slid her arms into the straps of her backpack. She pointed to Dimitre's suitcases of tracts and Bibles. "That man left everything for us to carry. Wait until I get my hands around his neck!"

Lord, we need every Bible and tract. How do I divide the luggage between us? The women do not have the strength to carry more than they already have!

I picked up one of Dimitre's suitcases and Yakov took the other.

We waved goodbye to our new brother in Christ as he bid us farewell. We walked ahead leaving Nina to walk behind as she kept mumbling. "I'm gonna get that Ukrainian. Wait till I get that guy."

She pulled out a butcher knife and repeated over and over, "I'm going to kill that man."

We tried to calm her down, but she grew angrier as we started for the tracks.

Lord, I thought I had made a big mistake, but You knew this man needed the Prince of Peace as his Savior. No missionary would purposefully come to this place.

Annya and I walked just ahead of Yakov and Sada. Nina, 10 meters behind, was still shrieking through the howling wind. We walked quickly to keep some distance between us. The tundra stretched out for miles.

The Value of One

The Desolate Arctic Tundra

At one point, I stopped and looked back at the man's village now invisible through the snow. The others followed my gaze. "I've been thinking. Only in the Lord's economy does it make sense to send us to this village so one man could be saved. Angels are rejoicing because of this one soul."

Sada shook her head. "I don't know if I like the Lord's economy. I'm cold and my feet hurt."

I paused and pointed towards the snow-covered mountains ahead. "I believe we'll make it to the hunting lodge."

The longer we walked, the more wrathful Nina got. She kept her mantra going, "I'm going to kill that man," and made stabbing motions with her knife.

I seriously feared for our safety but especially for Dimitre's life. Every 50 yards or so I checked to see if she was still there.

Lord, if You don't do something, we were going to have a huge fight and possibly bloodshed.

We walked in single file between the two rails.

They did not teach this in Bible College.

I began to pray.

Give me a miracle, Lord.

When we reached the mountains, we encountered a trestle that wound around the side of a mountain. The snow had picked up and we could not see far. I looked over the edge into a sea of white. When I reached the end of the trestle I stopped and looked back to see how Nina was faring. The Arctic Wind blew snow in blinding swirls.

Could things get any worse?

We had put about 100 yards between us, and I could barely see her. She had just reached the middle of the trestle.

I set my bags and boxes down, put a hand to my forehead, and squinted. In the distance, behind her, I saw a huge halogen light.

Another train! There is not supposed to be another train until tomorrow.

I ran toward her shouting, "A train is coming! Jump off!"

I directed the others to run to a small clearing along the mountainside and we leapt to safety. I stood on the embankment and looked back at her. Nina was so busy screaming she had no idea the train was coming! We waved our arms shouting, "A train is coming! A train is coming!" But she could not hear us in her rage and over the roaring of the Arctic wind.

We prayed as we watched in horror. When the train was about 100 yards behind her, the conductor blew the whistle. Suddenly Nina realized her predicament and started running, searching for an escape route. When she was almost to the end of the trestle, she jumped into what appeared to be a snowbank, but rolled down the mountainside.

After the long train of ore cars passed, we ran to her. We could hear her crying long before we reached her. I exclaimed, "I hope she's not hurt too badly. If she's broken any bones, I have no idea how we'll get her to a doctor!" I turned to Annya and Yakov. "Form a human chain and lower me down. I'll see how badly she's hurt."

Please, Lord, no broken bones.

As I approached, I shouted, "Nina! Are you okay? Where does it hurt? Is anything broken?"

She lifted her head and said, "God has judged me. I did wrong. I thought evil of Dimitre and wanted to harm him, but God has judged me. I'm so sorry for my sin!"

I reached down and helped her stand. She reached over, picked up her knife, and put it away. We gathered her gear and Bibles, then passed them up to the others. She had scrapes and bruises but no broken bones.

It took us 10 minutes to get her back on the tracks. Nina's mantra changed as she walked with us, crying the whole time, "O Lord, please forgive me for what I wanted to do to that man."

THOUGHTS
- Have you ever sought vengeance on someone only to have the Lord stop you and convict you of your wrong attitude?

CHAPTER FORTY-SIX

Polyarnyy Ural, Asia

Then came Peter to him, and said, Lord, how oft shall my brother sin against me, and I forgive him? till seven times? Jesus saith unto him, I say not unto thee, Until seven times: but, Until seventy times seven. Matthew 18:21-22

Cold and wet, bruised and tired, we finally arrived at the correct Polyarnyy Ural about 6 p.m. Thankfully, the storm had abated, and the skies cleared.

Lord, we made it with Your help. I've never felt so exhausted. If I look half as bad as the others, we're in bad shape.

Our feet scraped the ground between the tracks as we shuffled past the sign "Polyarnyy Ural". "Hey guys, the hunting lodge clerk said they are located up the hill, past the school, past the geological headquarters and near the foothills at the other end of town." I set my gear down. Yakov set his next to mine. Sada, Annya, and Nina came up behind us.

Our breath wafted in a stiff breeze. I pointed down the street, "I'm going to look for Dimitre. Stay with our luggage, and I'll look for the lodge while you rest."

They shook their heads. Yakov spoke up, "This little rest is enough. I just want to get out of these dirty, wet clothes." Everyone nodded, picked up their gear, and hurried up the hill. I ran to catch up.

We were runners sprinting for the finish line.

Lord, is it too much to ask for hot showers?

Our pace picked up. Past the school, past parked tanks, towards the far side of town. Minutes later, we walked through the lodge entrance. Everyone set their luggage in a corner and removed their coats, scarves, sweaters, and caps.

I could feel the warmth coming from a large fireplace. We rushed towards the fire. Several sat, removed their boots, and massaged their feet. Nina and Sada rubbed their hands over the open flames. I stood next to them and tilted my head towards the door. "I don't know if I'll ever thaw out from that hike."

"Ahh, that feels so good." Sada said as she straightened her clothes. "I can't wait to get a shower."

The front door opened, and a man entered. I left the team and headed towards him. Though my language skills had improved since coming to Russia, I had rehearsed the lines I wanted to say to the clerk.

I was halfway across the room when I heard my name being called. I turned and was immediately engulfed in a bear hug. Dimitre's bad breath watered my eyes. His beard was trimmed, hair combed, and he wore fresh clothes. "Brother Reasoner! All of you are safe. This is an answer to my prayers."

He turned to the others and pleaded. "I was so afraid of freezing to death, I panicked. I started the fire so you could warm up when you arrived. I'm sorry I abandoned you. Can you ever forgive me?"

Nina reached for her knife.

Lord no! She seemed so sincere in her apology.

Everyone's eyes widened and they held their breath as I started towards them.

Nina adjusted her knife scabbard which had slipped on her belt. She pushed a wisp of hair that had fallen across abrasions on the left side of her face, spread her scratched hands and pleaded. "Oh, my dear sweet man. Can you forgive me for the things I thought to do to you? I was wrong. God has punished me, and I have suffered. I will not have peace until you forgive me."

Before he could respond she reached out and hugged him. If my friends had known the words, we would have sung a verse of *Kumbaya*.

I moved back towards the stranger. Dimitre followed, "Brother Reasoner, this is the lodge owner. He allowed me to check in on the promise that you would soon be here to pay."

I offered my hand and the stranger accepted, "Please call me Vladimir Sergeiovich. The geologist said to expect you. We spoke on the satellite phone yesterday. As you can see, I am shut down and hiding from the government. I have no employees and the beds have no sheets."

I looked around the lobby. Cobwebs filled the corners, and our footprints left a trail in the dust on the floor. The lodge was in a state of general disrepair. "Is there another hotel in the town?" I asked.

Polyarnyy Ural, Asia

Vladimir laughed, "No, even I don't get enough business to turn a profit. That's why I'm in trouble with the government. They think I make more money than I do."

I pulled my wallet out, "I'd like to register our group."

Vladimir asked, "How many days?"

I turned and saw everyone but Dimitre dozing. "There are six of us and we'll be staying two nights. I know we must take our luggage when we leave each day, so it appears no one is staying here."

"Pay in US Dollars and I will take a chance. I'll let you leave your luggage here while you are out."

I pulled out a $50 bill and set it on a table.

Is this enough? $3x6=$18 x 2 nights =$36.

Vladimir swooped it up and handed me three sets of keys.

"Take the first three rooms on the right at the top of the stairs."

I guess the remaining $14 is a tip—at least we don't have to carry our luggage around.

I started to turn, and he added, "We are connected to the city generator. You have 10 minutes of hot water every hour. Plan your showers accordingly."

The women took showers first. When I finally took my turn, I let the remaining hot water cascade down my back.

After I dressed, I hurried down to the lobby where I found an empty seat next to Yakov. We had such sweet fellowship! Sitting around the fire, Dimitre stood and raised his cup of tea. "May God bless us with Reindeer People souls for the kingdom."

Everyone stood and the clinking of our cups chimed through the lobby. Unity was restored. I bowed my head, "Heavenly Father, we thank You for seeing us safely to the right village. We praise You that You allowed us to work through divisions in our ranks to become more unified in serving You. Amen."

I stopped Vladimir as he entered carrying a large load of firewood. "Excuse me, Vladimir Sergeiovich, we want to find the Reindeer People. I talked to a geologist yesterday on the phone. How do I find him?"

He scratched his bearded chin. He pointed toward the front door. "They should be arriving soon. The government insists they stay here free of charge. I will tell you when they arrive."

Within the hour, the front door opened, and a group of workers swaggered into the lobby. Vladimir motioned for me to follow him as he approached the group. He singled out a man and said, "Mr. Reasoner, this is the chief geologist for the region."

Serving God Behind Enemy Lines

The geologist frowned and sat to remove his boots. I stood in front of him and waited. When he looked up, I began, "I talked to one of your geologists on the phone yesterday and he said there are *chums* (teepees) not far from here."

He grunted, "So?"

"I'm from America and came to share the Gospel of Jesus Christ with the Reindeer People. I was told you could tell me where they are. Can you help me get there?"

"Yes, I know where they are." the geologist glared, "But they are six hours from here by tank." His scowl never left his face. The corners of his mouth turned down.

I pointed north. "Can we walk?"

He laughed, "No way, too dangerous. There are rivers everywhere; you might fall through the ice! You will get lost. Only Reindeer People and trained geologists with the proper equipment can maneuver their way through the tundra. Tanks are the only way you can travel in the Arctic."

Lord, I'm fresh out of tanks.

"Could I possibly use your tank and driver tomorrow?"

He looked at me as if I was crazy. "These are Russian Red Army tanks. You are American. Of course, you cannot use my tanks!"

Lord, here's another roadblock.

Without thinking, I reached into the secret pocket of my jeans and retrieved a $100 dollar bill and set it on the table.

His eyes flashed in anger. "Are you trying to bribe me?"

I shook my head. "No, Sir. I'd like to rent a tank and driver."

He took the bill and slid it into his pants. "Be outside tomorrow at 7 a.m."

THOUGHTS
- How do you resolve conflict between brothers and sisters in Christ?

Chapter Forty-Seven

The Tank Ride

I can do all things through Christ which strengtheneth me.
Philippians 4:13

At 7 a.m. the next morning I walked down the lodge steps with my rucksack slung over my shoulder. The weather was cold, around 25 degrees Fahrenheit. The wind blew my parka hood off, sending a chill down my back.

Should I put on another layer of clothing?

I had on a t-shirt, long johns, flannel shirt, sweater, and my parka. No, I already felt constricted.

Nina and Sada came out behind me, handing out food. Nina beamed with excitement, "One of the geologists told us about a store down the street that had fresh bread." She zipped the backpack up. "That bakery lady sent me to a butcher shop." She rose and adjusted her straps before she put it on. "I went to three stores. It wasn't expensive."

I turned my head eastward towards a rumbling noise. We heard a CLUNK as the vehicle came around a corner and drove over a large patch of ice. The cracking sound resonated throughout the foothills. Everyone turned as I said, "Sounds like our ride."

The engine idled, a balding Russian man stuck his head out of the driver's window, placed a knit wool cap on his head and climbed out. "Hello, I'm Elijah and I'm told you want to see the Reindeer People." His breath wafted in the air as he opened the back door and motioned us to enter. "You need to hurry. We have a six-hour drive, maybe more if we must ford many rivers. Snow melts, the terrain changes."

Standing in front of a Russian tank used in Polyarnyy Ural

We moved to the rear. Yakov held his wife's pack while she climbed in; he passed both their packs after she sat on the wood-slatted seat. Dimitre cinched his straps, and stooped, scraping his pack on the door jamb as he entered. He sat across from Yakov. Annya jumped in and put her backpack under the bench.

Meanwhile, Elijah did a final check on the tank. He tapped the links connecting his tank treads with a hammer.

Clink, clink, clunk. Clink, clink, clunk, clink. Clink, clink, clunk.

He put an 'X' on the outside of each link that sounded off key. After working around the entire vehicle, he pulled a prybar and a wrench from a box on top of his tank. He tightened the tread with the lever between a good and bad link with his right hand and turned a wrench clockwise with his left.

He grimaced as he struggled with the third link. "Uhh, urgh, there. That's good." He wiped his forehead with a sleeve and moved to the next bad one. "I'll be done soon. If I don't check the links the track comes off. I can't ford a river without tracks."

As Nina approached the tank, her eyes widened, her face paled, and she shook her head. "I don't like small places. I cannot do this."

The short Russian driver put his tools away and stood beside me. "We need to leave now. It's a long hard drive. We must go." He walked through a patch of ice to the front of the tank, put a foot on the left track, raised his body up, and crawled into the driver's hatch.

I pushed Nina toward the step of the tank, "You know God wants you to make this trip. We talked in class about how we might face

The Tank Ride

challenges." I turned my head as I heard the tank engine rev up. "You've been the most eager of my students to see the Reindeer People. Are you going to let Satan deprive you of a blessing?"

"Okay, I'll go." Nina put her arms through her straps and climbed the step. She paused, then closed her eyes. I smiled as she mouthed, "I can do all things through Christ which strengtheneth me."

Elijah exited the driver's seat, closed, and secured the rear hatch, then climbed into the cab.

I examined our small prison.

Lord, we're going to be squished in this box for six hours. Give us strength, lead us to the Reindeer People, and work even now in their hearts so they will accept Your Salvation when we proclaim Your Word.

It did not take long before my rear was sore. I had a padded seat. I could not imagine what the rest of the team was experiencing on the hard, wooden benches in the back. I looked behind me and realized there was a small, sliding window to communicate with the team. I slid it open and yelled, "Are you all ready for an adventure?" Several smiled and gave a thumbs up. Others looked as though they were hanging on for dear life. Nina still whispered, "I can do all things through Christ."

Thankfully, there were several windows to view the beautiful rock formations and rolling hills. The sun shone brightly. Its warmth continued to melt patches of winter snow on the tundra floor.

It might get above freezing today!

The tank pitched and rolled, Elijah shifted gears, revved the engine, and alternated pushing and pulling the two levers that took the place of a steering wheel. He worked with such ease and finesse, as if he had done this all his life. After banging my head against the ceiling three times I realized that it was not a good idea to press my body against the seat and side wall.

As I was getting used to the rhythm of the roller coaster ride, we reached a plateau and stopped. I stared into the abyss. Thirty feet below was a frozen river. Elijah grabbed his binoculars and surveyed his options. He pointed north, "The river is high." Then south, "The roads are washed out." He let his binoculars hang from its lanyard. "Okay, let's go."

I said, "What are we going to do?"

His eyes twinkled, "Watch."

As I fell forward, I heard five thuds behind me as the rest of the team hit the dividing wall. I flew into the windshield. Now I know how a bug feels. Panic set in. I thought we would do an end over end but soon we were on level ground staring at the frozen river. Elijah laughed at my white knuckles and face. He smiled, "Russian tank good?"

I managed to whisper, "Yes Russian tank is good."

Elijah proudly stated, "I was a Russian Army tank driver for 33 years. Let me show you what else a Russian tank can do!"

"No Elijah, that is not necessary. Russian tank is good."

No! Lord, he's not going to do what I—

At that moment, the tank angled down, crashing into the half-frozen river. I scrunched against the forward bulkhead, then back into my seat as the tank climbed over a sandbar, then back into the river. The inside temperature dropped as water enveloped our vehicle. Suddenly the engine died. I watched the water level rise through the windows. I was afraid to touch the glass for fear of it bursting. I listened to the rush of water flowing over the roof. I lifted my eyes and saw water dripping from a crack in the ceiling.

Are tanks waterproof?

I was not convinced; I held my breath.

Elijah took a moment to laugh at me, then turned the engine over. It started on the first try. He shifted into a lower gear, and we inched forward. The bow of our ship started to float and then sink. We hit the riverbed; his wide-eyed passengers grabbed anything they could hang onto.

Lord, we've spent a lot of time and money to get this far. Think of the souls that can be saved.

Elijah saw my lips moving. "Don't worry Holy Man, I do this all the time."

We drove across the river bottom and climbed up the bank on the other side. I let out my breath and praised God for dry land. Water flowed from every nook and cranny of the tank.

For the next three hours, Elijah showed me what else a Russian tank could do. Disneyland, eat your heart out. There is no greater roller coaster ride than going up and down cliffs, and fording rivers inside a Russian tank.

After six hours of continuous bumps, rattles, and rolls, we came to a clearing. Far in the distance, I saw a group of Reindeer *chums*.

THOUGHTS
- Describe a time when Philippians 4:13 became real in your life and enabled you to go forward in faith.

Chapter Forty-Eight

A Reindeer Village

To the weak became I as weak, that I might gain the weak: I am made all things to all men, that I might by all means save some. 1 Corinthians 9:22

Elijah stopped the tank about 200 yards from the *chums*. Everyone clambered from the belly of the tank. We rubbed our cramped muscles, stretched, and checked for injuries.

Lord, I've never hurt this much.

I flinched as I cinched the straps on my pack.

I don't think anything's busted, probably just bruises.

I checked on the others. "Is everyone okay?"

They nodded. I started towards the village motioning for everyone to follow. "Elijah, come introduce us to these Reindeer People."

Elijah's eyes widened; he zipped up his parka. "No way! I'm scared to death of these barbarians." He pointed to the *chums*. "Years ago, Moscow sent Political Commissars to educate them." His hand shook as he thrust it toward the village. "None were heard from again! Why do you think I parked here? They're used to us driving by this far away. They won't come out." He crossed his arms and his voice rose an octave. "I'm staying in the tank!"

Lord I'm only here because of Your Holy Spirit's guidance, I must meet them.

I moved in front of him. "You know their customs. You might have met some of them before. I need you."

He crossed his arms even tighter. "No. I don't know anyone in this tribe. I know those barbarians will use any excuse to kill." He relaxed his arms and tapped his chest with a finger. "It won't be me."

Lord, You can't want me to go into that village alone!

I frowned, "Listen, I met many Reindeer People on my first trip." I pointed to the nearby village. "This is the same tribe."

"Humph!" Elijah pulled his hat farther down on his head. "They were in public. They were on their best behavior."

I waved to the rest of the team, "Let's go."

They gave me blank looks. Dimitre stared at his boots, then pointed to the front of the tank where Elijah was cleaning the windshield, "We heard what he said. It sounds like the stories we heard back home are true. I guess reality has set in." He leaned on the side of the tank. "I'm staying here."

I turned to Yakov and Sada. Sada shook her head. "I remember you telling us about the Baptist missionaries who went to the Reindeer People and weren't heard from again." She took her husband's hand and squeezed. Yakov's lips moved silently.

Lord, I know I had a good experience on the first trip. That boat ride was a blessing. I remember hearing about those Baptists and the political commissars.

I closed my eyes and counted to 10.

Lord, I'm doing this because I feel Your Holy Spirit wants me to. I need You.

I moved my right hand towards the largest *chum*. "Yakov?"

He kissed his wife on the cheek. "This is why we came." He put his arm around her. "Remember when I passed out a tract to that woman on the street and a few hours later, she was murdered?" I stared at Yakov with new respect.

Here is a man who was saved out of new age religions and is now willing to risk his life in the middle of nowhere to share the true Gospel. Thank you, Lord.

Sada nodded, "The *militsiya* arrested you on suspicion of her murder!"

Yakov sighed, "I remembered Brother Ron's first Reindeer trip. When I was arrested, it encouraged me to preach to them for hours. They finally let me go." He smiled as he looked at the *chums*, "This is not as serious." He pushed his Siberian hat down. "I've prayed—I'm going!"

She grimaced, nodded, and let go of his hand.

Yakov and I walked through the lush tundra. As we neared the settlement the sled dogs signaled our arrival. I adjusted my ski cap as we approached the largest *chum*.

A Reindeer Village

Two men, apparently guards, stood on either side of the entrance. They looked like American Eskimos. They scowled as we approached. We stared back.

Lord, are they going to kill us?

The stench of rotting flesh wafted from the edges of the flap.

They gave me questioning looks as I held out a tract and Bible.

The man closest to me pushed it back and spoke to the other. Yakov started to shake. I gulped and looked up.

Lord, what're they saying? Are they going to kill us?

I slowly removed my backpack and cautiously pulled out apples. I do not know why I had carried them across the tundra, but I thought they might come in handy. The guards lunged for them and disappeared into the teepee. The flap remained open, and I saw them stuff the fruit under a stack of bear skins.

Soon, other men came out, and one of them held his hand out. We later learned he was the chief. He smiled when I handed him several apples.

I whispered to Yakov. "Apparently someone's told them about apples. They're treating them like gold."

Someone called from the next *chum*. I turned to see a skinny, short tribesman running across the tundra. He stopped to zip up his parka, then jammed his *ushanka* (fur hat) on his head. As he resumed his trek, he wove around several reindeer and jumped over piles of reindeer dung. He was breathing heavily when he stopped in front of us.

He asked in Russian, "I'm Andre, the village interpreter. What's going on?"

I held out the Bible and the tract the guards had refused. "I came to give them this."

The interpreter examined the material and nodded towards the tribesmen. "They refused your book because my people can't read Russian. Our Chief wants you to tell us what it says. Come inside." The Chief opened the flap with one hand and motioned for us to enter.

When my eyes adjusted to the light, I took a moment to survey the *chum* from the inside. I quickly discovered the source of the stench. There on the wood stove lay a freshly skinned reindeer hide. I directed my attention to a low table laden with food. I turned, reached into my pack, and set several loaves of bread in front of an old lady who had moved next to the chief.

Andre motioned for us to sit on either side of his leader. We sat where he pointed. "Gentlemen, this is Chief Ambal. He is interested in hearing what you have to say." He reached over, picked up an overflowing wooden bowl of raw fish, and passed it to Yakov and me.

We picked up flatbread from the table and wrapped them around the fish and ate.

Raw fish with bones?

It tasted terrible but I had to eat it. I nibbled slowly on the piece in my hand so they would not offer more.

The old lady smiled, spooned loose tea into a large teapot. After it steeped, she poured the strong black brew into our cups and then onto several saucers. As she set them down, Chief Ambal and Andre slurped tea from the flat dishes.

Andre pointed towards the Chief. "He wants to know where you are from."

I pointed toward where I thought was west. "I come from America. I live in a town with houses like you see in Salekhard. I want to tell your people about Jesus Christ."

Ambal gave me a blank stare. About that time, a lad returned, followed by 11 villagers, some carrying babies, others leading children. They filed in along the walls and stood the entire time I preached.

Andre shook his head. "He doesn't understand 'America'—make it simpler."

Again, I pointed west. "I live on the other side of a big lake. I flew on a big metal bird to come to Russia."

The chief's eyes widened with excitement. He had seen planes fly over the tundra and evidently understood 'big metal bird.'

I placed my hands together into a wedge and wiggled them. "Then I took a long iron snake to come to Polyarnyy Ural." I pointed towards the tank outside. "Finally, I rode in a turtle across the tundra and came to your village."

As I talked the Chief nodded.

Well, that's progress.

I pointed to him, then to the sky. "I want to tell you about God."

The chief smiled as Andre translated, "Yes, I want to know about this God of yours."

I opened my Bible to Genesis. "In the beginning God made everything in six days and rested on the seventh." I made sounds, used my hands to animate the story of creation. Everyone, even the children listened.

Lord, these people are friendly, how could anyone think they could kill someone?

A Reindeer Village

I pantomimed every Bible story: Noah, Tower of Babel, Abraham, Isaac, and Jacob. I gradually became accustomed to the smell of rotting flesh. After three hours I came to Calvary. "This man Jesus, remember, I told you he was God the Creator Who became a Man. He had 12 friends who helped Him tell their countrymen about God."

Lord, I need to give him a sense of Your power.

They smiled when I talked about Jesus healing the lame and blind. Their eyes widened when I read the story of Lazarus. I stopped pantomiming and looked at everyone, saw they were still enraptured and resumed. They gasped when I reached the part where Jesus leaned into the tomb and called: "Lazarus, come forth."

Andre tapped my knee. "He's impressed that your God conquered death."

Lord, maybe I'm getting through.

I smiled, "Yes, my Jesus has the power of life over death." I turned to the Gospel of John. "In this passage Jesus was in a garden praying, and Judas, one of His friends, approached with a band of soldiers."

The Chief smiled as if he anticipated what was going to happen. The chief's eyes widened and laughed when I told of Judas' betrayal.

I threw a questioning look at Andre.

He shook his head. "I don't think he understands what you said. He thinks it's admirable that Judas betrayed this Jesus."

Andre chuckled when I jerked my head between him and the chief. "You see in our culture deception is an admirable trait. It's best if you can deceive your friend before the betrayal. That's what this Judas did."

Yakov and I shared frightened glances. I spread my hands in front of me, moved them back and forth, and called out, "No, no, no!" I flipped to Matthew 27:5. "Listen to the rest of the story.

"And he cast down the pieces of silver in the temple, and departed, and went and hanged himself."

I held a finger on the page to make sure I had everyone's attention. "Judas did wrong, and he was so sorry. He killed himself."

The chief slowly nodded. I glanced at Andre. The two of them chatted and the translator turned to me. "Now he says this Judas must have been weak to commit suicide."

I told the story of Jesus' rigged trial and His walk up Mt. Calvary where He was crucified for the sins of the whole world. I told how the disciples took His body and buried him in a borrowed tomb. Everyone was quiet. I could see the confusion on their faces.

As I turned to Mark 16:6, I said, "Perhaps you wonder why I have come from so far away to tell you about my God Who died. Because three days later, the disciples came to Jesus' tomb, and this is what the Bible says happened:

> *"And he saith unto them, Be not affrighted: Ye seek Jesus of Nazareth, which was crucified: he is risen; he is not here: behold the place where they laid him.*

"Jesus Christ conquered death! He arose on the third day!"

Chief Ambal spoke rapidly. He held his hands palms up and kept flexing them towards his chest. Andre had a hard time keeping up. Finally, he turned to me. "He says come. He wants to have this God Who has power over death. He has enemies who want to harm him, and if Your God is his God he will be protected."

I folded my hands and bowed my head. "Andre, have him do what I do."

After he folded his hands, I prayed. "Jesus, I know I am a sinner and deserve to go to Hell. I accept the sacrifice You made for my sin on the cross. I believe You died for me and rose again. I beg You to forgive all my sins and come into my heart and life. Amen."

Tears flowed down Chief Ambal's cheeks. I felt 16 pairs of awestruck eyes looking from me to their leader and back. I looked at Andre, "Ask the rest of the people if they would like to receive Jesus as their Savior."

Andre asked. Everyone turned towards the chief. There was silence. He nodded. Then every one of the tribes' people bowed their head and repeated the sinner's prayer.

Yakov tapped me on the knee and turned his head towards the tank. It was then I heard the soft voices of my team outside.

So, they finally decided to join us!

The chief and I rose at the same time. I put a hand on Andre's shoulder and told the chief, "I will give him papers and books to help you learn more about Jesus."

Chief Ambal smiled, moved towards the back of his *chum*, pulled out a large rack of reindeer antlers from under a hide, then led us outside.

My eyes adjusted to the light even as my lungs gulped fresh air. I looked at Elijah and my team standing in a small group. "How long have you been here? I thought you were afraid?"

Dimitre spoke first. "When you entered, we didn't hear any screaming. We decided to creep closer and eavesdrop." He pointed to the indentations on the tundra. "We've been here at least three hours."

A Reindeer Village

Lord, at least they came through in the end.

I looked beyond the team and saw that Elijah had moved the tank closer.

**Me, Dimitre, Nina & Sada in the Reindeer chum
Kneeling is a Reindeer family**

Before Andre and I left his side, the chief held up the antlers. Andre moved between us. "He wants you to have these in return for giving him this Special Gift."

I clasped the base of the antlers and smiled through my tears. "It has been an honor to visit with you."

Lord, maybe he really does believe. He's giving me a special gift in return for the Gift You gave him.

Yakov and I followed Andre to his *chum*. We sat cross-legged in front of his table as his wife served us hot tea. "Andre? How did you become the village interpreter?"

The short tribesman put his hand about a foot off the ground. "When I was a young man, the chief wanted me to go to school to learn Russian so I could translate at the trading post." He sipped tea from his saucer. "That was 20 years ago."

I pointed back at the Chief's *chum*. "Tell me, why didn't any villagers ask questions? Why were they so interested in all the stories?"

The short man set his saucer down and wiped his mouth with his sleeve. "You see, in our culture we tell stories and listen." He leaned back on a pile of reindeer hides. "Our chief is a powerful man. But he has had an ongoing battle with a Shaman. The Shaman is evil. Chief Ambal believes your Jesus will be stronger than the evil one."

I nodded, "Our God is able!" I handed Andre a discipleship binder and Russian Bible, "Each page is a different lesson. Read this to them every week." I tapped his new Bible, "Then read the Scriptures noted in the lesson."

He sat in silence, unsure of the task set before him.

I tapped the Bible again. "I'm not asking you to be a pastor. All you need to do is read the Scriptures and lead the discussion."

I pulled several Bibles from my backpack, "Do any others in your tribe read Russian? Should I leave these with you?"

Andre shook his head, "No one else reads Russian. Perhaps someday the Bible will be translated into Nenets."

I laid five Bibles on the reindeer skinned stool, "I'll leave these just in case you meet someone who speaks Russian."

Looking out the Russian tank at the Reindeer Chums after Elijah moved the tank closer

I looked up when Elijah stuck his head inside. He pointed to the tank, "We need to go. My people will start searching if I don't return on time."

Chief Ambal and his tribe followed us to the tank. Laughing children scampered about, running between the adults and reindeer. The chief and the men of the village gathered around us and spoke what sounded like words of gratitude. The women of the village offered to make us reindeer outfits if we stayed longer.

A Reindeer Village

Nina & Sada to the left of the Reindeer Chum

Elijah paced between the *chums* and his tank. His eyes pleaded for us to hurry. We waved goodbye to the tribe as I called to the team, "Let's load up! We MUST leave now."

I spread my hands out, "We must go home to our families." I pointed to Elijah. "I only hired him for today. I'm sorry. You've been very kind, but we must go. God will guide you."

THOUGHTS
- How has God used you to do creative evangelism?

Chapter Forty-Nine

The Journey Back

Go ye therefore, and teach all nations, baptizing them in the name of the Father, and of the Son, and of the Holy Ghost: Teaching them to observe all things whatsoever I have commanded you: and, lo, I am with you always, even unto the end of the world. Amen. Matthew 28:19-20

My head hit the bulkhead when the tank lurched as Elijah pulled away from the village. Yakov slid the plexiglass panel between us and yelled, "I've never been this tired, but I've also never been this excited about God's work!"

I heard laughter and amens from the others. As we drove away, I wondered if I would ever see this tribe again, whether the Chief and his people were serious about getting saved, and if Andre would be faithful to teach the discipleship materials.

Lord, You brought us here. Thank You for using us to preach Your Gospel. Please be with these people and their newfound faith in You.

An hour after we left the village, Elijah brought the tank to a stop. With tears in his eyes, he pursed his lips, the noise level dropped several decibels as he put the transmission in neutral.

Elijah turned, "I don't care about being late. I must know!" He wiped an eye with a sleeve. "I listened outside the *chum* as you told those people about God's love, and Jesus' death on the cross. I heard those people pray."

He pulled out a handkerchief and blew his nose. "I have been a Red Army tank driver for 33 years. I have killed many people. Does God love me too? Will He forgive me? Can I pray that prayer?"

Yakov stuck his head through the plexiglass window and joined the conversation. "Elijah, there's no sin too great that God cannot forgive. The Apostle Paul murdered Christians before his salvation. Salvation is free. The only unforgiveable sin is refusing His free gift."

Elijah turned towards the rear and took the tract from Yakov. Yakov read John 3:16 out loud:

"For God so loved the world, that he gave his only begotten Son, that whosoever believeth in him should not perish, but have everlasting life."

Yakov raised his head, his breath wafted out my open window as he spoke, "God says whosoever—that means you too!"

For 20 minutes we talked. Every time I was stumped for a Russian word, Yakov chimed in. Whenever Yakov didn't have an answer for Elijah's questions, I interjected the right verse. Finally, Elijah's eyes widened. "So, what do I have to do?"

Muffled sounds came from the back as they shifted in their seats.

Hang on guys, we are doing the Lord's business!

"Elijah, repeat after me." He folded his hands and bowed his head as I did. "Dear Jesus, I know I am a sinner. I know I deserve to go to Hell, but I accept the sacrifice You made for me on the cross. Forgive my sins and come into my heart." I raised my head, "Amen."

It was 10 p.m. when we rolled into Polyarnyy Ural. As we crawled out of our metal prison, we refrained from kissing the ground. The team went into the lodge and straight to bed. I stayed to thank Elijah for an incredible day and the awesome opportunity to see God work miracles.

Elijah smiled, "I will give you a ride to the train tomorrow."

I turned, leaned in the tank's open passenger window, and retrieved the Russian Bible I had given him. I walked over as he closed the engine compartment after performing his maintenance checks. I placed the book in his hand. "I want you to read the first three chapters of the Gospel of John tonight. I'll have a few questions for you when you pick us up."

With tears in his eyes Elijah grabbed my hand, wrapped his other arm around me and gave me a bear hug. "Thank you. This has been the best day of my life."

A little before 8 a.m. we stood with our luggage outside the hunting lodge as Elijah pulled up. We managed to get all our belongings and team loaded without incident. I sat in front. As he put the tank in gear, I asked, "Did you read your Bible?"

Elijah smiled, "I've never had a Bible before. I did not know how wonderful God's words could be. I read about becoming His child when we believe and about that man who came to Jesus by night. The Word of God has many interesting stories!"

We were already at the railroad tracks when I reached into my backpack for my last discipleship book.

Oh no! Lord, I don't have any more! We gave the last one to Andre for Chief Ambal!

"Elijah, study your Bible every day. Learn it and then share God's Gospel with other Russians and other tribes you meet in the tundra."

We exited the tank, passing our gear and luggage from person to person until it was piled near the tracks. I turned back to Elijah, "Do you know what time the train comes for Labytnangi?"

Elijah answered, "Of course! It comes at 9 a.m."

I asked, "Is that 9 a.m. local time? Someone else said it was 9 a.m. Moscow time, which means we will have a four hour wait."

Elijah rubbed his chin, "I'm not sure. I am usually in the tundra when the train comes. Sorry, I must go to work. Thank you for telling me about God."

We shook hands and I watched as he climbed back in the tank and drove away. The team was in for a long wait. The train came at 9 a.m. Moscow time which meant we stood by the tracks for almost four hours fighting off mosquitoes and biting flies.

THOUGHTS
- Winning souls to Christ is the first part of the Great Commission.
- It is also our responsibility to baptize them and disciple them.
- What is your plan to help the spiritual babes you lead to Christ?

CHAPTER FIFTY

Back to Salekhard

The steps of a good man are ordered by the LORD: and he delighteth in his way. Psalm 37:23

Just when we thought the train would never come, we saw the halogen light in the distance. I gauged where the train would stop and guided the team, "Listen, we only have two minutes to get our luggage and team onboard the train."

Nina gasped, "How will we do that? There isn't a platform. We will be lucky just to get ourselves onboard, let alone the luggage."

I looked at the team. They were exhausted from yesterday in the tank and now four hours of fighting blood-sucking bugs.

Lord, we need help!

Suddenly this verse popped into my head.

Beloved, I wish above all things that thou mayest prosper and be in health, even as thy soul prospereth. (3 John 1:2)

Okay, Lord, I get it. You are with us and will help.

Surprisingly, Dimitre stepped up, "Okay, guys, we can do this. When the train stops, I'll jump on. Yakov, you stand at the bottom of the steps and throw the bags up to me. Brother Ron, you keep feeding Yakov bags until we get them all on."

Sada piped up, "What about us ladies? What can we do?"

I answered, "As soon as the train stops, help us get the luggage piled up at the closest ladder. Then, run down to the next ladder and get on. That way we won't have to worry about everyone getting on through the same door. Meet us where we pile the luggage, and we'll find our seats together."

The train slowed to a stop and our plan went into action. The ladies had the bags piled neatly within 30 seconds. I yelled, "Go!"

They took off running for the next ladder. I handed bags to Yakov as fast as he could take them. He threw them to Dimitre. The assembly line worked flawlessly.

Before I could hand Yakov the last bag, the train whistle blew. I jumped on the bottom rung and grabbed the train with one hand and the suitcase in the other. The train slowly moved. Dimitre pulled Yakov onto the train, and I flung the suitcase onboard. I then climbed the rest of the rungs and stumbled onto the train. The ladies walked towards us. Good—all six of us had made it.

Thank You, God!

Annya held our tickets up. "Well, we are close. We are on the number 13 wagon and our tickets are for number 10."

"Everyone, take a few bags, and we'll go find our seats." I ordered, then picked up the two heaviest bags and led the way. I nearly stumbled as the car lurched but maintained my balance. Years of standing on the subway as it jerked and wove its way through the underbelly of Moscow had taught me how to ride the iron horse.

We finally slumped into our seats. We slept until the train pulled into the station at Labytnangi. Yakov said to Sada, "I've never been more thankful for a train platform!"

Back at base camp, Winnie had a big pot of stew waiting. I thanked the Lord for it, and we gobbled it down while we anxiously awaited Joel, Oleg, and Glenn's return.

Several hours later, I heard footsteps running up the stairs. Joel opened the door and ran to me, "Dad! I'm glad to see you!"

I engulfed him in a bear hug. "How did it go?"

Joel smiled, "God worked mightily in Novyy Port. Twelve people got saved."

"Amen! Did Glenn give you any trouble?"

Joel looked at Glenn and smiled, "He was a blessing. At first, the town mayor didn't want us to pass out tracts and hold meetings, but when she saw Glenn she said, 'If this elderly American has come all the way across the world to talk to us, it must be important.' And she gave us free rein to preach, teach, and hand out Bibles."

I responded, "How did you get return tickets? I prayed God would provide."

"It was a God thing! One of the people we led to Christ had three tickets for today. He buys several dates every Spring in case he needs to come onto the mainland. I guess most of the residents in Novyy Port do that. They sell them later if they don't need them."

"Did you have enough money to buy them from the man?"

Joel smiled, "He was so thankful for the gift of eternal life that he gave them to us."

THOUGHTS
- Have you ever been in an impossible situation where you could do nothing but trust God?
- How did He come through?

Chapter Fifty-One

Train Ride of Terror

The LORD is my strength and my shield; my heart trusted in him, and I am helped: therefore my heart greatly rejoiceth; and with my song will I praise him. Psalm 28:7

Everyone tried to get a good night's rest, but with a 5 a.m. wakeup call, nerves were on edge. I finally dozed off about 3 a.m. but was awakened a few hours later by the aroma of Winnie's reindeer sausage.

We ate in silence, then gathered our bags. I looked at the remaining Bibles and tracts. We wanted to keep a few for the train ride, but I had an idea.

I looked for Dimitre and found him outside brushing his teeth with a cup of water. "Do you think it would be a blessing to the pastor if we left a box of tracts and Bibles?"

He spat his toothpaste on the ground and rinsed his mouth out, "That would be a huge blessing. They don't have access to a Christian bookstore out here."

I went back inside and set aside some Bibles and a discipleship notebook. Joel had brought back two notebooks from Novyy Port.

I wish I had this discipleship book when I said goodbye to Elijah.

I had Joel write a note in Russian to leave with the books. "Please accept our gift of thanks for your hospitality. God bless you."

We tidied up and we were off by 6:30 a.m. We had tickets for the 7:15 a.m. train to Moscow. We boarded as soon as we got to the station.

The babbling from passengers in many languages, the chugging of the engine three cars ahead of us, and the click-clack of the wheels as they ran down the tracks, made it hard for me to get everyone's attention. Waves of exhaustion flowed over me as I lay my head against the wall.

Train Ride of Terror

Lord, how are we going to pass out tracts today? We're so tired.

My hands fell to my side. I started to doze off.

No Lord, I can't sleep. I need to make sure everyone's settled in. But, Lord, I can only expect so much out of them.

I looked at the team lounging on their bunks. "Guys, we've had a great trip." I grabbed a pole to steady myself as the train jerked, slowed, then bolted forward. "I know we talked about what we'd do on this segment of our trip." I checked my watch, "We're exhausted. I don't think the Lord would mind if we took a nap before we pass out tracts. This is a 48-hour ride home."

They all smiled, lowered their heads onto their pillows and closed their eyes.

I was startled awake when a drunk Russian tripped over my legs which were dangling off my bunk. He sat on Sada's bed and put a hand on her leg. He reeked of alcohol. I spotted Yakov exiting the restroom down the hall. His jaw dropped when he glimpsed the man's hand on his wife's leg.

The drunk stroked a finger down her left cheek. Her eyes popped open as she gasped, sat up, and slapped his face. He grabbed her hand and laughed. I jumped down from my bunk and firmly placed my hand on his shoulder, pulling him away from Sada.

Her fear-filled eyes looked at me as she mouthed, "Thank you." Yakov, ever the gentleman, merely pointed down the corridor, "Please leave my wife alone!" The drunk nodded and stumbled away.

Too tired to climb back onto my bunk, wondering if I would need to defend the women again, I sat down on the first level. I leaned my head against the wall and fell asleep.

At the next station, I glanced out the window to see where we were.

Forty hours to go!

A young man walked past my bunk. I smiled, "Hello. Are you getting off at this station?"

He shook his head. "I am going to University in Moscow."

I switched to English, "Do you speak English?"

He glowed, "Yes, a little."

I motioned for him to sit across from me, "Please, sit down and you can practice with a native speaker."

He smiled, "This is very good. I am Vladimir."

I held out my hand, "I'm Ron. Sir, if you were to die today, do you know for sure that you would go to Heaven?"

Vladimir bowed his head, "I am Muslim."

I opened my Bible and read John 1:1. "The Bible says that Jesus is God, the God Who made Heaven and earth. This same God loves you so much that He sent His only begotten Son to die for your sins. Here, read this verse:"

> *"In the beginning was the Word, and the Word was with God, and the Word was God."*

As he finished reading, he teared up, "I have a friend who speaks to me of Jesus. She says her God gives while mine takes. I am tired of serving a god who demands I kill myself for his hatred. Tell me more about your God Who loves me enough to die for me."

I smiled as I opened my Bible to Romans 3:23. Ten minutes later, Vladimir bowed his head and asked Jesus to save him. Another soul for the kingdom of Heaven!

An hour and four drunks later, I heard boisterous singing from the rear. I turned to see a burly six-foot-five-inch Russian Army sergeant wobbly—marching towards us. Annya glanced towards me and back to the man as he headed to the empty seat on her bed.

Where was her husband, Oleg?

The drunk sat, put his arm around her and gave her a slobbery kiss before I got to her. She pushed him back. "Who is your mother? Is this how she taught you to treat a woman?"

Her comment struck his heart. He released her, put his head in his hands and sobbed. "Oh, Mama, I'm so sorry. But I'm so lonely."

She frowned and yelled, "That's no excuse. You should have more respect for women and yourself. Consider yourself lucky my husband is in the bathroom!"

I came up behind him, grabbed an arm and whispered, "Come on, soldier, move along." I gave him a gentle push toward the direction he came from.

Oleg returned and Annya scolded him for leaving her. He was both concerned and embarrassed, "Honey, when nature calls, you go!"

Eager to defuse the tense situation, I remarked, "I'm amazed they still let the toilets empty onto the tracks. Obviously, the environmentalists in Russia don't ride the long-distance trains."

Lord, I know You said in Philippians 4:13 that I can do all things through Christ which strengthens me. But this is the limit! My body aches— I'm exhausted; but someone needs to protect the women. Lord, help me!

By the next morning, we had a routine. Yakov and Oleg were next to me, Joel and Glenn sat against the window across the aisle. The women sat on the bunk across from us.

The first drunk of the day found me sitting on my bunk. I stood up, took him by the arm, and motioned for him to leave.

He shrugged me off and moved towards Annya. When Oleg sat beside his wife, and put his arm around her, the man moved on to Nina.

Yakov and Dimitre jumped up and stood between the women and the drunk. I followed, tapping his shoulder. "Where do you think you're going?"

He staggered, I nudged him toward the end of the wagon, "I've had enough of you drunk Russians. Stay away from our women!"

The man lowered his head. "I'm harmless." He turned his eyes toward Annya. "I know this girl. We were together last week."

I stood my ground, "Likely story, she's been with us in the tundra for over a week." I escorted him away

Thirty hours and many drunks later, we pulled into the Moscow station. During our entire trip we saw 77 people make professions of faith. Most of them were Reindeer People from different tribes. Imagine being so far removed from civilization that when I said, "I am from America," they had no idea where or what that was!

Preaching the Gospel where no one has ever preached before helps me fully understand what the Apostle Paul said to the church at Rome in Romans 15:20-21:

> *Yea, so have I strived to preach the gospel, not where Christ was named, lest I should build upon another man's foundation: But as it is written, To whom he was not spoken of, they shall see: and they that have not heard shall understand.*

THOUGHTS
- God is not willing that any should perish.
- He is preparing hearts all over the world at this very moment.
- Who will answer the call and harvest the souls?
- Will you?

Chapter Fifty-Two

Trust in the Lord

But my God shall supply all your need according to his riches in glory by Christ Jesus. Philippians 4:19

July 2003 — Joel's Testimony

Keturah called out, "Hey everybody! Get down here now. Dad's ready to start the family talk!"

Kathy frowned, poured me a cup of tea, and sighed, "I could've shouted." She lowered her head and pointed towards the staircase, "Go upstairs, get the others. Now."

Fourteen-year-old Keturah slid off her seat and moved towards the stairs. "Yes, ma'am."

I mixed cream with my tea, clinking loudly with my spoon to cover my laughter, "We have two more to go through this stage after her. Do you think we can survive?"

Kathy filled her cup, grabbed a potato cake, and broke it in half. "She's a good kid. She has a great heart. Remember what I said to you when Joel left for college last year?"

I thought for a moment, "You said, 'They are leaving us! We are still young! Let's have five more kids!'" I smiled, more to myself than to Kathy. "And I laughed at you!"

Now as I thought about it, I realized the truth. Last year Joel was an asset on the 2nd trip to the Reindeer People. Without any warning, a tear escaped my right eye. I swiped it away. "Micah is leaving this month as well. I now see your point—let's have five more children!"

Kathy threw her head back and laughed, "That was so 'last year'! Now we wait for grandchildren!"

Trust in the Lord

As if on cue, the other children clambered in and swarmed around the table, folded their hands, and looked at us.

Joel, home on summer break from Bible college, pulled his pocket New Testament from his shirt. "I think I know what this meeting is about. I heard you talking about how much money we need for the trip next week." He placed a thumb on a page. "This morning I was reading in Proverbs." He glanced at his siblings, then the two of us. "You've preached on this before—I think it's a good reminder."

He continued, "This is from Proverbs 3:5-6.

"Trust in the LORD with all thine heart; and lean not unto thine own understanding. In all thy ways acknowledge him, and he shall direct thy paths."

He closed his Bible. "Can I give a quick testimony of how God used this verse in my life?"

I leaned forward, anxious to hear how my God became Joel's God. He no longer needed to depend on my faith. God was real to him. "Please, we would love to hear how God worked in your life."

Joel cleared his throat, "You remember I had to get a new visa to come home. It took three weeks, and we didn't know exactly when it would arrive, so Mom booked my ticket for May 19th, but college ended on the 10th. I had to stay on campus those nine extra days and that cost $25 a day. My job in the computer lab was over. I had no money. I prayed to God for wisdom, and He directed me to open my Bible."

Joel opened his Bible and pulled out a token, "At college a pastor preached a sermon at chapel on 'This too shall pass.' He handed out these little round tokens that say, 'This' and told us to keep the token in our Bibles. The next time we had a trial, we should get the token out and ask God to make 'this' pass. He then asked, 'what is the 'this' in your life that needs to pass away?'

"At the time, I didn't have any trials or problems. Now I did. So, I asked God to remove my 'this'. No sooner than I said, 'amen' then there was a knock at my door. A student asked, 'Do you want to sign up to help with vacation Bible school? All the students who help don't have to pay room and board until May 20th.' I ran to the administration building and signed up. God removed my 'this.' I couldn't believe how quickly and perfectly He answered my prayer!"

Another tear slid down my cheek as I listened to Joel speak.

Thank You, Lord, for supplying his needs when we could not be there to do it. Lord, out of the mouths of babes.

I put my notes aside, reached and squeezed Kathy's hand.

"Joel, thanks." I tapped the folder in front of me. "We have two-thirds of the money we need; I haven't been able to get in touch with the owner of the hunting lodge, and I'm fighting with Winnie and Glenn about Glenn going. Winnie understands that only men are going this time."

I shook my head, "She thinks Glenn should be able to come but I'm worried about his age and diabetes without Winnie there to watch over him."

Kathy drank the last of her tea. "It will be easier without women on the trip. Nina has moved away, Yakov and Sada are ministering in Armenia, and Annya told me she would never go again. You men have sought the Lord on this." She set her cup on the saucer. "Let Him direct your path as He has before."

Planning the Next Trip

The next morning, Joel, Micah, Dimitre (the Ukrainian), and Oleg (the Moldovan) sat quietly on the couch. Glenn, and John, another American missionary sat in chairs. I stood before the group. "It'll be interesting to see how much has changed in the year since we've been with the Reindeer People."

Lord, I pray this group will do the job we need them to do.

I pointed to Micah, "Son, you are the first to tell us what you will be doing on our trip."

Micah nervously glanced around, stood up, and cleared his throat. "Uh, hi. My dad wants me to be his translator on this trip."

He picked up an EvangeCube from his trip packet. He read in Russian from the box to everyone: "This is a seven-picture cube that simply and clearly unfolds the Gospel of Jesus Christ. The cube begins showing the separation of man from God and progressively opens to reveal Christ's death on the cross, open tomb, Christ's resurrection, Heaven and Hell, and followers of Christ. Each cube comes packed in an attractive box with directions in English and Russian for presenting the salvation message." Everyone worked their cubes as he talked.

I pointed to my missionary friend that he was next. I motioned for Micah to translate for the Russians in the group. I introduced John when he reached the front. From the back of the room, I stated, "Next, we'll hear from Brother John. He's new to our group. He surrendered to be a missionary to Russia when I preached in his home church."

John ran his fingers through his thick black hair. He gave his testimony in English. "I'm excited about all the people who will accept

Trust in the Lord

Christ as their Savior on this trip. I've heard Brother Ron talk about the other trips." He straightened to his full height of 6' 3"and smiled, "I believe God's going to use me." While John returned to his seat, Micah translated what John had said into Russian.

Joel stood. "I'm going to ride with Oleg in the helicopter. This will be my second trip." He pointed to the map of the Arctic on the wall. "We hope to meet some Reindeer People again." He put his hands behind his back, "The old helicopter has seen better days, but it's the best way to travel. Trust in the Lord with all thine heart—" He quickly sat back down.

I nodded at Dimitre who took a sip of his tea, set the cup onto the saucer, and stood. He nervously shifted his feet. "I want many people to know my Jesus. I've contacted my friend in Labytnangi and he said we can stay in his dormitories again this year."

Lord, I see You're maturing him. He doesn't seem as arrogant this year.

Oleg raised his head and remained in his seat. "I'm excited to go back on the helicopter. I will try to meet people I saw last year. Maybe see more people accept Jesus as their Savior." He scratched his chin. "I want many opportunities to share the Gospel."

I rose to close our meeting with prayer, Glenn frowned from the back.

No matter what he says, Lord, I do not think he should go.

"Let's pray." Everyone bowed their heads. "Most gracious Heavenly Father, we thank You and praise You for another day to serve You." I felt eyes boring holes in my head, snuck a peek and stared into the eyes of my elderly friend. "Help us, Lord, to accept what You would have us do on this trip. May we all be submissive to Your will, Amen."

I scanned the room as I opened my eyes, "I look forward to seeing everyone Monday morning."

People started to leave when Winnie and Glenn stepped in front of me and spoke up. "So, what will it take for you to change your mind and let me go? I know you need $1,000 more and I'll pay it if I can go."

I don't care about his money. I care about his health. I focused my attention on Winnie. Surely, she could convince Glenn to stay home.

"Winnie, do you really think it is safe for Glenn to travel without you?"

She sighed. "He lives for this ministry. We love the Reindeer People." She put a hand on her husband's shoulder. "Please let him go!"

I shook my head, "I don't know—"

Winnie put her palms on the table between us and stopped with her head inches from my face. I leaned back as she moved closer and

Serving God Behind Enemy Lines

responded. "How many times have I heard you say, "When God calls, He enables. God has called Glenn to go, will you prevent him from fulfilling his calling?"

Lord, I never want to be that missionary who kept people from doing Your will. I'll let him come, but he's Your responsibility.

I relented, "You are right. If God has called you, I will not stand in your way."

My two elderly friends smiled. Glenn reached into his back pocket and pulled out his wallet. Gingerly, he counted out the ruble equivalent of $1,000. "I believe we are splitting the expenses into thirds between us missionaries. Here is my share."

Joel, Micah, me & Glenn on the Reindeer trip

THOUGHTS
- Can you recall a time when you needed financial help and God supplied through His riches in Glory?

Chapter Fifty-Three

The White Reindeer

For the which cause I also suffer these things: nevertheless I am not ashamed: for I know whom I have believed, and am persuaded that he is able to keep that which I have committed unto him against that day. 2 Timothy 1:12

The Team

- ✓ Joel — My Eldest son
- ✓ Micah — My Second son
- ✓ Oleg — The Moldovan
- ✓ Dimitre — The Ukrainian
- ✓ Glenn — The Elderly American
- ✓ John — The American Missionary
- ✓ Myself

The train trip to Labytnangi was the usual grueling ride. By this time, we—at least I—was used to it.

Joel, Micah, and I had just returned to our seats from passing out tracts when we passed Polyarnyy Ural, Europe. I pointed out the window at the piles of rubble, "Look Micah, this is where I led the hermit to Christ."

How is he doing Lord? Does he still live there?

Micah stared out the window for a few minutes and then remarked, "Were those Reindeer People there last time too?"

I looked where he was pointing and saw a small group of *chums* and army trucks just after we passed the village. "No, they weren't. Too bad we don't have time to stop and witness."

Two hours later, the air brakes spurted as the wheels came to a stop. Labytnangi at last.

This trip on the train gets longer and harder each time! Lord, please help us get helicopter tickets to Novyy Port for Joel's group and train tickets to Polyarnyy Ural for my team.

We gathered our gear and took our time exiting. The tracks from Moscow ended here. I immediately sent Dimitre and Micah into the *kassa* (ticket office) to buy four tickets to Polyarnyy Ural, Asia for the next morning.

When they returned, Dimitre led the way to the local church where we would spend the night. After we dropped off our bags, all of us boarded the ferry to Salekhard to buy helicopter tickets for the Novyy Port team. We showed John and Micah around the city and made it just in time to board the last ferry of the night back to Labytnangi.

The next morning, Joel, Glenn, and Oleg prepared to leave. With no women on the trip to cook for us, we were relegated to beef jerky and juice for breakfast.

I put my hand on Glenn's shoulder and prayed, "God bless Joel, Glenn, and Oleg as they head up to Novyy Port. May You be glorified and may souls be saved! In Jesus' Name we ask it, Amen."

With the three of them gone, the remaining four of us packed up our bags. Our train, to Polyarnyy Ural, Asia, left in ninety minutes. We got to the train station 30 minutes early and were among the first to board. We settled into our seats and awaited the jerky take-off.

As we approached Polyarnyy Ural, Asia, I coached the team about disembarking from the train. "We will have two minutes." I nodded to Dimitre, "I know this is old hat to you, but Micah and John have never experienced the fun we are about to enjoy."

I turned to them, "There is no platform. We must jump off the train onto the ground about six feet below us. I will stay up top and drop down our gear after you guys jump off. Be ready to catch it!"

As soon as the conductor stopped the train, Dimitre moved down the rebar ladder. Micah and John followed suit. I threw luggage at them as fast as they could catch it. After I tossed the last bag, I jumped down the ladder as the whistle blew and the train slowly moved down the tracks.

"That was intense!" John exclaimed.

Micah nodded, "Wow, it's a game changer without a platform."

We gathered our belongings and started towards the hunting lodge. A slight breeze blew in our faces.

I pointed to the center of town. "Micah, that's wh—"

The White Reindeer

Dimitre interrupted. "Brother Reasoner! Look, the town's deserted."

I checked both sides of the street ahead.

John came beside me, set his luggage down, "I thought you planned this trip. How're we going to save souls if there's nobody around?"

Micah stood on my other side. "Ummm, Dad? What have you gotten us into?"

I checked my watch. "It's 2 p.m. Moscow time. We need to check into the lodge and find food." I pointed in the direction of the hunting lodge, and I waved an arm for everyone to follow.

I bent down to pick up my backpack. "Pass out tracts to anyone you see."

My fellow missionary pushed his hat farther down on his head and shouted. "I hope you can salvage our trip. It's a failure so far."

Lord, what's with all this negativity? Doesn't he believe in Romans 8:28?

And we know that all things work together for good to them that love God, to them who are the called according to his purpose.

We trotted the quarter mile to the hunting lodge in a matter of minutes; We passed several boarded-up buildings, stores, and factories. A few citizens stared through their windows. I stopped at the foot of the stairs in front of the lodge. "It looks deserted. Let's go inside." I climbed the stairs and opened the door, "Hello?"

There was no answer. I turned to John and Dimitre, "Let's take our luggage into the lobby."

John held his nose and started towards the far wall. "It's so stuffy in here! Let's open some windows."

Dimitre frowned and pointed a finger at me. "You should've made sure we had accommodations. It was bad last time, but this time, it's a pigsty."

Lord, he's right. This wasn't a five-star hotel before, but now, there are rat droppings and various little creatures scurrying about.

After we set up our beds, I grabbed food from the supply bag. "Here Micah, you take these cups of top ramen. John, take this liter of water, and, Dimitre, you take this loaf of bread. I'll find forks and meet you in the kitchen where I hope there is an electric teapot to warm the water." I looked at the bread, "There's got to be a knife in the kitchen to cut that with."

Serving God Behind Enemy Lines

Both the teapot and the knife were found. We cleaned off a dusty table and sat down to enjoy our meager meal. Afterwards, I walked out onto the porch.

Lord, where are the geologists and tank drivers? Last year they were everywhere.

I called to the guys cleaning up the kitchen, "Let's take a walk around town and see if anyone is in charge. Perhaps we can get permission to stay here and find a geologist with a tank."

After asking several people, we were finally directed to the self-proclaimed 'mayor' of the town. He quickly granted us permission to stay in the lodge.

The town of Polyarnyy Ural, Asia
The lodge is in the bottom left corner

I smiled, "Thank you for your hospitality. Now if you could just direct me to a geologist with a tank, I'd appreciate it."

The mayor laughed, "They don't often come around here since the government moved the townspeople to Labytnangi."

"So, there's no one who can take us into the tundra?"

The mayor snapped his fingers, "I can't believe this! There IS a man in town for just this week. And, he has a tank. Come, I'll introduce you to Mars."

After introductions, I asked Mars, "Where is Elijah? He took me to the tundra last summer."

Mars shook his head, "He is on assignment in Germany. He won't be back this summer."

I sighed, "Mars, do you know where any *chums* are?"

The White Reindeer

Mars' eyes squinted. "The winter has been extremely hard this year and the Reindeer People haven't migrated back yet. I haven't seen any villages."

I scratched my chin. Micah came from behind me. "Dad, remember I pointed out some *chums* back in Polyarnyy Ural, Europe."

I exclaimed, "We saw a village about an hour west."

The mayor nodded. "Oh, that is where the reindeer come after the winter, but from what I've heard, they haven't arrived yet. Did you see any?"

I sighed and my shoulders slumped. "No, I didn't, just a few *chums*." I reached for my wallet. "But can we go there?" I held out a $100 bill.

Mars' right hand snatched the money. "Sure! Meet me here at the tank tomorrow morning at 8 a.m."

At 9 p.m. that night I smiled as I started our nightly prayer meeting. "In the late 1700s, William Carey preached a sermon. He said to 'expect great things from God. Attempt great things for God'."

I set my Bible down, "This phrase comes to my mind when I'm anticipating God's blessing. What will God do tomorrow among the Reindeer People? We need to focus on Him. Regardless of what happens, regardless of how we feel." Dimitre and John frowned.

I pointed a finger at the two of them. "The Lord doesn't guarantee any of us success. He tells us what to do. One sows, another waters, but God gives the increase. Let's get some sleep."

At 8 a.m. we walked to the tank. Mars looked up from checking the oil, wiped his hands on a grease rag, and smiled, "You may take pictures. I even have a rifle as a photo prop." Mars reached into his side of the tank and pulled out his hunting rifle.

We posed for a few photos before hopping in the tank.

I offered to let John sit in front. Micah, Dimitre, and I sat in the tank's belly.

The snow was melting, and the tracks slid several times. I opened the hatch and stood to admire the scenery as the tank trudged along. Suddenly the tank dropped 10 feet; I was unexpectedly even with the top of the snow. We had fallen through the ice into a frozen river. I quickly slammed the hatch shut before water could get in.

Micah turned white and called out, "We're going to drown."

I smiled. I was an experienced Russian tank rider. I already knew what a Russian tank could do.

Mars floored the accelerator, the tracks spun on the riverbed, churning water in our wake. After a few attempts, the tank climbed out of the river onto dry land. I leaned back and called out: "Never a dull moment in the tundra!"

Posing with the rifle and tank

We soon arrived at the clearing, where I saw three *chums* and two army tents. Mars parked away from the tents and was afraid to get out of the tank. "The Shaman is the chief of this tribe. He is evil. I'll wait."

Micah, John, Dimitre, and I scrambled out of the tank and spoke first to the best dressed Russian. I introduced us, "I'm a missionary. I've come to tell the Reindeer People about Jesus Christ. Can you tell me which is the Shaman's *chum*?"

The man pointed to the largest *chum*. "Over there, but you don't want to confront him." He frowned and jabbed a finger at me. "Don't go trying to change their ways. I pay them good money to bring me live reindeer." He leaned forward, "We're here to check on our investments. When the herds arrive, we will count them, thin the herd, and truck some to slaughterhouses."

My teammates reluctantly followed as I strode towards the Shaman's *chum*. Knowing that fruit would pave our way, I reached into the side pocket of my backpack for an apple.

I heard movement inside as I reached the entrance. Before I could call out, a short man threw the flap back. He shouted something in a language I didn't understand.

Micah translated into Russian as I held out an apple, "This is for you. I've come to tell you about Jesus."

The White Reindeer

Again, the man scowled and shouted in his native tongue.

I kept the apple in front of me and continued. "We've come a long way with Good News for you."

The man's eyes squeezed shut, he opened them, then reached back into his home.

Was he going for a weapon?

He faced me, shook a straw doll at me with one hand and jabbed a nail into its chest with the other; all the while screaming at the top of his lungs.

I rose to my full height and shouted. "Your power will not affect me because my God is the God of the universe. He will protect me from your evil powers. I want to tell you about my God because He loves you. He loves you so much that He sent His Son to die on the cross for your sins."

The Shaman looked shocked that his magic did not work. I was afraid he was going to reach for his rifle in his *chum*. Instead, he turned and ran into the tundra screaming and shouting like a wild man.

With her husband gone, the Shaman's wife came out. She invited us in for bread and raw fish. She listened as I shared God's love and the gift of salvation. I told her how the Great God of Heaven had sent my family on a big metal bird across the sky. We took an iron snake to a village where we rode in an iron turtle to come to their village to tell them of God and His love for them.

Dimitre & me eating raw fish in the chum

Serving God Behind Enemy Lines

After talking for a while, we stepped outside to get some fresh air. The Shaman's wife followed us out and I asked her if she would like to ask Jesus to be her Savior. She said, "Yes." We bowed our heads, and she asked Jesus to save her.

There were still two women and a man in the *chum*. I turned to Micah, "Son, go in and share the Gospel."

He hung his head. "Dad, I—"

"Son, just do it!" He obeyed.

The Shaman's wife and I exchanged glances and moved closer to the *chum* flap and leaned in.

Micah pulled an EvangeCube out and sat next to a young lady and her husband on a pile of hides. He asked, "May I tell you about my God?"

The young man rose and left. He called to his wife, speaking in a dialect we didn't understand. But the young lady ignored him and turned to Micah, "I would love to hear."

He told her of the story of sin, death, and the gift of God through salvation. Micah folded the EvangeCube over to the last section and asked, "Would you like to pray and ask God to save you?"

The young lady bowed her head and repeated the sinner's prayer with Micah. Another young lady came out from behind a sheet which concealed the kitchen area. She whispered, "I heard what you said, and I prayed that prayer too." These two Reindeer People were the first of many souls that Micah would lead to the Lord in Russia.

Micah & me praying with a Reindeer woman to receive Jesus Christ

To show their appreciation for the New Testament and for sharing the Gospel, they gave us a set of reindeer horns and hides. They also

The White Reindeer

pulled out bear skins and native Reindeer costumes for us to be photographed in. This was a special opportunity not offered to many strangers. We were thankful the Shaman never returned.

Dressed up in bear skins & Reindeer clothes

As we continued talking, the Russians came from behind the *chum*. The biggest Russian stood in front of me. "The reindeer have arrived!"

We walked toward the open field. To everyone's surprise, a reindeer herd came over the mountains and walked right up to us. Suddenly the Shaman's wife gasped, "Look, a white reindeer!"

I asked, "Are they rare?"

With the White Reindeer

Serving God Behind Enemy Lines

She nodded as tears came to her eyes, "Yes, they are and according to Reindeer tradition, it means that a Pure Spirit dwells among us."

God, You not only brought the reindeer herd in while we are there, but You put a white reindeer among them.

This Reindeer family got saved and a white reindeer appeared, confirming to them that a New Spirit now dwells among them. Our God is interested in each person. He works miracles everywhere, every day to orchestrate His power and majesty.

As the day came to an end, we said our good-byes and got into the tank to return to Polyarnyy Ural.

Micah, Dimitre & me with the Shaman's family

Along the route back to the village, Mars stopped the tank near the continental divide monument. He touched my arm, "Why was it so important for you to talk with the Reindeer People?"

I pulled out my Bible, "Do you believe in God?"

Mars thought for a moment before answering, "I think so. I was taught in school that God does not exist, but I look around me at the sun, the stars, even the flowers in the tundra and I understand that we did not create ourselves or these things. There must be Someone higher and more powerful than us."

"That Someone is God. This Bible is God's words to us. He created the world, He created us, and He wants to have a relationship with us. God made a perfect world, but humans spoiled it with sin. Romans 3:23 says:

"For all have sinned, and come short of the glory of God;

"Are you a sinner, Mars?" He nodded.
I smiled, "We all are. And in Romans 6:23 it says:

"For the wages of sin is death; but the gift of God is eternal life through Jesus Christ our Lord.

"God loves us so much, Mars, that He sent His son to die for us. John 3:16 says:

"For God so loved the world, that he gave his only begotten Son, that whosoever believeth in him should not perish, but have everlasting life.

"Mars, do you believe that God sent His only Son to die for you?"
Mars nodded, "I believe."
"I have one more verse to share with you — Romans 10:9-10:

"That if thou shalt confess with thy mouth the Lord Jesus, and shalt believe in thine heart that God hath raised him from the dead, thou shalt be saved. For with the heart man believeth unto righteousness; and with the mouth confession is made unto salvation.

"These verses say that if you believe Jesus died for your sins and rose again the third day, you can be saved. Would you like to ask Jesus to save you?"

Tears filled Mars' eyes as he nodded, "Yes. I need to be forgiven."

"Repeat after me, 'Lord, I know I am a sinner. I believe Jesus died for my sins. I believe He rose from the dead. Forgive me God. Come into my life and teach me to live for You. In Jesus' name, Amen.'."

After Mars repeated the prayer, he smiled. "Tell me, does this good feeling last long?"

I smiled, "The Christian life is a marathon, not a sprint. You see, Satan doesn't like to lose. He'll try to make it rough on you as you grow in your faith. You now have two desires within you. Your old man will want to go back to your life of sin, but the new man will desire to read God's Word and grow in Christ. One Indian described it like this, 'I now have a black dog and a white dog living inside of me fighting all the time. Who will win? The one I feed the most.' Do you understand that?"

Mars thought for a moment and slowly said, "I think so. If I think bad thoughts, I will do bad things. But if I think good thoughts, I will do good things."

I pulled a New Testament out and handed it to him, "Read this every day. God's Word will help you know God's plans for you."

Everyone finished taking pictures between the European and Asian continental divide and then jumped back into the tank.

Standing with one foot in Asia and Europe

We arrived at the hunting lodge in less than an hour. As we climbed the stairs, Micah turned back and asked. "When does the train leave tomorrow?" His voice trailed off as he headed towards our room. "I can't wait to share everything with Joel."

I put my hands to my mouth and shouted, "The train leaves at 9 a.m."

At 8 a.m., I turned to the team, "Did we get everything from the lodge? Did we leave it cleaner than we found it?" Heads nodded as we closed the door and headed through town.

Once on the train, Micah and I settled into our seats and watched the tundra whiz by. I tapped his knee. "I am so proud of you. You shared the Gospel with the Shaman's family with confidence."

Micah tilted his head. I shifted in my seat and continued. "Mostly when I told you to just go in and preach. You obeyed and the Lord blessed your obedience."

He smiled, "You know, I need to tell you something." He glanced out the window, then back at me. "Uh, Dad, I've been praying, uh—" He glanced out the window, down at the floor, then into my eyes. He took a breath, "You know I leave in a few weeks to go to Bible College. Before this trip, I was only going because you and Mom have a rule that we go to Heartland Baptist Bible College for one year before pursuing any other career."

I chimed in, "You know that's for your own good, right? Your first year away from home should be in a safe environment where there are rules and safeguards to help you make good choices."

The White Reindeer

Our heads bobbed with the train's movement. Micah sighed, "Yeah, I know." He paused, "What I'm trying to say is, I think God is calling me into the ministry. I'm going to college now, not because you are sending me, but because God is calling me!"

I let a tear slip out of my eye and I hugged my son.

Thank You, Lord! I am so blessed!

We returned to base camp rejoicing in all that God had done. I smiled as Dimitre unlocked the front door of the dormitory. "I call first shower!" I dropped my gear and ran for the bathroom. As I closed the door, a bag sitting on the sink caught my attention. I slowly unzipped it and looked inside.

Oh no, Lord! This can't be happening!

I opened the bathroom door and yelled, "Everyone, we need to pray!"

Micah came running, "What's the problem, Dad?"

As everyone gathered around, I opened the bag, "Glenn forgot his diabetes medication. They've been gone three days and we don't know when they will get helicopter tickets back. This is bad!"

John bowed his head, "Lord, we thank You that we can rest knowing that You are in control of everything that happens in our lives. While we stand here fretting, You are also in Novyy Port with Glenn, Joel, and Oleg. Protect them, Father, as only You can do. Amen."

Early the next morning, I heard a knock on the front door. I jumped out of bed, pulled on my pants, and ran to answer it. I was both shocked and amazed as Joel stood there with his arm around Glenn.

Without saying anything, Joel and I practically carried Glenn inside and sat him at the kitchen table. Joel was in full rescue mode. "Have you seen his medical kit? We need to test him and see how bad his blood sugar is."

I ran and grabbed the bag. Glenn took it as I approached. He quickly took out the tester and pricked his finger. We waited for the results. "Just over 200. I'll take a pill and be normal in no time."

I suddenly realized Oleg was missing. "Where is Oleg?"

Joel sat down, ran his hands through his hair and sighed. His reaction worried me.

Lord, what happened to Oleg?

Finally, Joel replied, "I had to leave him there. A Christian family we met only had two tickets. When Glenn started having fainting spells that we could not control, they offered to let us have their tickets in exchange for a box of Bibles."

Serving God Behind Enemy Lines

I leaned over and gave Joel a hug, "Son, I'm so sorry this happened." I looked at Glenn, "What were you thinking? You promised to be careful."

Glenn bowed his head in shame, but I was not finished, "You put my oldest son at risk. What if Joel had to deal with moving your dead body across the arctic? Did you think of the trauma that would put him through?" I took a couple of deep breaths to calm down.

Joel, always the diplomat said, "After the second fainting episode, we asked around and someone got us insulin from a diabetic."

Glenn raised his head, "I'm feeling better now. I have my kit. I think we should be concentrating on praying that God will get Oleg a ticket back."

I exhaled and turned to see Micah, John and Dimitre standing behind me. "How long have you been standing there?" I asked.

Micah cleared his throat, "Long enough to know Joel had an exciting trip and Oleg's stranded."

I took a moment to collect my thoughts, "That about sums it up. Let's pray. Father, we thank You for your protection of Glenn and Joel. We ask that you provide a helicopter ticket for Oleg either today or tomorrow. You know our schedule, that we have highly sought tickets to Moscow for the day after tomorrow."

I paused to recall Proverbs 3:5, "Lord, You said to

"Trust in the LORD with all thine heart; and lean not unto thine own understanding.

"Here we are, trusting, You. Amen."

We waited around base camp all day, but Oleg did not return.

Lord, You taught me a long time ago that You like to wait until the last minute to solve the problems. I'm going to bed and trusting You to get Oleg back to us tomorrow.

Early the next morning, I heard a knock. I ran to open it and engulfed Oleg in a bear hug. "Hallelujah! I knew God would answer our prayers."

As we entered, the rest of the team rose from their beds to welcome Oleg back. After hugs, Oleg asked Joel, "How is Glenn?"

Just then Glenn joined us from the bedroom. Oleg grabbed him and exclaimed in Russian, "Да. Слава Богу- вы живой!"

Joel smiled, "Yes. Praise God. Glenn is alive. How did you get a ticket back?"

Oleg exhaled slowly, "I flew standby. I've spent the past two days hanging out at the helicopter pad waiting for an available seat. Finally, this morning, there was an opening. I'm tired."

The White Reindeer

He looked at Glenn intensely before turning at me, "That was scary. I'm physically, emotionally, and spiritually worn out. I'm going to bed."

I patted his shoulder as he walked toward the bedroom, "Thank you, Oleg. You are a good man." I looked at the others and surmised that they had not slept any more than I had the night before. I smiled, "I think we all will join you."

Once on board the train for Moscow, Joel collapsed across from me. He leaned against the wall and rubbed his chin, "Dad, I know the ministry can be hard at times, but it also has great rewards. I don't know how you're going to take this, but I think the Lord is calling me to be a missionary specializing in Reindeer expeditions."

The middle and top bunks are folded up so we can sit down on the bottom bunk — My two sons, Joel & Micah

I raised both eyebrows, "Oh, Son! That's great." I shifted on my bunk and continued, "Your mother and I have always wondered how God would use you in Russia." I wiped a tear with the back of my hand. "But we've always known God had great plans for you!"

I soon drifted off to sleep. I was drained. This trip had not been the booming success the others had been. Between both excursions, only eight people were saved: four in the Shaman's village and four in Novyy Port.

Lord, Your ways are higher—

I was awakened when Glenn sat next to me. He sighed and bowed his head in evident disappointment.

I asked. "My friend, why are you so gloomy? Is your blood sugar okay?"

He lowered his chin into his chest, shook his head and sighed. "Yes, it's fine. I guess I'm just tired from the trip." He leaned his head on the bulkhead and closed his eyes. He let out another sigh.

"Glenn, why are you so sad? What's wrong? I know you are disappointed in yourself, but God worked everything out in the end."

The old man sighed. "Brother Reasoner, I don't know how many more trips I have before the Lord takes me home."

My head snapped up. "What's wrong? You said your diabetes was fine now!"

He sighed, "I have a bucket list. The Lord didn't fulfill my biggest wish."

I put a hand on his shoulder. "And what is that?"

Tears flowed down his cheeks as he leaned his head back on the wall and closed his eyes. "I am fascinated with stories of those who have died for the cause of Christ—from Stephen all the way to modern martyrs during the Soviet Union."

He opened his eyes and focused on my face. He pointed towards my two sons. "I see Joel and the success he had on the last trip and this one." He took a deep breath, then shook his head. "And your Micah, look at the success he's had on his very first trip."

I interrupted, "You came on this trip, and you helped finance it. You have a part in those souls being saved!"

He held his hands out. "I've always dreamed of being a martyr. I hoped to meet a Shaman who would kill me in Novyy Port. My story would be told around the world, and many would come to know the Lord because of my faith and sacrifice for the Gospel of Jesus Christ."

He frowned. "I didn't purposely leave my medical kit behind, but once I realized I didn't have it and started to get sick, I wondered if the Lord would count it as a martyr's death if I died there. But it didn't happen."

I drew in a deep breath and swallowed.

Lord, help me not to say anything rash to this old missionary! Thank You for protecting all of us!

THOUGHTS
- How does good health enhance your ministry?
- How can you take care of your physical body today so that it will not be a hindrance to your ministry in the future?

CHAPTER FIFTY-FOUR

The Safe Haven

The steps of a good man are ordered by the LORD: and he delighteth in his way. Psalm 37:23

One night, in early February 2004, Kathy sat in bed reading as I walked into our bedroom. I had endured a long day of language classes and a counseling session with a struggling family. "I'm so tired, I don't even know what day it is, and I have a terrible headache."

Kathy patted my side of the bed, "You better get some sleep. Tomorrow is Friday. It is your biggest day of ministry. You have language classes in Moscow, then you teach two hours of Bible College here in Domodedovo before we head out to Odintsovo for Friday night Bible study."

I crawled into bed and kissed her head, "I haven't even done my homework. I'm too sick and tired. I think I will skip class and sleep in."

Kathy smiled, "Sounds good to me." She put her book on the nightstand and turned the alarm off.

I awakened early the next morning and quietly got out of bed. I went downstairs and did my homework.

I'm feeling better. I think I'll go to class.

I climbed the stairs and turned on the light. "Up and at 'em, Honey. I'm feeling better and want to go to class."

Kathy rolled over and squinted, "Can't you just drive yourself?"

I smiled, "You know the deal we made when I signed up for this class. You drive me to the metro station. You know how impossible it is to find parking."

Kathy groaned as she rolled out of bed, "Give me 15 minutes."

I frowned, "I don't want to be late. I'll be waiting downstairs." She stood and stumbled toward the bathroom. I touched her shoulder as she passed, "Please hurry!"

Ten minutes later, I checked my watch and sighed. I walked to the stairs and yelled, "Kathy! Hurry up! I'm late!"

I handed her the keys and mumbled as she walked down the stairs, "It's about time!"

As we drove to Moscow, I sighed, "I can't believe how hard it is for me to learn Russian. No matter how many classes I take, I feel like I'm fighting a losing battle."

Kathy quickly pulled into the left lane to avoid a snow pile randomly dumped on the highway. She smiled, "Didn't you once tell me your dad and mom got together after your dad failed Latin while studying for the priesthood?"

I thought for a moment and coughed, "So, you are saying if my dad had an aptitude for languages, I might not be here today?"

"Right. Your dad would have become a priest and never married your mother. Without you, I don't think I would be in Russia."

Lord, thank You for working in the lives of my parents to bring us to where we are today ministering for You in Russia. How true Jeremiah 1:5 is:

Before I formed thee in the belly I knew thee; and before thou camest forth out of the womb I sanctified thee, and I ordained thee a prophet unto the nations.

As Kathy pulled up to the metro station entrance, she observed a large crowd, "I didn't realize how much difference 15 minutes makes on the morning commute. The metro entrance is packed." She kissed my cheek as I opened the car door, "Have fun with the crowds. I'll pick you up in the McDonald's parking lot at 2 p.m." I closed the door and she sped away.

I pushed through the throng, down the stairs to the underground entrance, only to find policemen blocking the way. "What happened?" I asked in Russian.

Stone-faced, the nearest *militsiya* ordered, "Bomb. Go away."

I looked at the panicked people surrounding me. I approached a young lady, "Did he say 'bomb'?"

She caught my accent and replied in broken English, "Yes, we are fortunate."

I pulled a church tract out of my pocket and handed it to her, "Not fortunate, blessed." I ran back up the stairs, hoping Kathy might still be waiting at the light, but she was gone. I had a cell phone, but she did not. I waited until she got home, called her and she met me at McDonald's an hour later.

She jumped out of the car and hugged me tightly, "Ron, you could have been on that train if we had been on time! I heard on the radio that 40 were killed and 125 injured." She wiped her tears, "That could have been you!"

I held her tightly for a few moments. Finally, I pushed away, took the keys, and walked to the driver's door. "You are too upset. I'll drive."

Kathy slumped into the passenger's seat. I took her hand, "Getting sick last night was God's way of protecting me."

She brightened up, "And me being so sluggish this morning was of God too!"

I kissed her hand, then I started the car and headed home. I still needed to prepare for Bible College class and the evening Bible study. While a bomb might stop all planned events in another country, this was normal for Russia and things would go on as scheduled.

On the drive home, my cell phone rang. Kathy answered it, listened for several minutes, then replied in Russian, "No, Pastor was late this morning too and wasn't on that train either. He is fine. Thank you for praying. Good-bye."

"Who was that?"

She smiled, "It was Vanya. He knows you take that train each morning and called to check on you."

"What did he say at the beginning of the conversation?"

Kathy grinned, "He was telling me how great our God is! His mother takes that train to work each morning as well. Yesterday she was pick-pocketed on the bus she takes from the metro station. This morning she decided to boycott the bus and walk. It caused her to be 15 minutes late as well. She missed the train."

It was my turn to grin, "Praise God. It is amazing how He can take a bad situation and turn it around for His glory. I'm sure she is thanking God right now for being pick-pocketed last night!"

That afternoon as I studied, my mind went back 20 years to Bible College when the campus carpool had left without me. I was just as frustrated for missing the ride that day, only to pass the tragic wreck. I lost friends in that wreck, and I never forgot that God had preserved my life. Today, God spared my life again. As I thought through the many Reindeer trips, I remembered how many times the Lord had preserved my life.

Serving God Behind Enemy Lines

It is daunting when God calls you into His work. It places enormous responsibility to go when others recoil in fear. In James 4:12-14, we are encouraged to be flexible when God changes our plans:

> *There is one lawgiver, who is able to save and to destroy: who art thou that judgest another? Go to now, ye that say, Today or tomorrow we will go into such a city, and continue there a year, and buy and sell, and get gain: Whereas ye know not what shall be on the morrow. For what is your life? It is even a vapour, that appeareth for a little time, and then vanisheth away.*

From left to right and top to bottom: Ron, Kathy, Jeremiah, Joel, Micah, Hannah & Keturah. 2004

THOUGHTS
- Can you think of a time when you thought God didn't come through, but you later found out He was "working all things together" for your good?

CHAPTER FIFTY-FIVE

The Camel People

The Spirit itself beareth witness with our spirit, that we are the children of God: Romans 8:16

A month after the bombing incident, I sat through a long Tuesday night Pastor's meeting. I was helping three young preacher boys start churches in the Moscow area. They attended our Bible Institute, and we met weekly to discuss the progress of their baby churches as I mentored them through the church planting process.

"Do we have any prayer requests before we close?" I asked.

Dimitre cleared his throat and scratched his neck. "I've mentioned my friend, Sergei, before. He is from the Russian Republic of Kalmykia."

I nodded as Dimitre continued, "I don't know if you remember, but Kalmykia is the only Buddhist region in Russia. Sergei was saved through the ministry of Athletes in Action. He is an Olympic wrestler. After his salvation, he came to Moscow, went to Bible College, and has returned to his hometown to start a church."

Our meeting had gone on longer than normal and everyone was ready to leave, but my interest was piqued. "I remember you talking about him. You mentioned the president of that republic vowed there would never be a Christian in their republic, yet Sergei has managed to gather about 20 believers."

Dimitre nodded, "I know you like going to the Reindeer People up North. You can call Sergei's tribe the Camel People. Reindeer People endure extremely cold temperatures in the winter and the Camel People endure extremely hot temperatures in the summer. It is a dry, desert climate by the Caspian Sea and some of the people there actually own camels. Most desert scenes in Russian movies are filmed there because of ample sand and domesticated camels."

I smiled at the 'Camel People' concept, as he continued, "Anyway, Sergei had a stroke last week. He is out of the hospital, but we need to pray for a full recovery. He has such a burden for his people to hear the Gospel." He paused, looked at each group member before landing his gaze on me, "Sergei also needs financial support. Athletes in Action has cut their funding in Russia—" His voice tapered off.

I looked around the table. Everyone was tired. We wanted to pray and go home. I stood, nodded acknowledgement of Sergei's need and bowed my head, "Put Sergei on your prayer list. Let's pray."

As Kathy and I got into the car to go home, she turned, "What do you think about supporting Sergei? He wasn't trained in our Bible Institute, so we really don't know what he believes."

I thought for a moment, "I'm not supporting anyone who doesn't agree with our beliefs. I'd like to meet this Sergei—maybe go out to Kalmykia and see his work."

Kathy smiled, "I agree. Let's pray about it. Maybe we can take a family vacation to Kalmykia. Joel and Micah will be coming home this summer from Heartland. Their friend, Ben, is coming too. It could be a working vacation."

I grunted, "Russia is a huge country. I recently heard that it is larger than the "planet" Pluto and it covers 11 time zones. We should probably get out a map and figure out where Kalmykia is."

A few weeks later in early April, my phone rang as I was driving to the Tuesday night Pastor's meeting. I nodded for Kathy to answer, "Allo?"

I heard Dimitre's voice jabbering away in Russian, but I could not make out the conversation. Kathy listened for a moment and put her hand over the mouthpiece, "He says Sergei is in town and would like to come to the pastors' meeting tonight. Is it okay?"

Intrigued, I nodded. "Sure. Tell him I've been praying for Sergei and would like to put a face to the name."

Kathy translated my message, "Ron says it would be nice to meet Sergei. Bring him along."

We were seated at the table and drinking tea when they arrived. Dimitre took off his coat, scarf, and shoes. The short, stocky Asian man did the same. I stood to greet them. Dimitre spoke first, "Brother Ron, I'd like to introduce you to Sergei from Kalmykia."

We shook hands and I gestured for them to sit and opened in prayer, "Father, bless this evening. Bless the food, the fellowship, and the future of Your work. In Jesus' Name, Amen." Plates of sliced bread, cheese, kielbasa, cucumbers, and tomatoes sat on the table. Kathy poured them tea into large porcelain cups.

We each took a slice of bread and topped it with meat, cheese, tomato, and cucumber. I observed that Sergei was about 30 years old without an ounce of body fat. His triceps bulged, making it hard for him to keep his arms against his sides. It was evident his nose had been broken more than once. His cauliflower ears stuck straight out. "Sergei, tell us about yourself."

He wiped his face with a napkin, "I am a professional wrestler. Where I come from, we are known for wrestling and playing chess. When I studied at the university, Athletes in Action visited our campus. They played sports with us and then preached the Gospel."

He smiled at the memory, "I saw how they were different in their actions, attitudes, and demeanor. I was intrigued when they explained that surrendering their lives to Jesus made them different. I served Buddha and he did not make me a better person. Several American wrestlers told how becoming a Christian had changed their lives for the better. They told of a God Who loved me so much, He sent His Son to die for my sins.

"After talking with them for hours, I bowed my head and asked Jesus to save me. My wife got saved a few weeks later. We wanted to tell everyone at home about Jesus, but we didn't know how. Someone told me about a Bible college here in Moscow. I came and learned how to preach. I had opportunities to stay and make money in Moscow, but I knew God wanted me to start a church in my hometown. We went home and now we have 20 faithful Christians. I want to start more churches. I have picked out six villages that need the Gospel."

As Sergei reached out to make another sandwich, I asked, "What do you believe about salvation? How does someone get to Heaven?"

Sergei hesitated, looked at Dimitre, then at me and asked, "Are you a Calvinist or an Arminianist?"

I countered, "Neither. I am a Biblicist. I believe what the Bible teaches about salvation."

Sergei jumped up, jarring the table as he stood. Everyone's teacups jiggled. Sergei was too excited to apologize, "You can do that? You don't have to be a Calvinist or Arminianist?"

Everyone smiled. The other young pastors had already been through this same conversation and were just as excited when they learned they could follow the Bible instead of men's doctrines.

By the end of the evening, I had a good feeling about Sergei and his doctrine. I handed him a copy of our Articles of Faith and a contract that young preachers sign who want our help, "Sergei, take these home; read them, pray over them, and if we both decide it is God's will to work together, we will come to Kalmykia this summer and help you evangelize those villages."

THOUGHTS
- Are your doctrines built around the traditions of man or founded upon the Word of God?

CHAPTER FIFTY-SIX

The College Boys & The Nenets Translation of Luke

And, ye fathers, provoke not your children to wrath: but bring them up in the nurture and admonition of the Lord. Ephesians 6:4

"Let's go!" I yelled loud enough for the whole neighborhood to hear, "If we don't leave now, we will be late!" It was mid-May 2004 and important guests were headed our way.

Kathy practically floated through the door from the kitchen, excitement written all over her face, "I can't believe all my children will be under one roof!"

Keturah, followed by Hannah and Jeremiah, stomped down the stairs, and raced to the mud room where each family member had their own closet. I could hear them rummaging through their shoes. Keturah sighed, "Hannah, have you seen my other tennis shoe?"

Hannah, the finder of the family, approached Keturah's closet, picked up a jacket and hung it up as she said, "If you keep organized, you can find anything." Hannah reached down, got the tennis shoe that had been hidden under the jacket, and handed it to Keturah, "See—it was right there."

It was Kathy's turn to hurry the family along. "Get your shoes on! Let's go!"

I went out to start the van while Kathy locked the front door. Keturah opened the sliding door and jumped in, announcing, "I'm sitting here, and Joel will sit beside me."

"Why do you get to choose?" Jeremiah complained.

"I'm the oldest until we pick up Joel and Micah at the airport! I'll be 16 soon." Keturah muttered under her breath, hoping I would not hear, "Obey your elders."

As Kathy opened the front passenger door, I threw the problem to her so I could concentrate on driving, "Mom, settle your kids down."

Kathy smiled, "Why are they always my kids when there's a problem?" Not even waiting for a reply, she looked behind her as she fastened her seatbelt, "What's the problem now?"

Hannah piped up, "Keturah is telling us where to sit and who will sit by us when we pick the boys up."

"Keturah, who do you want to sit by you?"

Keturah quickly replied, "Joel!"

Kathy looked at the seats, mentally counting in her head. "We will have to squeeze four people onto three seats. Hannah and Jeremiah, you are smaller, you can share with Micah and Ben." She stopped and looked at me, "You interviewed Ben when you took Joel and Micah to college. Is Ben skinny?"

I took a moment to pull the van onto the street before replying, "As a rail!"

Kathy looked back at Hannah and Jeremiah, "You four can fit in three seats. Keturah will sit with Joel on the other two." She pointed a finger at Hannah, "It's settled."

Traffic on the MKAD beltway was always horrendous, but we were driving through rush hour. Sadly, the tickets were $300 per person cheaper to fly into the airport on the other side of Moscow. A $900 savings warranted making the grueling drive. It took 3 hours to make the usual 45-minute trip.

I glanced at my watch as we exited the van and walked towards the terminal. "We are 20 minutes late. Perhaps they will be waiting."

Kathy snickered, "IF the plane was on time. IF they had enough border agents working at passport control, and IF the boys haven't lost any luggage, THEN they might be waiting for us."

I quickly checked the information board, "They just landed. Let's go find a place to sit. It's going to be awhile."

Kathy directed the children to follow me as she went in the opposite direction. "I'll find two copies of the *Moscow Times*." She returned a few minutes later and handed me a copy while she took a seat by Keturah. Hannah and Jeremiah pulled out their flip phones to play Tetris.

The College Boys & The Nenets Translation of Luke

Fifteen minutes later Jeremiah pulled us back to reality, "I see Joel!" The race was on as we ran to meet Joel, Micah, and Ben. Hugs were exchanged all around while Ben watched the family reunion. Finally, I reached my hand out to him, "Welcome to Russia! I trust God will do great things through you this summer." I stood back to admire my crew. "Okay let's go guys. The car is out this door." Everyone filed into their birth order with Ben walking next to Joel. Each of the young men pushed an airport cart.

"We have an exciting summer planned," I said as we loaded their luggage into our van. "Hopefully, you can go back to college this fall with exciting stories of the Reindeer People and the Camel People."

Micah waited for me to get settled behind the wheel and asked, "Yeah, what is this about the Camel People? You mentioned them the last time we talked on the phone. I looked the Kalmykia region up on the Internet. It looks desolate and wild."

I looked at Micah in the rearview mirror and laughed, "You sound like the people in our Moscow church. I announced last week that we were taking a trip to Kalmykia and all I heard were gasps and groans. Several came up after the services and said, 'Pastor Ron, you don't understand. Kalmykia is the wild, wild west of Russia. We are Russians and we would never go there. It is too dangerous! They are barbarians and will kill you if you look at them funny. You can't go!'"

Joel's eyes widened, "What did you say?"

I started the engine and shrugged, "I said that God has called us, so we will go. In fact, our whole family is going."

Ben sat quietly throughout the conversation. Finally, he spoke, "What did they think about you taking your whole family?"

I looked each of the young men in the eyes before answering, "They said, 'Let us have a picnic before you go because we want to say good-bye. We may never see you again.'"

All three raised their eyebrows and sat speechless as I pulled into the heavy Moscow traffic.

Lord, I trust You to do great things through us this summer!

It was a long two-hour drive back to the compound. The three men slept and snored the entire trip home.

The next morning, Joel, Micah, Ben, and I sat down to a breakfast of eggs and bacon that Kathy prepared. After we prayed, I asked her, "Did the younger three get off for school okay?"

Kathy smiled, "Yeah, but they are looking forward to summer break."

Joel stuffed a piece of bacon in his mouth, swallowed and said, "I don't miss those daily train trips to Moscow for school!"

Ben piped up, "I thought you homeschooled the children?"

Kathy smiled, "We did until they reached high school. The Southern Baptist and Campus Crusade ministries have a Christian school."

I explained, "We went on a furlough when Joel was 16 and noticed how awkward he acted around teens." Joel shot me a dirty look. I held up my hand, "Sorry, Joel, you were great with adults but quirky with teenagers. We decided when we came back to put him in Hinkson Christian Academy."

Joel interjected, "I had the coolest class and developed some great friends who helped me not be so socially awkward."

Kathy smiled, "We decided when the kids reached high school, they should go to Hinkson. The school was gracious and let our children memorize verses in the KJV. It has been a great experience for the children."

Ben nodded and added, "Brother Reasoner, I can't thank you enough for allowing me to come along to the Nenets tribe."

I buttered my toast, then answered, "I checked your references when you filled out the application last fall. Both the Dean and college President highly recommended you." Pushing my plate away, I looked at everyone. "I'm pleased you could join our little band. This is our fourth Reindeer trip. It's only been a year this time. It depends on resources, and the Lord's agenda." I sighed. "There are many unreached tribes, and we must continue until we reach them all."

Suddenly the front door opened, and Andre shouted, "Hallelujah!" We all headed to the living room, while Kathy followed with a pot of hot tea and scones.

"Ben, this is Andre. He helped us get our house documents legal. He went with me on our first Reindeer trip. Now he works at the Domodedovo airport. He contacted me last week and said there might be a translation of the Bible in the Reindeer Nenets language."

I pointed to Ben, "Andre, this is Ben. He goes to college with Joel and Micah." All three stood to shake Andre's hand. I turned my attention back to Andre, "So, it went well? Did you get in touch with someone at the Russian Bible Society?"

"It is nice to meet you, Ben." Turning to me, he continued, "I called three Russian Baptist Churches. The last one told me about a Brother Stepan Volkov with the Russian Bible Society. I called him yesterday."

The College Boys & The Nenets Translation of Luke

I stirred my tea and nodded. Andre reached for a scone and continued. "I asked him if he could locate the original Nenets manuscript of the Gospel of Luke that was rumored to exist. Surprisingly, he knew about it, so I asked if he could get permission for us to have 300 copies printed; and how much would it cost."

I took a sip of my tea and excitedly said, "Wow, that is amazing and an answer to prayer."

Andre buttered another scone. "He called this morning, and I came straight here."

Joel leaned forward, "Don't keep us in suspense. What'd he say?"

Andre chuckled at Joel's eagerness. "Bishop Varkov, the man in charge of the archives, informed him that if the manuscript didn't leave the monastery, he'd be willing to have our copies printed at 140 rubles a copy."

I grabbed a pen and some paper and started to do some figuring. "Why that's 42,000 rubles!" I wiped my forehead with the back of my hand and sighed. "Now I know why the Lord had me agree to Brother John's request to go with us on this trip."

Joel and Micah frowned. Joel shook his head. "You mean the complainer? You are letting him come again?"

I tapped my wallet and nodded. "None other. He told me he'd pay for half of all expenses." I shrugged, "He has seen the light, and wants to trust the Lord. He promised there wouldn't be any problem from him."

One month later, I pulled our van in front of the Russian Bible Society office which was inside a Moscow Russian Orthodox Monastery. Andre opened the passenger door and stepped out. He leaned his head back inside. "Brother Ron, I think your idea of letting me handle this is the only way we're getting the Nenets Gospel of Luke printed." He chuckled, "No offense, but if you said one word, they would know you are an American and they wouldn't even consider publishing the books."

I nodded, "You're right. By the way, do you have the cash?"

He tapped his coat pocket. "Right here, all 42,000 rubles."

I watched as he walked up the monastery steps.

Lord, go with him, thank You for giving me a friend with such strong faith.

I pulled out my Bible and started reading the Gospel of Luke. Forty minutes later I closed my Bible to pray.

Lord, he's been in there a long time. Is there a problem? Will we have them in time? I thought he'd be back by now. I need to get home, pack, and spend time with the family.

I opened my eyes and spotted Andre lugging three heavy boxes. I rushed out and opened the back of the van.

"Praise the Lord! Obviously, they got printed." I pointed to the entrance. "What took so long?"

Andre smiled. "The Lord was with us. Brother Stepan brought the books out and informed me that a Russian Baptist Church had placed an order as well. He bundled our order with theirs so it would be cheaper!" Andre reached into his pocket, retrieved the envelope, and handed it to me.

I looked inside. "Praise the Lord!"

He laughed. "All together we ordered a thousand copies. They charged us the equivalent of three dollars a copy rather than the original five."

I rubbed my chin. "At 28-rubles per dollar, which totals 16,800-rubles we got back. About $600. That'll give us a cushion in our budget."

We drove the 30 miles home singing and thanking the Lord for His mercy.

THOUGHTS

- Do you involve your family in your ministry?
- Does it give them a positive outlook on full-time service?

Chapter Fifty-Seven

Mother Russia

Not boasting of things without our measure, that is, of other men's labors; but having hope, when your faith is increased, that we shall be enlarged by you according to our rule abundantly, To preach the gospel in the regions beyond you, and not to boast in another man's line of things made ready to our hand. 2 Corinthians 10:15-16

"Is everyone packed? Do you know which bags you are responsible for?" I called out as we prepared to leave for the Camel People. It was July 16, 2004, and we were also celebrating our 20th wedding anniversary.

Everyone nodded. "Okay, let's begin with prayer." We bowed our heads as I prayed, "Father, we have a call from You to go to the uttermost parts of the Earth regardless of the consequences and obstacles we may face. We have been warned not to go to Kalmykia, but we claim the verse,

"We ought to obey God rather than men. From (Acts 5:29b)

"Please go before us and protect us on this journey. May many souls be saved, and churches started for Your glory. Amen."

We grabbed our assigned bags, including the extra supplies Sergei had requested. They contained Bibles, discipleship material, food, medicines, candy, props for skits and clothing. Each man carried a backpack, a satchel, and two large suitcases. My younger children each had a backpack, a duffle bag, and a rolling suitcase. Taxis could not carry all of our luggage, so we took the local train to Moscow.

As we boarded the *elektrichka* (local train), heads turned and stared. One lady gathered the courage to ask, "Who are you, and where are you going with so many bags?"

Kathy answered, "We are an American missionary family going to Kalmykia."

Everyone within earshot gasped. The lady's eyes widened. Quickly she composed herself and spoke evenly, "Oh, so you are going to visit the wild people of Russia? May I ask why?"

Kathy handed her a tract, "To tell them about Jesus."

She rolled her eyes, took the tract, and whispered, "Good luck."

Once we arrived at the Moscow Pavelestski Train Station, we unloaded our bags onto the platform. I motioned for Joel to follow me as I instructed the others, "Wait here while we find out which platform our train departs from. It will take 18 hours to travel 650 miles to Volgograd."

We soon returned, grabbed our bags and everyone followed to the long-distance platform. Our train was already at the station. I checked our tickets. "Here." I pointed. We got in line and waited for the wagon masters to open the doors.

Once we boarded, I directed Kathy, Keturah, Hannah, and Jeremiah to a second-class suite. There were four bunks and plenty of room to store the extra luggage under the beds and in the overhead compartment. The rest of us were relegated to third class—known by Russians as the plats-cart. It is a communal wagon with rows and rows of bunk beds stacked three high. While a first-class suite cost $120 per bed, second class cost $80, the plats-cart was only $17. The first- and second-class wagons did not have air conditioning, but our third-class plats-cart did.

Funny how the class envy of communism lingers on. The rich roast while the poor enjoy the cold air!

The farther southeast we went, the hotter it became. Kathy and the kids meandered into our air-conditioned car often during the trip. They were sitting on my bunk when Kathy jumped up and looked out the window. "What is that tall thing up ahead?"

We all looked to see a tall cement statue of a woman holding a sword high in the air and beckoning others to follow her. Kathy answered her own question as she squealed, "I think that is Mother Russia! I forgot she is in Volgograd! She is Russia's Statue of Liberty!" She turned to me, "Ron! I want to see it! I want to get pictures of it! She's on my bucket list! I'm so excited!" She turned to our three youngest and giggled, "Congratulations, you and I have just seen Russia's Statute of Liberty before seeing our own in New York Harbor."

We admired the beautiful monument through the train window. I knew I had to take Kathy. I stood beside her, took her hand, and explained,

Mother Russia

"A van is picking us up at the train station. One of the men in Sergei's church has a taxi business. We can ask him to take us there."

Upon arrival at the train station, it was not hard for Vlad, the Kalmykian taxi driver, to recognize our group of Americans. After we piled our bags into the van, Vlad offered to take us to see Mother Russia. What a beautiful and yet sobering edifice! She was built to commemorate the millions of Russians who died during W.W. II. In the basement beneath her feet, there is an eternal flame and plaque after plaque of local heroes' names. Nearly 9,000,000 Russian military men perished on behalf of their motherland during that war.

As I read the history on the commemorative inscriptions, I was moved to tears at the photos of Volgograd's (formerly Stalingrad) utter destruction by the German army. They estimate almost 60,000,000 Russian citizens died in World War II. Some of starvation, some from bombings, others from looting, and an estimated 25,000,000 under the direction of Stalin himself.

Gazing around at the beautiful statues and imagining the lives lost, I recalled a conversation years ago with Roman's father: "Ron, Russia suffers from a shortage of good men. Why? Because who goes to war—good men of character who love their country. When they die, who is left but the weak, the maimed, the selfish and the undesirable? That is why we struggle as a country. We have lost our good men."

I viewed the circular walls with names written from floor to ceiling. These were the names of good men. A large cement hand reached out of the ground in the center of the room, holding the eternal memorial flame.

Vlad caught my attention, bringing me back to the present. He tapped his wristwatch and arched his eyebrows. It was time to go. As we started back to the van, he smiled, "You know Mother Russia was designed with her sword high enough in the air to be taller than your Statue of Liberty."

I winked at our team. Part of team training was to understand we are visitors in a foreign country. We need not express our opinion when it differs from the host country. I turned to Vlad, gave him a thumbs up and said, "She's beautiful. Thank you for bringing us here. We are ready for Kalmykia."

Vlad stopped and pointed to the restrooms. "It is a four-hour drive over rough roads to our base village. These are the last restrooms with indoor plumbing you will see for ten days." Nothing further needed to be said. We all made a final pitstop before getting into the van.

Top Row: Me, Kathy, Keturah & Hannah at Mother Russia
Bottom Row: Micah, Joel, Jeremiah

Four painfully exhausting hours later, we pulled into the parking lot of a building we would later buy for Sergei's church. They had already remodeled it into a church building that sat 25 people. The upstairs was a dormitory for the men to use during our 10-day stay. There was an outhouse set off to the side of the property.

Mother Russia

Sergei met us at the front door, "I can't believe you came! I have great news. I have attempted several times to get into these six villages but have never had any success. This time I invited an orphanage cultural team to join us. When I said we would have orphans and Americans, it piqued the interest of the town administrators.

"They have agreed to allow us to use the cultural centers in their villages. We will arrive at each village a few hours before our scheduled meeting, go door to door, and invite everyone to the cultural center. We will have the orphans perform cultural dances, then your team can pantomime two skits, my wife will play her Kalmykian *dombra* (stringed musical instrument), and then we will show a Christian movie. We will give an invitation at the end."

I smiled as Sergei gave his detailed plan for evangelism. "What will happen to those who repent? How will they grow in Christ?" I asked.

Sergei put up his hand, "I'm not finished. I have a team ready to go back to each village the next day and immediately start a Bible study with those who repent."

I was impressed, but full of questions, "How far are the villages from here? Where are they located?"

Sergei smiled, "Interestingly enough, the six villages are in the shape of a cross. Two are north, two are south, one is east, and one is west. Each village is about 2-3 hours from here—it depends on the roads which are mostly dirt. If it rains, we may have to do some pushing."

Just then, Sergei's phone rang. I watched as he furrowed his brow, frowned, and spoke in Kalmykian to the caller. Finally, he hung up and grumbled, "That was bad news. The cultural dance team from the orphanage is under quarantine. I guess they were exposed to the flu and can't come. They have offered to send their youth band. I hope they will work into the program. I promised these village administrators that orphans were coming. I must let the band come."

I caught Kathy, Hannah, and Keturah out of the corner of my eye. They were headed to the outhouse. I watched with interest as they opened the door and quickly shut it. Kathy pulled out her camera and photographed the girls with their noses plugged, pointing to the outhouse. Sergei turned towards their laughter.

Lord, don't let him be offended, and thank You that the girls have a good attitude.

He turned back to me and smiled, "You deal with what God gives you, don't you? There used to be indoor plumbing in the apartments around here, but people used the toilets as garbage bins. The government got tired of plunging the sewer pipes, so they filled them with sand and built outhouses."

As Sergei spoke, the girls walked over to join us. Kathy asked, "Where will we be staying?"

Sergei clapped his hands and replied, "A lady in our church who has a small house. She is in Moscow for the month and offered for you to stay in her home."

Hannah disgusted with the outhouse

Hannah piped up, "Does she have indoor plumbing?"

Sergei laughed, "I just finished telling your dad that no one in the village has indoor plumbing. But" he said with excitement, "She has a *banya*!"

Thirteen-year-old Jeremiah approached our group just in time to hear the word *banya* and asked, "What's that?"

I smiled at Sergei, "I'll explain it later. Right now, we would love to go to this house and get some rest. My boys and Ben will be staying here at the church with Dimitre, right?"

Sergei nodded. As if on cue, Joel, Micah, Ben, and Dimitre exited the building. They joined Sergei on the steps and waved goodbye as Vlad took us in the van to our accommodations.

"How far is the house?" I asked as we pulled onto a narrow road.

Vlad smiled at my accent and replied in Russian, "Your Russian is not so bad. You will find that we villagers will not have a problem understanding you. We slaughter the Russian language as well."

I'll take that as a compliment, Lord. At least they will understand me.

Mother Russia

Vlad continued, "The house is my mother's, and it is five minutes from the church. I have the keys and I'll show you around."

Moments later, we slowly descended a steep driveway. The home, which would be considered nothing more than a shack by American standards, was one of the nicer houses on the block.

This is the place we stayed at on this trip to Kalmykia

We got out of the vehicle and Vlad began the guided tour. "This building on the left is our *banya*. Do you know what that is?"

I answered, "We've never used one, but I understand that it is like an outdoor sauna. There is usually a stove of some sort to heat a pot of water. You use a large ladle to pour the boiling water into a bucket of cold water. When you reach the desired water temperature in the bucket, you use the ladle to pour it over your body to cleanse yourself."

Vlad shrugged. "Close enough. I'll show you later how to start the fire. Mom had a natural gas stove installed a few years ago when the government brought gas lines down this street." We walked from the *banya* toward another building, passing through a beautiful flower garden. "This little garden is my mom's pride and joy."

Kathy admired the colorful peonies and roses. Climbing clematis decorated the small wooden fence around the garden's perimeter. She sniffed a pink rose and sighed, "Vlad, this is beautiful, and the flowers are so fragrant! Please tell your mother thank you for the hospitality and give her our compliments on the beautiful garden."

Vlad smiled and pointed to a small building in the corner of the property. "I think you can guess what this small shack is for.

Jeremiah opened the door, quickly closed it, and said in English, "It's an outhouse and it stinks!" Kathy and I gave Jeremiah the death stare. He quickly recovered by looking at Vlad and in his broken Russian said, "Thank you. It is good."

Vlad led us into the house. It was one large room. A small kitchen lined one wall; a closet lined an adjacent wall. A double bed hugged the third, and the fourth sported a futon. Vlad led Kathy to the kitchen and proudly announced, "I installed a working kitchen sink. A hose supplies the water, and I attached a pipe to the drain. The pipe flows underground to the garden."

Kathy turned the faucet on and grinned at Vlad, "Your mom must be very proud of you! This is great."

Vlad continued the tour, "The sheets on the bed are clean, and I see your children have sleeping bags for the floor. It looks like you are all set. I will come tomorrow morning at 8 a.m. for our first crusade."

As Vlad headed for the door, we yelled out in unison, "Thank you! See you in the morning."

A Kalmykian Girl

THOUGHTS
- Explain why flexibility, adaptability, and creativity are so important to missionary life.

Chapter Fifty-Eight

Buddhists & Spiritual Warfare

For we wrestle not against flesh and blood, but against principalities, against powers, against the rulers of the darkness of this world, against spiritual wickedness in high places. Ephesians 6:12

"Hurry up, Keturah! It's almost 8 a.m. Vlad should be here soon!" I said to my oldest daughter as she primped. "You may be 16 soon, but you know the rules—no dating until you get to college."

Keturah opened her mouth to protest, but Kathy was quick to back me up, "We are your parents. Nothing is hidden. We saw those young men at the church flirting with you."

Keturah sighed, gathered her belongings into her makeup bag and put it away. "Okay, okay. I'm ready."

I walked out last and locked the door. Hannah watched me and chuckled, "I don't know why you need to lock it. There is nothing in that house worth stealing."

I put my arm around her shoulder as we walked and squeezed it just enough to let her know a lecture was coming. "There may not be anything you want in that house, but compared to other people in this village, Vlad's mom is rich."

Fourteen-year-old Hannah countered, "But she doesn't even have cable TV."

Jeremiah rolled his eyes and said, "But she DOES have a TV. We wouldn't want that stolen on our watch."

Kathy and Keturah approached our little group. Kathy pointed to each child as she lectured them "Hannah, Jeremiah, Keturah, we are blessed from God with everything we have, but we should never ever think less of someone because they don't have a lot. She has worked hard her whole life to afford this house and is trusting us to take care of it. We WILL appreciate her hospitality and thank God for her giving spirit. We will also ask God to bless her kindness."

The three teens looked at each other and then at their mother, "Yes. Ma'am." They replied in unison.

Kathy checked her watch. It was 8:20 a.m. "Where is Vlad? You don't think he forgot?"

I smiled, "Don't worry, we are living on Kalmykian time. Apparently, it is even slower than Russian time. He'll be here soon."

I nodded toward the street, "There he is!"

Vlad pulled into the driveway. I slid open the van's side door, "Hurry up. We don't want to miss the fun."

At the church, I counted two other vehicles—a Lada and another van. Sergei approached as we got out. He looked at his clipboard, and immediately handed out orders, "Vlad, you drive this van with the Reasoners, John, and Ben in it. I will drive the other van with the Orphan band and their instruments. My wife, Elis, will drive the Lada with five other church members who will oversee evangelism, discipleship, and follow up."

A Kalmykian Boy

He turned to Joel and asked, "Do you have your props and the Bibles you brought?" Joel nodded. Sergei turned to Elis, "Do you have your *dombra*, the flyers, the projector, and the movie?" Elis double checked her

Buddhists & Spiritual Warfare

Lada's trunk and nodded. Sergei turned to the Orphan Band and asked, "Do you have everything you need to perform? Instruments? Microphones? Sound system? Everything?" They also nodded.

I peeked at the list and saw that Sergei had checked off everything except the last item. He turned back to me, "Ron, we will need food for the day. If you give Elis 3,000 rubles—$100, she can buy food for lunch and dinner at our local market."

I pulled out my wallet and handed him the money. I had brought several thousand dollars in rubles to finance our trip. Churches in America had responded favorably to my last prayer letter asking for help to finance this work among the Buddhists.

As Joel, Micah and Ben got into our van, Kathy gave the young men a quick hug. "Did you sleep well?" she asked.

They sighed. Micah spoke first, "Dimitre wanted to challenge us to ping pong. He could not accept defeat and insisted we play until we got tired enough to let him win. Then, he wanted to hear about life at an American Bible College. We did not get to sleep until 2 a.m."

Joel leaned his head against a side window and muttered, "Then someone started banging pots and pans in the kitchen around 6:30 a.m. Don't get me wrong, I appreciated the eggs, toast, coffee and *grechka* (buckwheat) but I would have liked two more hours of sleep."

Because our conversation took place in English, Vlad did not understand. He interrupted in Russian, "The first village is two hours away. It hasn't rained in a while, so the roads should be good."

We arrived just before noon and parked near the community center. I looked around. This village was tiny. There was a kiosk, a school, and the community center. Nothing else. I looked at Vlad, "This looks like a ghost town. How many people live here?"

Vlad pulled a bottle of water out and took a gulp, "Between 200-300 people, but most have left for the summer. I'd guess there aren't more than 150 people now. When Elis arrives with lunch, we will eat and then go two by two to all the houses we can find, pass out the flyers and invite people to our evening of live entertainment."

After the other cars arrived, we ate while Sergei went into the school/town hall building to meet with the mayor. He returned with the key to the community center.

Sergei instructed, "Let's set up, run through the program, and then go out and invite the villagers to attend our meeting."

Everyone hopped into action, helping to set up for the evangelistic crusade. My family went first doing the "Mask" mime. Sergei watched and when it was over, he applauded. "I like it, but I will call this mime 'Hypocrite' because 'mask' in Russian just doesn't have the same meaning."

Joel performing the "Mask" mime skit

We moved off the stage so the orphan band could practice. I stood in horror as they began their first song. It was not cultural music! It was not even classical! They were a "wanna-be" rock band.

Lord, help!

I watched Ben jump up and run out. I could tell he was offended and disappointed. I ran over to Sergei and yelled above the noise, "Did you know they were a rock band? I'm sponsoring these meetings and I can't condone this music!"

Surprised, Sergei turned to me, "You don't like this music? It's from America!"

Shaking my head I said, "No, I condemn rock music. Some people think music is amoral, but I don't! I know it changes people's moods and attitudes. I only allow godly music in our home and in evangelistic crusades. We need to find a solution."

Seeing Ben pacing back and forth, I touched Sergei's arm and said, "I must take care of Ben. This conversation is not over!"

Before reaching him, I called, "Brother Ben, I am so sorry. It was supposed to be a cultural team. I had no idea this would happen!"

In frustration, Ben said, "I was raised in a very conservative Christian home. I cannot participate if they are going to play that music."

Buddhists & Spiritual Warfare

"Ben, you need to understand we cannot always control the environment we minister in. Often souls are saved despite less-than-ideal conditions."

Joel, Micah, Kathy, Keturah, Hannah, and Jeremiah came walking towards us. Jeremiah, ever the jokester, played his air guitar while approaching.

Once we were gathered in a huddle I apologized, "Listen, guys, I'm sorry about that music. I don't know what to do. If we walk away from these scheduled evangelistic meetings, it will hurt Sergei's reputation because he cannot afford to do this without us."

Kathy put her hand on my arm, "Honey, we don't blame you. You have nothing to apologize for. You didn't know this would happen." She shook her head and continued, "The sad thing is, these kids probably think we are thrilled with their rock music because we are Americans from the land of rock and roll."

I bowed my head and everyone else followed suit, "Father, we came here to proclaim Your goodness and grace to a people who have never even heard Your Name. Give us wisdom to do right. When You were on the earth, You spent most Your time with sinners and publicans because You knew they needed Your salvation. Perhaps You have put these orphans in our lives that they might come to know You as their Savior. Perhaps they will even sing Your praises."

I went back to confront Sergei. He said, "Brother Ron, I'm sorry. You know this is not my fault. I booked the cultural dance team, but we got their rock band. I think we have them play first, and then take a 15-minute break while they pack away their equipment. We can then setup for mimes, the godly music, and the movie projector. There will be a distinction between their concert and our evangelistic meeting. Does that sound like a good compromise?"

Lord, what do You want? You said...

They that are whole have no need of the physician, but they that are sick: I came not to call the righteous, but sinners to repentance. (Mark 2:17b)

Okay, Lord, I'm trusting you.

I smiled, shook Sergei's hand, and said, "I just want God to be glorified!"

After the practice, we split up into groups and invited people to come. Door knocking was different in Kalmykia. We approached the edge of the property and yelled in Russian, "Is the owner home? May we speak to you?" We waited for someone to come to the door, then we asked, "May we approach?" If they nodded, we held out the flyer and invited them to the evening performance. If they said, "No, go away!" we simply said, "We will leave our invitation to a wonderful evening of music, theater, and a movie here on your front gate."

We had 100 people show up the first night. God was in it all. Everything worked smoothly. The band performed, tore down their set, we did two mimes, and Elis sang and played her *dombra*. Then a Kalmykian by the name of Baudma set up a fireside scene, sat on a rug, and told an old Kalmykian story about creation. It was surprisingly close to the Genesis account.

Lastly, we dimmed the lights and showed the movie *The Climb* dubbed over in Russian. It is a movie about two men who share a passion for climbing. One is a Christian, who continually witnesses to his friend who does not care about God nor the fact the Jesus died in his place. While on a difficult climb, the Christian sacrifices his life to save his friend. This bothers the friend, and he starts to understand that what the Christian did for him is exactly what Jesus did on the Cross. He later repents and becomes a born-again believer in the death, burial, and resurrection of Jesus Christ.

After the movie finished, Sergei stood and gave his testimony, "As a young Buddhist man, I felt there was more to life than Buddha and his teachings. Buddhism had not filled my spiritual needs. Life had no meaning and I fell into bouts of depression from the emptiness in my soul. But God sought me out. He sent a group of Christian American wrestlers to my university.

"We held exhibition matches. The Americans fought with passion but kindness. They never cheated. They played fair. I was impressed with their integrity. After the wrestling matches were over, they asked us if they could tell why they were different. They opened their Bibles and taught about Jesus. They told how God was the Creator of the Universe, yet He wanted to have a personal relationship with me.

"I accepted Christ as my Savior and Friend that night. I have never looked back, and I can tell you that God is real. He loves you; He sent His Son to die for you to prove His love, just like the Christian in this movie. If there is anyone here that would like to come to Christ, I ask you to stay after everyone else leaves. I will take a Bible, God's Words to us, and show you how you can be saved."

Buddhists & Spiritual Warfare

After Sergei concluded the message, five Buddhists stayed behind. They repented and got saved. Baudma planned to meet with them the next day to begin discipleship. A preaching station was established there.

Me in front of the Buddhist Temple

Lord, it makes hardships worth it when souls are eternally saved.

When we arrived back at our base camp, we learned that the van carrying the rock band, broke down.

Thank You, Lord.

Without the extra vehicle to carry the band, we left the rock band at base camp the next day. When we arrived at the village without the orphans, the administrator became furious and almost did not allow us to have our meeting. Sergei was able to calm her down, but we understood that we had to bring the orphans with us. At this second meeting, about 125 people came to hear the Gospel. Three raised their hands for salvation. A preaching station was started there as well.

The third village was the most difficult. Part of our team stayed at base camp to make room for the orphan band. Sergei had tried several times to get a meeting in this town and had always failed. God blessed us and we were able to get in.

As we prepared to canvass the village, I could feel the spiritual battle raging. I asked Ben to lead us in prayer, "Father, we are entering a battle for many souls today. I pray that You will protect us and keep our hearts and minds focused on Your business. Bless us as we represent You today. In Christ's name I ask, Amen."

I walked alongside Ben, "So you feel the darkness as well?" He nodded and I mused, "I think God has great plans here. We must be vigilant to defend the faith today!"

We went door to door inviting people to our meeting at 5 p.m. Everyone accepted our invitation and seemed excited. I was surprised when several of the elderly Buddhist grandmothers smiled at our invitation and asked, "Would your God fit on my shelf next to Buddha's statue?"

Sergei looked at me for an answer. I pulled out my Russian Bible and opened it to John 14:6.

> *"Jesus saith unto him, I am the way, the truth, and the life: no man cometh unto the Father, but by me."*

Sergei read it and explained that Jesus is the only way.

"I want to add to Buddha, not throw him away." One of the grandmothers exclaimed.

I turned to Acts 4:12 and Sergei read it to her:

> *"Neither is there salvation in any other: for there is none other name under heaven given among men, whereby we must be saved."*

While none of the ladies got saved at the door, they promised to come to the meeting.

At 4:45 p.m., we stood outside the cultural center, ready to welcome people. A group of several drunken Kalmykians and Buddhist priests came and blocked the way in. They started yelling at the approaching crowds, "Go home. We are Buddhists and will not abide Christians in our village."

"Excuse me," Sergei kindly said, "We are having a meeting here and everyone is welcome to attend. Please step aside so people can come in."

The crowd hesitated. People who intended to come, now backed away, afraid of what the repercussions would be if they entered the building against the priests' wishes.

I was taken aback by the aggressive nature of these priests. I was always told Buddhists are pacifists. Not so. They stood tall and threatened both our team and the villagers, "If you enter here, you will be punished." Turning to our team, they scowled, "Leave here, NOW, or else—!"

I admit, I had a moment in the flesh. We had several Olympic wrestlers on our team. The priests were drunk.

I think we can take them!

Buddhists & Spiritual Warfare

Immediately, the Holy Spirit convicted me.

Get on your knees and pray! This is not a fight against flesh and blood but against principalities and spiritual wickedness in high places.

I called my team together and fell on my knees, "We must pray! 'Father! We need You to intervene. I want to fight with my fists, but You have told us to fight on our knees. So, I pray You bind Satan and his demons. Cast them out of this place that Your Word may have free course.'" I opened one eye to watch God work a miracle. One by one, the drunken men and all but one priest walked away.

Sergei took the lingering priest aside, "I know you find no peace in your worship of Buddha. I know because I once worshipped him, and I felt empty. Then one day, I met the True and Living God Who made Heaven and earth. I learned He loves us so much that He sent His Son to die for our sins. I asked this God to forgive me, and He did! Would you like to meet the God Who made Heaven and earth?"

The priest fell on his knees and began to cry.

God was working in his heart!

Conviction was written all over his face. But Satan would not be so easily defeated. Suddenly the priest stood, grabbed his chest, and ran away. Perhaps he later got saved.

When the people saw what happened—how the priests and drunks mysteriously walked away, they returned to hear the Gospel and watch the Christian film. Five people got saved that evening.

Pastor Sergei on the left and me on the right with Kalmykian children

Serving God Behind Enemy Lines

We went to a total of six villages where we performed, preached, and gave an invitation. Souls were saved and Bible studies were started. On the last day, three of the six orphans in the band also got saved. They saw true Christianity for the first time in their lives and wanted to be a part of the family of God! The Kalmykian president had said there would never be a Christian in his republic, but today, there are six Bible Believing and Bible Preaching Churches!

Vlad became one of the main evangelists in Sergei's ministry. He traveled to the six villages to hold Bible studies. More than once, he was beaten for his unwavering Christian faith. He suffered broken ribs, black eyes, and even a broken collarbone when the village priests beat him up. One day he took a teenage boy fishing on the Volga River to witness to him. The teen fell into the raging river, which quickly swept him away for he could not swim. Vlad could not swim either, but he could never live with himself if he did not try to save the boy.

Greater love hath no man than this, that a man lay down his life for his friends. (John 15:13)

They both drowned that day.

Pastor Sergei left of me (my right) and Vlad sitting on the right
The others are unnamed Kalmykian pastors

Buddhists & Spiritual Warfare

As we boarded the train back to Moscow, Micah came and sat beside Kathy and me, "Dad, Mom, we hit the ground running when we got to Russia. I haven't had a chance to tell you yet what God did in my heart at Bible College. You know God called me into the ministry, but I wanted to live and minister in America. A few weeks before summer break, we had a missionary come and give a devotion in our dormitory. He talked about how most are willing to serve God in America, but few are brave enough to serve God on the foreign field. God pricked my heart. I heard the Holy Spirit say, 'You already know Russia and her culture. How long will it take another to learn what you already know? What is fearful for others, is home to you. Will you go for Me to Russia?' I—"

Kathy grabbed Micah, interrupting his prepared speech, "Oh honey! We are so proud of you!"

I pulled Kathy back, "I don't think he was done. Let him finish."

Micah smiled, "So I surrendered to come back to Russia as a missionary. I know it will make finding a wife harder, but I believe God is preparing her heart even now. I felt a great comradery with Sergei on this trip. I am burdened for these people in Kalmykia. I believe God is calling me to be a missionary among the Buddhists." Micah rubbed his hands down his thighs, "There. Now I'm done."

I grabbed my son into a big bear hug. Kathy joined in. Soon the whole Reasoner family fell into a group hug.

Thank You, Lord for making my God their God. Bless them as they follow You!

THOUGHTS
- When you are faced with opposition, do you fight with your fists or with your faith?

CHAPTER FIFTY-NINE

A Reindeer Pastor

He trusted on the LORD that he would deliver him: let him deliver him, seeing he delighted in him. Psalm 22:8

After returning from Kalmykia on the 26th, we did laundry, repacked, and had one good night's sleep. The next morning, we waited on the platform at the Moscow train station. I looked around at our team of six:

- ✓ Joel — My eldest son
- ✓ Micah — My second son
- ✓ John — The American Missionary
- ✓ Argum — An Armenian
- ✓ Ben — The American Bible College Student
- ✓ Myself

I walked over to John who was leaning against a pole with headphones on his head. After I waved a hand in front of his face, he slid them down.

"I hope you are listening to uplifting music which encourages you to serve the Lord with gladness."

His carotid artery bulged as his face turned red. "I'm a grown man and a missionary at that. Don't you think I can discern for myself what is God honoring and what is not?"

My eyes fell upon Argum the Armenian whom we had invited to accompany us. I returned my gaze to John, "What kind of testimony are you setting for Argum?"

John smirked, "He likes it. I gave him several CD's."

I was livid. "You've been giving that junk to him?"

He returned a blank stare, "He is a grown man who can make his own decisions. He asked me to run him off a CD. Besides, music is

A Reindeer Pastor

amoral." He tapped his headset. "It's the words that are important. The good beat makes the music more memorable." Having said that, he put the headphones back on and resumed listening.

After the now familiar 48-hour train ride, we took the ferry from Labytnangi to Salekhard and found a hotel. With Dimitre on vacation in Ukraine, we did not have the connection to stay at the church dormitory. The next morning, we bought breakfast from the local marketplace. As we sat in the hotel room feasting on reindeer sausage and bread, John piped up, "So what is the plan? You do have a plan, right?"

I stood, bowed my head, and prayed, "Father, we have come to the ends of the earth to share Christ with those who have never heard and will never hear if Your children don't go. We are trusting You to work out the details. Amen."

After asking the locals if they had seen any Reindeer People or *chums* in the area and hearing the usual, 'It's been a long winter, they aren't here yet,' we went back to the hotel to regroup. John piped up, "I was afraid this might happen, so I brought the name of a Wycliffe missionary in this area. I'll call him." John stepped outside and returned a few moments later.

"Well," I said, "Don't keep us waiting. What did they say?"

"There was no answer." John grumbled, "I'll try later."

That afternoon we handed out tracts and told people about Christ. John walked off when his phone rang. Momentarily he returned, "That was the Wycliffe missionary. He might have somebody who can help us. His name is Peytor Hoode, and he is coming over to meet us soon."

The Wycliffe Missionary and Peytor met us in our hotel lobby. We made quick introductions and listened to Peytor's testimony.

"I am from the village of Kazym-Mys. I left home to become a tradesman at 17, met some Christians during my studies, and became a born-again believer in Christ. I attended a Bible Seminary in Moscow. Now, I am back in Salekhard and want to take the Gospel to my village."

Peytor's face brightened as he continued, "I must start a church in my hometown. It is about 24 hours down the Obe River. Sadly, every time I plan a trip something happens personally, locally, or globally to stop me. I am ready to try again if you will go with me."

I looked at each of my traveling companions, "Well?" I asked, "What do you think?"

"Yes! Let's do it!" was everyone's ready reply.

I turned to him, "It looks like we are willing. Shall we meet you at the harbor tomorrow?" I noticed the look of surprise on the Wycliffe missionary's face when he realized we were willing to go.

Peytor raised his hands to Heaven in praise, "Amen! But I need you to meet me at the Russian Baptist church tomorrow. They have a huge canvas tent we can use. I need help getting it to the docks." He surveyed our young men and continued, "I think we can do it with your young men. We need to get it from the storage unit to a van, then from the van to the docks."

The next day, we stood on the dock staring at a 40-foot boat. I saw an older Russian man coming out of the boat's engine room. I moved to the boarding plank and called to the captain. "What time do you leave?"

The bearded seaman looked first at the sky, then our luggage, then me; "Soon." He pointed to our gear sitting on the dock. "You load—We go."

I called our men together. In moments, Peytor, Joel, Micah, and Ben grabbed the four corners of the heavy canvas and lowered one end onto the starboard railing. John, Argum and I stood on the deck, pulling it onboard. I struggled with the weight as it slid down the plank from the dock. The poles supporting the folded tent slid on the rail. Peytor and Micah jumped over the rail and grabbed the other end.

Thank You, Lord. That went smoothly. What a blessing!

I moved towards the pile of boxes we'd brought from the Russian Bible Society, grunting as I loaded them onboard. We quickly found seats and piled our luggage between our legs. Peytor removed his coat, pointed at the boxes, and asked, "What's in those?"

I opened a box and handed him a copy of the Nenets Gospel of Luke. Peytor's eyes welled up.

He grabbed the book from my hand and hugged it. For several minutes he sobbed. Finally, he said, "I can't thank you enough. Seventeen years ago, I translated the Gospel of Luke into my mother tongue. I gave it to a man who promised to give it to the Russian Bible Society to print it. It broke my heart when I heard it got filed away in the Russian Orthodox Archives." He smiled, "I never gave up hope that I'd see it in print."

Amazing, Lord. You brought us to the man who wrote the translation we printed and will be giving to a people he is called to preach to. Amen.

Ten minutes later, the seven of us grew silent as our converted military warship chugged out of the harbor towards the village of Kazym-Mys. Joel, Micah, Argum, and Ben chatted and talked amongst themselves. John and I were lulled to sleep as the boat worked her way south on the Obe River. Hours later I awoke to see Peytor still caressing a copy of his work.

Ben, Argum & Peytor on the boat — Notice the large pile of luggage

"Brother Reasoner, I can't thank you enough for getting this published. This is proof that I was right in ignoring my friends who said to not come with you."

I raised an eyebrow; "Were these Christian friends?"

Peytor nodded nervously. His eyes moistened as he strained his neck to see the horizon north of us. "A Shaman rules my people in the village and controls them. My friend said that I shouldn't risk my life going with your small, inexperienced group. He said the Shaman would be too powerful."

Sometime later, John woke up and rubbed his eyes. "Where are we?" He got up on one knee, glanced at the wheelhouse where the captain was taking another swig of vodka. "Oh, I remember." He reached for the headphones hanging from his neck and was soon rocking out to his music.

Peytor was curious. "Why is John engrossed in his music every waking moment?"

As if on cue, John stood, took the headphones off, laid them on his seat and said, "I'll be back in a few minutes."

Peytor walked over to John's seat, put the headphones on and pushed play. His eyes widened as he ripped the earphones off and stomped on them. "That is devil music!" His face was flushed, and his body shook.

John returned to see his headphones crushed on the ground. He immediately turned to accuse me, but Peytor was already in his face.

"Why do you listen to the music that the Shaman uses to summon evil spirits?"

John's face showed shock, anger, embarrassment, and finally pride. Though he opened his mouth several times to speak, nothing came out. Finally, he sat down, smugly pulled out a set of earbuds, and resumed listening.

Peytor ran over to me, "WHAT DO YOU MEAN BY BRINGING A DEVIL WORSHIPPER ON THIS TRIP?" He jabbed a finger towards John. "I don't understand the words, but the beat is satanic. It's music a Shaman would encourage."

I put my hand on his shoulder. "I've tried to convince him how bad his music is. I asked him not to bring it, but he is his own man and makes his own choices."

I looked back at John.

Lord, how does he justify making a weaker brother stumble? He may have liberty, but Peytor sure doesn't!

Suddenly John grabbed his stomach and headed for the restroom again. A few minutes later he came back, his sleeve and cellphone dripping wet. "I accidentally dropped it in the toilet. I hope it still works!" He wiped it repeatedly to dry it off but could not get it work.

Thank you, Lord. Will he understand that You are trying to direct him to quit listening to his worldly music?

John shrugged as he placed his broken cellphone into his pocket. He walked back to his seat, put in his headphones and resumed listening.

We stared on in disbelief.

Time dragged on. Everyone dozed off. Suddenly we were thrown forward as the boat came to a stop.

The first mate rushed from the bow. He climbed the ladder two rungs at a time. We could not tell what they were saying but we heard the two rivermen arguing over the throbbing engine.

The drunken captain staggered onto the walkway and stood next to the first mate. He frowned at his crew as he ordered them into the water to push the boat out of the sandbar. All able-bodied men, us included, were sent into the water to help. It took an hour to get the boat unstuck.

Finally, the first mate leaned over the rail as the boat slipped into the middle of the river. "All aboard, let's get going."

Cold and weary, I had just fallen asleep again when I felt a nudge. Peytor leaned over me, "Brother Reasoner, we're almost to Kazym-Mys. Time to wake up." He moved on to wake the others.

A Reindeer Pastor

Americans, Nenets, and Russians were waking up and stowing gear in preparation for disembarking. I strapped my sleeping bag onto my backpack and slung it over my shoulder. The captain sat in his perch, head in hand, as if he had a serious headache.

The first mate at the wheel was steering for a wide spot on the east side of the river.

John came up to me, dropped his gear at my feet, and said, "Do you see that dock?"

I scanned the shoreline, "What dock?"

"Exactly! It's just a plank on the water AND it's way higher than the boat rail. We will NEVER get this tent over the rails and up on the plank. Why did you agree to take this tent along if you didn't have a plan for getting it off? Even if we unpack it, the canvas will be impossible to unload."

The Russian and Nenets passengers tossed their luggage to family and friends who teetered on the plank.

The captain pointed to the tent. "We leave in 45 minutes whether you have that off or not. We lost too much time when we got stuck."

I turned to see John with a furrowed brow. The boys and Peytor looked expectantly at me.

I folded my hands and said in a calm voice, "Let's pray about this." I swallowed hard, closed my eyes, and took a deep breath. "Lord, I have no idea how we're going to get this tent off this boat. Please Lord, I call on You. Give us the means of lifting this out and onto shore. Amen!"

At that moment everyone turned towards a rumbling noise.

Joel shouted, "Dad! Look! An army truck and a crane."

I've never moved so fast in my life. "My prayer has been answered!" I leaped three steps over the ship's rail, jumped onto the plank, and ran waving my arms. The driver came to a screeching stop.

Peytor caught up and blurted. "We need to borrow your truck and crane for 30 minutes. We have a tent onboard that boat. Can you help us get it off?"

While Peytor talked, I pulled out my wallet. This was all the encouragement they needed. The driver nodded to his friend who got out and guided him to the ship. Within minutes, the tent was hanging from the crane above the truck.

I climbed back onboard and pointed to the tent. "I told you when we boarded that my God would help me." I pulled a tract out and handed it to the captain. "See, my God can do all things."

The Russian soldiers asked Peytor, "Where to?"

Peytor scanned the shore. "Take the tent to that clearing over there. Then I will go ask the mayor for permission to hold a meeting."

They placed the tent in the nearby clearing. I handed them a $20 bill and a couple of Bible tracts. "This is for you. Thanks for helping us." The men smiled and drove off.

Unloading the tent from the Army truck

Micah caught up to me. He slapped me on the back. "You are a man of faith! I'm impressed how the Lord answers your prayers."

I put my arm around Micah's shoulder. "It's amazing, God's answered our prayer with Peytor, a tent, a boat, and a crane."

Part of our group stayed with our stuff while the others went to town. As we walked along a side street, Peytor pointed to a building. "That's the mayor's office. We need his permission to set up the tent and have meetings."

As we entered the large building, I paused to let my eyes adjust to the dark. Peytor went straight to a woman sitting at a desk. "Is the mayor in?" She nodded. "May we see him?"

She pointed to a door, and I followed Peytor. A balding Russian stood by a window. He turned and nodded at Peytor, "What can I do for you?"

Peytor leaned forward. "We want to set up our large tent for three days of meetings. We will show a Christian movie each night. During the day we will walk through the town inviting people to attend. We request your approval."

The mayor frowned and rubbed his chin. "Is it a big tent?"

Peytor squinted then opened one eye. "It seats maybe 150."

A Reindeer Pastor

The mayor leaned back in his chair and shook his head. "The village Shaman is very powerful. He would not be happy."

Lord, this man's no different than the other officials I've met in Moscow. Maybe, just maybe—

I opened my backpack and pulled out the first thing I felt.

A can of spray deodorant? Lord, what kind of a gift is that?

I started to put it back when the mayor's face brightened.

I tilted my head, "Your honor, I would like to find a better—"

The mayor's chair slid back as he rose and came around his desk. "No, no, I want that. You give it to me?"

Peytor and I exchanged glances as I handed a can of Old Spice deodorant to his extended hand.

The mayor smiled as he caressed the red can. He ran his fingers over the trademark, then turned and set it on the right side of his desk. He spun around, "Yes, of course you may set up your tent. There's a large field near the port."

Thank You, Lord. That was where we already put our stuff.

We started to get up and then I paused. "Thank you for the use of the field, Mayor. It would be an honor to see you at one of our meetings."

The mayor smiled, "We'll see."

THOUGHTS

- Have you ever thought about how the other disciples felt when Peter walked on water?
- Were they critical or jealous?
- How do you suppose they told that story to their children?

Chapter Sixty

Idols & The Fishermen

For they themselves show of us what manner of entering in we had unto you, and how ye turned to God from idols to serve the living and true God; 1 Thessalonians 1:9

"What's the plan?" John asked. It was still morning as we sat down to a lunch of sausage and bread.

"The mayor said we can set up the tent in this field. I know we have plenty of time to do it later, but I think we should do it before we get too tired." I looked up into the sky and continued. "At this time of year, it never gets dark."

Just then, a group of boys waved at us. Peytor walked over to them. He came back laughing. "Brother Reasoner, I hope you don't mind, I accepted a soccer match." He looked at the others in our group. Ben, Micah, Argum, and Joel smiled.

They stood, stretched, and said in unison, "Bring it on."

John frowned. "I don't know, Brother Reasoner; this isn't on the schedule. We need to get the tent set up." He gestured towards the boys. "You know I'm not much of an athlete."

I smiled, "Come on, it'll be fun. It's an opportunity to invite them to the meeting. I'll be the goalie."

I laughed. "It doesn't matter if we lose. We need to build relationships."

An hour later, all of us, even John, lay on the tundra, breathlessly laughing and exhausted.

We waved goodbye to the boys as they headed home. After catching our breath, we put the tent up.

A little later, I leaned over to ask Peytor, "I noticed many of the townspeople wearing a hand-carved, wooden-doll necklace. What's that about?"

Peytor sighed, "Long ago, a young Reindeer girl wandered from her family's *chum*, fell through the ice, and drowned. They found her the next day frozen beneath the surface, but the little doll necklace her father carved her lay on the top of the ice. It became a superstition that the doll tried to save her. Fathers began to carve wooden dolls for their children to protect them. They must still do it."

I placed my hand on Peytor's shoulder, "God wants to save these people from their sins and superstitions! He is worthy to be praised and trusted. Wooden idols cannot save anyone!"

With the tent and generator set up, Ben walked over to Joel and Micah. "Let's finish setting up the projector and then rehearse the skits."

Setting up the tent — Notice our luggage in a pile

I fanned myself and called out, "It's too stuffy in here. Let's roll up the sides and get some circulation. Imagine 100 people in here."

After a brief snack, Ben and Joel set up a table of animal balloons. They began to make swords, dogs, hats, and giraffes. Soon children of all ages stood before them. Ben tossed his creations out to the crowd. The adults smiled as the children scrambled for their prizes.

Peytor saw the crowd and commented, "We should start before they get bored and leave. In the village, we have no set time. When people come, we begin."

I called everyone into the tent. "We are starting early." To Peytor, I said, "This is the moment you've been waiting for—you ready?"

He raised his eyes to Heaven and sighed. "Yes, Lord, I'm ready."

Serving God Behind Enemy Lines

As people got comfortable on the ground inside the tent, I smiled at the children sitting in front. I said in Russian, "My name is Ron Reasoner. I come from America." Peytor translated into Nenets.

I gave them the introduction I used on every trip. The children's eyes widened as I talked about a metal bird big enough to carry several hundred people. The adults shook their heads as I talked about the metal snake.

John signaled the soundtrack was ready. I ran off the stage to put on my costume so we could do our pantomime. Peytor stayed up front and introduced our "story with music."

Joel, Ben, Micah, John, and Argum approached the stage. Each had on a mask. Joel was first. He pretended to be a successful businessman with money and happiness, but when he was all alone and took his mask off, he was lonely and unfulfilled. I approached the stage dressed in white and red, representing Christ. Joel came to me, I touched him, and he was healed, signifying salvation. Next, Argum was a happy joker who was sad when he was alone. Micah was "Joe Cool" who needed healing. When the mime was over, Peytor explained, "No matter what hurts and pain you have, Jesus is the answer."

Next, John sang as Peytor translated it into Nenets. When he finished, the audience smiled. John walked over and turned the projector on. With the microphone in one hand, I pointed to the screen. "We will show you a movie about Jesus, His life, and why He lived and died for you and for me." I left the stage.

Peytor stood to the left of the screen and translated the entire film from Russian into Nenets. I watched the faces of the people as they took in the scenes from *The Jesus Film*.

When it finished, I spread my hands out. "Who here would like to receive Jesus into their heart and accept the gift of eternal life?"

I stared at their blank faces.

Lord, we've worked so hard, and not even one person is coming forward. How can we reach them?

I took a deep breath. "I'm going to pray. You can repeat the prayer silently to yourself right where you sit and receive His gift."

Lord, still blank stares. Is the Shaman's influence too strong?

"Please, fold your hands—close your eyes." I heard movement in the crowd, I peeked, saw they were following my instructions, then closed my eyes.

Well, at least they understand.

Idols & The Fishermen

"Heavenly Father, I thank You for the sacrifice You made on the cross for me." Peytor's melodic voice carried through the tent as he translated into Nenets. I continued, "God, I know that I am a sinner and sin cannot enter Heaven. I accept Jesus' death on the cross as the punishment for my sins and ask You for the gift of eternal life. Amen."

I gazed into the faces. "Is there anyone who'd like to come forward and acknowledge they've accepted Jesus as their Savior." No one moved.

I pointed to the exit. "We will be here two more nights. We will show a different film each night. Please bring your friends. As we walk around town tomorrow, we'd like to tell you more about Jesus." With that, the villagers left.

The boys put the equipment away as Peytor and I walked around unfurling the sides of the tent.

John came over and pointed outside the tent. "Tough crowd."

I nodded, "They've experienced the Shaman's oppression for hundreds of years. They are consumed by superstitions. We must ask God to break through their struggles."

John walked toward the corner where his bed roll was. "I'm tired. I'm going to bed."

The next afternoon, Ben set up his table with balloons. I introduced him. "This is my friend Ben. He's going to tell children's Bible stories." I leaned forward, "And, I promise a gift for each of you." I backed away and gave him center stage.

Ben & me outside the tent

Serving God Behind Enemy Lines

Ben spoke English—Joel translated into Russian—then Peytor translated into Nenets. With a balloon in his hand, he stretched it. "Let me tell a story of the God Who created the world. He made the animals, and He made you."

Ben paused to make a dog and a giraffe, then handed them to the two smallest children in the crowd. "God not only made you, He loves you. Come tonight and watch a movie about this God Who loves you!"

With that, Ben and Joel made hats and animals until each child got a gift.

Reindeer children with animal balloons

On the third afternoon, we gathered in the tent to pray—asking God to move. I checked my watch.

3:30 p.m.! Lord, we need to know how to reach these people. We've had services for two nights now. No one's come forward. The Shaman's control is strong. I feel Satan's presence. I need Your help. Please show me the way to their hearts.

There was a rustle at our tent flap. Peytor rose and spoke quietly with his uncle. He nodded, moved to my side, and tilted his head towards his uncle. "He's a fisherman. He and his crew want you to go fishing with them. He says if a holy man comes with them, they will have a good catch." I grabbed clean socks and laced my boots.

The others stood, and Peytor shook his head. "No, just Brother Ron. The boat's only big enough for one more person."

Micah and Joel exchanged glances and approached me, "Dad? Are you sure this is a good idea? We don't know this tribe. What if something happens?"

Idols & The Fishermen

I put an arm around each son, "We must find a way to get through to these people. Pray that God will bless this fishing expedition and they will take it as a sign that we are from the Lord God of Heaven."

I pointed to the village and addressed all the men, "I don't know how long I'll be gone. Why don't you guys take a nap before you start passing out tracts."

I grabbed my coat and hat and followed the fisherman. They helped me aboard. The fishermen chatted among themselves as they rowed their boat to their fishing grounds. They spoke to me in Nenets. I shook my head. Finally, one of the men said in simple Russian, "We will know if you good or bad 'holy man' soon."

Lord, could this be it? I want You to work, but my guess is if You do, I'll have raw fish for dinner. I'm willing Lord. Where You lead me, I will follow. What they feed me; I will swallow.

After the river made a westerly turn, they slid the oars into hooks on the inside of the dory. I watched in awe as they spread their handmade net between them and tossed it into the water.

The leader smiled. I leaned over the side and saw six large Arctic Cod floundering in the net. The Nenets gathered them into their boat.

Thank you, Jesus! Maybe this will help them understand Your power.

I helped pull the net in. They stowed the net and fish. They spoke happily to each other. They looked at me and smiled. One cautiously patted me on the back.

Lord, I was nervous about going on the boat alone with these men. When I saw how rickety the boat was, I almost backed out, but I understand now.

Once on shore, my team ran up. The grey-haired uncle pointed to a wooden shanty and said something to Peytor who translated, "Brother Reasoner, they've invited you and your team to a feast tonight. They usually catch one or two fish a day, but with you onboard, they caught six of the largest cod they have ever seen." He tapped a fish. "He gives you and your God the credit for their success."

Thirty minutes later we sat in the shack. My attention was drawn to the wooden idol displayed on a mantel.

Lord, save these people. Show them that wooden idols have no power, but You, Lord, are all powerful!

I picked up the doll as the men cut up one of the raw fish into a bowl. Suddenly all eyes were on me. I did not want them to think I condoned idolatry, so I spoke as I set it back in its place, "The God of Heaven has real ears to hear our prayers. He has a real mouth to speak His Word." The leader nodded as Peytor translated and then motioned for us to sit on the ground around a short table. I swallowed hard as they handed me the biggest piece. Again, I ate raw fish. I watched them eat everything: bones, head, guts, and scales. I nibbled.

Micah smiled as he ate the raw fish. He turned, "While you were gone, Joel and I started a fire and cooked fish kabobs we bought in the village. We offered some to the children. They hated it and spat it out."

Joel picked up on the awkwardness of the Nenets men wondering what our conversation was about. He translated it to Peytor, who repeated it in Nenets. The uncle frowned, "What a waste of good food!"

Lord, have we offended them? Will they still come tonight? Please Lord, we've worked so hard to get this far.

Joel nudged me. "Dad, it's time for tonight's service."

I checked my watch. "So, it is." I bowed to our host. "It's time for us to leave."

John's beautiful baritone voice reverberated off the canvas ceiling. A gentle breeze from the river swept through the tent. The Nenets sat in rapt attention. There was a commotion in the back, everyone turned and watched the fisherman escort his family into the middle of the front row.

Lord, let this be the night. We leave tomorrow.

John left the stage, and we started the movie. After it was over, I came to the microphone, "We've been here three days. We've told you of the God Who will give you relief from the oppression of the Shaman's gods. I want anyone who wants to accept Jesus as their Savior to come forward at this time." Nobody moved.

Lord, this isn't any different than—

From the middle of the front row, the fisherman rose. His wife, sons, and the rest of his family followed him.

Lord, thank You for these nine.

Peytor led them to a corner. The rest of the audience watched as they sat in a semi-circle in front of my friend.

I turned my attention to those who remained seated. I waved an arm at Joel, Micah, Ben, and John standing off to the side. "We'll be here until tomorrow morning." I gestured to Peytor, "He's staying here and will instruct you in the ways of the Lord. He will start a church for your tribe."

Lord, do they understand my heavily accented Russian? I pray Your message got through.

The few who understood Russian nodded as the crowd dispersed.

The next morning, Peytor, his uncle, the new believers, and a few Nenets children walked to the waiting boat. Ben and the others hurriedly

Idols & The Fishermen

made a few more balloons for the children before tossing their bags onto the boat and climbing in.

A Reindeer villager, Me & Peytor

I held back to bid farewell to Peytor. He shook my hand. "I can't thank you enough. I believe we broke the Shaman's hold on my people." He pointed to the crowd of Nenets. "Not many accepted Christ, but have you noticed that some aren't wearing their dolls." He smiled, "It's a start."

Our yearly trips to the Reindeer People stopped after we started the Reindeer church with Peytor. The government closed off the northern cities to both foreigners and Russian citizens. Our attempts to return failed because we could not get permission.

THOUGHTS
- Have you had to overcome superstitions when witnessing to others?
- What were they?

CHAPTER SIXTY-ONE

Winter Bible Conference

In weariness and painfulness, in watchings often, in hunger and thirst, in fastings often, in cold and nakedness. Beside those things that are without, that which cometh upon me daily, the care of all the churches. 2 Corinthians 11:27-28

One day, the phone rang. Kathy answered it, "Ron, it's Sergei."

I took the receiver, "Hello, Sergei. How have you been? How is the ministry in Kalmykia?"

Going to Kalmykia, which we called the *Camel People*, had become a yearly, often bi-annual, event for us. Sergei invited us to partake in several kinds of summer camps. Though other groups were deported for preaching in the region, God always protected us.

I wonder what Sergei wants to plan this time.

Sergei slowly answered, "Good, Brother Ron, good. Ummmm—I want to have a Bible Conference right after the New Year in 2008, perhaps January 7-12th? I want you to come and teach Baptist History. I want your wife to teach our ladies how to conduct a Sunday School. Will you both come?"

I put my hand over the receiver and asked Kathy, "Hey, Honey, do we have any plans January 7-12th?"

She went into the church office, examined the calendar, and yelled back, "Nope. That week is clear."

"Yes Sergei, we will come—yes, we will sponsor the event—how many will come? Are they all believers? Yes, we look forward to it. I'll see you on the evening of the 6th—amen—Lord bless you too."

I tore a piece of paper from the pad I'd been writing on. "Honey, we'll have 10 to 15 attendees. They are all believers and desire training for the

Winter Bible Conference

ministry. I went into my office and grabbed 20 copies of *The Trail of Blood*. The pamphlet records church history from the time of Christ to the present day. I handed them to Kathy. "Put these aside. I'll need them for the conference."

The night before we left, Katya, our new interpreter, a tall woman of 23, joined us in our home. "Thanks for asking me to come as an interpreter, and for letting me stay tonight. I'll get more sleep this way. I'm looking forward to this ministry experience. Since going through discipleship classes with Kathy, I've been praying for a way to use my talents for the Lord."

Kathy motioned for Katya to follow her into the spare bedroom. I stopped them before they left the office. "Let's pray before we go to bed. 'Father, thank You for the opportunity to serve You. Help us have willing hearts and open minds towards the lessons You want us to learn and to teach. In Jesus' name, Amen.'"

Kathy and I headed upstairs. She smiled, "The house is sure quiet tonight with Jeremiah and Hannah spending the week with friends in Moscow so they will be near the school."

I nodded, "I'm thankful for missionary friends who are willing to help us out. We'll have to bring them back a souvenir."

The next morning, Katya ordered a taxi. We were flying into Volgograd on S-7 Airlines, so we had to use Sherametovo Airport on the other side of Moscow. Traffic was slow as usual. The temperature had dropped to -35 Fahrenheit during the night. Although it was too cold to snow, the snowplows still staggered all eight lanes of traffic on the MKAD beltway.

I hurriedly paid the driver, gave him a tract, and we rushed to check in for our flight. We were the last to board.

Flying into Volgograd was like flying back in time. The plane parked in the middle of a field. As we deplaned, bitter cold winds hit our faces. My nostrils froze instantaneously. Kathy gasped and glared at me, "This is colder than Moscow! I thought you said it would be warmer. I should have brought my *shuba* (fur coat)."

Katya smiled, "That is why we dress in layers." She pulled a wool sweater from her backpack, took off her winter coat, put the sweater on, and then put her winter coat back on. "See, just like that. Each added layer gives more warmth."

We followed the other passengers to an outbuilding about 100 yards from our plane. After a tractor took the bags into the building, they proceeded to throw luggage out of the window. When ours flew out, I

Serving God Behind Enemy Lines

caught them one by one. I motioned for the women to follow, "The bus stop to town is this way."

An airport guard ran up to us.

Oh Lord, please not another arrest and interrogation!

"Please sir," he said in English, "Please me to help you!" He then broke into Russian and offered to drive us to the bus station for $40.00.

"Nyet!" I replied.

"For $30?" He counter offered.

Again, I refused. A van ride would take us straight to the bus station for $2.50 per person. We walked across the street to the bus stop and waited. Five minutes later, we were headed to the bus station for only $7.50.

"The heater feels so good on my feet!" Kathy exclaimed gratefully as we began our drive into the city. She pointed out the window and exclaimed, "Oh Katya—there is Mother Russia! Perhaps we can take you to her on our way back!"

Katya smiled at the grand lady towering over the city. She turned and asked, "When are we going back to Moscow? And how? I'd like to see Mother Russia, but I noticed you didn't buy round trip airline tickets."

I frowned, "I wanted to, but the return airline tickets were $300 because—"

Kathy joined me as I said, "Everyone wants to go to Moscow."

Katya was puzzled, "You didn't answer my question—how will we get back to Moscow?"

I smiled, "We are living by faith—God will provide a way."

We stood in line for over an hour to buy bus tickets to Tsagan Aman. When I finally got them, I turned to the ladies, "We have two hours before our van leaves—we should buy snacks. The ticket master said it is a five-to-six-hour drive depending on how many stops and how bad the roads are."

Kathy wrinkled her nose, "Ron, I'm freezing. I don't think I've ever been this cold. It is barely above freezing inside this bus station. Perhaps you could go out for supplies while Katya and I stay warm." I nodded and left to find food. I returned with sandwiches, chips, and hot coffee.

When our van pulled up, Kathy boarded first. She sat on a bench seat and motioned for Katya and me to sit on either side of her. She looked at the floor and gasped, "Ron! There is ice on this floorboard! I don't think the heater is working!"

I smiled, "Maybe it will heat up once we get going."

Winter Bible Conference

Forty-five minutes down the road, Kathy gave me the death stare, "Ron, I AM FROZEN! I can't feel my hands or my feet." She pulled the glove off her right hand and gasped, "My fingers are completely white!"

I grabbed her left hand, took the glove off, brought both hands to my mouth and blew into them repeatedly until some of their color returned. "Is that better?"

She frowned, "Probably, but my hands feel like pin cushions." Tears filled her eyes as she looked at me and whispered, "I'm sorry, but it hurts! It's so cold!"

I hugged her tightly and looked over the driver's shoulder at the dashboard. The digital thermostat read Fahrenheit: -22 outside, 23 inside. I positioned my body so Kathy could not see the thermostat and mumbled, "Aw Kathy, don't be a pessimist, it's not that cold!"

After an hour of holding my feet off the iced floor, my leg muscles began to spasm. I had to put them on the floor. My hands and feet were frozen by the time we exited the van at the Tsagan Aman bus stop.

Katya was the first to ask what we all were thinking, "Where is our ride? Weren't they supposed to be waiting here?"

I got out my cell phone and called Sergei. No answer.

Lord, we've fought spiritual battles against Satan and seen You defeat him, but how do we fight the battle of imminent hypothermia?

Kathy jumped up and down, "I'm dying! I'm going to freeze to death!" She looked up toward Heaven and almost screamed, "Oh God! Please send us help!" She ran over and stood under the little bus stop shelter, "This wind is freezing my eyes shut! It must be 30 below!"

I knew that it was colder than that. The wind had fingers that ripped our faces. -40 Celsius and -40 Fahrenheit are the same bone chilling monster.

I called Sergei again. This time he picked up, "Oh Brother Ron, where are you?"

"I'm at the bus stop on the main highway. I called you 30 minutes ago to say we were almost there, and you said someone would meet us here. Please send someone now! I can't feel my hands and toes."

"Yes! Right away."

We waited another 20 minutes in the frigid cold before Valarry drove up in the Renault Encore we had donated to the Kalmykian ministry. We jumped in. Kathy shrieked, "Hallelujah, heat!" She took off her gloves, leaned forward and caressed the heat vents through the bucket seats. I cringed at her stiff, white hands.

Lord, please don't let any of us have permanent damage!

Valarry apologized, "I'm sorry. Right after Sergei told me to come get you, someone grabbed me and wanted to talk about salvation. I'm sorry I got distracted."

O.K. Lord, I get it. It's not all about me. Souls for the kingdom are worth suffering the freezing temperatures.

Sergei and his wife greeted us as we entered the conference center. We had just thawed out in the car and were thrown right back into the cold. Normally Kathy is kind and patient with others. Her brain might have still been thawing. She demanded, "Why is it so cold in here?"

Sergei gave me a shocked look. When he saw I demanded an answer as well, he looked down and stuttered, "Well—ummm, our village is having an energy crisis. They are rationing the hot water that warms the pipes of the heating system. We had no idea this would happen when we rented this building for the conference. I'm sorry."

It was not Sergei's fault. The entire village was affected. Deserts are hot in the summer but cold in the winter. The last time I was in Kalmykia, it was so hot I could hardly stand it. This time, it was so cold I thought I would die! I looked at Kathy and Katya, "Well, the Bible says to endure hardness—"

Kathy finished before I could get the words out, "—as a good soldier of Jesus Christ. I know!" She looked at Katya and managed a feeble smile as she said, "We will be storing up big rewards in Heaven this week!"

I looked back at Sergei and smiled, "God is to be praised all the time. Where shall we put our bags?"

Sergei led us down a long hallway and eventually opened a door, "There are two rooms in this suite, one for you and Kathy and one for Katya. I'll let you get settled in. Tomorrow, we start with breakfast at 8 a.m."

Katya spoke to Sergei, "Where is the bathroom?"

He grimaced and motioned for us to follow. We dropped our luggage in the suite and fell in line behind him to an exit door. As we stepped outside, the freezing wind slapped our faces. Immediately our eyes stung, nostrils froze, and bones were chilled by the boisterous wind sucked into our lungs. It felt like knives were piercing my skin.

Sergei pointed to a cement building about 30 yards into a field, "The women's is on the right and the men's is on the left."

Kathy and Katya groaned. Sergei cleared his throat and continued, "We have worked out a system: if you only need to urinate, you simply come outside, position yourself out of sight from the door, and sing the whole time you are outside. No one else will come outside if they open

Winter Bible Conference

the door and hear singing. If you have serious business, you must walk in the freezing temperatures to the outhouse." Sergei looked at his watch, "It's late. I'll see you in the morning." He went back inside.

The girls frowned and shook their heads.

How bad could the outhouse be?

With a sigh and a look of determination, we walked through the bone-chilling cold. Once we got to the building, I went left, and the ladies went right. I almost slipped on a patch of ice on the floor. There was a block of ice on the toilet seat.

Is that ice made from snow flurries or—?

I shuddered at the thought. Though we had a cement wall between us, one large hole in the ground serviced both sides. I heard Katya and Kathy laugh.

Good, Lord. Help them keep a positive attitude!

We tramped through the snow back to our rooms. I reached in and turned on the light. Kathy took in a deep breath and held it. Finally, she let it out and sighed, "Um. Where are the mattresses? All we have here are springs."

Katya pulled her suitcase near the bed in the first room. She laughed, "These ARE the mattresses. We had them at Pioneer Camp during soviet times." She looked at Kathy's panicked face and assured her, "They aren't so bad. It's almost like sleeping in a hammock."

I nudged Kathy to the next room and shut the door. She stopped me as I started to pull two beds together, "I don't think we will need two beds. I'm not a cuddler, but like the Bible says, 'when two lie together, they make heat.' Heat is exactly what I need! I think you and I will be doing a lot of cuddling the next few days!"

We opened our suitcases and proceeded to put on every article of clothing we brought with us: two sets of long johns, two pairs of pants, three sweaters and two pairs of socks.

Kathy zipped our sleeping bags together. We did not have any pillows, so we folded our coats and placed them on the 'hammock'. We slipped into the freezing sleeping bags and held each other.

Lord, we need sleep, but we are so cold. I beg You to help us!

Thankfully, the trip had been long and exhausting. Soon we were fast asleep.

Four hours later, I awakened to Kathy sitting up in bed. What little heat we had generated in the sleeping bags quickly escaped. "What are you doing?" I murmured.

She whispered, "I'm sorry to wake you. I am so cold I'm putting my coat on; I'd rather sleep without a pillow." I could feel her frown in the darkness, "Oh Ron! If we are this cold while cuddling, how will Katya not freeze to death?"

I pulled Kathy a little closer as she crawled back under the covers and nudged my mouth to her ear, "God will protect us!" We hardly slept at all.

The next morning, we followed the voices to the breakfast room. Kathy and Katya made a break for the hot beverage station. Elis, Sergei's wife, stood nearby, "Would you like me to make you a cup of Kalmyski Chai?"

Katya and Kathy looked at each other and shrugged, "Sure."

She poured a third of cup of hot water, added a one-third cup of concentrated tea, and finished the concoction with milk, sugar, and salt.

Kathy took a cup, put it to her mouth, blew on it, and took a small sip. I could see from the look in her eyes that even though she loves salt, she did not love it in tea. She smiled at Elis and brought the cup over for me to try. I pushed it away, "No thank you. I've had Kalmyski chai—I'm not a fan." I reached for a bowl of *grechka* (buckwheat) and a small plate of eggs.

After breakfast we met in the auditorium.

I helped Sergei set chairs on the sides of the tables facing the podium. He gave out the schedule, "We'll have an introduction time—maybe 30 minutes." He pointed to my wife, "Then she can give her talk on teaching Sunday School to young children."

"On the second night, you will talk about how members can serve in the church. I'd also like you to include Baptist History." Sergei smiled, "On the third day, we will make gift boxes for the children in a nearby village from the candy and toys you brought with you. The village will allow us to have a Christmas Concert on January 9th."

I frowned, "Isn't Russian Christmas on January 7th?"

Sergei smiled, "Yes, but the community center was busy that day. January 9th is the best we can do. We will have ample opportunity to preach the Gospel."

The first night of the conference, Kathy stood bundled in two sweaters, and a fur hat. She gave her Christmas flannelgraph lesson from her Sunday School class. She had a handout of how to lead a child to Christ, how to teach Bible stories to children, and how to discipline unruly children through affirmation and motivation.

Winter Bible Conference

The second night, I preached from the *Trail of Blood* pamphlet. We passed out copies of the pamphlet in Russian. Everyone gasped when I explained that Baptists are not Protestants. "Protestants came out of the Catholic Church. Baptists were never a part of the Catholic Church. We are the church that Jesus built."

I could see that some doubted. "Turn to the back of the pamphlet. Unfold the chart that shows church history. In the first century, there was only one line but by the second century, there became two lines—one would become the Catholic Church while the other became known in history as the heretics."

I stopped, looked around the room and pointed to my chest. "We are the heretics, the line of Christians who died for their faith in Christ alone for salvation and the Word of God as their only rule of practice. We come from a line of martyrs who believed that doctrine mattered. Don't let the prosperity preachers and television evangelists tell you that doctrine doesn't matter. Thousands of our Christian forefathers were burned at the stake, crucified, beheaded, sawn asunder, drowned and all manner of evil deaths so that we could have the Gospel today."

After I preached, Sergei rose to introduce an elderly man named Zhenya. He struggled to the front, dragging his left leg. Sergei put his arm around Zhenya, "This man suffered for Christ in ways that most of us can't imagine. I've asked him to give his testimony."

Zhenya scratched his broken nose. His left forearm stuck out at an awkward angle as he told how he was imprisoned during the Soviet Times for the Gospel's sake. His family secretly listened to the radio broadcast of *Voice of the Martyrs* and got saved through that ministry. Sadly, they lived in a communal apartment, and their neighbors turned them in for listening to "American Propaganda." At 15 years of age, he was arrested by the *militsiya* and taken to their headquarters. Once in police custody, they told Zhenya if he renounced Christ and testified against his family, they would ignore that he broke the law. He refused, so they put him in prison, where he was able to lead several inmates to Christ.

He suffered persecution but remained true to his Lord. He was confined to cell block 37.

Years later, after the fall of the Communist regime, Zhenya was able to go back to that same prison and hold a Bible study in their newly renovated library. Something seemed familiar. Zhenya discovered that the library was in the very spot of cell block 37. There, where he had suffered for the cause of Christ, is where he now freely preaches the Gospel of Christ.

Serving God Behind Enemy Lines

Lord, Your timing is perfect to provide this testimony. What an honor to meet this man who has suffered so willingly for You!

When Zhenya finished, Sergei put his arm around him. "Here we have an example of the type of Christian Brother Ron talked about in Baptist History. The struggles he went through were real. I pray his testimony encourages all of us to be strong in the Lord."

The next morning, Sergei came to us, "Remember, if you stay more than three days, we must register you with the government. I need your passports and migration cards."

Kathy got out her passport but panicked when her migration card, which you must always carry, was missing.

Most clouds have a silver lining if you look hard enough: without Kathy's migration card, we could not register. If we could not register, we would have to leave the conference the next day. If we left the conference, we would leave the frozen desert.

Thank You, Lord—three days, and three nights in the belly of the frozen desert was enough! I think our mission here is done.

Zhenya and me at the Winter Bible Conference in Kalmykia

We got up early the next morning, said our good-byes, and Valarry drove us to the bus stop. We waited 30 minutes in the subzero temperature for the Volgograd bus. As I paid the driver for three tickets, Kathy slipped past me.

Where did she go?

Winter Bible Conference

I found her grinning from ear to ear as she pointed to a big heater blasting warm air above her seat.

Five hours later, back in Volgograd, we went to the train station to buy tickets to Moscow only to find out there were no tickets until next week. I spoke to a bus driver with the marquee "Moscow" scrolling on the front of his bus, "Do you have three tickets on a bus leaving today?"

He shook his head, "No. Everyone wants to get back to Moscow for university. All the buses are sold out until tomorrow. I can sell you tickets for tomorrow."

I hesitated and felt the Lord telling me to wait. "Thanks, I'll keep looking."

"You will come back. There are no other rides to Moscow."

I walked away. Katya gave me a troubled look. Finally, she spoke, "I've been worried about this since we landed." She held her hands out, "How will we get back to Moscow?"

I shook my head, "Katya, the Lord will provide!"

Kathy grabbed my arm, "I just heard an announcement over there saying they have bus tickets to Moscow on a bus leaving in four hours. Let's check it out."

We walked over to the lone bus parked in a corner. I asked, "Do you have three tickets to Moscow today?"

The driver nodded, "Yes. This bus leaves in three-and-a-half hours. Would you like tickets?"

I pulled out my wallet and gladly paid $45 per person. The driver handed me three tickets, "Be here by 3:45 p.m. sharp. We leave at 4 p.m. with or without you."

Katya smiled as she took her ticket, "You were right, the Lord did provide."

Kathy interjected, "This is perfect. Let's take our bags into the heated train station. I will stay with the bags while you two see Mother Russia."

Katya hesitated, "No, it's okay. I saw it from the van coming into town. You know I'm originally from Moldova, so it doesn't mean that much to me."

Kathy pushed her toward the train station, "No, I insist, there is plenty of time. Just help me get settled with our bags."

After we settled Kathy near a heater in the train station, Katya and I jumped on a local bus. Within five minutes, we were standing at the bottom of 200 steps leading to Mother Russia. I took on the role of tour guide, "We will now ascend 200 steps symbolizing the 200-day Battle for

Stalingrad during the war." We slowly ascended the steps passing through the Ruined Walls Memorial, dotted with bullet holes.

Katya stopped to put her finger in a bullet hole. I watched as her whole demeanor changed, "This is really interesting—" We continued past the Lake of Tears into a round building. I walked behind her. I wanted to see her reaction to the grand memorial called The Hall of Military Glory. She stopped at the first plaque that covered a large portion of the tall, golden walls. The names of men and women who died during World War II were inscribed on the plates. Volgograd (formerly Stalingrad during the war) was destroyed by the Germans. Katya turned to me with tears in her eyes. She motioned to the plaques and whispered, "7,200 names of soldiers who tried to defend Stalingrad are written on this wall!" She scurried to another plaque, "Over three million people died in the Battle of Stalingrad. I remember learning about it in history—the starving, the bombs, the utter destruction—but it was just facts to learn for a test. This makes it come alive!"

I took Katya's camera as she stood before the flaming torch held by a hand coming out of the floor. Mother Russia was visible from the opening in the roof. I knelt on my knee to get the best angle. "That should make a good memory for your children someday." I said as I handed her back her camera.

We continued past the Square of Grief. I paused while Katya grabbed photos of the beautiful statues. She lingered at the one of a mother holding her fallen son. Finally, we stood at the bottom of Mother Russia.

"Wow! It's even bigger as you stand at her feet," Katya said. She handed me her camera, "Here, take a picture of me!"

"Open your mouth like Mother Russia's." I joked after taking several normal shots.

Katya turned to look at the giant woman. She turned back, "She is calling for the people to defend the Motherland. She's brave, she's beautiful. She makes me proud."

Two hours later, we found Kathy sleeping on our bags. She roused as we approached, "Oh hi! Did you get good pictures?"

Katya beamed, "Yes, thank you for making me go. It was wonderful. I have never been very patriotic but seeing all those names and reading the call to arms and the charge to protect the motherland, I felt proud to be Russian."

I sat down beside Kathy and we both looked at Katya. I mused, "I think everyone should be proud of the country God birthed them in. God has a purpose and a plan in everything He does."

Winter Bible Conference

As we boarded the bus, I settled next to Kathy, and Katya sat across the table from us. We smiled and pointed to the heat vent above our heads. *Praise God for working heaters!*

The flaming torch coming out of the floor (from a summer trip)

As the bus pulled out of the parking lot, Kathy, already falling asleep on my shoulder mumbled, "I can endure anything if I know the end date. Thank You, Lord, for only three days and three nights in the frozen desert."

Not long after this evangelistic adventure, Katya got a full scholarship to Harvard University. She married an American, has three children and is a professor of Theology in a major US university.

THOUGHTS
- Have you ever suffered for the cause of Christ to the point you thought you would die?

Chapter Sixty-Two

Our Last Reindeer Trip

Being confident of this very thing, that he which hath begun a good work in you will perform it until the day of Jesus Christ: Philippians 1:6

In January 2011, I popped my head into the back bedroom. "Is everything ready for Joel and Michelle's arrival tomorrow?"

Atop the ladder, Kathy turned around. She smiled as she moved her hand in presentation around the room, "I just finished putting up the curtains. I made a bedspread and pillows to match! What do you think?"

I nodded. "I like the color. It looks great, Honey. I know you've worked hard on this room. Good job."

Kathy climbed down the ladder and motioned for me to take it away, "I'm so excited to have Joel back. When he left 10 years ago, I thought this day would never arrive, but he's coming home a married man! God is good."

She picked up the drill and extra screws, holding them in one hand as she straightened the pillows. She directed me toward the door, shutting it behind us. We walked to the basement to put the tools away.

"Oh no!" Kathy said, "The basement is flooded again! The sump pump must have quit."

"When was the last time you were down here?" I asked, "It has been raining the last few days."

"I was down here this morning to find screws. It was fine then." Kathy sighed as she stepped into two inches of water. I watched as she grabbed a stick and pushed the pump float until it bobbed in the water, and we heard it turn on. She smiled, "It will be so nice to have a few more people in the house to keep an eye on all the pumps and Russian nuances in this huge ministry compound."

"Tomorrow," I said, "Tomorrow."

The next morning, Kathy tugged at my arm as we awaited in the arrival area at Domodedovo Airport. "Do you see them yet?" I shook my head as I continued to watch the entry door from customs. Kathy looked around nervously, "This is the exact place the bomb went off last year killing 37 people. I wish they would hurry!"

I looked down, "Kathy, whatsoever things are lovely and of good report—think on those things—that's them!" I waved and moved toward the front of the crowd. Joel saw me and waved. His tiny, brunette bride of five years, Michelle, walked beside him. I could tell the trip had been rough on her. Her normally well-groomed hair was pulled into a fluffy ponytail and there were bags under her eyes. I grabbed Joel and pulled him into a bear hug as soon as he was in reach, "Welcome home, Joel!"

Kathy grabbed Michelle and give her a hug. We switched kids and hugged again. I took the luggage cart from Michelle and Kathy led the way to the car. She turned to me, "The car is over there. Why don't you take them to the car while I pay for the parking?"

As we placed their bags in the trunk, Joel said, "Dad, I went on deputation with the idea of having a ministry among the Reindeer People. When do you think we can take a trip?"

Kathy reappeared, handed me the exit ticket, and sat in back with Michelle. I motioned for Joel to sit beside me. Once we were settled in the car, I answered Joel's question, "Well, I see no reason why we can't do it next summer. That gives us a year to plan."

Kathy leaned forward and remarked, "Don't forget we have four interns coming for a missions trip next year."

Already Michelle was looking pale and trying not to get carsick. She mustered the energy to ask, "Who's coming?"

Kathy looked at Michelle's queasy face, and stated, "Ron, don't forget that Michelle has a sensitive stomach. Try not to drive too *Russian* (fast)!" Leaning back, she answered Michelle's question, "We have two college students, a retired widow who loves to visit missionaries, and a preacher's kid who is just graduating from high school."

Joel laughed, "I can't believe you are having more students from Heartland Baptist Bible College after the last ones were so troublesome."

I refused to dwell on the bad memories of the last students. "We had rough spots but three of the young men on that trip are now preparing to

Serving God Behind Enemy Lines

come back to Russia as career missionaries. God worked despite the trials."

Making Plans

Time passed quickly as we spent hours preparing for the Reindeer trip. One day in May of the next year, as we were sitting together in my office, Joel looked up from his computer with a frown. "Dad, I can't find anything on the Internet about Salekhard being a closed city. I think we should just fly in there and see what happens."

"I like that we can fly this time. This group will be only Americans; You, me, Michelle, Kathy, Jack, Rebecca, and Chelsey." I counted as I named each person, "Seven—God's number."

Joel grinned, "I remember you used to stress over the budget of the Reindeer trips. I think the best part of this trip for you is that each person is paying their own way." He continued, "Do you think it would be a good idea for Michelle and me to fly to Salekhard early, find a hotel and search out leads on the Reindeer People?"

I nodded, "I say 'yes' to you two going early, but I beg to differ with you on the other point. Perhaps the best part about this trip is that you are in charge and must do all the planning."

Joel sighed, "I'm not excited about being in charge of Jack!"

I smiled, "I've spoken to him about his behavior last summer."

Joel interrupted, "Isn't he the one who went to the store, bought a toy AK-47 with lights and sounds, dressed in fatigues, painted his face, and went into the birch forest behind our compound at twilight?

The Birch Forest behind the compound
Me playing Dodgeball with some friends

Our Last Reindeer Trip

"He ran from tree to tree shooting his toy gun and playing commando. And don't I remember you telling me one of our neighbors must have seen it and called the police because the next week, a full platoon of young soldiers showed up in our forest to camp and do a week of military exercises? They had never done this before and have never done it since. Isn't that the story you told me?"

I leaned back in my favorite office chair, "I almost did not let Jack come again, but he promised to be respectful as a guest in a foreign country. If he isn't, he'll be on the first plane out."

Joel grimaced and returned to his computer, "Well, the good news is there are plenty of plane tickets going to Salekhard for only $100 each. I guess only crazy people leave the comforts of Moscow and fly to the Arctic North. But the bad news is to fly back to Moscow, the tickets are $500 each."

Simultaneously Joel and I said, "Because everyone wants to come to Moscow!"

He continued typing, then sighed, "But train tickets back are only $45 each."

I groaned, "None of us can afford $500 for return plane tickets, which means we have to take another long ride on the train."

Joel stood and walked to the office window. The sun was just starting to set. Finally, he sighed, "I remember that train ride home from Salekhard when we had the girls with us. It was a fulltime job keeping the drunks and 'lewd fellows of baser sort' away from them. I don't want to go through that again. Didn't we vow to never take women with us again? I remember thinking that if God ever gave me a wife, I wouldn't let her be exposed to that."

"Yet, here we are," I stated, "We either suffer through that again or tell them they can't go."

Joel shook his head adamantly. "No, Michelle must go. We are praying about going there to live and minister. She must go. We are a team."

I stood and joined Joel as we watched the sunset, "And if we let her go, we must let all the women go. Besides, your mom has never been on a Reindeer trip. She's listened to my stories, and she's thrilled to finally be going. With Keturah and Jeremiah in college and Hannah teaching English here at Moscow State University, she no longer needs to stay home with the children. We'll pray for God's grace."

The Big Day Arrives

"I'm a little nervous," Michelle said as she pulled her backpack onto her shoulders and grabbed her jacket off the couch. "But I'm excited! I know God has great things in store!"

Kathy smiled as she took the car keys off their hook, "Yep! God always has great things in store!" She turned to Joel as he grabbed the large luggage, "Ты готов?"

Joel and Michelle answered in unison, "We are ready!"

Kathy drove them to Venukovo Airport in the wee hours of the morning on July 3, 2011. She dropped them off curbside. "I'll see you guys tomorrow! Godspeed! We will be praying for you! Text me and let us know how it goes!"

Later that evening, Kathy got a text on her phone, "Things are complicated, but you still need to come as planned."

I immediately called Joel, "What happened? Are you guys okay?"

Joel answered in a whisper, "They were waiting for us when we got off the plane. They let us gather our bags then drove us to a secret military base where the FSB interrogated us."

"How did Michelle handle everything? Is she okay?" I interjected.

Kathy, hearing the concern in my voice, rushed to my side, and listened.

"They separated us, but she took it like a trooper! At first, I insisted Michelle come with me, but they put her in a waiting room and promised she would not be bothered and would still be there when I returned. She got a book out of her bag, sat down, and read until I returned five hours later. God sat right there with her and kept her calm!"

Kathy talked into the speakerphone, "Praise the Lord for His loving arms around her!"

Joel continued, "It was hard, Dad. I always thought you were embellishing your arrest stories, but it happened just like you always said."

I wanted the whole story, "What about you? What happened to you?"

"Well, Dad, Salekhard is indeed a closed city. At first, they accused me of being a spy. But I was ready. Remember, I didn't bring any Bibles and tracts in my luggage in case it was illegal. I took out the only Bible and tract I brought with me, handed it to the interrogator and asked, 'If you were to die today, do you know whether you would go to Heaven?' I told him about Jesus dying on the cross for his sins and all the while he kept accusing me of being a spy. Finally, he asked how I could prove I'm not a

Our Last Reindeer Trip

spy. I told him that my parents and three other Americans will be on tomorrow's flight with boxes of Bibles, tracts, and discipleship mat—".

I interrupted, "Maybe we shouldn't fly out tomorrow."

"No!" Joel said a little louder.

He settled back into a whisper, "They released me, drove us to a hotel, and told me that proof of my story would be when my parents get off the plane at the Salekhard airport. You must come, or Michelle and I will be detained indefinitely or perhaps deported. You must arrive with Bibles and tracts."

I took a moment to savor the irony. We thought that bringing Bibles might pose a problem for Joel. Instead, it was the absence of Bibles in his suitcase that almost got him sent to the *Gulag*. "Don't worry, Son, we'll be on that plane with plenty of Bibles. I'll see you tomorrow. Godspeed."

Lord, You are in this. Please be with us as we travel tomorrow to spread Your Word.

I gathered the group around the kitchen table, "I've got good news and I've got bad news. The good news is our trip is still on. The bad news is we will be arrested as soon as we get off the plane."

Gasps were heard around the table. I held my hand up and continued, "Technically, only Kathy and I must go. Joel and Michelle were arrested and will be detained indefinitely if we don't show up with suitcases of tracts and Bibles. If anyone wants to back out, you are welcome to stay here with Hannah and the retired widow."

All three interns looked at each other. Jack spoke first, "This sounds like an adventure! I'm in."

Rebecca chimed in, "Me too!"

Chelsey was more thoughtful. She took a few moments to silently pray before looking up, "God wants me to go."

I looked around the table at these four people whom God had given to my charge.

Do they understand the gravity of the situation?

I repeated, "We WILL be arrested when we get off the plane." There was a long silence, but everyone seemed to accept their decision. I looked around at our team and thought of Joel and Michelle.

✓	Joel and Michelle	My Eldest Son and His Wife
✓	Chelsey	American Bible College Student
✓	Jack	American Bible College Student
✓	Rebecca	American High-School Graduate
✓	Kathy & Myself	

The next morning, as we boarded the plane for Salekhard, I was amazed to see that aside from our group of five, there were only two other passengers. We sat together and prayed, read our Bibles, and asked God for guidance as we anticipated what awaited us.

About two hours into the flight, Jack tapped me on the shoulder and whispered, "Do you think those other passengers are FSB?"

I frowned at the thought then whispered back, "I doubt it, but perhaps. We'll never know."

I watched out the window as the plane began its descent. Lush green grass danced as a breeze blew through the valley. The hilltops were still covered in snow. Kathy leaned over and commented, "The trees look so small. Surely they are taller than they look!"

I mumbled, "Their growing season is only three months. The other nine, they are dormant. Their roots work hard to break through the permafrost. Under those conditions, it's amazing there are any trees here."

A few minutes later, the plane landed. We looked nervously at each other, grabbed hands, and prayed together one last time.

As soon as we exited, as if on cue, three officers approached. The highest-ranking officer held out his hand and casually stated, "Give me your passports." We reached into our backpacks and handed them over. As if he had rehearsed the phrase all night, he said in English, "Follow me!"

The officer took us to baggage claim and ordered us to gather our bags. I grabbed mine, then looked to the team, "Did everyone get their bags?" They nodded. I turned to the officer and said in Russian, "We are ready."

One officer led the way, and the others followed behind with their AK-47's held ready. Their stern faces and weapons were reminders to keep a steady pace and behave.

Once in the parking lot, the head officer opened the back of a paddy wagon. I started to get in, but the officer stopped me, "No—you two—in front." I went around and got in the front seat. Kathy followed me while the others filed in the back. After I settled in, I turned around to see how the girls were doing. They were huddled in fear. Silent tears streamed down their faces. I pointed toward Heaven and smiled.

God's got this!

All I got was grunts when I attempted to engage the officer in conversation. Kathy also asked a few questions about where we were going and why the trees were so small, but she could not engage the officer either.

Our Last Reindeer Trip

Forty-five minutes later, the wagon pulled up to a secret compound in the middle of nowhere. A guard, standing outside an iron gate, approached us with his hand resting on his holstered gun. He conversed with the driver, looked at us, and opened the gate. I shuddered as I heard the gate close behind us. We had arrived.

The officer turned off the engine, opened his door and commanded, "Come with me."

Kathy asked in Russian, "What about our bags?"

He motioned for us to take them out and leave them on the front steps outside the building. Jack whined, "But I have important stuff in my bags. I don't want it stolen."

I gave him a death stare.

Really? We are in a secret FSB military encampment in the middle of the Arctic, and you are worried about your stuff?

He reluctantly put his bags with ours and we followed the officer.

We stood in the entry hall as the officer commanded, "Wait here." He walked away with our passports, and we never saw him again. It seemed like hours before the head officer of the compound came out to meet us. He spoke only Russian, "Which of you is the best Russian speaker?" We all looked at Kathy and she replied, "Я."

The FSB officer sized me up, then said, "Are you in charge? I want to speak with you first. Follow me."

Kathy and I followed him into a small, cramped office. I took a quick look around the room. Outdated computers on the desk. A dot matrix printer. Piles of paper strung across the desk and on top of file cabinets. I felt as though I had stepped back 20 years in time. President Putin's photo on the wall seemed to be the only updated item in the room. My eyes caught a glimpse of our passports neatly piled on his desk.

I turned my attention to the officer as he settled into his chair. He took his hat off, slowly ran his fingers through his dark hair with one hand as he gently tossed his hat on the desk in front of him.

He's thin—maybe that's a good sign that he doesn't solicit bribes. The chubby ones are often the ones given to dainties and delights. They take bribes to enhance their lifestyles. Maybe he is one of the good guys. We'll soon find out.

He looked through the stack of our passports until he found mine and Kathy's. He examined them, looking through each page with a magnifying glass. He paid particular attention to our visas. Finally, he spoke, "I see you have religious visas, but I suspect that you are spies!"

Not knowing what else to do, I took out a tract and Bible from my backpack, pushed it across the desk and asked, "If you were to die today, do you know for sure whether or not you will go to Heaven?"

The Officer pushed it back, reached into his top drawer and took out an identical Bible. "Your son already gave me a Bible and told us all of that yesterday." He leaned back and scowled, "Why are you really here?"

Here we go again! How long will it take for me to convince this man I am not a spy?

I answered, "To preach the Gospel to the Reindeer People. I was here 10 years ago, and I got to meet many Reindeer People. I have returned to tell more of them about God's love and gift of salvation."

The Officer furrowed his brow, "You were here 10 years ago? We have no record of that."

"I arrived by train."

"The officer scribbled on a paper in front of him. Finally, he looked up and said, "Russian law only allows those with certifications and degrees in theology to do religious work. I want to see your diploma or certificate!"

Really, Lord? Who carries a copy of their ordination certificate in Siberia?

I looked at Kathy. I could tell she was silently praying. Suddenly she looked at me and smiled, "You have a copy in your wallet!"

I gave her a 'you must be crazy' look as I pulled out my wallet, "Where?"

"Remember when you had to give a copy of your ordination certificate to the city office in Ada, Oklahoma so you could perform Micah and Sarah's wedding? I made a credit-card sized copy and put it in your wallet. Is it still there?"

I pulled out some receipts and handed them to Kathy. Next, I pulled out my credit cards and handed them to her. I looked everywhere. Finally, in a hidden compartment, I felt a piece of paper. I pulled it out and unfolded it. "Here it is!" I said as I handed it to the Officer. He took it and made a photocopy.

I looked at Kathy and smiled. She and I were thinking the same thing:

We serve an awesome God Who knows the beginning to the end. Only God could have known I would need that piece of paper in the Arctic Circle.

"Well done," The officer half smiled, "As the leader of this team, if you hadn't given this to us, we would have deported you for unlawful propagation of the Gospel." He handed me back my papers, "You may go. Send in the next person."

Our Last Reindeer Trip

I took a final look at Kathy. She nodded for me to go. In English she whispered, "I know how to scream."

I sent in Chelsey and Rebecca together. They were young, pretty and had sweet spirits which I thought might make the Officer go easy on them.

I was wrong. As they entered, the officer looked for their passports. Having found them, he asked them to take a seat. Kathy interpreted. The officer took the magnifying glass and went over Chelsey's passport. He smiled when he saw her visa, "You have a tourist visa, yet you come here for religious work. This is very bad!" His voice was gruff and accusatory.

Kathy cringed at the officer's hard words. She turned to see Chelsey nervously wringing her hands. Tears filled her eyes, ready to spill over at the slightest confrontation. Kathy softened the language for Chelsey, "He's concerned about your visa. Remember how you didn't apply early enough to get a religious visa, so I sent you to a site that gave you a tourist visa?" Chelsey nodded, "Well, he's not happy about it."

The officer looked at Kathy. He clicked his tongue as he shook his head. "I could arrest and deport her for this violation! This is very serious!" He picked up Rebecca's passport and discovered the same problem. By now, both girls had tears silently streaming down their faces.

Kathy felt her chest tighten. Her stomach was in knots, but she needed to concentrate on the girls and their well-being. She had to do something to keep the situation from escalating further. First, she addressed the girls in a calm and matter-of-fact manner, "God is able—pray." Then she turned to the officer, cleared her throat, and humbly apologized in Russian, "I'm so sorry Officer. This is my fault. I gave Chelsey and Rebecca the wrong website to apply for a visa. I'm sorry."

The officer looked at the girls who were ready to burst into uncontrollable sobs, and then at Kathy who seemed genuinely remorseful for creating the problem. Evidently, he had no desire to create an international incident over a misunderstanding. He relaxed and almost smiled. Turning around, he scanned the passports, and returned them to Chelsey and Rebecca. "They may go," he said as he looked at the last passport on his desk. "Tell this Jack to come in."

Kathy smiled at the girls, "You may go." They hopped up out of the chairs and practically ran out. As they opened the door, Kathy could hear singing in the hallway.

As Chelsey and Rebecca entered the hall, they saw Jack standing with his hand over his heart, singing the National Anthem in this secret military compound, in a closed city, in Northern Russia.

Really Jack? I know it's the 4th of July but celebrating in a secret military base while in custody of the Russian government is not wise. Come on. THINK, Jack!

I was livid. I jumped up, rushed over to him, and yelled, "Jack! What are you doing?"

Everyone checked to see if any Russians were present. The one guard who was supposed to be guarding us had left a moment earlier. No other Russians were around giving Jack the courage to stand and sing, "*By the dawn's early light, what so proudly—*"

"Stop it! You are putting us in danger!"

Yet he continued, "*The bombs bursting in air, gave proof through the night—*"

Upon seeing the girls return, I pushed Jack toward the office, "It's your turn. Show some respect like you promised!"

Jack strutted into the office as the FSB Officer picked up his passport. "Please sit down."

Jack hesitated, so Kathy repeated, "Jack, please sit down." Begrudgingly, he sat.

The Officer took the magnifying glass to Jack's passport and immediately noticed that there was only a middle initial written down, "What is your middle name?"

My wife interpreted the question to Jack, but he answered, "If I won't tell the American government my middle name, why would I tell you?"

Kathy lowered her voice and repeated the question, "Jack! What is your middle name? This is serious!"

He shrugged and said nothing. Finally, my wife turned to the officer and said in Russian, "Middle names aren't important in America. We don't carry our father's name like you do in Russia. It's nice that you do that; it lets everyone know how important family is to Russian culture."

The military officer stared at Jack, then looked at Kathy who was pleading with her eyes to disregard the proud American boy. Finally, he decided to move on. Jack had a religious visa, so he merely scanned his passport and handed it back. Happy to be rid of him, the officer told Jack to leave and ask me to come back.

As I sat down again, the officer handed me a stack of papers, "In order to come to our city, you must have a sponsor. You have entered without written permission from one of our citizens. This is a violation of the law. These papers are the fines you must pay."

I immediately took the papers and asked, "Where do I pay the fine?"

The officer scribbled down the address of the closest Cber Bank and handed it to me. He continued, "In addition to the fine, you will have a black mark put next to your name in our governmental system. Three black marks and you will be deported for five years."

I put the papers in my backpack and smiled, "Can we hold evangelistic meetings and pass out tracts and Bibles in your city?"

He thought for a moment, "You may pass out Bibles and tracts, but you may not have public meetings without written permission from the mayor and he is out of town."

I nodded and asked one more question, "Do you know where any tribes of Reindeer People are that we might share the Gospel with?"

The Officer sighed, rolled his eyes, and shook his head. As Kathy and I stood to go, I held out my hand to the Officer, "Thank you." He took my hand and said in English, "Good-bye."

He did not ask for a bribe; he did not overstep his authority. This FSB officer was a good one.

We walked out of the office and rejoined the others, "We may go," I said. Jack ran out the door to check on our bags. They were exactly as we had left them. If someone went through them, they did a good job placing everything as it was.

I picked up my bags, "Gather your things and let's get out of here while we still can."

We walked to the iron gate.

The guard hesitated. He looked at the entrance for permission to let us go.

I turned to see the FSB officer standing on the front steps. He nodded and the guard opened the gate.

We were free.

THOUGHTS

- Have you suffered persecution for the cause of Christ? How did you react?
- If not, are you prepared to suffer for His Name's Sake?

CHAPTER SIXTY-THREE

The Red Brick Church

Those things, which ye have both learned, and received, and heard, and seen in me, do: and the God of peace shall be with you. Philippians 4:9

Joel and Michelle were waiting just outside the gate. Joel smiled, "Welcome to Siberia. How did it go?"

I motioned for us to keep walking down the gravel road. Joel took my cue and led the way toward town. He pointed with his hand and whispered, "The town is a 15-minute walk."

We dragged our suitcases down the gravel road, occasionally looking behind us, fearful they might change their minds. It was a somber walk.

Once we found civilization, I took the address of the bank from my pocket. "Our first order of business is to pay these fines. Where did you go to pay yours, Joel?"

Joel looked puzzled, "He didn't give us a fine. Maybe he gave it to you. Give me the papers." I handed Joel the stack.

He quickly counted, "There are only five fines. He must have let Michelle and me slide."

I took one of the papers but could not read the scribbles. "How much is the fine Joel? Can you read the chicken scratch?"

Joel looked closely at the first and then the second one. He laughed, "They are the equivalent of five dollars each! Imagine, all this trouble for $25.00."

I shook my head, "No, this had nothing to do with $25.00 and everything to do with intimidating Americans. They are still fighting the Cold War." I sighed, "The FSB guy said we would get a black mark on our

The Red Brick Church

names. He was probably the first honest agent we ever met. I wonder if we have gotten black marks and don't know."

We found the bank, stood in line, and paid the fines. As we walked out, I yawned, turned to Joel, and muttered, "We are beat. Where is the hotel?"

Joel smiled, "Not far. They dropped me off at the nearest hotel from their base so they could keep an eye on us."

As we walked into the hotel parking lot, two police vehicles pulled in. Out jumped several of the officers from the FSB headquarters. Kathy drew near and whispered, "Those are the guys who met us at the airport. I saw them at the base too. If they were going to follow us, why didn't they just offer us a ride?"

I furrowed my brow and replied, "Remember? It's all about intimidation! My guess is we will see them this entire trip. We are the most exciting thing to happen to them this whole summer—perhaps their entire careers."

I turned to the group, "Stay out here while we get rooms. We'll put the girls in one, and the guys in the other. Joel and Michelle already have their own room."

The clerk recognized Joel. After getting a nod from the FSB officer seated in the lobby, she asked, "How many rooms?"

Joel answered, "My wife and I will stay another day. We would like two more rooms."

The clerk nodded, asked for all our passports so she could legally register us in the city and charge us an extra $10 each for her kind service. She also charged us $25 a night per person for the rooms. I paid the bill, and she handed me two keys.

Jack was the first to ask where his passport was. I explained, "When you come to a city in Russia, you must register with the local government. She took our passports and said they would be ready in a few hours."

Kathy looked at the FSB officers outside in their car and frowned, "You would think after this morning's escapade, we would already be registered with the local government."

She must be tired to say that in front of the others. She knows we are guests in this country and must obey their laws as much as possible. Being in that office and interpreting must have been harder than she let on. Lord, help her!

I handed Kathy a key and said, "The good news is we have rooms and, although the showers and bathrooms are communal, they have hot water!"

Two hours later, I knocked on the girls' door. Kathy opened. Her hair was a mess as she yawned, "What's up?"

I kissed her cheek, "Now that we've had naps, let's get some food. Tell the girls to grab a backpack of tracts and we'll pass them out on the way to the market."

Kathy looked behind her at the sleeping girls, "You'll have to give us 15 minutes."

We met in the hotel lobby 20 minutes later. Joel and I went to the front desk to retrieve everyone's passports.

"Where's Jack?" Joel asked.

"I tried to wake him, but he wouldn't budge." I replied as we headed out.

Joel walked with me and pointed to our left, "The hotel receptionist told me about an indoor marketplace down this way."

I looked behind me to see Chelsey handing a tract to an elderly lady. Kathy stepped up to translate when the woman asked questions. "Slow down Joel, your mom is witnessing to a lady."

Momentarily, the elderly woman smiled and walked away. Kathy rushed up to walk with me, "She is Russian Orthodox and believes the ground won't accept her body when she dies if she listens to anyone but a priest talk about God's Word. It's so sad."

When we arrived at the market, the smell of blood and spoiled meat overwhelmed us. Kathy turned to the girls, "Don't buy fresh meat. We'll get kielbasa and cooked sausages for dinner."

We went to several vendors. One for bread, one for mayonnaise, another for vegetables, yet another for a block of reindeer sausage, and goat cheese. I was proud to see each of the team passing out tracts to everyone they met. When all our tracts were gone, we headed back.

As we entered the hotel, Jack was standing in the lobby, "Hey!" He shouted, "Where were you?"

I motioned for him to quiet down as he stomped toward us. "We went to the local market and passed out tracts. I tried to wake you, but you refused to get up." I reached into my pocket and handed Jack his passport.

Jack frowned, "I'm a heavy sleeper! You should have tried harder."

I moved towards the stairs, "Let's go, team."

We were soon eating sandwiches while Joel gave the group an overview of the schedule, "Tonight is the Wednesday evening Bible study at the little Russian Baptist Church. This is where Oleg and I visited ten years ago. Seven visitors will be a blessing to them."

The Red Brick Church

We gathered our Bibles, locked our hotel doors, and walked onto the street. Joel led the way to a bus stop, "According to *Yandex (*Russia's map system) we take bus 14."

Six stops later, we deboarded. The church was across the street about a block away. Joel held his phone with the online map pulled up and continued giving us directions. "The underground crosswalk is this way."

A cold blast hit us in the face as we climbed the stairs to street level.

"What a quaint little building!" Michelle exclaimed as we approached the red and white brick structure.

I climbed the stairs and tried the door. It was locked. Joel quickly looked down at his phone at the church's website. "It says services start at 7 p.m." He looked at his watch, "It's 6:45 p.m.—maybe the pastor is running late."

A few minutes later, a young man approached. His eyes widened as he saw us waiting on the steps. "Can I help you?"

Joel smiled, "We are Americans who have come to preach the Gospel to the Reindeer People. Tonight, we want to worship with you."

The Pastor smiled, "That's wonderful. We are a small group. But we love the Lord."

I stepped forward and asked, "Have you seen any Reindeer People in town?"

He shook his head as he unlocked the door. "They usually come at the end of summer to trade for winter supplies. I haven't seen any in town."

Our group doubled the size of the church that night! Halfway through the first song, a group of young people with backpacks entered. The Pastor finished leading the song and then asked, "Where have you come from?"

The leader of the new group stood and said, "We bring greetings from the church at Penza."

The Pastor nodded for Joel to introduce our group, "We send greetings from the church in Domodedovo."

"Welcome to Salekhard," The Pastor answered, "It is an honor to have so many visitors. While our governments may not always agree, we understand that we are one in Christ and our citizenship is in Heaven. Let's sing *As the Deer Panteth for the Water* together. I would like the Americans to sing in English and we will sing in Russian."

After singing this song so many years in Russian, I struggled to remember the English words, so I sang in both.

Next the pastor asked each group to give a testimony.

Joel stood, "We have been in Russia as missionaries for over 18 years. Although we mostly minister in Moscow, we also take trips to preach the Gospel to the Reindeer People. God has worked miracles and we have seen many saved. We have taken helicopters to Novyy Port and tanks into the tundra. We have come in search of more Reindeer People."

I heard gasps and whispers from the young Russian travelers.

Their leader stood, "We have heard stories of American missionaries who went into the tundra on tanks to find Reindeer People and tell them of God." He paused to admire our group, "Perhaps it was your stories we heard." He smiled and continued, "After hearing the stories, we decided we should be concerned about the souls of our fellow countrymen as well. We spent the whole spring planning a backpacking trip through the tundra in search of Reindeer People to share the Gospel with."

The Red Brick Church

Tears filled my eyes as I wondered if our adventures had reached across Russia. If they had heard our Reindeer stories in Penza, where else had God used our ministry to motivate others to surrender their lives to the Gospel?

On the steps of the church with the other group

THOUGHTS
- Has your zeal for the Gospel influenced others to serve our Lord?

Chapter Sixty-Four

An Old Friend

For this cause also thank we God without ceasing, because, when ye received the word of God which ye heard of us, ye received it not as the word of men, but as it is in truth, the word of God, which effectually worketh also in you that believe. 1 Thessalonians 2:13

The next morning, as we ate leftover reindeer sausage on bread for breakfast, Jack asked, "What will we do today? Will we see any Reindeer People?"

Joel responded quickly as he stuffed the last bite in his mouth, "I've hired a van to take us around the city and into a neighboring village where Reindeer People might live."

Michelle sniffed the sausage and remarked, "I think this is the last time we should eat this. Without refrigeration, it is going bad."

Jack took the remaining sausage from Michelle. "I'll take it. I have a strong stomach." He wrapped it in plastic and stuffed it into his backpack.

Joel stood up and said, "Everyone use the bathroom. Our ride should be here in 10 minutes."

Our first stop was the Reindeer People Museum, a place I always took first-timers to. As we meandered the wooden path, Jack peeked into the first teepee. "Hey, we can dress up in Reindeer outfits."

Michelle handed Joel an outfit as she put on another. She handed Kathy her camera. "Please take several photos of us in front of this teepee. This is awesome."

After everyone had their photo shoot, we continued to the gift shop. We viewed artifacts and photos of the Reindeer People's tragic and arduous history. Locals claim that when the Russian government

An Old Friend

discovered the Reindeer People early in the 20th century, they were amazed at the vast number who roamed the tundra. They welcomed them 'into Russia' by dropping crates of vodka off at the villages. It is said that thousands died that first winter from getting drunk, passing out, and freezing in the subzero Arctic temperature.

Kathy & me in Reindeer clothes

Kathy lingered in the museum gift shop. A history buff, she insisted on examining each exhibit. As she viewed some photographs, a man approached. He pointed to the photos, "I took these photos. I am the Chief of the Reindeer People in this area. You should buy some of my photos."

Pulling the Gospel of John from her pocket, Kathy said, "I'll buy photos if you'll take this booklet."

He looked at the pamphlet, wrinkled his nose and asked, "Are you a Baptist?"

She replied, "Yes, I am."

He stood tall and boasted, "I follow the religion of my ancestors. I worship the sun. It is my god."

My wife smiled, leaned toward the Chief, and whispered in formal, respectful Russian, "Мой Бог создал Вашего бога (My God made your god)."

She then stood erect and motioned all around as she continued in Russian, "My God is Creator of all that is in the universe, including you. He loves you. He loves you so much, that He sent His Son to die for your sins. It's all written in this booklet. Here, take it."

The Chief and Kathy had a stare down. Neither wanted to be the first to look away. Finally, the chief sighed, looked down at the Book of John, grabbed it from her hands, and walked away. Kathy proceeded to buy photographs as promised.

After viewing the Mammoth Museum and seeing a replica of a baby female mammoth discovered a few years earlier in Siberia, we were ready to get to work. We loaded into the van and drove into the tundra. The van dropped the men off on the outskirts of town.

The driver gave instructions as we exited, "Follow this road into town. I will pick you up in two hours at the town square. I will drop the women off at the square and they can talk to people there."

We knocked on doors of small shacks, "Hi, I'm Ron, this is my son Joel. We have traveled from America to give you the Gospel. Do you believe in God?" The answers varied, but all homeowners took tracts and thanked us for stopping. We eventually found the girls at the Town Square. They had given all the shopkeepers and people on the streets a tract.

Kathy had the opportunity to talk at length to one elderly man. He cried as she spoke of God's love for him and His sacrifice on Calvary for his sins. He said, "My grandmother used to tell me this story. She had a Bible hidden in her house. Sometimes she got it out and read to me. They told me in school that God was dead, but Grandma said she knew better, that God lived in her heart. I had forgotten about this."

"Would you like to ask God to save your soul today? If Jesus is your Savior, you will see your grandmother in Heaven." Kathy opened the tract, *You Are Special*, and began to go through the plan of salvation with the elderly man. Tears continued to pour down his cheeks as he listened to the Gospel plan of salvation.

An Old Friend

Finally, he shook his head, "No, I must think about this. I was so convinced that God was not real, but you stir up old memories."

Kathy gave him the tract and the Gospel of John, "Take this home and read it. God will reveal Himself to you through His Word." With his hands shaking and his heart breaking, the elderly man took the material.

It had been 10 years since our last trip to a Siberian village. My heart broke that no one seemed to be interested in God anymore. Apathy and materialism had overcome the desire to know God even out here on the Siberian tundra.

We continually asked people if they knew where any Reindeer People were. No one seemed to know of any.

The van dropped us off at the hotel. We needed a new plan. Joel stood before the group, "We have done all we can do here. The police are watching our every move. I suggest we take the ferry over to Labytnangi tomorrow morning and head to Polyarnyy Ural where Dad has met Reindeer People in the past. Get your things together by 6 a.m. We'll take a bus to the ferry, a ferry to the train station, and then a train to Polyarnyy Ural."

Polyarnyy Ural, Asia

Early the next morning, Joel and I talked to the ticket agent at the train station. "We have tickets to go back to Moscow tomorrow morning. We would like to buy tickets to Polyarnyy Ural, spend the night there and join the train to Moscow when it passes through Polyarnyy Ural tomorrow. Can we do that?"

The ticket agent gave us a puzzled look and shrugged. "Yeah, if you want to do that, you may. It will cost $10 per person, and you must sit in coach. I'll make a note that you will be joining the train to Moscow in Polyarnyy Ural, which was renamed Camp 133. Hopefully, the wagon master won't sell your tickets when you don't show up in Labytnangi."

Two hours later, the train approached Camp 133, and we stood to gather our stuff. The passengers looked at us as though we were crazy. One elderly woman asked, "Are you sure this is your stop?"

I smiled, "Yes, we have been here before. We know what we are doing."

She was not the only one to roll her eyes and say, "Well, good luck to you—"

As we deboarded, another passenger got off, and a tank came down to meet him. We took longer to get our bags off and so missed the opportunity to ask for a ride. We walked up the hill into the village.

Serving God Behind Enemy Lines

*Walking to the town after deboarding
Notice no train platform*

Chelsey & Rebecca carrying their luggage after deboarding

Kathy was the first to say, "Ummm, are we in the right spot? Is this the abandoned village you accidentally stopped at on your second journey—you know the one with the hermit?"

Truly something was wrong. The whole village was in shambles, much worse than a decade ago. I set my bags down, rubbed my chin, and thought.

Lord, have we done it again? Is this the wrong town? Give me wisdom.

I looked at Joel, "Is this Polyarnyy Ural, Asia? The one with the hunting lodge?"

Joel looked at our train tickets, "Yes. That's what the ticket master said when he sold us the tickets." Joel ran after the tank driver, who had parked and was headed to a group of workers, "Excuse me, are we at Camp 133? Where are all the people?"

An Old Friend

The driver laughed, "The government shut down this village years ago. They moved everyone into another town. We geologists and a few dissidents stayed behind. There are maybe 15 people in the whole town."

Joel pressed further, "Can we stay in the old lodge up on the hill?"

Another geologist piped up, "That lodge hasn't been lived in for years. We live in these containers. With the school and grocery stores gone, we moved down here by the tracks. Water and electricity no longer go up to the lodge."

I spoke up, "We are stranded here until the train comes tomorrow. Where can we spend the night?"

As the group of men looked at our team, their eyes popped out of their heads. I overheard one of the men whisper to another, "Красивые женщины! Как долго мы не видели!"

Joel quickly turned to me and said in English, "We have a problem. They just said, 'Beautiful women—we haven't seen any in so long.' There are only men here, and they want our women."

Lord, we need Your help! Protect our women—Your children—from evil.

Eyeing the women in our group, one of the geologists pointed at two abandoned containers and walked me over to them, "You can stay in these two containers. One for the women, and one for the men."

He winked at his fellow geologists as he directed us to put the women in the container closer to theirs. He popped his head inside the container to see the layout. "I'm sorry they aren't cleaned up. We weren't expecting visitors. They don't have locks either." He shrugged, tossed a lustful look toward the women, and muttered, "It's all we have."

He turned to walk back to his group, but I stopped him and asked, "Do you know if there are any tribes of Reindeer People nearby? I've been here before, and a tank driver has taken me to various tribes. We come from America and want to give the Gospel of Jesus Christ to the Reindeer People."

The man shook his head, "It's been a long winter. We go out in the tanks every day in search of minerals. I haven't seen any *chums*."

I walked back to the group. Kathy whispered, "Don't they say that every time—it's been a long winter?"

I sighed, "Yeah. I wonder when they will figure out that all their winters are long?"

Michelle walked into one of the containers and walked back out, "That is filthy. I can't do this."

Kathy poked her head in, looked around, then walked into the other container. She called from inside, "This one isn't any better." She came outside and faced the ladies, "Listen, I've learned in life that I can endure anything provided I know the expiration date. We must survive these conditions for only 24 hours. We can do this!"

I gathered the group together. I looked at the men, "Did you see the way those geologists looked at our women? This is going to be a problem. We will have to stand guard in shifts." Both Jack and Joel nodded.

We put our bags in one of the containers. I looked at everyone's dejected faces and smiled, "I think we need something to cheer us up. Let's eat! This situation is exactly why I said to carry emergency food. There is no store in this town, and we will have to live off our rations."

Several in the group gave me a horrified look. I quickly asked, "Is something wrong?"

Rebecca puckered her lips before admitting, "I ate my rations several days ago. I've been bumming off Chelsey. I think hers are almost gone too."

Chelsey nodded. She opened her backpack and pulled out two packages of Top Ramen. Kathy and I also had packets of soup. "Well," I said, "It looks like it is soup for lunch. Let's go outside and find a way to cook this over an open fire."

We found three long sticks for a tripod and Jack had packed a camping pan. After several attempts, we finally managed to heat the soup. We scarfed it down, but we were still hungry.

Rebecca took a 16oz mayonnaise squeeze bottle from the table. We all watched in astonishment as she said, "I'm so hungry, I can eat this whole package of mayonnaise!" And she did, grossing out the rest of us. We were not hungry anymore, a definite blessing in disguise.

I looked at our disgruntled and defeated team, "Let's go see the town. I'll show you the old hunting lodge and the graveyard. Take tracts along— we'll witness to anyone we see."

Jack headed back to the container. "I'll stay with the stuff and take a nap. I'm not feeling very well. I finished that reindeer sausage on the train ride. I think Michelle was right, it was rotten."

The rest of us walked through this ghost town. There was the old school, the deserted bakery, the abandoned hospital clinic, and in the back corner of the town, the hunting lodge. Its doors were off their hinges. We did not dare walk inside.

Joel saw a man approaching and started a conversation, "Hi, we aren't from around here."

An Old Friend

Really, Joel?

The man nodded, and Joel continued, "We have come to find the Reindeer People. Have any come through this village?"

The man shook his head and asked, "Where are you from?"

Joel replied, "I have come from America. We came to tell you about Jesus."

While Joel witnessed to this man, I caught the girls about 20 feet away trying not to make a commotion. I walked over to them, "What's the problem?"

"Look at Miss Kathy's hair!" Michelle exclaimed, "It has bugs in it. Hundreds of bugs!"

I looked and saw gnats crawling all over her head. "Do they itch?" I asked.

Kathy was trying to stay calm for the sake of the other girls, "No, I can't tell they are there." She looked at the girls and smiled, "You know they are in your hair too; you just can't see them because you have dark hair." Rebecca, Chelsey, and Michelle held their hands over their mouths to keep from screaming.

I pointed to Joel witnessing to the man and put my finger to my lips, "Shhh, God is working in that man's heart."

Eventually Joel shook the man's hand, gave him a tract and Gospel of John. As the man walked away, Joel turned to me, "Almost persuaded. I pray God continues to work on his heart until he surrenders his life to Christ."

I pointed to the hill above the hunting lodge. Let's walk up this hill and get a team photo. I took the lead and started up the hill.

Rebecca was close behind. "Ummm, Brother Reasoner, are there any bears in these hills?"

I paused to look around. A gentle breeze danced with the prairie grass, but there were no signs of bears. I glanced back at Rebecca and smiled, "Don't worry. I come from pioneer blood. My Grandmother once killed a bear. I'm sure I can do the same." My eyes twinkled as I talked.

Joel laughed, "Tell them the story, Dad. I've heard it a hundred times. It gets better each time."

Turning to face everyone, I begin my Reasoner history lesson. "In a small way, it's probably part of the reason we are here today. You see, my grandmother used to tell me stories of her pioneer days. It made me want to be a pioneer." I paused to swat a mosquito from my jacket.

"Her parents moved to Oregon in the late 1800s and settled in Sumpter, a village not much larger than this one." I pointed to Camp 133 below us. "They built a log cabin just outside of town. Grandmother was taught at the young age of seven how to use a rifle to protect their homestead from enemies, whether human or animal."

Several of the girls gasped. Kathy explained, "It was the Wild West with plenty of hostile criminals hiding out in the mountains. She had to know how to handle a gun."

I continued, "One day when Grandma was 19 years old, her Ma and Pa went to the village for supplies. She was alone when a terrible roar came from just outside the front door. 'It must be a bear come to eat the livestock!' she reasoned. Grandma knew they would not survive the winter if a bear got their cow, or horse, or goats. Grabbing the gun, and opening the front door, she—"

I looked around as if to check for attacking bears. Everyone followed my gaze. Satisfied everyone was boiling with anticipation, I continued, "She pointed her rifle, aimed for the bear standing 50 feet from her and shot. The bear let out a blood-curdling scream and ran away."

"Did she kill it?" Michelle asked.

I raised my eyebrows and held my breath for dramatic effect. Finally, I exhaled, "It ran about 100 yards and fell over dead. She had it gutted and mostly skinned by the time her parents got home. They ate off the meat for several months. She became a town hero."

I turned around and started up the mountain again. "Grandma Hutchinson did lots of great things like that. She tamed wild horses, ran a boarding house, was the local postmaster, and survived two husbands. She even had twins when she was in her forties. One of those twins is my mother."

Kathy piped up, "Then she had two more children after the twins. I was privileged to know her for a few years before she passed away. She was a pioneer woman if ever there was one." She grabbed my hand. "I'm glad you got her pioneering spirit. Without it, we might never have come to Russia, and we definitely wouldn't be out here searching for Reindeer People."

Joel added. "They say some things run in the blood. I guess we have pioneer blood."

We reached the top of the hill. I looked up to Heaven.

Thank You, Lord, for a grandmother who was strong, determined and most of all, a Christian who loved You.

Kathy snapped me out of my thoughts, "Everyone, line up against the beautiful sky and Ural Mountains. Chelsey, can you take the picture? I'll take the next with you in it."

Joel & Michelle, Kathy & me, Rebecca (Chelsey taking picture)

"Well," I sighed as we walked back down the hill towards our container, "I think we have witnessed to everyone in town."

Meeting an Old Friend

As we walked past a container, a man exited. I ran up to him and said, "I would like to tell you about God." The man looked at me, then at the tract I held out. His eyes bulged as he said, "Wait a moment." And ran back into his container.

Within seconds, he returned waving something in his hand. As he got closer, I realized it was my family's prayer card from 10 years ago. I grabbed the man and exclaimed, "Elijah? Is that you?"

He held the prayer card up to my face and asked, "Ron, is that you?"

We embraced as old friends who had not seen each other for 10 years! Tears filled both of our eyes. I called the team over, "This is Elijah the Tank Driver!"

Kathy grabbed his hand, "Elijah, I have heard so much about you! I am so excited to meet you."

Joel approached Elijah and offered his hand, "Elijah, I am Joel, Ron's eldest son." He pointed to himself in the picture, "That is me. It is a pleasure to meet you!"

Elijah was elated at our presence. He said, "Come into my home. My friend has come from the city, and we have prepared a big meal."

We filed into his container. It was standing room only as the six of us tried to stay out of his way. Elijah asked, "Are you hungry? We have prepared Shashlik and vegetables. Please eat with us."

I whispered to the group, "God always provides!" Then I turned to our host, "Thank you Elijah! You are a blessing."

As Elijah instructed us where to sit, he excitedly told us about his Christian walk, "I remember how you told me of Jesus. I used to be afraid of the Reindeer People, but now I am their friend. When they travel through our village, I tell them what you told me about God and how He loves us. I still read the New Testament that you gave me." Elijah pulled out a tattered Book from the side table near his chair.

I smiled, "I have some gifts for you!" I pulled a whole Bible and discipleship notebook out of my backpack and gave them to him.

Finally, Lord, Elijah has discipleship material!

I also left him with a handful of tracts and Bibles to give to Reindeer People.

I took another piece of shashlik and used it to point to Joel, "Elijah, my son Joel, would like to go with you out to see many more Reindeer People Tribes. Do you have a phone number?"

Elijah nodded as Joel got out his cell phone and they exchanged numbers. "Call me a month before you come, and I will tell you if Reindeer People are in the area. It will be my pleasure to introduce you. Together we can tell them about the Great God in Heaven!"

Although Jack was not with us, I did not feel the liberty to ask for any extra food for him. I stood and the team did the same, "Elijah, this has been a great blessing to see you again and know that you have a ministry among the Reindeer People! But we must go. Your friend has come a long way to see you and we do not want to intrude."

I turned to Elijah's friend and asked, "Has Elijah ever told you about the God Who loves you so much, He sent His Son to die for you?"

The friend smiled, "Yes, he has. I read the tract you gave him ten years ago and I prayed that prayer."

Elijah is a soul winner, Lord! Thank You for showing me this!

"Amen!" I beamed. I turned to Elijah, "Thank you again for the food and great fellowship!"

Elijah rose and walked us back to our containers. He laughed as he saw the piles of rubble in the container, "I wish I had room in my container."

"Don't worry about us, Elijah. We are missionaries and we are used to surviving wherever God puts us."

Me, Elijah & Joel in his container

"I will come tomorrow and drive you in the tank down to the train tracks. What time does your train arrive?"

"We don't really know," I said as I pulled my ticket from my pocket. "We bought our tickets to leave from Labytnangi but came a day early to Camp 133. Do you know what time the train comes?"

Elijah scratched his chin and chuckled, "Didn't we have this conversation 10 years ago? I think it comes at 9 a.m."

I laughed, "Deja Vu. But is that Local time or Moscow?"

"I am not sure. I will come get you at 8:30 a.m. to be sure you are there in time."

"Thank you, Elijah. Thank you for everything."

I watched as he left our container and went over to the geologists and tank drivers. He spoke to them quietly. They nodded, shook his hand, and waved goodnight. I wondered if he had witnessed to his co-workers in the past and if any of them had gotten saved.

Inside the container, Jack had awakened and was sad to hear that he had once again missed out on the evangelism. The nap had been good, but he was still sick to his stomach.

"I will take the first watch." He said as the girls started to get ready for bed, arranging their sleeping bags on old bedframes.

"We need to be up and ready to go by 8:30 a.m. Elijah will be here with his tank to take us to the train tracks. Let's pray that God will protect us all tonight; 'Heavenly Father, thank You for the grand gift of seeing Elijah again and hearing how he has continued to read his Bible, learn of You, and share what he knows with the Reindeer People. I pray that as we sleep tonight, You will protect us from any evil that is planned against us. Help us make the train in the morning and may You be glorified on the trip home.'"

It was a fitful night. No one got much sleep. I could not shake the image in my mind of the way the geologists had gawked at the girls. I needed to be vigilant.

When my alarm went off at 8 a.m., I found Jack asleep next to Joel. I quickly checked on the girls. They were up, dressed, and ready.

Thank You, Lord for answered prayers!

Elijah and the tank arrived at exactly 8:30 a.m. We loaded our bags, and I helped the girls into the back. Jack jumped in, opened the hatch, and proceeded to take selfies. We all took turns getting photos of the tank.

Elijah saw the bags under my eyes and asked, "You did not sleep last night?"

"I admit, I stayed up most of the night to guard our ladies from any evil intentions someone had." I nodded toward the group of geologists sitting near a tank smoking cigarettes and shamelessly staring.

Elijah waved his hand as if to dismiss any thought of them, "After I left you, I stopped by their camp. I told them you were dear friends and they needed to treat you all as they would treat my family. They dared not bother you."

Oh Lord, me of little faith! I prayed for Your protection and then proceeded to handle it myself when all along You had already taken care of it!

Elijah drove us to the train tracks and helped us unload our gear, "I'm sorry I can't stay with you, but I have work to do."

I shook Elijah's hand, half hugged him and patted him on the back, "Oh Elijah, you have done more than enough! Thank you!"

Elijah shook everyone's hand as we lined up to say, 'thank you' and 'goodbye.'

We wondered in amazement at God's Divine appointment with a man I had led to the Lord ten years ago. I never thought I would see him again and yet, God let us meet. I saw how God continued to use this 'Russian army tank driver of 33 years who had killed many people' to give the Gospel to the Reindeer People.

An Old Friend

Inside the Russia Tank – Chelsey, Michelle & Me

The train was to arrive at 9 a.m., but no one knew if it was 9 a.m. Moscow time, Camp 133 time, or Salekhard time. So, we had to be at the train stop at 8:30 a.m. I looked at the group and pounded my fist in the air, "God is so good! Did you all just see that miracle?"

"Ouch! What was that?" Michelle asked, "Something just bit me!"

"Ouch!" Rebecca echoed, "It got me too! What is it?"

I pulled out my Deet Mosquito repellant. I walked over to each of the girls and sprayed them.

"It's not helping!" Kathy shouted as she kept hitting her legs, "They are biting right through the repellant!"

Joel ran over to a tall bush, pulled out a knife and cut off branches for everyone. We grabbed them and began hitting ourselves to keep the flies and mosquitoes away.

We waited four hours by the train tracks. One of the girls, I will not name names, lost her mind for a few hours. Thankfully, it returned once we finally got on the train.

The women were in tears by the time we saw the halogen light in the distance. Kathy echoed our sentiments when she yelled, "Oh Praise God! A more beautiful sight has never been seen! The train!"

Everyone grabbed their bag and prepared to jump up four feet to the first rung of the ladder to board the train. I stood beside the women, held their bag in one hand, gave them a step up with my knee and then handed them their bags.

Serving God Behind Enemy Lines

The whistle let out a piercing sound. Kathy got onboard and reached for my bags, and screamed over the noise, "Its leaving! Hurry! Jump up!"

I looked around to ensure we had everything. Winded from helping the ladies, I jumped onboard and barely made it after waiting so long.

We quickly walked through the long aisles to get to our wagon and bunk numbers. Joel whispered, "I hope they didn't sell our bunks when we didn't get on the train in Labytnangi."

I nodded. That very thought had been nagging me. The moment of truth arrived as we came upon our assigned bunks. They were empty!

Thank You, God!

Back to Moscow

There was nothing I wanted to do more than take a nap, but I needed to make sure everyone got settled in. Jack's bed was a few aisles away from ours. I went to make sure he found it and to see if he needed anything. I was astonished at how pasty he looked. I felt his forehead. It was burning up, "Jack, you look awful."

He managed to mumble, "I feel awful. I should have never eaten that spoiled reindeer sausage."

I managed a half smile, "Get some rest. Your body heals best when you are sleeping. I'll go pray for you with the others."

I passed Chelsey's bunk. She was already asleep. I was not the only one who did not sleep last night.

The train had no air conditioning and a heat wave had hit the tundra. The inside temperature of the train hovered at 90 degrees. Russians have a fear of the wind blowing on their backs. They believe it causes pneumonia. Thus, we could not open the windows. The air was stifling.

Over the years, Kathy appreciated how much God blessed her when He called us to Russia and not Africa. She loathes the heat. She grabbed my arm, "Ron, this heat is awful! I don't know how I can handle 48 hours of this! I'm having trouble breathing. I think I might pass out!"

I put an arm around her, "Kathy, it's all in your head. Don't let Satan scare you. You can do this! Didn't I overhear you tell the girls yesterday that you can endure anything if you know the expiration date? Well, this trip is only 48 hours. Chin up."

If looks could kill, I might have died right then, but Kathy's cold stare softened as she murmured, "I guess—Endure hardness as a good soldier of Jesus Christ, right?"

I sat down on my bunk to relax. But it was not to be. Almost immediately the drunks and soldiers came calling. One man sat down next to Rebecca and offered her a bag of chips and cheese. She gladly accepted. I jumped off my bunk and wedged between them before he could reach for her. Realizing that Rebecca did not speak Russian, the man asked me to interpret. "Would you like some vodka?" He asked.

I did not bother interpreting. I answered, "We are Christians. We do not drink alcohol."

Offended, the man objected, "I am a Christian and I drink."

"Really?" I countered, "Tell me about the day that you asked Jesus to forgive your sins and come into your heart. Where were you? How old were you?"

"I am Russian Orthodox! I was baptized three years ago. I follow the Patriarch religiously!"

The man bent across me and asked Rebecca in broken English, "We go to toilet?" He pointed to himself and then to Rebecca."

Rebecca stood, "I do need to use the restroom."

I grabbed her arm and pulled her back, "Rebecca! This man thinks you owe him because he gave you food. He wants to go to the bathroom with you to do evil! Sit down, and do not take any more food from men!"

I turned to the man, "Leave us alone. We are tired and want to rest. Good-bye."

I stood and towered over him. He gave me a cruel stare, took a lingering look at Rebecca, and made the correct decision to move on.

I turned back to Rebecca, controlling my voice as I said, "We will be stopping soon in a larger village. There will be vendors and grandmas selling food on the train platform. We can load up on drinks, bread, salami, and snacks. Until then, please do not accept any more food from anyone. Their food is not free. It comes at a price much higher than you, or I are willing to pay. Do you understand?"

Rebecca, who had just graduated from high school, nodded.

Hoping my trials were over, I started toward my bunk. Looking behind me to ensure Rebecca was obeying, I almost ran into Joel who was holding his stomach in pain. "What's wrong?"

Joel rolled his eyes and sighed, "I did something stupid. I drank some leftover juice I bought when we were still in Salekhard. I opened it two days ago and finished it off this morning. Obviously, it was bad. I'm sick out both ends, and this heat is making it worse. I'm sorry Dad. I know you need me to help, but I need to sleep."

"Go, Son, don't worry. You need to get better. I'm sure Michelle will take good care of you, and I'll keep a watch out for her."

Oh Lord! Jack is sick. Joel is sick. I alone am left to protect the ladies. I need Your grace and help!

As I slumped onto my bed to relax, I could not sleep so I began to think about our trip and a great burden overcame me. I prayed:

Lord, when I first came to Russia, there was no Internet, no cable television, no cell phones, and no hope. The Russian people were ripe for the Gospel. I preached and hundreds of people came forward for salvation. This week, we have given the Gospel over and over to people, but not one of them was willing to give their heart and life to You. Now I understand when You said:

Say not ye, There are yet four months, and then cometh harvest? behold, I say unto you, Lift up your eyes, and look on the fields; for they are white already to harvest. (John 4:35)

When You prepare a people for harvest, Satan knows, and he comes to spoil it so Your servants cannot reap the souls. Thank You for the thousands that have been saved in Russia. Help me to be faithful even if the harvest is one soul at a time.

Those two days on the train were probably the longest days of my life; protecting the women and constantly checking on the men to make sure they were not getting worse. I thought we would never get back home, but we serve a Great God Who protects us even on the Trans-Siberian Railroad!

We experienced situations on this trip above and beyond what any of us had expected: we were arrested, detained, fined, famished, threatened, and endured pestilence, heat stroke and sickness. Yet, praise God, everyone made it back with no lasting repercussions.

This had been a scouting trip and we came back with Elijah's phone number and got discipleship material into his hands. We gave the Gospel to a Chief. Not every trip sees hundreds of people getting saved, but that is not up to us. We will only know in eternity the results of meeting the Chief and getting a whole Bible and discipleship materials into the hands of Elijah. We go as God directs and He does the rest.

Chelsey and Rebecca went back to America after their adventure in Russia. They got married and serve the Lord in their home churches. Jack married an M.K. (missionary kid) and serves the Lord in Ukraine.

THOUGHTS

- Can you recall a time when God gave you more responsibility than you thought you could handle?
- How did God come through for you?

Chapter Sixty-Five

Ever the Spy Suspect

Nevertheless the foundation of God standeth sure, having this seal, The Lord knoweth them that are his. And, Let every one that nameth the name of Christ depart from iniquity.
2 Timothy 2:19

Surveillance from the U.S. Embassy

Several years passed. One day in 2015, I walked into the kitchen, leaned over the stove, and asked hungrily, "What's for dinner?"

The kids were doing their own things. Joel and Michelle were living with us at the compound as Associate Pastor. Micah was now married to Sarah, and they were on deputation in America raising funds to come back to Russia as missionaries. Keturah and Jeremiah were at college in the states. And Hannah was living with us at the compound teaching English in Moscow.

Kathy hollered from the computer desk in the dining room, "Leftover *borscht* from lunch. I'm reheating it. It's ready now if you want to dish yourself up a bowl. Oh, and before I forget, that American family who works at the American Embassy will be coming to church Sunday."

I sighed, "Another spy, I suppose. Remember when we saw Jeff last year, he said almost all embassy personnel are spies."

My brother had finally retired from the military, so I was able to now have contact with him.

"Well," Kathy came over to the stove and served herself a bowl of *borscht* as well. "We passed last time, I'm sure we will be fine this time as well. This new family will either be a blessing or a curse, but we will endure hardness as good soldiers of Jesus Christ."

Serving God Behind Enemy Lines

That Sunday, as George and Lily entered the church with their five children, Kathy and I greeted them, "Hi, I'm Pastor Reasoner, and this is my wife, Kathy. You must be the Floor Family."

George stepped forward, took my hand, and smiled, "It's so nice to finally meet you, Pastor. Thank you for all the encouragement and advice during our move to Moscow."

I nodded at Kathy as she smiled and shook Lily's hand and said, "It was no problem. We are happy you found our ministry compound." She bent down and introduced herself to each of the children, "I'm Miss Kathy, you will be in my Sunday School class. We stay up here for singing and then go downstairs. I teach the class in both English and Russian so you can grow in Christ as well as the Russian children."

The Floor family became faithful members of our Church. Later, George confided that once the embassy found out he was attending our church, he was asked to fill out an updated report on whether we were a security risk. By this time, we had been in Russia for 20 years. George also reported that we were truly missionaries trying to see Russians saved to the glory of God.

Interrogations

Unknown to us, one Sunday, a Russian spy followed the Floor Family to church, putting our ministry compound on the radar. It was also during this time that Micah, his wife Sarah, and our three grandchildren—Chloe, Leah, and Micah Jack—arrived in Russia as missionaries.

One Monday evening, while everyone was sleeping upstairs, I heard pounding on the front door.

Someone forgot to lock the front gate and a homeless man is in the yard.

I went to the front door with Kathy on my heels. I slowly unlocked the door. It burst open, knocking me back a few feet. Two policemen ran through the door and began shouting questions.

"Slow down!" Kathy demanded in Russian, "Мы плохо говорим порусски. Что вы хотите? (We don't speak Russian very well. What do you want?)"

The lead officer approached Kathy, pointed at me, and said, "Do you speak Russian better than him?"

I slipped between the officer and my wife and spoke in English, "Kathy, translate for me. Yes, my wife speaks better Russian than I do, but please direct your questions to me."

"Give me your passports!" the policeman demanded.

Kathy answered, "They are upstairs. I will go get them." She turned and hurried upstairs, found Micah, and whispered, "The police are here.

Hide the children and Sarah and keep everyone quiet. I don't want them to know you are up here." She grabbed our passports and came downstairs.

After snatching our passports, the lead officer looked through them and asked, "You live here by visa?"

I answered, "Yes. All our papers are up to date and legal."

The Officer looked at our registration papers and smiled, "You are not registered at this address. That is illegal!"

Kathy quickly answered, "That is because this house is in my name. Only I can be registered here. Your government does not allow an American to invite other Americans into the country. We must register in a Russian's home."

The officer decided not to pursue it. He finished looking at the documents. Satisfied that all were in order, he said, "I need a copy of all of your documents."

Kathy took the passports and registrations from the officer and went into my office. Both officers and I followed. Kathy turned and grimaced, "I ran out of ink in the copier yesterday. We haven't been to the store to get refills." She repeated the problem to the officers.

The lead officer took our passports from Kathy and said, "Then you must follow us to headquarters. Come!"

The other policeman wandered around the office, looking at everything. My eyes followed his gaze to a pile of Russian Bibles. I grabbed two off the top and presented one to each of the policemen. They looked at each other, then to the Bibles, and reluctantly took them. "За мной!" he commanded me.

It was a command I knew well. My mind raced back to the first time I heard that phrase:

> *I had driven a friend home from a meeting one Friday morning. Jeremiah and Hannah, who were about five and six years old, were with me in the car. Our newly purchased Volvo was a lemon. As the snow fell, the windshield began to fog up. I kept rubbing a spot so I could see but I had tunnel vision. Apparently, I drove through a police checkpoint without stopping.*
>
> *A police car pursued us, pulled in front of me, and slammed on the brakes. Typical Russian approach to stopping cars. I screeched to a halt, just inches from his car. The policeman jumped out, opened my door, and yanked me out by the collar.*

I turned to Hannah and Jeremiah as the policeman threw me against the car. "Stay in the car!" I screamed in English.

Startled that I spoke English to my children, the officer jerked his hands away from me. He asked, "You American?"

"Yes!" I answered.

"Give me documents!" he demanded.

I handed him my car documents but would not allow him to have my passport. The officer took the car documents and said, "За мной!" He got in his car and drove away.

I got in my car and drove home. Upon entering our apartment, I called Kathy to my side, "What does, за мной mean?"

Kathy frowned, "Follow me. Why?"

My face turned white as I realized the error I had made. I was supposed to follow the police officer. The man still had my car documents.

I called Roman and asked him what to do. He laughed, "The man was trying to get you into a back alley to rob you. Now he has egg on his face because he has your documents and no way to get them back to you. Both you and he are in trouble—him because he obviously wanted a bribe from you—and you because you have lost your car documents."

It happened to be a Russian holiday, and all local police stations were closed. We would have to wait three days for them to open and inquire about the location of my documents.

The next morning our doorbell rang. Kathy went to answer it. A lady asked, "Have you lost any documents?"

At first Kathy was confused, but then she smiled, "Yes."

"What kind?"

"Car documents."

"I found these outside in the snow." The lady handed Kathy my car documents.

Kathy took them, "Wait a moment." She turned and ran back into the apartment to grab a Russian Bible. As she handed it to the lady, Kathy said, "Thank you so much!" The lady took the Russian Bible, smiled, and happily walked away. God had solved yet another of my missionary problems!

I pulled my mind back to our present dilemma.

So, they want us to follow them. God will solve this one too!

We got in our car and followed them to their headquarters in the basement of an old building. They led us down some stairs and locked the door behind us. We were stuck. Now they began to interrogate us, "Do you have a church in your home?"

"We have a Bible study—yes." Kathy used the term *Bible Study* because to have a church in a home was illegal.

The policeman continued, "How many people attend?"

"Twenty or so—"

"What are their names?"

"Tanya, Tanya, Tanya, Oleg, Oleg—"

"What are their last names?"

Kathy and I smiled. Years ago, we decided not to keep a church roll and to not learn the last names of our church members just in case we ever got arrested. If the police ever asked their names, we could honestly answer that we did not know. That day had arrived.

They wrote out a page of statements. They handed it to Kathy and said, "Sign this paper and we will give you back your documents."

Kathy and I looked over the document. We understood nothing. I asked if we could have a Russian friend come down to explain it to us. They emphatically said, "NO!"

We saw no option but to sign the documents, get our passports back and quickly exit. To this day, we have no idea what we signed.

From that day forward, we noticed a car randomly parked outside our gate. Sometimes it followed Hannah (now 20). Sometimes it followed our housekeeper. We learned to look outside our balcony before we left. If there was a car parked outside, we waited.

On another occasion, we had gone to the store, when I received a call on my cell from our Russian Associate Pastor, Vee. He said in Russian, "We have visitors at the house. When will you be home? They want to talk to you."

"We will be home in two hours."

Vee said, "Okay." And hung up.

When I got home, Vee knocked on our door. We invited him in and as he sat in a chair, he explained, "It was the local police. I forgot to look before opening the gate, and there they were—waiting. They wanted to talk to you. That's why I called."

I sat down and sighed, "They were gone when I drove in. What did they say?"

Serving God Behind Enemy Lines

Vee frowned, "They gave me their phone number and told me to call tomorrow to arrange a meeting."

I spent a sleepless night of prayer and questions, awaiting another encounter with the police.

The next day, we prepared for a 'meeting.' Vee called the number he was given, "I am calling to arrange a meeting for the Americans."

I watched as Vee talked on the phone. First, he frowned and then smiled, "Да—спасибо." Hanging up the phone, turned to me and said, "That's interesting."

"What?" I nervously asked.

Vee shook his head, "Normal Russian politics. The guy said he was instructed yesterday from 'higher-up' to cause trouble for the Americans. But today, it has blown over and they are on to someone else. They don't need to meet with you anymore."

We both let out a huge sigh of relief. Vee stood to go, "Next time, I'll be more careful to check for police before opening the gate!"

To this day, random cars park outside our gate for hours on end. Did the police plant a bug in the compound those many years ago? Are they listening in? Perhaps a parishioner is a spy, and they planted a bug? Nevertheless, we continue to preach the Gospel that souls might be saved.

THOUGHTS
- Do you have safeguards in place to protect those with whom you serve the Lord?

Chapter Sixty-Six

Many Other Things

Thou therefore endure hardness, as a good soldier of Jesus Christ. 2 Timothy 2:3

Time and space do not allow us to tell all the amazing missions trips God allowed us to go on. There were two more Reindeer trips, five more to Kalmykia, three trips to Romania, three to Estonia, and one trip each to Moldova, Armenia, Belorussia, Slovakia, Belgium, Finland, and Greece.

Each journey had its own victories and defeats. We were robbed at a train station in Estonia, robbed on the train to Ukraine, slept with mice in Moldova, saw a young man give his life to Jesus in Greece, and fished for men around Lake Sevan in Armenia. I preached in the gypsy villages of Romania, led a young lady to Christ in Helsinki, and helped one of our Bible Institute students start a church in Moldova. I have stood in the amphitheater where The Apostle Paul preached in Ephesus, and I proclaimed the Gospel to the tourists there. I stood on Mars Hill in Athens and preached the Gospel to hundreds of refugees.

On one trip to Kalmykia, we almost starved. Sergei entrusted the care of 15 Americans to his associate pastor who secretly hated Americans. He took us to a tent on the Volga River 20 miles from civilization and left us there for two days without food and water in temperatures of over 100 degrees. I had given him money for a summer camp to buy food for everyone. He bought food for the Russians, kept the rest, and left us in the middle of nowhere to starve. At the end of the second day, Sergei asked his associate where we were, how we were doing, and what we were eating? Sergei came bearing food, water, and a huge apology when he found out what his associate had done. God always comes through.

The entrance to the dormitories at the compound at a combined church picnic

On many other occasions, we were arrested by FSB and detained. How many FSB agents infiltrated our services and came to the saving knowledge of Christ? At least four that we know of; perhaps many more. Two of those agents followed the Lord in believer's baptism.

We are humbled that God would take a poor, young family from Hillsboro, Oregon and transplant us to Moscow, Russia. I worried my children would become communists, but God protected them. They are patriotic Americans whose worldview far exceeds the borders of the USA.

As America moves closer and closer to a socialistic country, my children are in the forefront begging their fellow countrymen to turn to God and not the government for their salvation. They have seen the result of a country who turned its back on God, and they have no desire to see the USA succumb to the same demise as the Soviet Union.

I find myself wistful, watching these young missionaries just starting out—their lives ahead of them and my life in the twilight years. I can only imagine the adventures they will have, the souls they will touch, the fruit abounding to their account if they will but call unto God and ask Him to show them great and mighty things. I would gladly do it all over again.

I do not believe that God calls every young person to go to the mission field. Some are called to hold the ropes while others go. However,

Many Other Things

I firmly believe that every Christian should surrender to go, and then GO if that is what God calls them to do.

I have no regrets that I decided to follow Jesus. What a great reunion some day in Heaven when we see people from every tribe and nation gathered around the throne of God because we had the courage and resolve to trust God's command, "Go ye therefore to all nations."

Often people ask me if thousands really got saved. I cannot answer that question. I only preach the Gospel. It is the Holy Spirit who convicts and Christ who saves them.

I will share a story of one person who was saved and committed her life to following Jesus Christ.

We first met Angela in August of 1996. She came to an evangelistic campaign we did in Odintsovo, where she got saved.

Several months later, Angela walked through the door of our weekly Bible study. She smiled as she approached me, "Brother Ron, I would like to give a testimony."

I smiled and turned to a group of about 30 people. "Angela would like to share what God has done in her life."

She played nervously with her hands as she began, "My name is Angela, I just moved here from Armenia with my husband and two daughters. We were living with relatives and looking for jobs. Every day I felt more and more discouraged. When I was at my lowest, someone handed me an invitation to your revival meeting. I came the first night and got saved. I went home and told my family about the great news of Jesus and showed them my new Bible. I prayed that evening that God would change our lives. Within a few days, my husband got a job. Then I got a job. Next, we found an apartment. God answered all my prayers, immediately.

"I called my relatives and told them how I had humbled myself in repentance and met the God Who changes lives." She smiled for the first time since she began her story. "There is so much that has changed in our lives since I accepted the Lord." She sighed, "Since I repented. I just want to let everyone know how good God is." She looked at me, smiled, and sat down.

Angela became the most faithful attendee to our Bible study. She constantly witnessed to people and invited them to attend as well. Eventually her children got saved. Her mother, father, sisters, and brothers came to know the Lord as their Savior. Finally, even her husband received Christ through our ministry.

Ultimately, I turned the Odintsovo Bible study over to one of our Bible College graduates. He was not successful, and the Bible study died. Angela and her family started attending our Moscow East Church. After I turned that church over to another pastor, we rarely heard from Angela.

Then in April 2015, our house phone rang. We had been in Russia for 21 years at this point. I walked into the dining room and picked up the receiver. I recognized the thick Armenian accent as the caller spoke Russian. "Angela, it's been a long time. I've wondered what happened to you." I pulled up a chair to sit, "How have you been? How is your family?"

"Brother Reasoner, I am so glad to reach you on the first try. My youngest daughter is getting married in two months. I would so much like it if you and Sister Kathy would attend."

I motioned for Kathy to come to me, "We'd love to come, Angela. Let me pass you off to Kathy and you can give her all the details."

"Angela, so good to hear your voice."

On Saturday, June 10th, we headed out from Domodedovo for Domnikovo in the Northern Moscow Region. I maneuvered our VW Touran around the Moscow Ring Road while Kathy double-checked Google. "Follow this road to the Tver region. It'll take almost two hours. Then continue to Domnikovo. We should arrive around 4 p.m."

We were quiet for a while as I drove. Finally, Kathy broke the silence, "I've been thinking about Angela's family. What a blessing! She got saved at that revival meeting and then her two girls got saved."

I nodded as I reminisced, "And remember when we gave each family in the church a copy of the movie, *Facing the Giants*, for Christmas? The next week her husband, Felix, came to church and said, 'I know everyone thinks I'm a Christian, but until I watched that movie and saw how God works in people's lives, I did not see a need for Him as my Savior. This week, I bowed my head and asked Jesus to save me.'."

"I remember," Kathy mused, "God has been good to us and to them, hasn't He?"

"Amen!"

We arrived 30 minutes late after taking several accidental detours in the surrounding area. Being late did not matter though; the guests of honor had not yet arrived.

We saw Angela and Felix greeting guests. Angela excused herself from a group and ran to hug us, "Oh, I'm so glad you came! It is an honor to have you at the wedding of our youngest daughter."

"Where are the bride and groom?" Kathy asked.

Many Other Things

Angela threw her hands in the air and said, "Last I heard they were in Red Square taking photos in front of St. Basil's and then putting a bouquet at the tomb of the Unknown Soldier. I'm afraid Leela has several places she wants to stop at along the way for more photos."

"Oh, yes!" I replied, "The Russian tradition of going around the city and taking photos in their wedding attire at all the famous landmarks."

"I think it's wonderful!" Kathy exclaimed. "You only get one wedding day and it should be full of great memories and photos,"

"Come!" Angela grabbed Kathy's hand and motioned for me to follow, "I want to show you where you will sit. It is an incredibly special table."

Kathy and I gave each other that, *'Oh no! What have we gotten into?'* look and followed Angela.

Almost immediately, someone stopped us, "Angela! Is this your Ron Reasoner?"

Kathy's puzzled look did not escape me as I concentrated on what Angela was saying, "Pastor Ron, I want to introduce you to my sister, Lena. When I got saved at the Odintsovo Revival almost 20 years ago, I immediately called Lena and shared the wonderful news of Jesus with her. She also asked Jesus to saved her. Our lives have never been the same. God has truly blessed us as His children."

Lena grabbed my hand and kissed it, "Спасибо! Спасибо что прехали в Россию!" Another lady ran up to us and repeated the phrase, but in heavily accented English, "Yes! Thank you for coming to Russia." Then she added, "I also know Jesus now."

Angela introduced another, "Pastor Ron, this is Tanya. She is the one who gave me a job after I got saved. When I shared with her how Jesus saved me and blessed me, she also got saved."

Tanya hugged me and commented, "Well, I did not get saved right away but when I saw how Angela loved and shared Christ with everyone, I took notice. I watched how she treated all people with respect and love. She prayed when she was troubled and trusted God when trials came. Eventually, I realized that God was real in her life and could also be real in my life as well. Thank you for coming. Because of Angela, I also became a Christian."

Angela sat us at her 'special table.' People began to introduce themselves and kept thanking me for coming to Russia and preaching the Gospel. Because I had come, Angela had been saved. Because Angela was saved, all 20 people at that table had heard her testimony and received

Christ. One had been suicidal, and Angela led her to Christ, saving not just her life but her soul.

Another said, "My mother also got saved at the Odintsovo Revival. As a result, I grew up in a Christian home and love the Lord. Thank you!"

Felix, me, Kathy & Angela

We were humbled. That night, God gave us a rare glimpse at what happened in the life of just one of the people who got saved in our many revival meetings. I was privileged to see how God took Angela's life and wove a beautiful tapestry of souls that were saved by her testimony of

Many Other Things

God's grace. Those people continue to tell others who become Christians, and then the newly saved tell others. The tapestry continues to grow as one soul tells another about Jesus.

Angela still works at an open marketplace but now owns her own company. Many of the other sellers and clients are Muslim. Angela gets excited when someone tells her they are Muslim because she loves to brag on her God, "Oh, you serve Allah? I serve the True and Living God—the God Who loves me so much that He sent His only Son to die for me. And not only did Jesus die for me, but He arose again from the dead and now intercedes for me in Heaven. He answers my prayers and gives me joy and peace in my life. That's how much my God loves me. Does Allah love you like that?"

What a great day it will be in Heaven when we meet all the people who came to know Christ through our labor and testimony!

THOUGHTS

- Can you trace the tapestry of your salvation?
- Who led you to the Lord?
- Do you know who led them to the Lord?
- Have you led someone else to the Lord to continue the tapestry of souls?

Chapter Sixty-Seven

Health Problems

Therefore I take pleasure in infirmities, in reproaches, in necessities, in persecutions, in distresses for Christ's sake: for when I am weak, then am I strong. 2 Corinthians 12:10

"Are you feeling any better today?" Kathy asked as I descended the stairs. Something was not quite right with me.

I walked into the kitchen and started to grab the teapot, but Luba, our live-in helper, got to it first.

She scolded me in Russian, "Ron, sit down! I'll pour tea and fry you potatoes. I heard you were sick—." She stopped short. Her shocked look did not escape me. She quickly poured the tea, handed it to me and rushed to prepare the potatoes.

"Are you feeling better?" Kathy repeated.

"Oh, a little." I rubbed my chest, "I still have congestion and my throat is sore."

"Maybe the tea will help."

Kathy and I both observed as Luba kept nervously looking in our direction. Finally, Kathy asked, "Luba, is there a problem?"

She hurried to the table, sat down, and spoke so quickly in Russian that I held up my hand, "Slow down."

She repeated, "Ron, there is something on your neck."

I put both hands around it, trying to find what Luba was talking about. I finally found it. A large lump on the left side. "I don't know how long this has been there! I haven't felt well and haven't shaved for three days." I turned to my wife, "Kathy, have you noticed it before?"

She moved toward me to get a better look. "It must have appeared this weekend. I don't remember seeing it."

She pushed on it, "It's soft. Does it hurt?"

"A little. Maybe my lymph nodes are just swollen. Let's not worry about it for a few days. Perhaps the swelling will go down."

By the following Monday, the mass had not receded. As Kathy and I sat at the dining room table, Luba joined us. Though we were speaking English, she understood enough to know we were talking about making a doctor's appointment for the lump.

With tears in her eyes, she cautioned, "Ron, you must be very careful with the Russian healthcare system. Remember when my sister died?"

I nodded, and she continued. "She had an ulcer. That's all—an ulcer. Her pain was controlled by medication. She lived in a village. She knew better than to go to the village doctor. Her doctor was in the city. On that fateful weekend, she ran out of pain medication. She tried to survive the weekend without it, but by Saturday night, it was unbearable.

She went to the village doctor, explained she just needed pain medication to last the weekend and would go to her city doctor on Monday. The village doctor demanded he examine her. He saw her swollen intestines and without her permission, sedated her for surgery. He removed her small intestine, leaving only two inches. When she awakened, he told her that he had removed her problems, and if her intestines grew back, she would be healed." Luba wiped her tears, "She died two days later."

I patted Luba's arm, "I remember when this happened, Luba. I'm so sorry you couldn't get to Ukraine before she died."

"Ron, you must remember that our healthcare often causes more problems than solutions."

Kathy nodded. "Yeah, Ron, don't forget about the time we visited my friend Julia when she had pneumonia. She kept getting worse. It was two days before the doctor visited her and realized the nurses were giving her the wrong medicine. Remember all the bad things that happened to her roommates there!"

I tried to interrupt, but she plowed ahead, "One of the women almost died when the nurse let her IV drip dry. The air in the IV bag entered her arm and it swelled up like a balloon. The nurse almost did not get there in time to remove it."

Kathy paused, squinted, and sighed, "I'll never forget the smell of urine and blood stains all over that hospital—on the walls, the floors, the sheets!

I tried to interrupt again, but she continued, "I'm still haunted by the memory of that young lady who came to Julia for help because she was a

Christian. The girl claimed that the police were bringing in young ladies off the street. They were coming in healthy and leaving a few days later in body bags. Julia thought they were harvesting the organs of homeless people and prostitutes."

Kathy fell silent, but soon continued, "And what about our American missionary friend who died this past summer. She was experiencing heart problems and the Russian hospital sent her home and told her to come back after the weekend. She died on Monday morning before they would admit her. Oh, Ron, I don't want you to go to a Russian hospital!"

Just as Kathy broke down in tears, I heard the back door open.

Vee poked his head around the corner. "Brother Ron, I've come to check on you. How are you today?"

I motioned for him to take a seat at the table. "Not so well. We have prayed for this lump to go away, and it hasn't. I need to get it checked out."

Vee nodded, "I am free today. I will go with you to the local clinic. They have done several ultrasounds on my esophagus, and it's been helpful. It will cost you less than $20 and maybe we can learn something. Let's go."

As I drove my VW Touran into the clinic parking lot, a woman almost side-swiped us with her Lada. She quickly turned and drove straight into a snowbank. Vee and I thought we would have to push her out, but she left the car there and went into the clinic. I figured she was a drunk going in for treatment. It turned out she was my doctor.

This 'doctor' did an ultrasound and determined that one side of my neck muscles was larger than the other side. The diagnosis was that I needed to wear a neck brace the rest of my life.

She proceeded to provide instructions, "At any moment, your head might fall to the side, and you will never be able to get it up again. You must wear this brace day and night. You may take it off to shower but put it back on immediately!"

As one might imagine, my family laughed me to scorn when I came home with a neck brace on. I took it off and Kathy booked us flights to America.

THOUGHTS

- What is your worst medical story?
- In Contrast, write down your prayer to God, thanking Him for access to the greatest doctors in the world!

Chapter Sixty-Eight

The Valley of Decision

For none of us liveth to himself, and no man dieth to himself. For whether we live, we live unto the Lord; and whether we die, we die unto the Lord: whether we live therefore, or die, we are the Lord's. Romans 14:7-8

In early 2016, we flew back to the United States, where I met with an American doctor. He sat me down, "This tumor is in a dangerous place near your carotid artery. It must be watched. If it grows toward your artery, it could cut off your blood supply."

The doctor then looked down at my chart. His eyes widened, "This tumor is the least of your problems! You have extremely high blood pressure, your cholesterol is off the charts, you are pre-diabetic, and you have heart disease. You are at risk for a heart attack. You can't go back to Russia."

When I arrived back at Keturah's home in Hillsboro, I sat Kathy down. "Honey, the doctor said my health is way worse than we thought. The tumor must be watched, but it is my other health issues that the doctor is more concerned about." I plodded on through her looks of shock, anger, and despair, "But, you know what? No doctor can tell me God's will for my life! God alone can do that!"

Kathy wagged her finger at me, "Ron! We must pray! You know I love Russia and I hate the idea of leaving the mission field, but I can't lose you!" She clenched both of my forearms with her fists, "I don't like change and I don't like surprises, but I know I must follow you."

I pulled my wife's hand down to the table and caressed it for a moment, "You are right, we should pray about God's will, but I repeat, no doctor can dictate God's will for me! God will tell us when it's time to

Serving God Behind Enemy Lines

leave Russia. At the very least, I must go back to transition the work into new hands."

We bowed our heads and I prayed, "Father, we love You. I am so honored and humbled to be Your servant. Thank You for the opportunity to serve in Russia these past 22 years. I told You from the beginning that I would give 20 years of my life to Your service in Russia. We are past that time, Lord. I've been listening for You to change our ministry direction, I have felt the change coming, but I have asked You for a clear sign of when to leave Russia. Is this Your sign? The doctors are saying it is too dangerous." I paused for a moment to collect my thoughts, "But, God, I know the most dangerous place in the world is out of Your Will. We want to be in Your perfect Will. You made it apparent when You called us to Russia. I believe You will make it just as clear when it's time to leave. Help me, Father, to know Your Will and to have the wisdom to follow it. In Jesus' name we pray, amen."

I looked into Kathy's tear-filled eyes and smiled, "Honey, I know you want to stay in Russia until they kick us out or we die of old age."

Kathy sniffled, blew her nose with a napkin on the table and reminisced, "Funny thing; I went to Russia kicking and screaming in my heart; I did not want to go. Now I am kicking and screaming in my heart because I do not want to leave! God has been so good to us in Russia. Souls saved, lives changed, churches started—oh Ron! I wish we could be young again so we could do it all over! It's been that good!"

She paused, looked Heavenward, then looked back, "I remember the challenges we faced when we first started Corridor Baptist in Hillsboro. I agreed we should not take welfare, or WIC. I'm afraid of going back to that kind of poverty. I don't know if I have the faith." She wiped a tear with the back of her hand, "I fought God about going to Russia. I asked for a sign and tanks surrounded the *Duma*. People died. That was my fault. Long ago I promised God that I would NOT cause another civil war to conform me to His will. So, I will go where you go, and I will serve God where you serve God; where you go and when you go."

Six months later, Kathy was smiling from ear to ear as we took our seats. I brought her hand to my lips and laughed, "You'd think this was your first time on an airplane. You are so giddy."

Kathy pulled her eyes from the runway and looked me in the eye as she responded, "I am so happy to be going back. I was afraid this day would not happen. But we have new three-year visas in hand, your medications in my purse, and we are going home!"

The Valley of Decision

"Don't get too comfortable. We'll see how my health is in six months when we must leave Russia for re-registration."

I softly added, "I'll need your help to keep an eye on the tumor to make sure it isn't growing. If all is well, we can go to a neighboring country for a short vacation but if I'm not well, we will have to return to the States for more testing."

She nodded and looked out the window, "The first time we took off on an airplane to go to Russia, I was so scared—the unknowns and fear for the wellbeing of my children had me convinced God was punishing me for my childhood. But now as we take off, I thank God for allowing us to be His servants in Russia. It's not a curse, it's a blessing!"

Calling a New Pastor

We settled back into life in Russia. We had peace that God had given me this time to transition the church into another pastor's hands. Our ministry was functional. All it needed was a qualified, dedicated pastor. I began the search. Joel (my eldest son) and Michelle were praying about God's will for their lives. They had struggled with infertility for over 10 years and wondered if they should return to the States on a prolonged sabbatical. They could establish residency and start the process of adoption. This uncertainty meant Joel was not a candidate for taking over the Domodedovo church.

Our second son, Micah, and his wife Sarah, along with their three children had come to Russia as full-time missionaries in 2015. Their sights were set on moving to Kalmykia and working among the Buddhist people. Therefore, he was not a candidate.

Vee walked into my office at my bidding. "Vee, you graduated from Heartland Baptist Bible College with a major in pastoral studies. Have you considered that God might want you to take over this work?"

He sat on the couch as I settled into the leather chair across from him. He was silent, shuffled his feet and finally looked up, "Pastor Ron, to be honest, I never felt the call of God to pastor. I am happy as a second man."

"I can't stay here forever. Joel and Michelle aren't sure of God's will, Micah and Sarah are headed to Kalmykia, and while we have one other missionary in our ministry here, you and I both know he is not the same doctrinally as we are. Would you pray with me that God will reveal His Will?"

Vee nodded and stood to pray, "Father, this is Your church, not ours. Please lead us into Your plan. Give us confidence in the right man and the right timing. In Jesus' name, Amen."

Lord, I think he would be a good pastor, but Your ways are not my ways. If not Vee, who will take my place?

One year later in January of 2018, Sergei from Kalmykia came to Moscow. As Kathy set tea and cookies before us, he began his story, "Last month we had a group of Americans visit. The FSB invaded our services, arrested the Americans, and deported them. I think we have a spy in our church."

Startled, Micah spilled his tea. Kathy hurried to get a towel as Micah turned to Sergei. "So, you are saying it is not safe for Americans to work in the ministry there?"

Sergei frowned, "I'm afraid your family's plans will put both your family and our church in danger. I have come to ask you to reconsider. Perhaps in the future, the door may open, but for now, it is better if your family stayed away."

Disappointment was written all over Micah's face, but I felt a stirring within me.

Is this Your doing Lord? Is he my replacement?

Around this time, we had a Youth Camp where Kathy and I played the treasure hunters — a whole other story

Later that evening I pulled Micah aside, "Son, I know you had your heart set on Kalmykia, but perhaps God wants you to stay here in the ministry compound and take over this church. Consider it, won't you?"

The Valley of Decision

Micah shook his head, "I can't believe this. I raised money on deputation with the idea of going to Kalmykia. Now, it won't happen."

I put my hand on Micah's shoulder, "Pray about this ministry here, Micah. The people know you; they love you, and the youth group has multiplied under your leadership. Pray about it!"

Micah sighed, "I'll talk to Sarah. Perhaps God has a plan we have not considered."

A couple months later in the spring, Micah, Sarah, Kathy, and I sat across the table from Vee and his wife, Vera. I began, "Vee, I want you to be the first to know that God has been stirring in my heart for several years that a change was coming. I thought it was that my sons would serve with me, and our ministry would explode. But my health is declining. I must go back to America. This is the change God was preparing me for. I don't know the exact date, but I promised God 20 years in Russia. September of this year will be the 25th anniversary of our ministry. I stayed another five years waiting for God to move me."

He smiled, "Brother Ron, God has used you greatly. You have been a big part of our family's life and training. Thank you for coming."

I smiled, "Praise the Lord for His goodness. I would like to offer Micah up as the candidate for the next pastor of this church. Is that something you can get behind?"

Vee turned to Micah and teased, "You, Micah?"

Micah laughed, "I know, I know—I was a troublemaker when we were in Bible College. But God has worked mightily in my life, and I believe He would have me to pastor this church."

"Yes, I have seen God transform you from a boy to a man of God. I would support you as the next pastor of Domodedovo Bible Baptist Church."

In the following weeks, we met individually with each family of the church and presented to them the idea of Micah as the next pastor. Everyone agreed. They hated to see us leave, but they understood about my health and God's stirring.

One family was a blessing to me. We invited Victor and Tatiana over for dinner and asked them if they would consider Micah as their next pastor. They both wiped tears from their eyes as Tatiana said, "Brother Ron, you will always be my pastor. The first time we came to this church. Misha was only eight and had not yet learned to filter his comments. We already knew he had Asperger's but didn't know how to control him. He blurted out comments during your sermon."

My mind flew back to that eventful week.

> After Wednesday evening Bible study, a young man in our ministry approached me. He wanted to pray with me for more visitors to come to our church. As we knelt praying, we heard a knock on the front door. Together we went to answer it. Victor, Tatiana and two other individuals stood there. "We heard a church meets here. Is that true?"
>
> The young man excitedly answered, "We were just praying for you to come! Yes, we meet here on Sunday mornings and Wednesday nights!"
>
> They came the next Sunday, joined a few weeks later and were faithful members of the church.

Tatiana's voice brought me back to the present, "You came to me after the service, and I thought you were going to ask us not to come back as other pastors had done. But instead of reprimanding Misha, you said, 'It's not a problem. Children are always welcome.' That's when I knew this would be our church home. We want to go with you to America, but if we must stay here, Micah will do well as our pastor."

I hugged them, "Your family has been a blessing to us. We will miss you terribly."

That spring, Joel and Michelle requested a family meeting. They were leaving the next day for a short trip to America and had an announcement. I thought they were going to tell us they were leaving Russia. Instead, they announced that Michelle was pregnant, and they would be going to a doctor in America to see if all was well.

God was answering prayers left and right!

THOUGHTS

- God's timing is not ours.
- Hold on Christian, God is working out the details—patience.
- When God doesn't answer your prayers right away, do you have the faith to keep praying?

Chapter Sixty-Nine

I Left My Heart in Russia

Only let your conversation be as it becometh the gospel of Christ: that whether I come and see you, or else be absent, I may hear of your affairs, that ye stand fast in one spirit, with one mind striving together for the faith of the gospel; Philippians 1:27

The day finally came in August of 2018. I turned Kathy to face me. Her eyes were red and swollen. I could tell she spent the night crying. I kissed the top of her head and engulfed her in a hug. "I know this is hard. You hate change. You love these people. But we promised we will come back to visit." I tenderly pulled her chin up, so she had to look me in the eye, "This isn't our last service forever. It is just our last service as Pastor and pastor's wife. Are you going to be, okay?"

Kathy took a deep breath, slowly let it out and forced a smile, "I guess I have to be." Another round of tears flowed as she sighed, lips quivered, and her voice cracked, "I can't believe we are leaving tomorrow. I've packed up everything I hold near and dear. I've tried, but I can't fit the Russian people in our suitcases."

More tears. Lord, help her! Help me comfort her!

I gave her one more hug, wiped a tear from her eye and whispered, "Be strong in the Lord and in the power of His might!" Kathy gave me a weak smile. I took her hand and insisted, "We need to be strong. If they see us sad and moping, they will follow suit."

Kathy turned toward the bathroom door. I heard her mutter under her breath, "I'll be glad when this day is over. I hate, hate, good-byes!"

The people came early, bearing precious gifts. Mariam, Yakov and Sada's daughter, was the first to arrive with a bouquet of flowers. "Brother

Ron and Miss Kathy, I bring you greetings from my parents. They are so sorry they could not be here today. Their ministry in Armenia keeps them from traveling. They asked me to pass on their thanks for the many years you invested in all our lives. They still talk about their trip to the Reindeer People. We serve God today because you encouraged us to trust God in the hard times and never give place to the Devil!"

While Mariam yet spoke, Angela and Felix walked through the door. Kathy excused herself. She ran to hug Angela, "Thank you for coming."

Angela kissed both of Kathy's cheeks and immediately started to cry, "It is I who must say, 'thank you for coming.'"

She looked at Felix and continued, "We cannot even imagine where we would be today if God had not sent you to Russia! Oh, praise God for His mercies and for you obeying His Will!" Angela reached into her shopping bag and pulled out a box of Ballerina Chocolates. "I know these are your favorites."

I watched as Kathy pulled her shoulders back just a bit.

Give her strength, Lord. Help her through this day!

"Thank you, Angela, and Felix. You are a blessing."

I grabbed the next group to enter the church. It was our Filipino ladies who came three hours each way to church. "Welcome, ladies. Thank you for coming."

"Pastor, we will miss your smile and greeting each Sunday. After spending hours on public transportation to get here, we are always encouraged by your smile and challenge to serve God."

Kathy moved over to hug each of them. I saw a tear escape as she wiped it away, "Oh please, ladies. It is you who are the blessings! I don't know how we ever survived picnics without your help."

"Speaking of, we are headed to the kitchen to oversee the meal. We want everything to be perfect on your last day. That is our gift to you." CeCe led the ladies down the stairs to the kitchen.

Victor, Tatiana, and Misha walked through the door. Tatiana handed Kathy a gift bag, "Open it now. I want to make sure you understand its significance."

Kathy pulled out a lacquer jewelry box. "It's beautiful. Thank you."

Tatiana smiled, "Open it."

I watched as my wife opened the box. She gave me that 'I'm going to lose it' look as I raced to her side and looked inside the box. I saw seven glass hearts.

Tatiana put an arm around each of us, "Seven is God's number of completion but it's also the number of hearts you brought to Russia so many years ago. Those seven hearts—your family—have touched so many people. Thank you for coming to Russia."

People continued to come. Some gave Kathy bouquets of flowers. Others brought what they knew to be our favorite Russian cuisine. The church children drew us pictures. By 11 a.m. the church auditorium was packed. Some of the people in the congregation had not been to our home in over five years. They had all come to say goodbye.

As I stood to preach, I saw Andre and Gala slip in the back door.

Lord, the trials Andre and I endured on that first trip to the Reindeer People! Thank You for such a faithful friend.

"Open your Bibles to Joshua 1:8-9,

"This book of the law shall not depart out of thy mouth; but thou shalt meditate therein day and night, that thou mayest observe to do according to all that is written therein: for then thou shalt make thy way prosperous, and then thou shalt have good success. Have not I commanded thee? Be strong and of a good courage; be not afraid, neither be thou dismayed: for the LORD thy God is with thee whithersoever thou goest."

God, as I begin this sermon, please give me courage to finish well!

After a silent prayer, I continued, "The book of Joshua was written during a time of transition in Israel. Moses is gone and their new leader is Joshua. The Lord encourages Joshua in this passage to keep going, keep serving, and keep trusting in God. This is a great message for us today. God is calling me back to America, but He has raised up another man, my son, Micah, to take over. This message is for you and for him—keep going, keep serving, and keep trusting God."

I held up well until the service was over and we began the transition of laying my mantel onto Micah's shoulders. Before I could start the ceremony, Micah took the microphone from me. One of our young Russian teens went to the piano and began the introduction to, *Friends*. The whole congregation stood to sing in Russian that heart wrenching song by Michael W. Smith, Gary Chapman, and Amy Grant about saying goodbye:

Packing up the dreams God planted
In the fertile soil of you
Can't believe the hopes He's granted
Means a chapter in your life is through
But we'll keep you close as always
It won't even seem you've gone

Serving God Behind Enemy Lines

>'Cause our hearts in big and small ways
>Will keep the love that keeps us strong
>
>And friends are friends forever
>If the Lord's the Lord of them
>And a friend will not say never
>'Cause the welcome will not end
>Though it's hard to let you go
>In the Father's hands we know
>That a lifetime's not too long
>To live as friends

Through my tears, I could see Kathy by my side sobbing uncontrollably. First, they sang in Russian, then English, and then the Filipinos sang the chorus in Tagalog. There was not a dry eye in the house. My eyes focused on my three grandchildren in the front row. Even their young faces had tears rolling down their cheeks.

When the music faded, I called for us to vote Micah in as the new pastor. It was a 100% vote. There was one last order of business to be accomplished. Micah knelt as I called Vee and Andre up front to lay hands on Micah with me. We each prayed for God to bless him as the new pastor of this church.

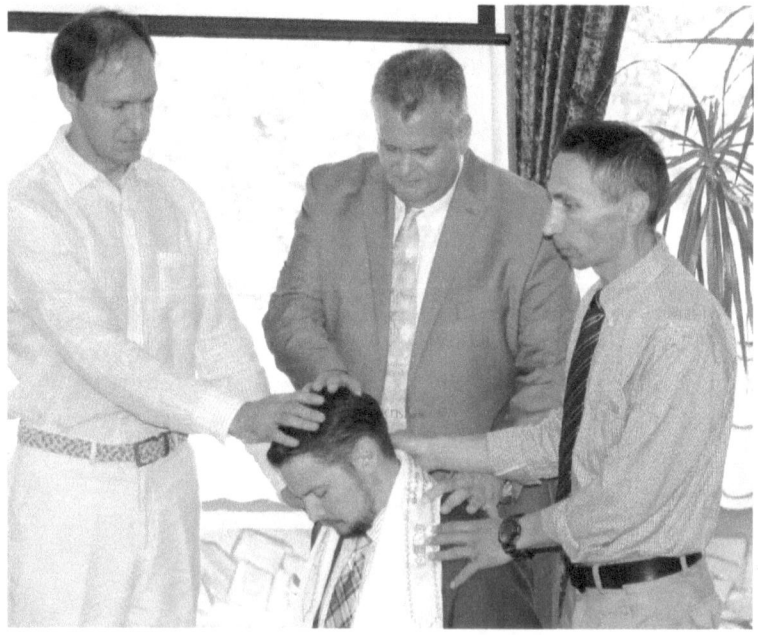

Andre, me & Vee praying over Micah

With the final 'amen', Micah stood. Kathy handed me gifts for my son. He reached out as I gave him each one.

"This is my Russian/English Bible symbolizing that you are now the shepherd of this flock." I turned and picked up a decorative sword, "This sword symbolizes the spiritual battle you are about to enter as a pastor." Lastly, on Micah's shoulders, I placed the prayer cloth/mantel I had been given by a group of Israeli Christians during my tour of the Holy Land, "Let this prayer cloth remind you that without prayer, you will surely fail."

After closing in prayer, we went outside for a group photo. One by one, the people came to thank us for our years of service and shared their favorite memory of us. It was emotionally draining. New tears flowed with each family.

Last Sunday before leaving Russia

As Andre and Gala approached, we engulfed them in hugs. "Where are the children?" Kathy asked.

Gala smiled, "Masha is studying in Germany. I told her we were coming here today, and she asked me to tell you 'Thank you' for fixing her cleft palette when she was a child. My other girls teach Sunday School at our church in Odintsovo."

I shook Gala's hand, "Gala, you can't imagine how many hours Kathy and I spent in prayer for your salvation! It is such a joy to hear that not only are you a faithful Christian now, but your daughters have also embraced the God of their father."

I patted Andre on the shoulder as he beamed, "Brother Ron! I can't believe how much we have gone through together. You are a big part of why my family serves God today. Thank you for coming to Russia."

The last guest left at 7 p.m. I turned to Kathy and smiled, "It is finished. We survived 25 years in Russia. Ten churches established, a Bible Institute, and thousands of souls later, God is calling us back to headquarters."

Kathy took my hand as we ascended the steps to our living quarters. She pondered, "God's been good, hasn't He? I can't imagine a better life than the one He gave us. Why do people resist Him?"

I stopped and tugged on Kathy, "It's not over yet, Kathy. God still has plans! We aren't leaving for Heaven yet!"

Kathy continued to our room and spoke. "He will take care of us, won't He?" The desperate look in her eye was gut-wrenching!

"Is that a question or a statement?" I asked.

Kathy exhaled as new tears appeared, "Both I suppose." She broke into a sob, "Please, God, don't make us as poor as we were before we came. I know You always supply, but please don't—" Her voice trailed off as she fell on the bed sobbing uncontrollably.

I sat down beside her and stroked her back. Suddenly an encouraging thought came to my mind, and I formulated it out loud, "We will always be Americans to the Russian people. We were raised during the Cold War, and I have a thick accent when I speak."

She rolled over and through her tears, she smiled, "Mine isn't much better."

I continued, "Our sons, however, are accepted by the community as Russians because they were raised here, and both speak Russian well. They will be able to take the churches in Russia to a new level. It is always a blessing when a father sees his sons do better than himself."

Kathy thought for a moment, "Remember that preacher on deputation who put one hand on Joel's shoulder, the other on Micah's and told you, 'I have a feeling God is calling you to Russia so you can raise these boys to be missionaries there. Second generation missionaries are much more successful!'" She smiled, "He was right!"

I reminisced about God's great blessings.

You are so good, God! Wow!

Kathy tilted her head, "What are you thinking about?"

"I'm praising God for His goodness. Just think of it, Kathy, five grown children serving the Lord. Joel and Michelle are preparing to welcome their miracle boy into the world next month. They'll return to

Russia after the New Year as soon as they get Jonathan Daniel a passport and visa."

She smiled, "Can we go for his birth? I have prayed so many years for God to give them a child."

I thought aloud, "Michelle will probably have the baby in Wichita, Kansas. Plane tickets can't be that much from Portland to Wichita. Surely, we can work it out."

Kathy grinned, "Speaking of children serving the Lord, the service today making Micah the pastor was beautiful—emotional—but beautiful. Micah and Sarah with their three children are serving God here in Russia. He is raising another generation of missionaries in Chloe, Leah, and Micah Jack!"

I sighed, "Even Keturah is faithfully serving God in our sending church after all she has been through—betrayal, abandonment, and divorce. She, Reaia and Jadon have had a rough go of it, but they have clung to God's promises, and He is faithful."

Kathy continued, "Remember when Hannah came back to Russia to teach English while she waited on God to send her soulmate. We told her to be patient, that God would send a man all the way from America, and she would know he was God's will for her."

In unison we exclaimed, "And He did!"

Kathy continued, "Royce came over twice on construction crews for this ministry compound. The first time, he scoped Hannah out. The second time he swept her off her feet."

I finished off our child checklist, "We can't forget the doctor in the family. Jeremiah and his wife, Kayla, are faithfully serving in their local church while he completes his residency in Temple, Texas. Perhaps when he finishes, God will bring him to Vancouver!"

Kathy clapped her hands, "Wouldn't that just be the icing on the cake? Do you think God would do that for us!"

I nodded, "My God can do anything."

Kathy rose from the bed and walked to our bedroom window. I rose to stand beside her. She took my hand and squeezed it tightly. "You are right. God is good! He is faithful!"

She sighed, "However, back to the task at hand—it's 7:30 p.m. and we leave at 4 a.m. I've set my alarm and Ivan will take us to the airport." Her eyes sparkled, "Remember, that's how Ivan came to be a part of our ministry—we called a taxi and witnessed to him all the way to Sheremetyevo Airport. He took a tract and started attending church while we were on furlough. Now his whole family is saved and serving the Lord faithfully at Domodedovo Bible Baptist Church."

The memory replayed itself in my mind. "I remember. I guess it is fitting that he would take us to the airport."

We changed into causal clothes and went into the shared living room with Micah's family. His three children sat on the couch.

Chloe's lip stuck out a mile. I sat between her and Micah Jack. I put my arm around her, "What's wrong?"

Her lip quivered, she sniffled. "No more walks in the forest, walking to Baskin Robbins for ice cream, or toy days at the mall. I won't ever see you again, Grandpa."

I squeezed her shoulder, "Honey, God has made it clear to me that my work here in Russia is done. I need to go back to the States where doctors can keep a close eye on me." I raised her sagging chin so she had to look at me, "Besides, I'll come back and visit as often as I can and as soon as God clears me to start another church, our first missionaries we support will be both Reasoner families in Russia! That way, you will have to come and visit us when you are in the States."

She smiled, "Promise?"

Ivan the taxicab driver and his wife, Alona, getting baptized in 2018

I held out my pinky finger and motioned for her to do the same. As they locked, I vowed, "Pinky promise."

I played a video game with Chloe, a game of Slap Jack with Leah and read a good night book to Micah Jack. I gave Micah a few words of wisdom, and a long fatherly hug. I gently hugged Sarah before we retired to bed.

Kathy hugged each of the family members as well. She addressed Micah, "You guys don't need to get up at 4 a.m. to see us off. Let's say good-bye right now." She turned to speak to Sarah, "For the past three years we had shared the living quarters with your family. Tomorrow, you will become the single residents."

I grabbed Kathy's arm. "Come on Honey, let's get some shut-eye."

"You go ahead Ron; I'll be there in a few minutes. I want to say goodbye to the house. It has so many, many great memories. I want to reminisce."

I watched as Kathy headed down the stairs.

Lord, give her strength—give us BOTH strength—to face whatever is ahead.

About an hour later, Kathy came to lie beside me. I was half asleep, but I still heard her as she prayed, "Lord, we are Your servants, ready to do Your will. Lead us where You need us, until we are home with You."

THOUGHTS
- Can you understand the turmoil of missionaries when they leave their families to go to the field?
- What about the pain when they have to say goodbye to the country they have grown to love?
- Describe a time you were forced to say 'goodbye' to someone you loved.

CHAPTER SEVENTY

Back in the U.S.A.

Not that I speak in respect of want: for I have learned, in whatsoever state I am, therewith to be content. Philippians 4:11

"Welcome Home!" Hannah grabbed me as we exited the secure area of the airport in Portland, Oregon. I engulfed her in a bear hug. Out of the corner of my eye I saw Kathy being attacked by Reaia, Jadon and Keturah. I lightly hugged Royce, Hannah's husband, and then we all switched until hugs were given all around.

The culture shock was immediate. The familiar restaurant smells floated throughout the airport. I suddenly craved cheeseburgers and pizza. I felt like an intruder into the conversations surrounding me. With almost everyone speaking English, I overheard and understood everything. The teenager behind me broke into Russian as she hugged her parents. I struggled to understand her. She had gone to be a counselor at an English Camp outside of Moscow. My heart was torn—the English conversations came naturally but the Russian conversation tugged at my heart.

"The house is ready," Hannah said pulling me back to the family as she and Royce each grabbed a bag and led the way to the car. "We moved out last week into a house in Battleground. We appreciate renting your home in Vancouver for the past year."

Kathy had an arm around each grandchild as Keturah chatted away, "Mom, I'm so glad you and Daddy are back! It's been hard raising these two hooligans by myself." Keturah pointed to me, and I overheard her whisper, "It will be nice for them to have a godly male influence in their lives."

Back in the U.S.A.

I pulled back and rubbed Jadon's hair. "Have you been giving your mother trouble?"

Jadon smiled, "Well, sometimes. I got in trouble last week at school—I spend a lot of time in the principal's office."

I gave him a disappointed look, "Son, Reasoners don't get in trouble. We obey the rules and make everyone happy. Do you understand me?"

He looked down at his feet, then lifted his eyes to me, "Yes, sir."

Lord, is Jadon one of the reasons You called me back? I know he and Reaia have had a tough time since their father left.

We loaded into our Honda Pilot Royce had driven to the airport. It was a tight squeeze, but we made it work. "Do you want to drive?" Royce asked, offering me the keys.

"Absolutely not! We have been traveling for almost 24 hours fresh from Moscow traffic. There is no telling how I might drive."

Kathy chuckled, "Once Ron drove in the emergency lane on I-5 all the way through downtown Seattle. It wasn't until I noticed people gawking at us that we realized it wasn't legal in America to do that."

Royce pulled the keys back and got into the driver's seat. "I'll drive."

As we turned onto our street, Kathy and I said, "The lawns are so beautiful."

Keturah asked, "Are they that bad in Russia? I don't remember. I've been gone for 11 years."

I answered, "Who knows? Every Russian yard is hidden by an eight-foot fence. It's just interesting to see open, well-maintained front lawns."

"We're here," Hannah announced as we pulled into the driveway. "Welcome to your home in America."

Kathy had made an appointment for me to see a holistic doctor. It was two years since I had seen an American doctor. I sat on the bed as the nurse took my blood pressure. I immediately saw concern in her eyes as she scribbled down numbers and excused herself. A few moments later, the doctor entered the room, "Your blood pressure is high. Do you have any other medical concerns?"

"I have this lump on my neck. It appeared a few years ago and I've had an ultrasound. They say it is a lipoma. I think it may have grown some since it was last checked."

The doctor felt my neck tumor and then wrote down a few notes on his computer. "I'll schedule an ultrasound and retrieve your old medical records for comparison. I'd also like to draw some blood and test your cholesterol and blood sugar. I'm sure you saw that I practice holistic medicine—preferring to use diet and natural medicines to treat illnesses. I only prescribe medicine in extreme cases."

"Yes, my wife studied up on holistic medicine and sought you out. We are Christians and believe that God made our bodies to heal themselves with the right diet and proper exercise."

The doctor nodded, "I'll send you over to the lab. You should have the results in your online portal by tomorrow morning. Thank you for coming in."

Later that afternoon, the doctor called. "I need to prescribe blood pressure, cholesterol, and diabetic medication. You need them all!"

I struggled to wrap my mind around his tone. "I thought you were a holistic doc—"

He interrupted, "And I said I prescribe medication in extreme circumstances. You are an extreme circumstance. Frankly, I'm surprised you haven't already had a heart attack. You need to be on all these medications today. I have already sent them to your pharmacist."

"Wow!" was all I could say.

"I've also made you an appointment for an ultrasound tomorrow morning. I'll call you on Monday with the results."

On Monday, when the doctor called, he asked, "Did you get your medications? Are you taking them faithfully?"

"Yes, and my wife and I started the Mediterranean diet as you suggested. I've lost five pounds already."

"Good, good. Now about your ultrasound. I'm sorry to say that your lipoma has grown slightly. However, it isn't growing toward your throat or carotid artery, it is growing toward your collarbone. This is good news. We must keep an eye on it. I will send you to a specialist and see what he thinks."

Weeks later, the specialist examined the ultrasound and declared, "Removing this would be purely cosmetic and I would not recommend it. In fact, I would not do such a surgery. I believe there are less than 10 surgeons in the USA who would dare attempt this. It is too close to the carotid artery and if it isn't obstructing your breathing or blood flow, it should not be touched. According to my records, you have had this tumor for three years. We need to keep tabs on it."

I opened my car door where Kathy was waiting. "What did he say?"

Sitting in the driver's seat, I turned to Kathy's anxious eyes, "He said he would never do the operation. It is too precarious, but we need to keep an eye on it. If I feel discomfort, I need to come back immediately."

"Did he say what he thought caused it?"

"I asked and he can't be sure. I mentioned my trips to Northern Siberia to nuclear radiated places and he seemed to think that very well could have caused it, but we will never know. It could be just part of getting old."

Kathy mustered a smile, "What is that Russian saying? 'Growing old is not joyful!'"

I smiled, "But growing old with God in control of our lives is. He always has and always will carry us through storms!"

Kathy wrinkled her nose with a smile, "So you're saying it ain't over until the fat lady sings?"

I rolled my eyes, grabbed her hand, and began our family prayer, "Lord, we are Your servants, ready to do Your will. Lead us where You need us, until we are home with You."

THOUGHTS
- What health issues have you or someone you know had to endure?
- How did it change your/their ministry?

CHAPTER SEVENTY-ONE

The Next Journey

And ye shall seek me, and find me, when ye shall search for me with all your heart. Jeremiah 29:13

When we came back in 2018, Kathy and I endured immense reverse culture shock. The United States is not the same country we left 25 years ago. God, the office of President, the flag, police officers, and the laws of the land were once honored and respected regardless of political preferences. That is no longer true. In horror, we watched the Portland riots as people destroyed government property night after night without arrest or repercussion.

We struggled with the free use of profanity by adults and children. The kindness that was once afforded strangers had disappeared. The rules of driving have changed with road rage and impatience being the new norm.

When I went door to door and invited people to church in the 1980s, they were courteous 90% of the time. Today they are overtly rude, often not even answering the door, just staring me down through the front window. The coldness of hearts towards the Gospel is heart wrenching! The Light has grown dim in this land I love.

There is more work to be done.

God prompted me to start one more church for Him. There are over 120,000 Russian speaking people in the Portland metropolitan area with a great number of them residing in Vancouver. One in six people speak Russian in our area.

I am a novelty amongst the Russian community. I survived 25 years in Russia. Some Russians left when the Soviet Union broke up in 1991 and are anxious to hear how it has changed. Other Russians were born in

America and though they attend Russian churches, schools, and surround themselves with the Russian community, they have never been to Russia and want to know what it is like. They love to hear stories of how an American family with five small children thrived in Moscow.

God builds beautiful lives when we surrender. I look back in amazement how God called a young preacher boy who was planting a church in Hillsboro, Oregon to Moscow. I love how He used our experiences in America to enhance our ministry in Russia. As I trained young Russian preacher men how to start churches, they often asked, "Have you done this before? Did you start a church in America?" God knew that question would often be asked, and He provided me with an answer years ahead of time.

Our church in Russia has Russians, Ukrainians, Moldovans, Armenians, Syrians, Belarusians, Filipinos, Peruvians, Americans, and Canadians. I desire to replicate that in Vancouver by building an international church with people from all nations.

Domodedovo Bible Baptist Church Representing Philippines, America, Russia, Ukraine, Armenia & Guam (2015)

On January 6, 2019, Corridor Baptist Church sent us to plant Bridgeway Baptist Church in Vancouver. Age and life experience has taught me that building a Godly church in any culture is a long and slow process. I have no desire to build a mega church by preaching a prosperity Gospel or by tickling peoples' ears. I desire to build a church on the Gospel of Jesus Christ, Him crucified, resurrected, and coming again. It is a church where attenders are compelled to live each moment for Christ. The sermons call us into the spiritual battle—to gird up our loins and live boldly for God. Romans 12:1-2 calls on us to be living sacrifices 100% of the time—not just on Sunday morning.

First service at Bridgeway Baptist Church

One month after starting the church, my younger brother, Jeff, had a widow maker heart attack. Having retired from the military several years earlier, he was working as an independent military contractor.

I was at a preachers' conference in California when my mom called me with the devastating news that Jeff was near death. I gathered 50 pastors and asked them to pray with me that God would spare Jeff's life until I could get back to Portland to witness to him.

I went to the hospital as soon as I returned from California, witnessed to Jeff, and he was gloriously saved! Then his wife, Cindy, received Christ. We now serve the Lord together. Jeff has a burden to work with Veterans and help them adjust back to civilian life.

A few months after Jeff was saved and baptized, my mom called to tell me that my great nephew had cancer and needed a liver transplant. As a church, we prayed for a miracle. My great nephew got his liver transplant and as soon as he was well enough to visit, he and his mother, my niece, came to church to thank us for our prayers. After the service, I led them both to Christ! God answers prayers!

My brother Jeff and me at a survivor ceremony after his heart attack

The Next Journey

Often as missionaries, we go to the foreign fields wondering who will stay behind to witness to our friends and family. God has allowed me the privilege to enjoy serving Him on the mission field, and then come home to see members of my family saved as well!

God is saving people through the ministry of Bridgeway Baptist Church. Some are from my family, others from the street, and still others right in our services!

We support five missionaries through our faith promise missions program. We continue to fulfil the Great Commission. Once we went, now we send.

During our second year, Bridgeway Baptist Church was able to buy property to build a House of Prayer for the believers in Vancouver, Washington. We continue to be astonished at our circumstances and amazed how God comes through!

Bridgeway Baptist Church

In the Summer of 2022, our youngest son, Dr. Jeremiah Reasoner, moved to Vancouver with his lovely wife, Kayla, and our grandson, Evryn. God answered our prayers, and he got a job in Portland as an Anesthesiologist. Wow! God is able! Psalm 37:4 says:

Delight thyself also in the LORD; and he shall give thee the desires of thine heart.

God had me in mind when He preserved my Mayflower ancestors from the great famine. He thought of me as He protected my grandma from bears and wild horses. God formed my character through all the troublesome situations I got into as a child. He guided me as I spent years

Serving God Behind Enemy Lines

searching for Him until He found me when I reached out in absolute surrender. I do not know why God chose me for the ministry, but I am thankful He did.

I called unto God and He answered me. I asked Him to show me great and mighty things, and He did.

God has a plan and work for you too. He will answer when you humbly offer yourself for His service. What great and mighty things will He show you?

Call unto me, and I will answer thee, and show thee great and mighty things, which thou knowest not. (Jeremiah 33:3)

THOUGHTS
- What kind of legacy are you leaving for your children and future generations?
- Will they find you faithful?

Epilogue

And when they were come, and had gathered the church together, they rehearsed all that God had done with them, and how he had opened the door of faith unto the Gentiles.
Acts 14:27

Someday, we will gather in Heaven as friends who invested time and money to reach the lost. You might ask how many people in this book are made up characters. The answer is zero. Each was used by God at a perfect, divine moment. At times, in this book, I explained what eventually happened to certain people, but some require a longer explanation.

My Parents

My parents are still alive. They supported the work we did in Russia and attend Bridgeway Baptist Church in Vancouver, Washington. I am grateful for their encouragement to go on this journey. Kathy's dad, who came to Russia in 2000 to build the kitchen at the compound, went home to Heaven in 2020. Kathy's mother still lives in Emmett, Idaho.

My Family

God is good and worthy to be praised. Missionary families understand that life on earth is short, but eternity lasts forever. It is rare when they are blessed to minister together when the children reach adulthood. God has uniquely blessed us. Keturah, Hannah, and Jeremiah, along with their families, attend Bridgeway Baptist Church where their families are heavily involved in the ministry. Keturah got married in 2019 to Alan Brown. They added another grandson to our family tree.

Micah is an Associate Pastor with me at Bridgeway Baptist Church and every Sunday preaches in Russian to the Slavic community who attend our church.

Joel and his family visit us often. They accepted the pastorate in Bellingham, Washington, about 4.5 hours north of Vancouver. There is a large Russian community there too, and several families have started attending services. Joel also preaches once a month at a Russian Baptist Church in their area. God is giving him opportunities to minister to the Slavic people.

We are confident God will direct each of our children as they seek His will for ministry.

Pacific Coast Baptist Bible College

In 1998, Pacific Coast Baptist Bible College Board of Directors voted to sell the decaying campus in San Dimas, California. This is the college that we attended. The sale of that property was divided among three groups who desired to continue educating young people for the ministry. The largest group moved to Oklahoma City, Oklahoma where they purchased a campus—known as Heartland Baptist Bible College.

Heartland Baptist Bible College

I required my children to go to our alma mater for one year when they graduated from High School. It was a positive experience for them. Four of my five children found their spouses there. Over the years, I have hosted students on internship programs in Russia and continue to host one student each summer at Bridgeway Baptist Church.

Corridor Baptist Church

Pastor Steve House is still my pastor. 35 years later, there are still members there who were there when I pastored. One family I led to the Lord as a young couple still attends with their children and their grandchildren. What a heritage when we serve the Lord!

Roman, the Interpreter

I have no idea how we would have made such quick progress in Russia without Roman. I am grateful that he agreed to be my interpreter our first 10 years in Russia. Because his English skills improved so much while working with us, he was able to get a job working for the National Aeronautics & Science Administration office in Russia. Today, he is married with children.

Andre

If it had not been for Andre, I am not sure we would have gone on any Reindeer trips. Once we went, it encouraged me to go on other mission trips within Russia. His help when building the compound was invaluable. Andre and his wife, Gala, serve in a Russian Baptist Church in Odintsovo. Andre is a CEO for Domodedovo Airport and attributes his years of working and learning English with us as a key reason he has advanced his career. His daughter, Masha, studies in Germany. They have three other daughters.

Epilogue

Smolensk Church

We started the Smolensk church when I went on the survey trip and did the meetings in the communist hall. The Bible College student we put in charge, stole the church's money, and disappeared. The church merged with another Independent Baptist Church. Today, the church has over a thousand members.

Associate Pastor Vee

Vee grew up in Uzbekistan and was saved through the ministry of an American missionary there. This missionary directed him to Heartland Baptist Bible College where he met our sons, Joel, and Micah. After he graduated, he moved to Russia. He attended our church, and eventually moved into the compound with us. He became my right-hand man for construction, documents, and dealing with the police. He is now married to Vera, a Ukrainian Baptist. They have two sons. They moved to Vancouver, Washington in 2022, seeking political and religious asylum from the war Russia waged on Ukraine. Had he stayed, Vee would have been drafted and forced to go to Ukraine and kill his own family.

Dimitre the Ukrainian

It was Dimitre who first told us of the Reindeer and Camel People. He opened many opportunities, and we are grateful for his support. We helped him start a church in Western Moscow which he still pastors.

Pastor Igor

Though Igor cheated me on the bricks, I forgave him. He continues to pastor a church in Moscow.

Glenn & Winnie

After the Reindeer trip where Glenn forgot his diabetic medicine, they went back to the States for a visa renewal. His doctor told him he absolutely could not go back to Russia. They continued to serve the Lord in their local church until God called first Glenn home, and then Winnie several years later. In Heaven, Glenn and Winnie will meet the souls that were saved because of their earthly sacrifices for the cause of Christ.

Elijah, the Tank Driver

It was a Heavenly blessing to meet with Elijah after ten years and to learn that he was evangelizing the Reindeer People. That is the last contact we had with him. I look forward to seeing him in Heaven and talking about the great things God did for and through him.

Serving God Behind Enemy Lines

Nenets Tribe Church

Pastor Peytor Hoode still pastors the church. While we only saw that one family saved on the 4th Reindeer trip, the church has grown with many converts.

Moscow East Church

We started this church before moving to Domodedovo. Today it is an Armenian church that still preaches the Gospel.

Domodedovo Church (Compound)

As this book goes to press, Micah and Joel preach Sundays and Wednesdays remotely by video conference to the church families still in Russia.

Micah and his family have moved to Vancouver to pastor the Russians and Ukrainians who fled the war and migrated to Bridgeway Baptist Church.

Both sons are adapting to pastoring in America. After ministering most of their lives in Russia, it is hard to pick up the shattered dreams and start over in a new country. Sadly, Putin threatened to draft American men living in Russia and ship them to the front lines. Also, the economic sanctions prevent them from living there without any way to get funds. When governments go to war, spiritual ground is lost on the mission field. Of course, that is part of Satan's plan.

Kalmykian Churches

In this republic where we helped start six churches, Sergei continues to have a great ministry among his people. God is raising a generation of Christians in this former Buddhist region.

President Vladimir Putin

President Putin indeed brought his country into the 21st century, rebuilt the economy, and restored national pride to Russians. Had he been satisfied with these great accomplishments; he would have gone down in history as a national hero. But, alas, in August of 2008, he invaded the country of Georgia and took 20% of its land mass. In February 2014, immediately after hosting the Winter Olympics in Sochi, Putin invaded and confiscated the Crimea from Ukraine as the world looked on with half-hearted protests. Finally, on February 24, 2022, Putin declared war on Ukraine when he sent missiles, troops, and airstrikes to "de-militarize and de-nazify" Ukraine. This time the world protested by sending billions of dollars in aid and modern weapons of warfare to Ukraine, and economically isolating Russia from most of the modern world.

Epilogue

Any good Putin did for Russia and for the world at large is forgotten. He will be remembered as a bitter old dictator who dreamed of ruling the former Soviet Union and would stop at nothing to reassemble it. Consequently, world history will not treat him kindly.

My Health

After reading this book you probably wonder about my health. God is faithful, having put me in the ministry. I walk every day and try to eat healthy. My tumor is still visible but has not caused any blockage problems. For as long as I live and breathe, I want to serve the Lord. I have had COVID19 twice and have no lingering side effects.

Conclusion

My friend, thank you for taking the time to read this book. I hope it blessed you. If you found Jesus or decided to go into missions, please write me. I would be encouraged to hear how the Lord is using you to reach others.

If you are ever in Vancouver, Washington please drop by Bridgeway Baptist Church. We always have a seat open for visitors. Our website is: https://www.bridgewaybaptistchurch.com/

Thank You

THOUGHTS
- Leaving Russia was one of the hardest things I ever did.
- Now I see how God used us leaving as preparation for our faithful Russian brothers and sisters in Christ to have a place to escape war and famine.
- What are you going through that God will use in the future to help others?

Special Thanks

I want to thank my wife and children. They graciously let me drag them across the globe, to the ends of the world to reach the lost. They endured extreme hardships, starvation, cultural ridicule, prejudice, and many dangerous adventures. I could not have done this ministry without their enduring encouragement, faithfulness, and love. Thank you.

Thank you to Westgate Baptist Church for making this book possible. I started writing this in 2012 and preached the "Reindeer Story" at their church in 2020. Two men approached us to help write this testament to God's Greatness. We showed them the 100-page manuscript and that was the seed for the book you just read. Their church helped with many beta readers and donated funds for this book.

Thank you to the Coalition of Christian Homeschool Families who provided many beta readers and also donated funds.

Thank you to the 9 Bridges Tuesday night critique group, Cedar Mills Writers group, and to Roger Shipman from Reify Press for their work on the original manuscript.

Thank you to Jim Elstad, Don Stackpole, Sarah Burley, Gwendolyn Harmon who did the final book review.

I am blessed with people around me who like to write and research. My wife was a great help in editing this book. She kept a journal while we were on the mission field which we often referred to for details of the stories. The Scriptures tell us what a blessing it is to find a good wife. When I think of my wife, I think of Proverbs 31:30b:

A woman that feareth the LORD, she shall be praised.

Praise God for a godly wife. We complement each other perfectly. Together we raised five children who love and serve the Lord today.

Most of all, we are grateful to God! To Him be all the glory forever and ever amen!

And every creature which is in heaven, and on the earth, and under the earth, and such as are in the sea, and all that are in them, heard I saying, Blessing, and honor, and glory, and power, be unto him that sitteth upon the throne, and unto the Lamb forever and ever. (Revelation 5:13)

Scripture Index

The Bible is rich with wisdom and instructions in righteousness. It explains our relationship to God and His relationship to us. Maybe you have thought about memorizing Scripture. Here is a list of verses I recommend. They will help you share the Gospel and know what God says on various topics. The Word of God will bless you the more you study, memorize, and apply it.

1

1 Corinthians 9:22	309
1 John 1:7	17
1 John 4:4	67
1 Peter 3:15	112
1 Samuel 17:34-35a	1
1 Samuel 3:1	186
1 Thessalonians 1:9	390
1 Thessalonians 2:13	428
1 Thessalonians 5:17	155

2

2 Corinthians 10:15-16	363
2 Corinthians 11:27-28	398
2 Corinthians 12:10	458
2 Corinthians 6:17-18	202
2 Corinthians 8:3-4	x
2 Kings 6:15-16	219
2 Thessalonians 3:1	146
2 Timothy 1:12	333
2 Timothy 1:6-7	177
2 Timothy 2:15	32
2 Timothy 2:19	445
2 Timothy 2:2	230
2 Timothy 2:3	451

3

3 John 1:2	321
3 John 1:3	275

A

Acts 1:8	ix
Acts 14:27	271, xv
Acts 16:30	12
Acts 18:25	22
Acts 20:24	256
Acts 20:28	80
Acts 4:12	378
Acts 5:29b	363
Acts 8:25	287

C

Colossians 3:23	32
Colossians 3:23-24	240

E

Ecclesiastes 5:4	74
Ephesians 2:8-9	18
Ephesians 5:15-16	181
Ephesians 6:12	371
Ephesians 6:4	357

H

Hebrews 13:17	72
Hebrews 7:25	142

I

Isaiah 40:31	151
Isaiah 55:9	214
Isaiah 6:8	247
Isaiah 64:6	33

J

James 4:12-14	352
James 5:16	62
Jeremiah 1:5	350
Jeremiah 29:11	37, 84
Jeremiah 29:13	480
Jeremiah 31:3	76

Jeremiah 33:3 .... iii, 273, 484
Job 13:15a 258
John 1:1 326
John 14:6 378
John 15:13 380
John 3:16. 17, 19, 99, 254, 319, 343
John 4:35 444
John 8:32,36 128
Joshua 1:8-9 469
Joshua 1:9 .... 106, 241

L

Luke 14:23 282
Luke 15:10 294
Luke 16:13 226
Luke 17:5 46
Luke 4:18 119
Luke 9:62 87

M

Mark 1:38 53
Mark 16:15-16 247
Mark 16:6 314
Mark 2:17b 375
Matthew 18:21-22 301
Matthew 19:29 211
Matthew 27:5 313
Matthew 28:19-20 318
Matthew 9:37-38 x

N

Numbers 6:24-26 156

P

Philippians 1:27 467
Philippians 1:29 251
Philippians 1:6 410
Philippians 3:10 71
Philippians 4:11 476
Philippians 4:13 .... 305, 308, 326
Philippians 4:17 x
Philippians 4:19 328
Philippians 4:6 294
Philippians 4:6-7 211
Philippians 4:6-8 293
Philippians 4:9 422
Proverbs 16:7 123
Proverbs 18:22 40
Proverbs 18:24 28
Proverbs 22:6 193
Proverbs 3:5 346
Proverbs 3:5-6 .... 139, 329
Proverbs 31:30 .... 38, xxi
Psalm 119:105 ix
Psalm 139:7-8 162
Psalm 2:8 245
Psalm 22:8 382
Psalm 27:13-14 263
Psalm 28:7 324
Psalm 32:8 171
Psalm 37:23 .... 321, 349
Psalm 37:4 483

R

Revelation 5:13 xxi
Romans 1:15 101
Romans 10:9-10 343
Romans 10:9-13 19
Romans 12:12 222
Romans 12:1-2 481
Romans 12:13 268
Romans 14:7-8 461
Romans 15:20-21 .... 53, 188, 327
Romans 3:23 .... 17, 19, 342
Romans 6:23 .... 17, 19, 343
Romans 8:16 353
Romans 8:28 335

Maps

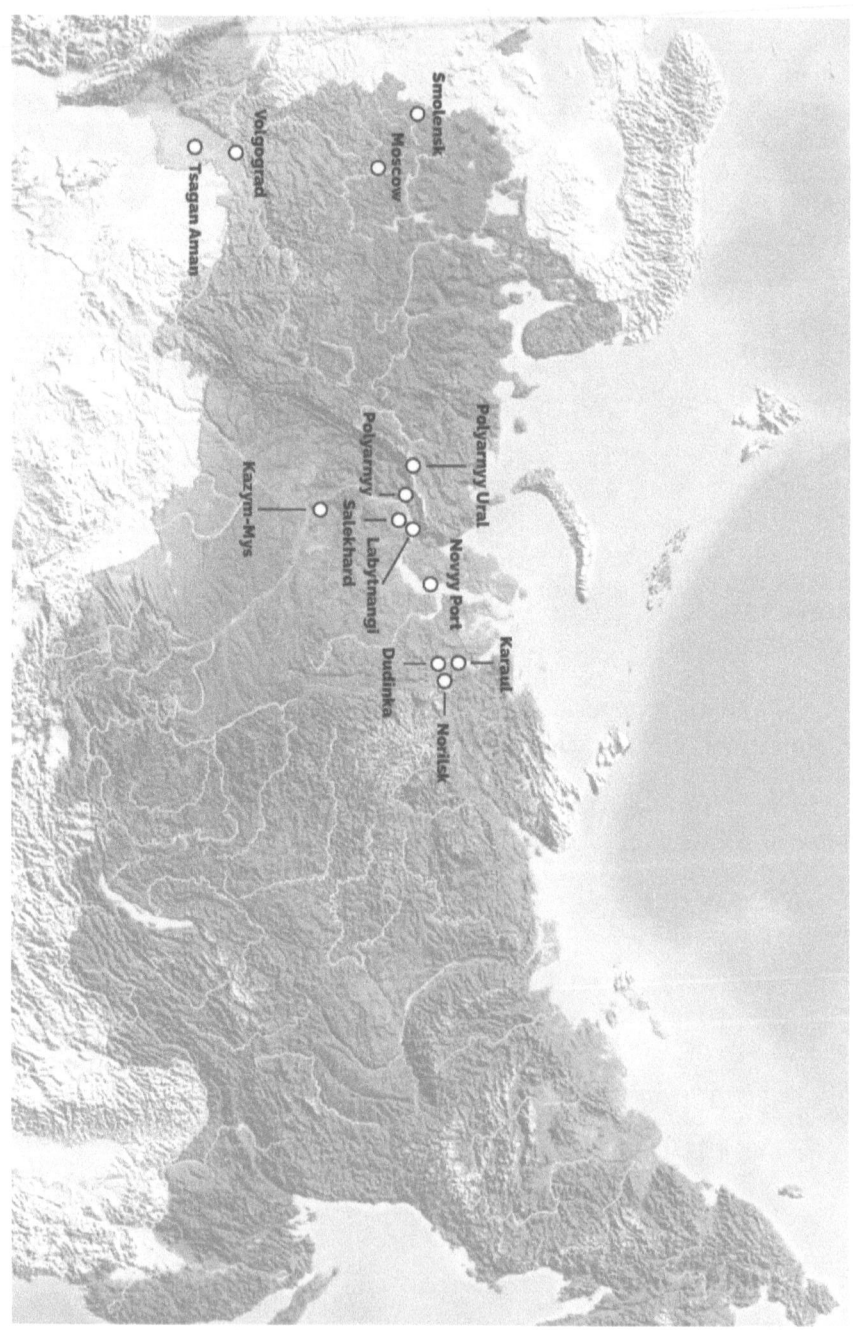

Reindeer & Camel People Trips, Smolensk Campaigns

1st Reindeer Trip

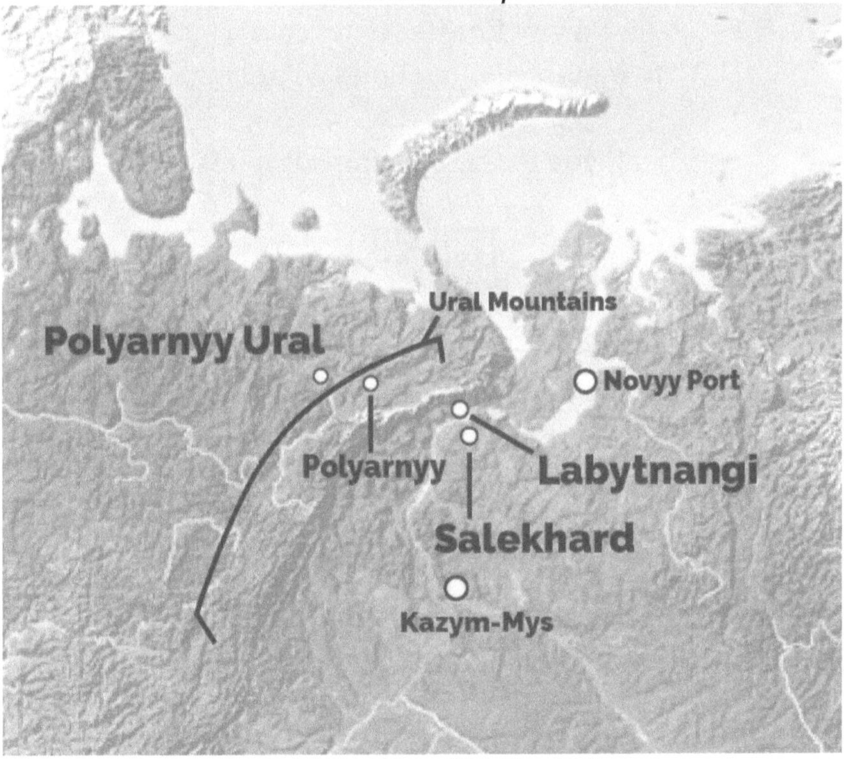

2nd, 3rd, 4th and Last Reindeer Trips
In the book, Polyarnyy is called Polyarnyy Ural Asia and Polyarnyy Ural is called Polyarnyy Ural Europe

Wholesale Book Orders

Please contact me at
www.RonReasoner.com
to inquire about wholesale pricing.

Thank you for supporting our ministry.